HERBERT SPENCER

The Evolution of a Sociologist

HERBERT SPENCER
the evolution of a sociologist

J. D. Y. PEEL

BASIC BOOKS, INC., PUBLISHERS

NEW YORK

Library of Congress Catalog Card Number: 77–156915
SBN 465–02922–1

Printed in the United States of America

Contents

Preface

In writing this book I have been pursuing a number of distinct aims, which it should be helpful to indicate briefly at the beginning. The first is straightforward: to produce an account of Spencer's life and ideas, set against enough of their background to make them comprehensible, which might serve to correct some of the many prevalent misconceptions about this much referred-to but little-read author. Despite a revival of interest in Spencer in the last decade (giving rise to several new selections from his works with introductory essays and to chapter-length treatment in a number of histories of sociology), there has been no book-length study of any aspect of Spencer's thought since J. Rumney's *Herbert Spencer's Sociology* (1934) and, as far as I know, no full attempt to place Spencer in his own times or in the history of sociology at all. The corpus of Spencer's writings fills a fat shelf and my account of them is far from complete. I have cut down the 'external biography' to the barest summary (in Chapter 1), though there is much of quaint interest in Spencer's manner of life; and my treatment of much of his writing on philosophy in the narrow sense, psychology, ethics and biology is cursory and patchy. With regard to his sociology, I have not tried to give an inventory of his views on different topics—religion, kinship, the professions etc.—but to present a series of focal points or problem areas relevant to understanding Spencer's sociological vision as a whole.

Sociology, more than any other kind of thought, only makes sense when it is set in the social context which has produced it and provided its chief subject-matter. This is particularly important when we are considering the founders of sociology (and Spencer, let us remember, was the first person in the English-speaking world, excepting only that oddity, George Fitzhugh of Virginia, to call his analysis of society 'sociology'); for they did not have clear areas of professional interest, agreed criteria of significance, or established methods and concepts to guide their work. Spencer did not even set out to do sociology, but to produce a prescriptive interpretation of his developing society, a species of moral philosophy, that derived much of its plausibility from its being set within a universal philosophy of nature. England at the close of the heroic period of her industrialization was the context, subject-matter and audience. Spencer's assumptions and outlook belonged to provincial Dissent, whose traditions, albeit in a rather secularized form, had shaped him.

I hope it does not seem excessive that Chapters 2 and 3 are not directly about Spencer at all, but about this austere yet fertile and persistently underestimated culture. We must acknowledge its great spread and variety, the connexions with the Scottish Enlightenment and the revolutionary movements of America and France, the continuous spectrum from its greatest figures such as Priestley and Godwin to the social movements of ordinary men in the provincial towns, the important variations between the world-views of different religious confessions and between the social structures of different towns. Spencer was heir to the whole broad tradition, but his particular matrix was the hosiery towns of the North Midlands, and a combination of Methodism and Quaker/Socinian rationalism. It has been difficult to do justice to this background, especially relying very largely on secondary sources. These have been fewer and weaker on the religious and cultural side than on the social and political.

In pointing out similarities of argument, assumption or even phraseology between Spencer and such figures as Smith, Ferguson, Paine, Priestley, Erasmus Darwin, Godwin, Hodgskin, Cobden and Harriet Martineau, or, among the less-well known, Miall, Sturge, Wade, Mackinnon, Bray, Spence and Combe, my aim has not been mere *Quellenforschung*, the affiliation of Spencer's ideas to their source. This would be difficult to do in any case with Spencer. He hated acknowledging intellectual debts, very rarely engaged in detailed criticism of anyone else's views, and in his autobiographical essay 'The Filiation of Ideas' neglected the deepest roots of his thought (which he may have been only dimly aware of, like most of us) for a number of late and specific borrowings of ideas from scientific sources. With some of the writers mentioned above, we *know* that he had actually read them himself (though that does not explain agreement or affinity); with others, we know that they were widely read in the circles where Spencer grew up (and since he avoided formal education almost entirely, this sort of spontaneous ingestion of belief is likely to have been important); but others of them were direct contemporaries, merely products of a similar environment, whose writings agree with, or supplement and dovetail into those of Spencer's. Where our purpose is to relate social thought to its social context, that is to write sociology of knowledge rather than intellectual history, it does not much matter whether Spencer was influenced by, say, Godwin, or whether Spencer was merely responding to social circumstances in a similar way to Godwin. The one does not exclude the other, of course; and, unless the fact of influence is just to be taken for granted, the first will tend to lead to the second.

It might, conceivably, be possible to study Spencer's thought and the origins of sociology simply as historical phenomena interesting enough in their own right—without taking up any position as to what sociology (and even, by implication, other disciplines) is, and ought to be. But it would be as undesirable as difficult to do so. We would have to disavow our chief reason for being interested in Spencer, as a founder of sociology in whom there is now a revival of interest for reasons rooted in contemporary concerns, and also relinquish our hope that we might learn something about the nature of sociology by examining the successes and failures (judged so by some present criteria) of this founding father. Traditions of thought are continually remade, not merely by new circumstances, but by self-reflexion. Up to a point, at least, we can choose our ancestors. Even such important questions (which I have hardly been able to answer here) as whether 'sociology' existed before the name, and, if not, what is the authentic character of this form of social awareness that seems peculiar to industrial and would-be industrial men—these can hardly be answered unless we have some idea as to what sociology properly is in our own day. (Perhaps for this reason the emergence of sociology has been rather neglected by the 'culture and society' tradition of literary criticism, despite its obvious impact on the novel and other literary expressions of our response to society). The danger is that the history of sociology is merely quarried to provide spurious pedigrees for current claimants to sociological legitimacy. Spencer above all has suffered from this myth-making. He has been disregarded or misrepresented where dichotomous stereotypes of conservative and radical are used to characterize classical sociology. An excessive tendency to see social theory as, above all, a projection of political ideology has concealed the extent of his area of contact with Marx. So much emphasis has been placed on Weber, Durkheim and the 1890s as the starting point of basically sound, modern sociology, that their relations with the real 'founding fathers' have been obscured, and the nature of their innovations misconceived. But these are mostly matters of simple historical error and ignorance, which may be corrected without much difficulty.

But Spencer's place in the sociological tradition can only ever be located tentatively. It *must* be seen in relation to the present state of sociology's development. This need not simply mean that Spencer's works are to be praised where they anticipate modern orthodoxies, and criticized for falling short of them. If that were all, there would be little serious point in modern sociology paying any attention to them. Nor do I propose to champion Spencer, as some have championed Marx, as an unwisely neglected thinker (though he is indeed that), whose writings contain badly needed correctives and solutions to our contemporary problems. Rather, I hope it is the case that this study is infused with a particular view as to what sociology ought to be, is permitted by its subject matter to be, and required by our purposes to be. This is expanded in Chapters 9 and 10, where Spencer's relation to his immediate successors, and his contemporary relevance, are discussed in some detail.

The history of sociology only becomes functionally necessary for the practice of sociology when sociology itself is conceived in ways radically distinct from natural science. Here it is enough to state my view baldly. Every age's sociology, our own as well as Spencer's, is irretrievably specific in its problems, both practical and theoretical. Despite its ambition to produce a universal theory of society after an *a priori* ideal drawn from natural science, it is necessarily attached to those models, metaphors and theories which best seem to capture the complex actuality which is each period of sociology's chief subject-matter: contemporary society. Spencer is superseded, as is his contemporary Marx, not primarily because his theories are wrong about Society (though insofar as each made universalist claims, each has paid the penalty), but because they refer to a very different social reality from that which confronts us. Sociologists always need to comprehend their own society first of all. But in order to do this they are obliged to create a framework for the comparative analysis of other societies, contemporary and historical, similar or alien to varying degrees; for it is only possible to see how a thing is by comparing it with what it is not, or is no longer. Thus there grows up the noble ambition for a general theory of society, rewarding as long as it does not lead to the ignoring of the variability and the specificity of human societies which gave rise to it. We can learn the most profound lessons from the history of sociology when we use it to point up the particular features of our own society and the requirements of our purposes in theorizing, both so different from Spencer's. If, as some seem to believe, a timeless and placeless Theory of Society were to be had and should be the final goal of sociology, then history, whether of sociology or of human society, would indeed be useless. It is an added poignancy that Spencer can only be of other than antiquarian interest if we abandon his own scientistic view of sociology.

As I have remarked, this book is an essay in the sociology of knowledge. In its traditional form this had two connected purposes. Firstly, it was intended as a kind of intellectual prophylaxis to enable social thought itself to free itself, as much as was possible, of 'social determination' and so approximate to the condition of natural science, taken to be the touchstone of certitude and cognitive purity; and secondly, as a consequence, it was to be a general programme for the understanding of thought as a function of its social context. But the second, sociological, purpose is in the end incompatible with the first, epistemological one. For the comparative analysis of the very variable functions of different kinds of thought in relation to patterns of social action, can only be incomplete as long as one type of thought, natural science, is excluded from its purview by being regarded as above sociological comprehension because it is an epistemological touchstone. The criteria of validity are in any case prejudged in this instance. But as T. S. Kuhn and others have shown, science itself can and should be analysed sociologically. The relevant distinction in the sociology of knowledge should not be between true thought and corrupt (i.e. socially determined) thought, but between different modes of relation between thought and action. I do not wish to assert that there is no connexion between the sociological analysis of thought, and the 'philosophical' discussion of criteria of validity (for this study is proposing to move from the first to the second). For though a genuine sociology of knowledge will not produce *directives* from prejudged criteria, it can, if it is epistemologically disinterested, yield us a measure of *guidance*. By comparing modes of thought and their functions it can enable us to choose more rationally our own criteria of fitness, in the light of our purposes and our subject matter.

I have consulted three principal collections of letters and manuscripts relating to Spencer: the Huxley Collection at Imperial College (many letters, few of them important, to and from Spencer), the Passfield Collection at the British Library of Political and Economic Science (letters between Spencer and the Potters and Webbs), and what survive of Spencer's own papers (mostly letters to Spencer) at the Athenaeum, where Spencer's Trustees deposited them in 1908. The majority of these belong to Spencer's later years; and most of the interesting and significant letters are reproduced, in whole or in part, in Duncan's *Life and Letters*. It is difficult to know how much is lost, particularly from his earlier period, when his parents and his uncle were his chief correspondents. I suspect a great deal. But the missing correspondence is unlikely to be anywhere else than at the Athenaeum. Perhaps I should add that, to judge from the surviving correspondence, Spencer does not seem to have been a particularly interesting or revealing correspondent. I would like to express my sincere thanks to the Librarians of these institutions, as of those of the Public Libraries of Derby and Nottingham and of Nottingham University, for their ready assistance—mentioning particularly Mrs. J. Pingree of Imperial College and Miss Penhaligon and Miss J. Clarke of the Athenaeum.

In writing this book I have also incurred a great many intellectual debts, some of them too diffuse to be properly acknowledged. Colleagues at Nottingham, especially M. D. King, J. S. McClelland, Daniel Lawrence and Professor Julius Gould have discussed issues and criticized drafts, to my great benefit. Outside Nottingham I would like to thank especially Dr. Steven Lukes of Balliol College Oxford and Professor D. G. MacRae of the London School of Economics for their advice; Dr. R. M. Young of King's College Cambridge for allowing me to read before publication his recent book on nineteenth-century psychology; Mr. F. R. Cowell for expediting access to the Spencer Papers at the Athenaeum; and

Mr. Clive Bemrose of Derby (whose great-grandfather saved Spencer from drowning as a boy) for showing me family papers relating to Spencer. Mrs. Eileen Davis and Mrs. Mildred Pare have earned my gratitude by the care, efficiency and good humour with which they have typed the manuscript. Finally, I would like to thank my wife Jenny; for whatever this book has of clarity of argument and expression is owed in great part to her.

J. D. Y. Peel

1: The Man and His Work

I

Posterity is cruellest to those who sum up for their contemporaries in an all-embracing synthesis the accumulated knowledge of their age. This was what Spencer did for the Victorians. So of all the great Victorian sages, Spencer lost his repute soonest; it needed no Lytton Strachey to proclaim to the Edwardians that this giant had his flaws. When he died in 1903 he was already a figure of the past whose synthesis of knowledge was not so much disproved as needed no longer. This drop into obscurity came the sooner, because, more than any other leading Victorian intellectual, he was, despite his immense popular reputation in the 1880s, an institutional outsider, attached to no parties, institutes or universities which might continue his work. Mill, Darwin, Arnold, Marshall, T. H. Green, even the journalist Bagehot, made sure of their posterity.

It is well to remind ourselves of the extent of his reputation. William James, whose obituary essay is one of the fairest and most balanced short accounts of Spencer, and by no means uncritical, wrote that he had 'enlarged the imagination and set free the speculative mind of countless doctors, engineers and lawyers, of many physicists and chemists, and of thoughtful laymen generally. To be able to say this of any man is great praise. . . .'[1] Certainly few philosophers or sociologists have ever had such a wide popular appeal, to people of all classes and nations. Captain Ross the discoverer of the cause of malaria considered himself a Spencerian.[2] *Social Statics* was much read 'by the officers on the northern frontier of India', and the Chief Commissioner of Scinde 'swears by it and acts completely on its principles'.[3] Beatrice Webb's sister once came across three farm labourers and a minister discussing *First Principles* in a train in the north of Scotland.[4] A letter arrived at his home in the early 1890s (we don't know where from) addressed to 'Herbt. Spencer,

England, and if the postman doesn't know where he lives, why, he ought to.'[5]

Spencer's appeal was strongest in the U.S.A., where hundreds of thousands of his books were sold and where his theories were an acknowledged pressure on legislation.[6] His most celebrated admirer was Andrew Carnegie, whose letters were sometimes worshipping in tone:

> Dear Master Teacher [to Spencer in 1903 during his last illness], you come to me every day in thought, and the everlasting 'why?' intrudes—Why lies he? Why must he go? and I follow. . . . The World jogs on unconscious of its greatest mind in Brighton lying silently brooding. But it will waken some day to its teachings and decree Spencer's place is with the greatest.
>
> I am ever gratefully, My Master, Your Devoted pupil
>
> Andrew Carnegie.[7]

The secret of Spencer's message in America was far deeper than its obvious ideological utility for expansionist big business. It was the promise of order in seeming chaos. This is put most eloquently by Jack London in his largely autobiographical novel *Martin Eden*, whose hero is an intelligent but ill-educated merchant seaman:

> Martin Eden had been mastered by curiosity all his days. He wanted to know and it was this desire that had sent him adventuring all over the world. But he was now learning from Spencer that he never had known and that he never could have known, had he continued his sailing and wandering for ever. He had merely skimmed over the surface of things, observing detached phenomena, making superficial little generalizations—and all and everything quite unrelated in a capricious and disorderly world of whim and chance.
>
> And here was the man Spencer, organizing knowledge for him, reducing everything to unity, elaborating ultimate realities and presenting to his startled gaze a universe so concrete of realization that it was like the model of a ship such as sailors make and put into glass bottles. There was no caprice, no chance. All was Law. . . .
>
> Martin had ascended from pitch to pitch of intellectual living and here he was at a higher pitch than ever. All the hidden things were laying their secrets bare. He was drunken with comprehension. . . .[8]

Spencer struck American universities like lightning in the early 1860s and dominated them for thirty years.[9] His visit to the United States in 1882 was a triumphal progress.

But his ideas also found ready listeners in more remote and alien places—Russia, China, Japan and other Asian countries. Here Spencer stood for science, reason, progress, the conquest of backwardness and tradition, enlightenment and the ideals of youth. In Chekhov's short story *The Duel* (1891) a female character recalls the idyllic beginnings of a relationship:

> . . . to begin with we had kisses, and calm evenings, and vows, and Spencer, and ideals and interests in common. . . .[10]

Spencer's best-selling and most translated book *Education*, with its businesslike question 'What Knowledge is of most use?' seemed the key to the regeneration of society. Against the arbitrary conventions of tradition stood the calm directives of nature and necessity. The sociology suggested a necessary path by which backward nations might progress. Spencer was consulted about both general policy and the reorganization of education by leading Japanese diplomats and ministers.[11] Chairman Mao was influenced by Spencer in his youth.

But in Europe both events and theories rapidly came to make him seem redundant. His theories were abandoned if they seemed false or irrelevant, and if they were true or useful, like many of his sociological concepts, they were absorbed into a tradition and their author forgotten. The view of G. Simpson, Durkheim's translator, that 'there would seem to be no reason for being interested in Spencer's ideas after Durkheim has finished with them', was characteristic.[12] They were totally discredited because they were so obviously intended as part of a system that was unacceptable as a whole. Spencer's relations with Beatrice Webb (née Potter) illustrate neatly his failure to impress posterity.[13] She was the daughter of one of his oldest friends, and intended by Spencer as his literary executor and intellectual heir. Despite personal friendship and intellectual tutelage from Spencer, she drifted away from his ideas in the late 1880s—first criticizing *laissez-faire*, becoming socialist and imperialist. Not only her political opinions, but her notion of what 'social science' should be—the accumulation of data needed to implement a social policy—diverged widely from Spencer's, and long dominated the British sociological tradition.

By the 1930s people were finding it difficult to understand how Spencer had ever had his great reputation, and were speaking of his writings as if they were the fossil remains of an extinct megasaur. 'Who now reads Spencer?' asked Crane Brinton in 1933, 'It is difficult for us to realize how great a stir he made in the world. . . . We have evolved beyond Spencer.'[14] Socialists and fascists could only see in Spencer the characteristic thinker of a liberal and individualist, confident and optimistic world which lay in ruins about them. He could be nothing more than a 'curious and in many ways absurd philosopher whose theories of political society are now little more than academic dodos preserved in American university courses.'[15] It is not possible for an English intellectual to be more contemptuous.

Since 1950 the rediscovery, exegesis and criticism of Victorian literary figures has become a minor but flourishing industry, but even here we have been slow to look at Spencer again, either to find what it was in him that stirred his contemporaries, or to see if there is anything of enduring value in him that has not been absorbed or reacted against already. It is not hard to see why those of a moralistic or literary bent find the reading of Spencer tedious and unrewarding. Spencer is to be read for his *ideas*, which means reading beyond his fascinating and amazing (though still highly intellectual) *Autobiography*. Although his essays and occasional articles are often pungent, colloquial and simply expressed (usually excellent pieces of scientific writing, at once popular and original), the main substance of his thought, *The System of Synthetic Philosophy*, is conveyed in tough, powerful, ugly prose—difficult but nearly always clear.

Some will not treat Spencer as a scientific thinker because, evidently, they cannot. A. O. J. Cockshut, who considers Spencer 'a failure of course . . . a bore, of course,' though 'a heartening portent' that human behaviour cannot be made the subject of science, says Spencer was not a scientist at all, but 'a failed Wordsworth'! His system was an attempt to provide 'a viable view of life when religion was lost' (which is part of the truth), and is only to be considered as one might consider a poem, as the expression of an interior state of feeling.[16] Naturally, there are very few references to the thousands of pages of scientific argument. It is fashionable to contrast Spencer with Darwin, whom everyone respects. Cockshut contrasts Spencer's use of principles to 'cut through the tangle of evidence' with Darwin's 'great strength as a scientist'—that 'he had few general ideas and none of great significance. He followed the evidence. . . .' Gertrude Himmelfarb, on the other hand, speaks of

Darwin's 'amiable credulity', and claims (surely correctly), that his theoretical notions directed his selection of the facts; but nonethless finds Spencer's work 'a parody of philosophy' and 'comic and pathetic'. She finds it 'surprising' that T. H. Huxley, 'who did not suffer fools readily, found him sufficiently well-informed to discuss anatomy with him'.[17] (Cockshut can only explain the Victorian regard for Spencer as one of the 'weaknesses' of the age.)

The practising scientists, whether Spencer's contemporaries or ours, tend to rate Spencer's scientific abilities differently. Hooker, Darwin, Huxley, Galton and A. R. Wallace all spoke highly of both his intellect and its scientific achievements. Wallace wrote of 'the sun of his great intellectual powers',[18] and Galton, who disagreed profoundly in his theories, of his 'magnificent intellect'.[19] Hooker, writing to Darwin about a new book of the latter's, says that 'not one Naturalist in a hundred can follow it. . . . Spencer, Huxley and Lubbock may'.[20] In our own day Sir Peter Medawar, almost the only natural scientist to have discussed Spencer, has rated his system of knowledge among the greatest examples of a now unfashionable genre—a serious attempt, if in the end unsuccessful, to generalize important scientific ideas.[21]

The kind of universal synthesis of science in a philosophical system, or *Naturphilosophie*, of which Spencer produced such a noteable instance, has no appeal to the scientists of today, nor very much to other professional academics (though the popular success of Teilhard de Chardin shows that its appeal to the wider circle of the reading public is by no means extinct). But Spencer's venture seemed worthwhile to the leading professional scientists as well as to the public which was eager to know. Huxley, for example, on reading the proofs of *First Principles* in 1860 wrote that it was important 'that somebody should think out into a connected system the loose notions that are floating about more or less distinctly in all the best minds'.[22] He likened his own work to hemp-yarn and Spencer's to rope—'Work away then, excellent ropemaker, and make us more ropes to hold on against the devil and the parsons'. Wallace, impressed by a reading of *First Principles* in 1862–3, went to visit Spencer, for 'Our thoughts were full of the great unsolved problem of the origin of life . . . and we looked to Spencer as the one man living who could give us some clue to it.'[23] Even J. S. Mill, no scientist and one whose conception of philosophy was very different from Spencer's, considered *First Principles* 'a remarkable [book] in many respects and its far-reaching systemization of so many heterogeneous elements is very imposing.'[24] Spencer's understanding of what philosophy is probably most distances him from us. It was not a critique of reason or a methodology for science but simply the coping-stone of science, the most general knowledge to be had of nature. The word 'scientist' had only recently been coined (by Whewell in 1840) and 'natural philosophy' was not yet wholly an archaism. But the change in ideas about the proper field of philosophy (and the growth of a specialized subject 'philosophy', due partly to the eventual unacceptability of Spencer's system) occurred in the course of his lifetime.

Today it is sociologists and anthropologists who have reason to take more than an antiquarian interest in Spencer. It is, as I shall discuss in the final chapter, proper that this should be so, but it comes after decades of neglect. There is no tradition of Spencer studies, no recognized cruxes and points of dispute, no shared focuses of debate. The intellectual biographer or interpreter of Spencer has, therefore, a freedom which the student of Marx, for example, does not have. But a convenient point of orientation is provided by the context in which the present revival of interest in Spencer is occurring. The relation of the theory of social evolution to the actual course of historical change will be the main focus of interest here.

II

Spencer's *Autobiography*, the bulk of which was written when he was in his late sixties, is entirely typical of the man. It centres on his ideas and at a conscious level is very candid and revealing of his intellectual habits and development. It also fully confirms George Eliot's remark that 'the life of this philosopher, like that of the great Kant, offers little material for the narrator'.[25] Spencer's extraordinary character offers great scope for ill-founded speculations, and his contemporaries kept record of, or invented, a large number of absurd anecdotes about his quaint habits. But his real life was the working out of his ideas. The biographer must concentrate on these, and on the various intellectual traditions and social influences which fashioned his thought. The most important of these influences will be considered in the next few chapters. Since their order is not chronological I give in this section a brief outline of the main events of Spencer's life.

Herbert Spencer was born on 27 April 1820 at Derby, in a red-brick terrace of little houses (demolished in 1969) on what was then the edge of the town. His father, William George Spencer, was a private teacher of some reputation among the well-to-do of the neighbourhood. Herbert was the eldest of seven children, of whom no other survived infancy. Of his uncles, one was a solicitor, and led a secession of the Wesleyans at Derby before emigrating to California; another, the Rev. Thomas Spencer, went to Cambridge and entered the ministry of the Established Church, of Simeon's evangelical party; a third was also a teacher. His Spencer relatives were electors, and figure in the town directories of the early nineteenth century. The Spencers had lands at Wirksworth and Kirk Ireton, places a few miles north of Derby, whence they had moved a few generations back; other ancestors came from Scotland and the Black Country. His grandparents on all four sides were Wesleyan Methodists (including lay preachers and class leaders), and further back Independents, Calvinists and Unitarians, besides Churchmen. Spencer proudly regarded himself as having inherited Dissenting habits, and considered his own life a continuation of their traditions.

His father and his uncle Thomas were the main influences on the boy. They left strong impressions on those who knew them. George Eliot (who met Thomas Spencer, and later William George, in the circle of friends of Charles Bray, radical editor and ribbon manufacturer of Coventry) found Spencer's father 'a large-brained, highly-informed man, with a certain quaintness and simplicity, altogether very pleasing'. The Rev. T. Mozley, a prominent Tractarian who had been taught by Spencer senior as a boy, described him as tall, spare, upright, a good talker and listener, popular and highly speculative, and said 'he could not appear in a street without everybody in it becoming immediately sensible of the fact'.[26] He was an unusual and excellent teacher, and though not given to doubt in his own mind, taught others to question, doubt all authority and to learn by experience and discovery. He upheld what have come to be regarded as very modern methods of learning, by self-instruction;[27] and his book *Inventional Geometry* 'presented [it] . . . as a field of discovery'.[28] His son lists a number of traits which they both shared: punctuality, inventiveness, impracticality, finicky attachments to peculiar ways of doing things; and adds coolly that he was not kind to his wife Harriet, Herbert Spencer's mother. Like many provincial radicals of the period he was possessed of an apolitical zeal for general improvement which expressed itself in speculation about nature and society, and in schemes for the re-ordering of society according to a perfect unitary system. 'He was always supposing a state of things that in his opinion ought to be, but which confessedly was not, and was not likely to be in our time.'[29]

Mrs. Spencer was unremarkable in any way, an orthodox and piously observant Wesleyan. Her husband retained the industry, sobriety and sense of duty which the evangelical revival stimulated, but became highly unorthodox in his beliefs. Though a member of the Library Committee of the Derby Methodists, he drifted away from them, objecting, said his son, to the power of the ministers over them, and began attending Quaker services, taking Herbert with him, because he liked the quiet reflexion, free of doctrinal restraints. There was later a controversy between Herbert Spencer and Mozley respecting his actual beliefs.[30] Spencer objected to Mozley's opinion that 'Mr. (W. G.) Spencer had no religion in the sense I then attached to that word' and that 'he avowed no doctrines except for those of a purely ethical or philosophical character'. But to a churchman like Mozley, many advanced Quakers or Unitarians must have seemed like this. It seems that though Spencer senior came to regard his son's beliefs as far more radical than his own, his own beliefs may be regarded as a scientific deism. Herbert Spencer attributed his own basic scientific outlook to his father's hostility to any kind of supernaturalism in explanation of things.[31] So his non-conforming contempt for the customary usages of orthodoxy, and his rationalist distrust of its intellectual content, had left the moral residue of evangelicalism (here he did differ from such eighteenth-century deists as Hume or Erasmus Darwin) wrapped in the scantiest deism.

Spencer's early boyhood was spent at Derby, except for three years when his father gave up teaching to go to Nottingham to try lace manufacture on the new machines, at which he was not successful.[32] He was sent to day school, and was a quick though reluctant rote learner; his real education he provided for himself in roaming the countryside collecting specimens, drawing, day-dreaming, associating with his father's scientific friends (members of the Derby Philosophical Society, of which W. G. Spencer was secretary), reading their scientific books and periodicals—in sum doing whatever his curious and speculative fancy prompted. There was also, says Spencer the son, his father's habit of asking questions about the causes of the phenomena he came across. It seems to have been a happy childhood, and an excellent preparation for scientific activity.

When Spencer was 13, it was decided he should go and live with his uncle Thomas, who had a living at Hinton Charterhouse, near Bath, in order to acquire a more thorough and orthodox education. The Rev. Thomas Spencer, an impressive-looking man, was that rarity, a rural parson who was eager for church reform and the repeal of the Corn Laws, and who wore the white hat of radicalism. He was respected but not liked in the parish, for his talk was all 'dogma and commandment', says Mozley, and 'he had none of the small coinage of courtesy'.[32] He exhibited what must be a typically Victorian character-syndrome, a restlessness which never found release, aggravated by the strain of perpetual conscientiousness. He died of overwork, his nephew tells us, and in his restless energy he outdid Mr. Gladstone, for he used to break stones in a quarry with a crow-bar to let off steam. Uncle Thomas was the author of that celebrated remark in front of his teenage nephew at a dance—'No Spencer ever dances!'[34]

Apart from an occasion a few weeks after arriving at Hinton when out of homesickness he ran away to Derby (reaching it in three days, and walking most of the way), Herbert Spencer enjoyed his stay with his uncle, whose company he grew to like more as he grew older. By the age of 16 he had acquired a reasonable if narrow education—plenty of mathematics, mechanics, physics, chemistry; some logic and political economy, with much discussion of social topics; but scanty French and Classics; and hardly any history, literature or poetry. It is a significant range of subjects when we consider Spencer's subsequent intellectual interests. Under his uncle's aegis, his literary career had already begun, with short articles critical of the Poor Laws in a local general magazine. It was now time to think of a proper career, and, having considered and rejected teaching, he joined the staff of the London and Birmingham

Railway to become a civil engineer, where his supervisor was Mr. (later Sir) Charles Fox, son of Dr. Fox of Derby, a friend of his father.

To have entered railway engineering in 1837, on the eve of the period of construction of the greatest lines, and to have continued in it intermittently until 1846, to have surveyed cuttings and inclines, designed and prepared schemes for Parliamentary Bills, is to have been an intimate participant in the last great battle of the Industrial Revolution in England, and the final opening up of the country. It was the railways, and their consequences for the movement of goods, people and ideas, which the Victorian novelists singled out as a change so important that it served best to symbolize the whole social transformation.[35] It was Spencer's only direct experience of industrial life, and, though he does not seem to have seen its great significance at the time, it enabled him to speak to the mid-Victorians with a peculiarly appropriate sense of the times. His duties were very varied and took him all over the Midlands, moving from one railway as it was finished to another. He had plenty of free time to pursue his scientific and speculative interests; the fossils excavated in line-building led him to read Lyell's *Principles of Geology*, and, a significant event, so to become acquainted with the ideas of Lamarck. He read papers on engineering subjects to a railway staff club, and had some published in engineering magazines. He even had published articles on phrenology, which was at the height of its short-lived popularity. He made a few simple inventions, of which he was inordinately proud. (This remained a typical little weakness of Spencer.)

The appeal of phrenology to a young autodidact like Spencer is appropriate and significant. He had become a believer when Spurzheim, a leading disciple of the founder F. J. Gall, visited Derby about 1830 on a lecture tour. The main British phrenologist, George Combe, said it 'advances . . . rapidly in the humbler grades of the middle rank . . . not so among philosophers of the old school, professors and literati'.[36] It ran through the newly founded Mechanics' Institutes like a fire, and soon became a middle-class parlour-game. The biologist A. R. Wallace, at that time, like Spencer, a self-taught railway surveyor who had slipped from orthodoxy, was an adherent;[37] and so was Richard Cobden, to whom 'it seemed like a transcript of his own familiar thoughts' and who wrote a play called 'The Phrenologist'.[39] Combe's book, *The Constitution of Man* (1828), which John Morley said was 'seen on shelves where there was nothing else save the Bible and Pilgrim's Progress', furnished a bridge between traditional religion and purely secular amelioration. It stressed the values of self-help and adaptive change, and in its popular, Combean form, was still part of a deistic, this-wordly, natural religion; but it was one of the general agencies of popular secularization. Combe said that phrenology 'as a branch of physical science gives scope to the talents of those who are fond of observation and love to approach nature in her most palpable form';[39] and those who felt for the organs of adhesiveness, eventuality or philo-progenitiveness must have been gratified that science, religion and self-improvement coincided so well. Phrenology was, in its way, an exploration, if a futile one, of the boundaries between mind and body, the main focus of nineteenth-century mental science; and as will be seen, Spencer's writings on psychology, composed after he had abandoned belief in phrenology, hover continually round the same problems, and shared some of its assumptions.

When Spencer moved from the London and Birmingham Railway in 1838 to join the Birmingham and Gloucester he entered 'social surroundings of a previously unknown kind'.[40] At the former, under Mr. Fox, his companions had been like himself, two of them sons of dissenting ministers; now the staff 'belonged largely to the ruling classes, and had corresponding notions and habits'. Spencer thus joined that great tide of middle-class and dissenting feeling whose leaders were Cobden, Bright and the Anti-Corn Law Leaguers. Class-feeling, especially among the middle-class against first the 'ruling-class' and later the working class, reached one of its peaks in the 1840s, and Spencer took up radical politics, though his passionate and utopian belief in progress meant that he could not be wholly serious about political agitation. For he was 'quite satisfied that whatever temporary stoppages there may be in the progress of Reform, we shall continually advance towards a better state'.[41]

In 1842 he gave up railway work for a while and returned to Derby, restlessly trying his hand at various projects. One of these was his first work of consequence, a series of letters entitled 'The Proper Sphere of Government', to *The Nonconformist*, a Dissenting paper whose editor, Edward Miall, a Congregational minister at

Leicester, was acquainted with Uncle Thomas. These letters are very indicative of what was to come later—society is governed by laws just as nature is, and man's mind just as his body is; only harm can come from these laws being disregarded; the sphere of government should be restricted as much as possible. These theses fitted well in a paper which proclaimed 'the Dissidence of Dissent' and concentrated its attacks on the Church Establishment.

Later in 1842 Miall joined with Joseph Sturge, the prominent Birmingham Quaker, to establish the Complete Suffrage Union, whose aim was to contact Lovett and the 'moral-force' Chartists and to form a common front with them. Spencer became secretary of the Derby branch of the C.S.U. and reported relevant local doings in *The Nonconformist*. A meeting between the C.S.U. and the Chartists at Birmingham, at which John Bright and Rev. Thomas Spencer were leading delegates, came to nothing, and for a year or two Spencer went back to his sundry projects, which came to have a more consistently literary bent. But in 1844 he was invited by Joseph Sturge to return to Birmingham to be sub-editor of *The Pilot*, a radical paper, and wrote leaders on political and commercial topics. His acquaintance with middle-class radical politics deepened. He became friendly with Lawrence Heyworth (the maternal grandfather of Beatrice Webb), a Unitarian merchant from Liverpool, for whose successful candidacy for Liberal M.P. for Derby in 1848 Spencer was an eager supporter. The political radicalism of this provincial Dissenting and manufacturing leadership, which demanded a reduction on the powers of the government, the Established Church, the aristocracy and the landed interest, and, less strongly, a great extension of the franchise, had not yet been turned aside by their absorption into the upper classes after 1850.

Spencer did not stay in journalism long. The Sturges were financing another railway in the Black Country, and Spencer was released from his duties to take up engineering again. The great 'Railway Mania' was at hand, and Spencer now saw much more of the promotional and administrative sides of railway construction; his attendance on committees at Westminster did not impress him with the competence of M.P.s. Underlying his surveying activities was a continual restlessness, trying one enthusiasm and then another. He finally left engineering in 1846, and after a period in which he turned again to inventions, finally secured what looked like a firm job: in 1848 he moved to London to be sub-editor of *The Economist*, a post acquired through Uncle Thomas' influence with its owner, Mr. James Wilson.

It was an ideal job. Spencer's duties were not arduous, and he was soon a guest at the house of the publisher John Chapman, along the Strand. So came his entry into the intellectual circles of London. At Chapman's he met Froude, F. W. Newman, and G. H. Lewes, with whom he established a serious intellectual friendship. *Social Statics*, on which he had been working for several years, a summation of the experience of provincial radicalism in the 1840s, appeared in late 1850, and was, on the whole, well received. This period seems to have been the happiest and most settled in Spencer's life. In 1851 he met Marian Evans (yet to become George Eliot) at Chapman's, and developed a close friendship with 'the translatress of Strauss'.[42] They began to go to the theatre and opera together, and Spencer wrote to his friend Lott at Derby:

> We have been for some time past on very intimate terms. I am very frequently at Chapman's and the greatness of her intellect conjoined with her womanly qualities and manner, generally keep me by her side most of the evening.[43]

She described their relationship in these terms:

> My brightest spot, next to my love of *old* friends, is the deliciously calm *new* friendship that Herbert Spencer gives me. We see each other every day, and have a delightful camaraderie in everything. But for him my life would be wretched enough.[44]

The details of the relationship are obscure, but it is clear that Marian Evans felt much more deeply for Spencer than he for her; and even then it was intellectual friendship rather than her sexual nature which attracted him. Yet his behaviour was equivocal enough for him afterwards to issue somewhat excessively strenuous denials that there had been any possibility of an engagement. He justified himself a bit too much, one feels, and made ungallant references to her ugliness. When, through Spencer, Marian Evans met G. H. Lewes, their friendship became less close, though it was maintained until her death in 1880. She wrote to him as 'Dear friend . . .', and Lewes seems to have been one of the most intimate and jovial of his correspondents.[45] Yet George Eliot had sized up the egotism of

Spencer's character, which had lain behind the failure of their love affair:

> His mind rejects everything that cannot be wrought into the web of his own production. . . . We have long given up vain expectations from him and can therefore enjoy our regard for him without disturbance by his negations. He comes and consults us about his own affairs, and that is his way of showing friendship. We never dream of telling him *our* affairs, which would certainly not interest him.[46]

After *Social Statics* came a flood of articles some of which, notably 'The Development Hypothesis' (1852–4) and 'A Theory of Population' (1852), published in the leading reviews, foreshadow later work. These were the years of his greatest intellectual excitement and discovery. His acquaintances with T. H. Huxley, and later Tyndall and other scientific figures, led him to read the French and German biologists, and to attend lectures on science at the Royal Institution. His work as a reviewer gave him sufficient knowledge of the dispute between Mill and Whewell to wish to contribute to this epistemological debate, and *The Principles of Psychology* originates in these years. An idea of what was to be his life's work was now gelling in his mind; the main formative influences were there; and in 1853, on his uncle's death, a legacy under his will enabled him to give up his post at *The Economist* to devote himself, an entirely independent man, to his writing.

When the *Psychology* came out in 1854 Spencer went so far as to confess in a letter that 'my private opinion is that it will ultimately stand by Newton's *Principia*'.[47] In 1852 he had begun to read Comte, and gave it up in disgust unfinished, though reading Harriet Martineau's abridgment and conversations with Lewes, who avowed himself a positivist (a term Spencer always rejected for himself), gave him a better acquaintance with his ideas. In 1856 he visited Comte in Paris to give him a remittance from John Chapman. It was a very unmomentous meeting; Spencer found him 'a very undignified little old man',[48] They had an argument in French 'in a very slipshod style', and Comte advised Spencer to cure his depressions (which had now begun) by getting married.

As he always protested, perhaps overmuch, he was little affected by Comte's influence, and mostly to react against it. The growth of Spencer's system was merely a wave in a swelling tide of English opinion. The idea of progress had been a stock notion since the eighteenth century, and had become popularly diffused in a biological form largely through the anonymous *Vestiges of the Natural History of Creation* (1843). Spencer had been discussing 'the development hypothesis' with Lewes in 1850 and had helped put the word 'evolution' into common parlance during the 1850s. If ever an idea was vaguely in the air before it was made concrete in one work, it was this. At the house of Baden-Powell, a progressive clergyman, 'talk ran terribly on material evolution' at gatherings in 1855;[49] and in the same year Spencer sent Tennyson a copy of his *Psychology* because of the words 'Or if thro' lower lives I came . . .' in 'The Two Voices'. (The references to the struggle of nature in 'In Memoriam' are better known.) So the work of synthesizing his ideas around this great central theme went on until in 1857 he decided on a massive system of philosophy, beginning with the humble biological origins, and ending with the highest ethical principles. This was to be his life-work.

III

Spencer's existence now assumed the general pattern that remained for the rest of his eighty-three years. In 1855 tension and overwork had precipitated a nervous breakdown which inaugurated the valetudinarian condition which never again wholly left him. For a few years his financial position, despite further family legacies, remained precarious. An attempt to secure a post at the India Office through J. S. Mill came to nothing; but eventually the sales of his works, particularly his little book *Education* (1861), gave him financial independence. In those days too, it was possible to make some sort of living as a freelance reviewer and writer of articles for the great reviews, the *Westminster*, the *Contemporary* and the *Nineteenth Century*. By 1860 he had managed to collect about six hundred subscribers for the *System of Synthetic Philosophy*, which he outlined in a printed programme. With extraordinary doggedness this neurotic semi-invalid, for nearly forty years, forged ahead along the lines thus laid down, producing volume after volume (besides other occasional books and articles), until, with ten volumes, the system was substantially complete. The first volume, *First Principles* (1862) contained the foundations of this evolutionary *Naturphilosophie*, and was, when it came out, modern and radical in a way that the subsequent volumes were not. The judicious Mill, who found Spencer 'a considerable thinker though anything but a safe one', wrote to Alexander Bain in 1866 describing him as 'the rising philosophical name of the present'.[50]

The Principles of Biology appeared in 1864 and 1867, by which time interest in Spencer was being shown overseas, particularly America, where Spencer's champion was E. L. Youmans. The late 1860s saw the revising of *First Principles*, the beginning of reading on sociology (now so-called), and the complete overhaul of the *Psychology*, whose second edition, in two volumes, came out in 1870 and 1872. At the suggestion of his American friends Spencer now turned aside from the *System* to produce, first in the form of articles in *The Popular Science Monthly*, and later in book form, *The Study of Sociology* (1874) —a methodology for social science, critical of historiography and preparatory to his later work. It sold well, which is not surprising, for it is clear and vigorously written in Spencer's best popular style.

Besides *The Study of Sociology*, Spencer had already, in 1867, engaged a young Scot, David Duncan, to search histories and ethnographies to 'put in fitly classified groups and tables, facts of all kinds, presented by numerous races, which illustrate social evolution under its various aspects'.[51] It was a forerunner of the joint research project under supervision, and resulted in a series called *Descriptive Sociology*—vast folio volumes with the facts duly classified in columns. The first one was issued in 1873, and they continued to come out, different races and societies by different hands, all in the same format, for years, even after Spencer's own death. The columns of facts, arranged by structure and function, look quaint; the volumes are unwieldly and unread; but they were notice that sociology was a new and serious subject. The first part of *The Principles of Sociology* came out in 1873, and subsequent ones, as well as *The Principles of Ethics*, were published at irregular intervals till 1896 when the whole series was concluded, though not in quite the form initially projected. Spencer merely remarked to his amanuensis, when the last sentence was complete: 'I have finished the task I have lived for.'[52]

His writing was undertaken intermittently as his nervous condition permitted. Towards the end of his life he allowed himself very little social intercourse at all, but in the 1860s and 1870s his life was active enough. As a prominent intellectual radical he attended J. S. Mill's Saturday dinner parties at Blackheath—where Grote, John Morley, Louis Blanc, Fawcett and Cairnes the economists, were frequent guests. On one such occasion Mill challenged Spencer to expound his philosophy, which he did in twenty minutes; his ability at exposition was much admired.[53] Despite serious disagreements with Mill—about the latter's *Logic*, and his leanings towards socialism and Comtean positivism—Spencer stood squarely with Mill on the radical side. The radicals, for all their divisions, still formed a coherent party. The ferment over *The Origin of Species* provided them with one issue; the prosecution of Governor Eyre in 1865 another.[54] As Governor of Jamaica, Eyre had suppressed an uprising with extraordinary brutality; opinion was mobilized against him by Dissenting anti-slavery circles—the names of Spencer's friends Edward Miall and T. B. Potter were prominent—and under Mill's chairmanship the Jamaica Committe was set up to prosecute Eyre for murder. Few issues so polarized the leaders of opinion; as Huxley (anti-Eyre) wrote to Kingsley (pro-Eyre), 'the great use of the prosecution . . . is that it will help a great many people to find out what their profoundest political beliefs are'.[55] Besides the Dissenters, the positivists (Lewes and Harrison), the leading liberal intellectuals (Dicey, Mill, T. H. Green) and the evolutionists (Lyell, Huxley, Darwin) aligned themselves against Eyre; and on several counts Spencer stood with them. Their opponents, said Huxley, were the hero-worshippers, the supporters of force and violence; and their number included Carlyle, Ruskin, Kingsley, Dickens and Tennyson.

Spencer was a regular contributor to the organs of the 'party of humanity'. There was the short-lived *Leader* managed by Holyoake and edited by Lewes; and later the famous *Fortnightly Review* edited by Morley, whose opening number in November 1865 took up the Jamaican cause. Spencer became increasingly alienated from the political radicalism of these journals in so far as 'radicalism' came to mean socialism or state intervention. His opposition to all kinds of militarism and imperial expansion (a relic of the older Dissenting radicalism of John Bright), and his support of educational reform and science, however, aligned him with the progressive party. In 1865 he actually became co-editor of *The Reader*, a weekly journal for the wide dissemination of science. It had been founded in 1863, and collapsed in 1866; a fellow-editor, Francis Galton, remarked that Spencer 'wasted the time of the committee in discussing first principles'.[56]

The cynosure of scientific radicalism was the X Club, an unofficial but highly influential group of nine scientists, who met once a month to dine and to discuss matters of interest to science.[57] It soon acquired the reputation of a scientific caucus: 'they govern scientific affairs', said someone at the Athenaeum, 'and really on the whole they don't do it badly'. Huxley, Tyndall, Lubbock and Hooker were among the members, and except for Spencer all were Fellows of the Royal Society; Darwin and Galton were not members, but attended occasionally as guests. Elections to Educational Boards, the presidencies of the various scientific societies, general scientific policy, opposing the 'theological party', were their typical concerns. In the summer they went with their wives on picnics and boating trips up the Thames. For nineteen years after its foundation in 1864 its membership was unchanged; it never elected new members and when in 1893 it dissolved itself it had met 240 times. John Fiske, a leading American evolutionist, attended one of their dinners, and recalled:

> It was a jolly company . . . the ordering of a dinner was usually entrusted to Spencer, who was an expert in gastronomy and as eminent in the synthesis of a *menu* as in any other branch of synthetic philosophy.[58]

Spencer was elected to the Athenaeum in 1867, and it became the focus of his social life in London. His range of acquaintances was now very wide, and helped provide him with the changes of scenery and diversions he liked. He never bought a house himself, but changed lodgings several times. Fiske speaks of 'dainty little suppers at Spencer's lodgings . . . on which occasions I have known men berated as materialists to join in singing psalm-tunes'.[59] For many years he lived in a boarding house in Bayswater, where he played the flute and enjoyed the intellectually unexacting company of retired military men. A bizarre, and in the end ludicrous episode, was his living with two unmarried ladies who kept house for him—a relationship which ended with Spencer's accusing them of mismanagement. As 'Two' they later wrote a book of memoirs absurd even among Spenceriana. His closest friends were the Huxleys; the Leweses; the Potters, whose house at Standish in Gloucestershire he used to visit, and with whose growing family he became good friends; the Smiths, wealthy ex-Dissenting brewers who owned an estate at Ardtornish in Argyll, where the fishing was excellent;[60] Edward Lott, a lifelong friend from boyhood days in Derby; and E. L. Youmans, his chief American disciple who arranged his successful American tour in 1882. Throughout his life he lacked neither friends, nor, despite his nervous condition, rude physical health and the capacity for strenuous exercise—walking, rackets, rowing, fishing, climbing, skating.

Spencer's life is marked by a series of steps down from his eager, optimistic and active condition in the early 1850s. In 1855 his nervous invalidism commenced. In the 1860s, despite the heroic labours of synthesis, the social ideals of *Social Statics* which had seemed so radical for 1848, came to seem old fashioned in the climate of the new liberalism, and Spencer adopted more consciously the position of defending attitudes and ideals which looked increasingly irrelevant. The book of essays he published in 1884, *The Man versus the State,* got him the reputation of being a conservative (though he attacked socialism as 'The New Toryism', indicating how much his argument rested on the assumptions of the radicalism of 1832–48). He remarked in a letter to Youmans: 'oddly enough, I am patted on the back by the Conservatives, which is a new experience for me.'[61] One whose views on land-ownership in *Social Statics* had caused many to regard him as a Communist was now sought after by bodies like the London Ratepayers Defence League.[62] It was not only that progressive opinion had left Spencer behind; with age (and with sociology?) he had become more relativistic and hence able to countenance views which his youthful radicalism would have dismissed outright. To justify his opposing Home Rule for Ireland he wrote in 1892:

> In my early days I held the unhesitating opinion that self-government was good for all people, but a life passed in acquiring knowledge of societies in all stages has brought a decided change of opinion. The goodness of these or those institutions is purely relative to the natures of the men living under them.[63]

The outdating of Spencer's opinions, to be discussed further in Chapter 10, came from several quarters. His political ideals were already passé by the early 1850s, and were utterly irrelevant by the 1880s, when 'Social Darwinism', to which he was supposed to adhere, was being widely used to justify policies he abhorred. His scientific ideas came under serious attack somewhat later. Most painful were the criticisms of his biology, especially his defence of the inheritance of acquired characteristics, since they came from his friends Huxley and Hooker. In the early 1890s Spencer was engaged in a controversy on this topic with August Weismann, and though William James considered this his best work, 'genuine labor over a puzzle, genuine research',[64] he was judged to have lost. The philosophical climate, too, at the end of the century, turned cold for Spencer—the Hegelianism of Green and Bosanquet was consciously opposed to his style of utilitarianism and individualism. Moreover, developments in physics, workings out of the second law of thermodynamics, suggested that if there was a movement in the universe it was entropy, a tendency to 'mixed-upness', and not to the increasing order and heterogeneity which Spencer described in *First Principles*. Spencer disregarded Clark Maxwell's careful exposition, though, as Bertrand Russell told Beatrice Potter, 'this used to worry optimists about the time when Spencer was old'.[65]

But Spencer was no longer an optimist. As he grew older, his hopes were increasingly dashed aside. The great system was fixed, and he could only become embattled behind its assertions, attempting to salvage what he could. His psychological misery increased apace with the decomposition of his synthesis. He came to have an almost morbid fear of being misquoted and misrepresented, and open intellectual debate became impossible to bear. This self-imposed protective isolation was made worse by the deaths of his closest friends, in whose company he had talked out his ideas—Lewes died in 1878, George Eliot in 1880, Lott in 1886, Youmans in 1887, Huxley in 1895. Those that remained were, in the main, lesser men, dull secretaries, sycophants, or remote adoring Syrians and Punjaubees.[66] He longed for the company of children and found most peace with the family of Richard Potter, whose daughter Beatrice called him 'guide, philosopher and friend'.[67] Yet even her he did not see often. A letter written to her a few months before he died says he could take no pleasure at all in his past achievements;

when to tried to recollect 'the average colour of the whole consciousness produced is grey'.[68]

IV

The nature of Spencer's system, and the way he thought, are intimately related to his personal character. One should not reduce the content of his thought, or belittle its general significance, by remarking on this, but one cannot understand the thought apart from the man, or, more even than with most thinkers, the man apart from his intellectual achievements. It has been said of some thinkers —Freud,[69] or T. H. Huxley, for example—that impressive as their works are, their lives, as we see them in their actions, their letters and the testimonies of their friends, show them to have been greater men still. Such is not the case with Spencer. Of him William James wrote, unkindly but not unfairly, that never were greatness and pettiness so oddly mixed.[70] Monotonous, petty, cantankerous, small-minded, self-pitying he was; but he grasped a great idea, evolution, and in working out all its implications and ramifications, he achieved an intellectual tour-de-force. For us the content of his theories is everything; the character of the man significant only so far as it is necessary for an understanding of the thought.

It is convenient to begin with the nervous condition which came on when he was 35 and got steadily worse throughout the rest of his life.[71] It began during a holiday in North Wales when he was, as he wrote to Huxley, 'knocked . . . up with hard work'.[72] 'The mischief', as he usually referred to it, began with 'a sensation in [his] head—not pain, nor heat, nor fulness, nor tension, but simply a sensation, bearable enough but abnormal'.[73] Thereafter he was only able to work in short bursts, alternately with walking, or playing a game, or resting; and he became progressively less able to engage in intellectual debate, and at times any kind of social intercourse, lest he suffer from insomnia. An incident described by an elderly uncle, on visiting Spencer at his lodgings, seems typical:

> We had tea with my nephew, Herbert Spencer, who allowed us 10 minutes by his watch and then departed to his study, leaving us to finish our tea and enjoy the excellent madeira cake to which we did full justice. We were shown out by the servant who informed us civilly that his master was engaged and hoped we would excuse him.[74]

The ear-muffs with which he used to shut out the unwanted excitement of conversation have become legendary, but they were not an affectation. He wrote to Huxley many years later: 'My history is always the same—improvement, avoidance for a time of dangers and mischiefs, and then some incident which puts me off my guard, resulting in disaster.'[75] Though excitement had in the past caused sleeplessness, his terrible insomnia now became persistent. The only other physical symptoms, in a man who had singular bodily health, were palpitations, a racing pulse, and dyspepsia. Most of the doctors could find nothing wrong with him, but Spencer had a fine contempt for their opinions, and evolved his own methods of dealing with it, though he admitted (in 1887!) that he had 'discovered fundamental errors in [his] system of treatment'.[76] The main method was to avoid anything that might excite him. There is a very pathetic ring about some of the replies he sent to invitations: 'I am so out of condition I dare not face social excitements.' He replies to Mrs. Huxley that he can come 'provided always you will promise to keep me out of discussion or any other undue excitement'.[77] Huxley once visited Spencer, to find him 'having taken to the horizontal, partly on theoretical, and partly on practical grounds —he is in a queer state—but my own belief is that it is all dyspeptic —not that that makes it any better . . . he looks healthy enough'. But a few months later found him 'in boisterous spirits', and 'as lively as a cricket'.[78]

It is worth noting that similar nervous symptoms—melancholia, inability to concentrate, a manic-depressive cycle—troubled many other Victorian intellectuals, seemingly associated with the strain of very hard work and intellectual tension.[79] Huxley himself was a victim of the acutest melancholy; Darwin virtually bedridden; Max Weber, unable to concentrate for a period of many years; Mill, Faraday, Kingsley all similarly subject. The symptoms often seem to have first come on in the early thirties; and we wonder what was in the mind of John Morley when he described this period as 'that earlier climacteric when the men with vision first feel conscious of a past and reflectively mark its shadow'.[80] In Spencer's case the advent of the mischief did come at a crucial turning point of his life, when his earlier impressions and thoughts crystallized to form a system which he spent the rest of his life in working out.

The modern reader, steeped in a diffuse vulgar Freudianism, is inclined to wonder if sex had anything to do with it. Spencer was a bachelor at the time of the breakdown, and despite the advice of Huxley, Comte and Richard Potter to get married (a course of treatment called 'gynopathy' by Huxley), he remained one. It is impossible to suppose that Spencer, like some other Victorians, had a secret sex-life to which neither he nor anyone else made any reference. He refers to only two instances of what might be called amorous attachments. There was a girl whom he knew when engineering at Worcester when twenty years old, of which he writes 'the intimacy which thus sprang up with one just growing into womanhood, was extremely agreeable; the more so because my previous life had kept me almost wholly out of female society'. But before any 'entanglement of feeling' occurred, he discovered she was engaged and the matter was over.[81] The other was Marian Evans (George Eliot). This was his most serious relationship with any woman, and came at a time when he was thinking, in general terms, of getting married, shortly before the breakdown. He told the closest friend of his later years, the young Beatrice Potter, that she reminded him of George Eliot—an old man's sentimentality?[82] In 1845 he had written to Lott saying that the problem of marriage was to maintain in the other the representation of one's ideal; and that the idea of the husband exercising power over the wife, by legal or other means, rendered this difficult.[83] This attitude recalls the unconsummated feelings of two other early upholders of the equality of woman, J. S. Mill towards Harriet Taylor, and Auguste Comte towards Clotilde de Vaux. Does this represent the rationalizing of a fear or reluctance to get married? Later it was bolstered with the argument that Spencer's profession was financially precarious and that for marriage one needed a sure income.[84]

The one-sidedness of Spencer's character struck his friends forcibly. 'If an abstract logical concept could come to life its life would be like Spencer's'.[85] Beatrice Potter, preparing biographical notes in 1886 and proof-reading the *Autobiography*, wrote in her diary:

> there . . . is an unconscious sacrifice of the whole nature of the man to the one aim. His mind, from the first intensely theoretical, taking in the hypotheses of positive science, dwelling on them till he had found the formula which would include all. . . . Though there has been a great struggle with outside circumstances, grandly borne; yet there has

> been and is no sign of a struggle with his own nature. It was all plain sailing—his aims clear and definite—no other qualities in his nature, crying out, sometimes with agony, for fulfilment. Except this one intellectual passion. . . . He told me there had been no feeling of sacrifice in pursuing his work and giving up all things to it. . . . Strange, a nature with so perfect an intellect and little else—save friendliness and the uprightness of a truth-loving mind.[86]

Spencer told her that he had 'never been in love and my only conception of life was an existence devoted to working out my ideas—there were no other qualities to sacrifice'. As far as our evidence goes, it seems that, at a conscious level, Spencer's life-activities were the natural and proper expression of his nature. His life-work grew upon him 'organically' (to use a favourite word of his), and his troubles did not seem to stem from any self-denial or repression. There was never any agonizing break with his past, such as the loss of religious faith so characteristic of the great Victorian agnostics, no great shattered emotional attachment, no felt loss. If we must regard his neurosis as symptomatic of a loss or frustration, it was deep in his evangelical-dissenting background.

The central paradox of Spencer's character was that the peculiar rigours, obligations, moral assumptions and tastes of evangelicalism (a creed which began by emphasizing the sinfulness of man's 'natural' inclinations, and prescribing a counter-code) had become so ingrained that they were 'natural' for him; and, drawing his arguments from the liberal deism which was the intellectual side of the religious heritage which shaped his childhood, he proceeded to justify the bulk of them as natural. Never was there a man who so wholeheartedly espoused what was liberal, natural, unfettered (passages in his *Education* sound modern even today), and whose own life was so quaintly consistent and rule-governed. He was rigid in his libertarianism, for his rule was the Law of Nature and to be natural was the only way of being free. When he visited the Potters, 'to the children of the house the philosopher always appeared in the guise of liberator':[87] he was for allowing them to do what they wanted, for abandoning all rituals and ceremonies, for relaxing the strictness of rote-learning for the informal delights of nature-study. Yet Hooker wrote in exasperation to Huxley, during one of their disagreements:

> At my house at Kew he was always a damper. Comprehensive as his intellect and capacity is, his views are so cribbed, cabined and confined that you have no freedom of motion in conversing with him. . . .[88]

He was, like his father and his uncle, so persistently unfrivolous that we can sympathize with Tyndall's remark that he would like him better if he would swear now and again.[89] He had no natural taste for common pleasures. When Galton took him to the races, 'he could not be roused to enthusiasm. . . . He said the crowd of men on the grass looked disagreeable, like flies on a plate.'[90]

Spencer greatly prided himself on his nonconformity. But the other side of Dissent was consistency. As he refused to wear evening dress, rejected all the many honours and titles which were offered to him, and became well known for his quaint behaviour at what ceremonies he did attend, so he multiplied rules for his own behaviour. When in the days of his social success Lady Derby asked him to meet the Tsar of Russia at a reception, he declined; for though she kindly said it wouldn't be necessary for him to wear levée dress like the others, he yet did not like to be conspicuous without it. His oddities were well known. A guest said of the wedding of Beatrice Webb's sister: 'that wedding is not forgotten . . . how Mr. Herbert Spencer behaved during the service. . . .'[91] (It is left to the imagination.) He was notably punctilious and truthful; the notion of keeping the contracts one freely made was very deeply ingrained in him. The inexorability of cause and effect in nature as he saw it echoes the justice of the Puritan divine Bookkeeper. He remarks of his boyhood exploit in walking from Bath to Derby that, though there seemed at the time to be no bad effects, 'the cost has to be met somehow, and is met, no doubt, by a falling short of ultimate perfection of structure'.[92]

In his *Autobiography* Spencer frequently criticizes the principles upon which he was brought up. He denounces the asceticism of so much of English life, and proclaims:

> the industrialism of modern life has so strongly associated the ideas of duty and labour, that a man has come to be regarded as the more praiseworthy the harder he toils; and if he relaxes greatly in his activities, it is tacitly assumed that some apology or explanation is needed. But the whole thing is a superstition. Life is not for work, but work is for life. . . .[93]

Is this just another paradox of his character or is it a final judgment on his life? For he also writes: 'I was [at the age of fourteen] as always before and ever after, very idle unless under the stimulus of some powerful motive: usually the desire to compass some large end'.[94] This he found: his life-work fulfilled the demands of his evangelical superego. But the agnostic and libertarian in him (this was inherited from the easy-going milieu of Erasmus Darwin, before the marriage with the evangelical spirit) provided all the arguments for overthrowing such a regimen, but was unable to furnish new goals or the means to attain them. So the effect of paradox remains. Emotionally undemonstrative himself, he stressed the importance of parents demonstrating openly their affection for their children. The most intensely intellectual of men, he continually insisted that it was not intellectual education and book learning, but character and circumstance which effected change; and the following of his intellectual bent resulted in him writing, 'What I want is a life which does not tax the intellect in any degree while it brings the emotions into play'.[95] Was Beatrice Webb's diagnosis wrong, or is Spencer simply, from the outside in his misery, regretting his inability to feel as others did? He coined the phrase 'survival of the fittest' and called the underlying principle of his system 'the persistence of force'; but he was a humanitarian, hating wars and loathing hero-worship of any kind. He saw strict self-control as the correlate of freedom; and in his unbelief he could be so dogmatic and defensive as any Victorian bishop.

Spencer's paradoxical, or contradictory, combination of evangelical spirit and rationalist substance was peculiarly congenial to the mid-Victorians—a generation which, looking back on the years from 1815 to 1851, could regard the political repression and turmoil, the economic distress and achievement, as a triumph, though hard-won, at considerable spiritual cost. Spencer's achievement was virtually the answer to the plea which Coleridge made years before: 'Socinianism moonlight; Methodism a stove. O for some sun to unite heat and light!'[96]

There were other reasons why Spencer was so fitted to producing a total system of explanation and exhortation for the mid-Victorians. Although, as I have said, Spencer cannot be accused of scientific ignorance, the creation of a system such as his does require that one has a guiding principle which will enable one to order, cajole, stretch or dismiss the detailed facts which the specialists provided. Spencer's vast superiority as a synthetic philosopher to, say, Teilhard de Chardin, lies in the fact that his analysis does not lie loosely on top of the facts, like oil on a pool, but really does integrate, order, and illuminate them, and prompt further investigation. The Oxford biologist Romanes owed a series of 'beautiful experiments' on nerves to Spencer's work;[97] while H. T. Buckle, an unjustly-neglected historian, wrote:

> rarely, very rarely, have I read a volume containing so much thought. Indeed, some of your views almost trouble me with their wealth—the ideas, in spite of their clearness, being so suggestive as to fatigue.[98]

The *Psychology* was a direct acknowledged influence on the famous experiments of Pavlov.[99] George Eliot applied his psychology to the *detailed* creation of her characters,[100] and there were the innumerable doctors, teachers, officers, artisans who called themselves Spencerians, and applied his theories to the conduct of life.

But it is fair to call Spencer 'a dogmatist of genius', as Houghton does.[101] Such systems can only be achieved, and maintained, by certain intellectual bad habits. (Typically, Spencer was quite open and honest about these.) Spencer was, above the elementary levels, a self-taught man—and this was probably one secret of his popular appeal in an age of widespread ignorance (and desire to learn) which a popular press, Mechanics' Institutes, and bodies like the Society for the Diffusion of Useful Knowledge were only just beginning to disperse. Consequently his knowledge was patchy, and his need for a synthesis great. His scientific education as a boy was sound enough, and in the 1850s, he took care to keep up with the latest thought in England and Europe. But his treatment of the philosophy, history and theology of the day leaves one aghast at his temerity. At the age of 24 when the only 'mental science' he knew was phrenology, he started to read Kant's *Critique of Pure Reason*. He had not got far when he decided that Kant's theory that time and space are subjective forms was utterly absurd. 'Being then, as always, an impatient reader, even of things which in large measure interest me and meet with a general acceptance, it has always been out of the question for me to go on reading a book, the fundamental principles of which I entirely dissent from.'[102] The same happened with Comte. He began at George Eliot's instigation to read the

Politique Positive, disagreed with Comte's classification of the sciences, was glad to drop it, and then, like any self-improving mechanic, proceeded to pick up the outlines of Comte's system from a popular summary by Lewes in *The Leader*.[103] Comte was not the only person to have practised 'cerebral hygiene'.

It was as if the ideas of others would disrupt the natural spontaneous development of Spencer's ideas. He has given us an account of how his ideas developed which is also an excellent description of one common method of creative thought. (It is much recommended to those who see conscious hypothesis-formulation and testing as the only road to scientific truth.) George Eliot once remarked on Spencer having no lines on his forehead. He replied it was because he was never puzzled, by which he meant:

> It has never been my way to set before myself a problem and puzzle out an answer. The conclusions at which I have from time to time arrived, have not been arrived at as solutions of questions raised; but have been arrived at unawares—each as the ultimate outcome of a body of thoughts which slowly grew from a germ. . . .[104]

The organic imagery is significant and very typical. He describes how a fact or observation would dwell with him, its meaning not clearly perceived, as if by an 'instinctive interest'; it would be remembered, parallel instances would be noted, other cases would be thought up, their bearings considered, a generalization would gradually emerge, anomalies and difficulties first passed over and then used to modify the incipient theory.

> Eventually the growing generalization, thus far inductive, might take a deductive form: being all at once recognized as a necessary consequence of some . . . principle, some established law. And thus, little by little, without conscious intention or appreciable effort, there would grow up a coherent and organized theory. Habitually, the process was one of slow unforced development, often extending over years. . . .

He goes on to stress the advantages of not forcing one's thought but allowing 'the true association of ideas' to assert itself. Thought arrived at in this way is more likely to be true, says Spencer, than strained thought. A comment by Fiske, who liked and admired him, is entirely consistent with this:

> Of historical and literary knowledge, such as one usually gets from books, Spencer had a great deal, and of an accurate and well-digested sort; he had some incomprehensible way of absorbing it through the pores of his skin—at least he never seemed to read books.[105]

Translating these observations into sociological terms, we may say that Spencer was able to speak to the mid-Victorians with such effect because he allowed the experiences, hopes, fears, desires and assumptions of his contemporaries to express themselves in his thought. Until the synthesis was complete, he opened his mental pores, so to speak, and absorbed the spirit of the times.

The resulting system, its sources so heterogeneous, had a very coherent, unique, original, rounded form. T. H. Huxley expressed this supremely well:

> Spencer . . . elaborated his theory from his inner consciousness. He is the most original of thinkers, though he has never invented a new thought. He never reads merely picks up what will help him to illustrate his theories. He is a great constructor: the form he has given to his gigantic system is entirely original: not one of the component factors is new, but he has not borrowed them.[106]

It is a description of the *bricoleur* at work, a cultural handyman on an enormous scale.

Towards the end of the century, when the synthesis was complete and out-of-date, Spencer was taken as the prime example of the deductivist, dogmatic, theoretical, academic thinker, opposed to reality and experience. Yet this was not the case before 1860, when the outlines of the synthetic philosophy were established. Spencer despised the classical education of the universities as being irrelevant or harmful for the conduct of industrial life, and though his own system became a dogma, it was a dogma shaped by his own experiences, which were more appropriate, typical, timely, strategic ones than those of almost any other thinker of the age. One of the demi-gods of the age was Bacon, the great philosopher of experience and utility, and Spencer attacked the philosophies and psychologies of others as not being properly based on experience.[107] The mid-Victorians, a nation of self-taught artisans, wanted a dogma, a guide for life, but they would have none which they could not believe was based on experience. Spencer's experience admirably fitted him to gratify their desire—and his own nature at the same time. It was a later generation, that of the 1870s and 1880s, whose characteristic figures were John Morley and W. H. Mallock, who valued flexibility and felt they had outgrown the need for dogmatic systems.

This was the period in which Spencer's methods came under severe criticism. Here is a typical anecdote, told by Francis Galton.[108] Spencer had been discussing finger-prints with him.

> He asked me to show him my laboratory and to take his prints, which I did. Then I spoke of the failure to discover the origins of these patterns, and how the fingers of unborn children had been dissected to discover their earliest stages, and so forth. Spencer remarked that this was beginning in the wrong way; that I ought to consider the purposes the ridges had to fulfil and work backwards. . . .
> [Sociologists, by the way, will note that this is the perfect paradigm of functionalist explanation.]

Spencer went on to argue that their purpose must be to protect the mouths of the sudorific glands, and, Galton says, 'elaborated a consistent and ingenious hypothesis at great length'. Galton said the theory 'was beautiful, and deserved to be true' but that the mouths of the sweat-ducts were on the ridges. Spencer laughed good-humouredly and told the well-known story of how, in a discussion about literature at the Athenaeum, he had said he had once written a tragedy. Huxley remarked he knew what the dénouement was: 'a beautiful theory killed by a nasty, ugly, little fact'.

Spencer had a good idea of what a theory is, and well appreciated the important role that deduction must play in it. This was an important stand, for, under the influence of J. S. Mill's *Logic*, it had got about that the only valid kind of scientific reasoning was inductive. Spencer knew that unless one does have a theory, one will probably not know what to look for. The trouble was that for Spencer the empirical side consisted of illustrating, rather than testing, his theory. So he writes to Huxley, during the argument about use-inheritance: 'I want an example of a rudimentary organ that is inconvenient or mischievous. . . . Send me a *postcard* and then you cannot write more than a few words'.[109] This method is really the same as only reading the books one agrees with, lest one's theories are challenged or qualified. Opponents of his theories, such as Galton, greatly admired his ability to support his theories with instances: 'his wealth of ready explanations was marvellous'.[110]

Mill wrote that he had 'a great mastery over the obscurer applications of the associative principle',[111] and Wallace that 'he was always interesting from the often unexpected way in which he would apply the principles of evolution to the commonest topics of conversation'.[112] Spencer's ultimate aim was to use his theory (which he did not shrink to call a 'doctrine'), to make inferences and show how new things were not puzzling, because they conformed to it. Hence the practice observed throughout the *System of Synthetic Philosophy*, of establishing the doctrine in a very general way, or, assuming its truth *a priori*, showing *a posteriori* how the facts fitted it. The ideal is a total explanatory doctrine, so over-arching that all other theories dealing with the phenomena covered must be special cases of it (or else false), which the puzzled man might carry around with him to apply in any circumstance or experience of life. Utterly alien would be the notions that theories deal with parts of the truth and that the other theories may explain other parts better; that progress is a gradual reduction of the 'uncleared' area from many sides; and that often scientists must put up with a very untidy, partially inconsistent body of general theory. There is, nonetheless, a certain benefit for the collective scientific venture in stubborn attachment to one's theories; it means that theories are given a run for their money, and their strengths and weakness are thus manifest—to others, if not to their creators.

Spencer's reluctance to admit that his theory was in its totality unacceptable became extreme, part of his neurosis. The man who had in 1851 paced up and down arguing positivism with George Eliot became so sensitive to criticism that the slightest excitement brought on insomnia and the whole 'mischief'. Galton found him 'far too opinionated for candid argument', and said that 'wicked friends' asserted that when getting the worst of an argument, he would finger his pulse and say 'I must talk no more'. So he probably did; they fought to win an argument, he to save his only peace of mind. Here lies the real root of Spencer's nervous condition. It came on at the climacteric of his life, and whatever its specific causes (overwork certainly, sexual anxiety perhaps), it worsened as the system of thought, to which he had worked for years and which became the great obsession of his life, became subject to increasingly persistent and telling criticisms—political, logical and scientific. He had given himself so totally to his philosophy that any attack on its integrity struck to the root of his self-esteem. He protected himself.

At a terrible cost. In his letters and conversations with Beatrice Webb in his last years, he seems to have regretted, too late, his one-sided obsession. People admired the immense structure of his thought, wondered at the idiosyncracies of the man who produced it, and came to pity him in his wretchedness. During their quarrel in 1890 Sir Joseph Hooker, a friend of many years standing, wrote to Huxley:

> . . . his Egoism is so crushing that I prefer getting out of its way—he has humiliated himself by [his last outbreak], and when I look at the poor devil's antecedents and surroundings, the attending of flattery he has had in America and elsewhere, and the throne he fancies he occupies, high above that of any sage that ever lived, I rather feel a profound pity (far indeed from love) than even contempt.[113]

Beatrice Webb was more kind, when she wrote, after a visit to Spencer:

> How sad! Poor old man. . . . All the pain that comes from that one passion in human nature seems almost to outweigh the happiness of pure affection.[114]

The biographer comes to share this pity for the man; but the sociologist sees that it is the work which survives.

2: Enthusiasts and Lunaticks

I

A provincial, a Methodist, the son of a private schoolteacher. It seems a dreary background, for most of us have been influenced by Matthew Arnold's sweetly-expressed caricature of provincialism; and what is dull, petty and mechanical in Spencer's thought has been largely attributed to it.[1] Yet this is to ignore what a rich variety, creativity and seriousness there was in the English provinces from the mid-eighteenth to the late nineteenth century.

Despite the importance of London's growth in the steady ascent to what we properly call the Industrial Revolution, the great transformation itself, in the late eighteenth century, was engineered in provincial towns like Birmingham, Derby and Newcastle. They rose to hitherto undreamed-of splendour and importance: their wealth, the restless innovation of their political and intellectual life, the ominous aspect of their swelling populations, all compelled attention. For the smaller towns such as Derby and Norwich, the construction of the railways in the late 1830s, opening them up to London and the larger centres, ended this golden age. Only the biggest cities, like Birmingham and Manchester, really maintained a proud separateness in the latter part of the nineteenth century. Although Derby's great period was behind her by 1820, when Spencer was born, the Derby of the 1780s and 1790s still exerted its cultural influence on him.

In 1700 Derby was a typical county town whose social and political life was dominated by the oligarchic Corporation and the gentry and nobility of the neighbourhood, above all the Dukes of Devonshire, who had houses in the town.[2] There were five parish churches in the town, and one Presbyterian congregation; sixty years were to elapse before the advent of Methodism. Industry came early, in the form of the silk-weaving factory (the first in England), which the Lombe brothers established in 1718. The population increased steadily, but still it only reached 10,000 in the 1790s. Thereafter the population shot up (the rate of increase being 47 per cent between 1821 and 1841) and passed 40,000 in the 1840s. Until the building of the railways there was no single dominant industry, and despite the social predominance of one family of manufacturers, the Strutts, the economic life of Derby was dominated by its small manufacturers and merchants—the 'shopocracy', shot through with Dissent and Methodism (for at this time these were distinct forces), and the main seat of the liberalism which was the central, if not unchallenged, political stance of the town.[3]

Compared with its neighbours Leicester, and more particularly Nottingham, Derby was politically rather quiet. In 1817 it witnessed the trial and execution of the leaders of the Pentrich rebellion, an inept uprising of labourers, quarrymen and stockingers from the villages of East Derbyshire, which has been called the last of the peasants' revolts—it is certainly not to be classed with Luddism.[4] Spencer's father went to court to sketch the main prisoner Brandreth during his trial. But this was remote from the town politics of Derby, which were placid. A disinterested observer, Sir Richard Philips, considered in 1829 that Derby was outdone by Leicester and Nottingham alike in poverty, 'religious fervour' and 'party spirit'.[5] Derby was smaller, and more of a deferential county town. There were, it is true, riots in 1832 in which a bookshop which stocked anti-Reform petitions was ransacked;[6] and for several months in 1833–4 there occurred the renowned silk factory strike and lockout, in which the workers were defeated and the local branch of Owen's Grand National Consolidated Trade Union crushed.[7] Between these two events lay a watershed of some importance—the emergence of specifically proletarian interests from the general current of radicalism. Yet this remained muted in Derby, even during Chartism, and the mid-century saw the social peace described by J. A. Hobson, who was a native of the town.[8]

Dr. Vincent's general claim that 'the Liberals [represented] the essence and core of the town—business, shopkeeping and craftsmanship—the general self-esteem of the townspeople, and their social ethic and common culture' was true of Derby.[9] And as at Leicester and Nottingham the intellectual leadership of the Radicals (especially before 1832) was provided by the Unitarian manufacturers and the members of their chapels. The chief local aim of the reforming party was to throw off the dominance of the landed gentry, their party and their church. This is what lay behind the bitter complaint of one anonymous Tory:

> . . . Derby was one of the most peaceful and pleasant little towns in England. Then it was indeed the *county* town, and the best feeling and fellowship subsisted between the county gentlemen and the tradesmen, the agriculturist and the mechanic. . . .
>
> [How Derby has changed since the days of 'good King George the Third']. . . . Go where you will, and ask a stranger what sort of a town is Derby? What sort of answer will you get? Derby! 'Why Derby is one of the most *riotous*, *revolutionary* and *disunited* towns in all England.' Was it not Derby that first set the example of plunder, riot and incendiarism in 1832? and ever since has been noted for bitterness and strife and party violence? Is it pleasant *now* for the country gentleman, or the country clergyman to walk the streets of Derby? or to meet the sullen look, to hear the coarse jest or the muttered curse, at every corner of the street.[10]

At Derby the Strutts were foremost among what their opponents denounced as 'a motley assemblage of infidels, Socinians (i.e. Unitarians), revolutionists and political Dissenters'.[11] The Strutts, once considered 'right true Jacobins', had welcomed the French Revolution, and deplored the Pentrich executions.[12] 'The merchant princes of Derby, the Medici of their day',[13] as a fellow Unitarian and the leading Radical at Leicester called them, were noted for their successful, though paternalistic labour relations (somewhat like Owen's at New Lanark) and their benefactions to the town—a library, an arboretum, a hospital, chapels and schools. Although the edge was taken off their Radicalism in 1835, when the Corporation was reformed, and one Strutt became Mayor and his brother M.P., they continued to lead organized Radical Liberalism. The Tories were no more pleased by their policies in the 1840s, when Edward Strutt, and his successor Lawrence Heyworth (elected M.P. in 1848), attracted Chartist votes, and were denounced as republicans. The Tory *Derby Mercury's* admission then that 'Derby has hitherto been prominent among the manufacturing towns of Great Britain for the quiet and orderly behaviour of the artisans and labourers who reside within it'[14] (despite the silk lockout) was due to the acceptance of the manufacturers as Radical leaders by the artisans of Derby.

The Tories, besides being churchmen, inclined to be drawn from the old professions rather than from trade; and were in a permanent minority. For within Derby, as many other provincial towns, the parties were distinguished not so much by class as by religion and the cultural assumptions linked with it. Religion was of crucial importance as a mark of social identity.

II

All four of Spencer's grandparents were Wesleyan. Catherine Spencer (1758–1843) had heard John Wesley himself preach at Derby in 1777 and to the end of her days wore the simple Quaker-like costume adopted by the early Methodists.[15] The other grandfather John Holmes was also an eager adherent, preaching in the villages of the circuit and entertaining preachers at his house in Derby; his wife Jane came from the West Midlands where her brothers, John and Jeremiah Brettell, were among the earliest Methodist preachers. The first Methodist chapel was opened in Derby in 1765, and the society expanded along with the growth of the town. It is probable that new immigrants to Derby were attracted to the flexible and outgoing Methodist organization rather than into the Established Church or to Friargate Chapel with its prosperous congregation, Strutts and lesser men, by now rapidly moving from its original austere and embattled Calvinism to an accommodating, rationalistic and unemotional Unitarianism. Matthew Spencer, the grandfather, probably joined when he moved into Derby from Kirk Ireton, sometime in the 1780s.

At this time Methodism was still a society for religious enthusiasts, many of whom, like Wesley himself, retained an active membership in the Established Church; they would express the view that 'Methodism is Church of Englandism *felt*'.[16] But after Wesley's death in 1791, with the rapid growth in numbers, the separation of the Methodist congregations (many of whose poorer members effectively knew no other church) was inevitable. Social differentiation within the Methodist body became more marked, and in the 1790s, beginning at Nottingham, occurred the first secessions.[17] In 1821 the Wesleyan Methodists at Derby, yet undivided, comprised 554 full adult members—though children and other adherents would raise their effective strength considerably. The secessions did not prevent numerical increase, until by the time of the religious census in 1851 the various Methodist groups came to a quarter of the church-going strength in a town which was more pious than most of its size.[18]

It is much harder to speak about the social history, or rather anthropology of the early Methodists, than about the theological and political opinions of their leaders. The social history of nonconformity has not enticed historians; and we hardly have the evidence about the nature and effects of Methodism which we need in order to assess its importance. Yet some sort of picture must be offered—pieced together from odd remarks in local church histories, fragments of sermons, diaries and autobiographies. For Methodism in Derbyshire we also have a unique source—George Eliot's novels, in particular *Adam Bede*, whose heroine, Dinah Morris the Wesleyan preacher, was directly modelled on Elizabeth Evans, George Eliot's aunt, who was born in Leicestershire, preached in the North Midlands, and died at Wirksworth, a few miles from the ancestral village of the Spencers at Kirk Ireton.[19] (George Eliot's father lived at Kirk Hallam, between Derby and Nottingham.) There is a more direct connexion with Spencer: Elizabeth Evans and her husband (the original of Seth Bede), were for several years adherents of the 'Derby Faith', or the self-styled 'Arminian Methodists', a local secession of some importance, among whose leaders was John Spencer, Herbert's uncle, of Green Hill Chapel, whose three Bible classes made up nearly half of the seceders in the town.[20]

George Eliot reminds us of the varied and changeable aspect of Methodism as it moved from the early years of heroic preaching through the war years to its later prosperity, when she writes:

> It is too possible that to some of my readers Methodism may mean nothing more than low-pitched gables up dingy streets, sleek grocers, sponging preachers, and hypocritical jargon—elements which are regarded as an exhaustive analysis of Methodism in many quarters.
>
> That would be a pity; for I cannot pretend that Seth and Dinah were anything else but Methodists—not indeed of that modern type which reads quarterly reviews and attends in chapels with pillared porticoes; but of a very old-fashioned kind. They believed in present miracles, in instantaneous conversion, in revelations by dreams and visions; they drew lots, and sought for divine guidance by opening the Bible

at hazard; having a literal way of interpreting the Scriptures, which is not at all sanctioned by approved commentators; and it is impossible for me to represent their diction as correct, or their instruction as liberal.[21]

This religion which was so other-worldly in some respects was markedly this-worldly, or 'magical', in that supernatural truth was to be manifest to the believer by signs, the most important of which was the conscious *assurance* of Salvation. Wesley describing 'the character of a Methodist' emphasized that his follower was not to be distinguished by his opinions, but by his feeling the truth of religion: 'God is the joy of his heart and the desire of his soul'.[22] This sense of assurance is the most important psychological result of Methodism. Orthodox Calvinists, however admiring of Methodist vitality, criticized the Wesleyans for scriptural ignorance or naivety, and argued that 'attention to undefined impulses of mind, to dreams, visions, and impressions of scripture on the memory . . . violent corporeal effects . . . pretended effusions of the Spirit' amounted to a subjectivism which made 'our faith itself, and not Christ the object of it the ground of our justification'.[23] But nonetheless, in a smaller social compass, Methodism's insistence on *experience* as the test of religion, and the consequent security for the individual in chaotic times, are perhaps a truer recreation of the psychological character of seventeeth-century puritanism than the polite, etiolated Calvinism of latter-day Dissent, either orthodox or rational. The theological underpinning of Wesleyan teaching, 'Arminianism', is less important for our purposes than its effects; for as other evangelical enthusiasts such as Whitefield showed, it was possible for a revised Calvinism to have similar results. A variety of theological balances were struck between the inevitableness of sin, and the possibility of assurance, perfection and salvation, on the one hand; and between the relative importance of God's decrees, and the individual's efforts, on the other.

The security resulting from the individual's acknowledgement of his sinfulness and his acceptance of Christ's promise of total remission was undoubtedly further sustained by the community spirit and group relations within the Methodist societies. The disorientation of the new immigrants to the cities was a unitary condition—an absence of both viable social standards and social institutions to sustain them—to which Methodism brought an answer which can only be analytically divided into theological and social elements. Wesley was a Tory, and likened the society to a family. 'As long as I live', he wrote in 1790, 'the people shall have no share in choosing either stewards or leaders among the Methodists—we are no Republicans.'[24] (Here he is also excusing his followers from the charge of political disloyalty which clung to Dissent.) Moreover, the preachers should submit to Wesley himself, 'as a father-in-God over loving sons'. In the Bands and Class meetings the idiom was rather one of fellowship or brotherhood. And for most of Spencer's relatives (though not, as we shall see, his father) the Methodist Society was a tight-knit and all-embracing social world of its own.

Within the societies locally there were various cross-currents at work, militating against the preacher's control advocated by Wesley. The emphasis on experience, perhaps at the expense of learning or 'correct diction', and the need for local preachers, gave the societies a popular, if not a democratic, aspect compared with the older Dissent or the Church. Wesley's was a theology of mission, of universal salvation, of open access to the benefits of religion; his movement was the most singular piece of mass-communication of the age, and despite his Toryism, a notable blow against the pre-industrial 'idiocy' of the lower orders. In one sense Wesley's authoritarian ecclesiastical policy could best succeed when the members were overwhelmingly drawn from the working classes, as in the earliest years; and as Wesley himself saw, the attraction of middle-class adherents (like the Spencers) or the growing prosperity of the poorer ones, could lead to the 'decay of pure religion' and to demands for democratization. 'For the Methodists in every place grow diligent and frugal; consequently they increase in goods. Hence they proportionately increase in pride, in anger, in the desire of the flesh, the desire of the eyes and the pride of life'.[25] It was the 'middle class' members who led the demand for a more congregational method of government, such as lay behind the Kilhamite secession at Nottingham in 1797. 'Who can deny that we are a society in which the people have no voice?' complained a Kilhamite layman in 1796, 'in which they are not permitted to deliberate on the choice of their own officers, the formation of their own laws or the distribution of their own property'.[26] Whatever may have been John

Spencer's connexions with the Kilhamites, his own breakaway was very similar in its characteristics: argument with the clerical Superintendent, calling themselves the 'People's Meeting', alterations in the Methodist order.[27] Of the Kilhamites too we read, what would have horrified Wesley and his orthodox successors, that 'revolutionary principles were actively propagated, the writings of Thomas Paine were extensively read and also attempts were made to model the Methodist government, as well as the Nation, upon new and popular policies'.[28] Paine's writings are susceptible of middle-class, as well as working class, interpretation and here the call for freedom from conference meant, as it had for the older Dissenters, that leadership in the congregation would devolve upon those local figures who paid most.[29] So understandably John Spencer (a solicitor) took over a third of the Derby members with him in the 'Derby faith' to a new chapel built by him in Babington Lane. Even within the Wesleyans local middle-class leadership was important; it does not sound as if the 'three butchers' who founded Green Hill Chapel (hence known as 'Marrowbone Chapel') which Spencer's mother attended, were poor men; for it had 'numerous and respectable congregations'.[30]

In such congregations the 'enthusiasm', and visionary and magical aspect of Methodism, as well as the strong sense of community, gave way to restrained Biblicism and a middle-class ethic of individual attainment. Methodism drew closer to Dissent and the passionate disputes of Arminian and Calvinist were forgotten. It is difficult to know how such middle-class Methodists as the Spencers came to view the rather anti-intellectual heritage of the early days. This should not be exaggerated. Wesley himself was prepared, like the deists whom he loathed, to see science as revealing God's work in the Creation.[31] Yet there was a readiness to admit also non-scientific views of the world—belief in witches, and supernatural causation as in his sermon 'The Cause and Cure of Earthquakes' (1750)[32]—which permeated and were further confirmed by the magical beliefs of the common people. The emphasis on the specifically spiritual detracted from much attention to purely secular knowledge, and that tended to be justified on rather narrowly utilitarian grounds. Then there were the phenomena of enthusiasm, widespread despite Wesley's own reluctance to sanction many of them as of divine origin. A mild form was commonplace at the main Wesleyan Chapel in Derby in the early 1840s: there was one 'Holy John' Bowring, and 'when his knees were heard pattering on the floor and that peculiar noise he used to make, a sort of suppressed attempt at sneezing, it was well known that spiritual power was present'.[33] Spencer always defined the essence of his own 'theory of things' in contrast to the religious world-view and attitudes which he had known from his Wesleyan connexions.

The intellectual culture of Methodism was slight. Its dull and insipid tracts, moralistic and devotional, 'full of anecdotes about happy deaths, special providences and divine judgments on the ungodly'[34] (for the sense of assurance rested solidly on the belief in God's continued intervention in this world), are directed rather to the creation of a moral character which would sustain men who reasonably feared social fragmentation and moral uncertainty.[35] The doctrine of Original Sin which the old Dissenters, as they became prosperous, optimistic and rationalist, found implausible and irrelevant to their experience, was convincing to these disoriented immigrants; and the severe moral codes to which they consequently subjected themselves created corresponding virtues—orderliness, diligence, industry, self-help, neighbourliness. Methodism undoubtedly helped inculcate the new work-discipline which capitalist production demanded. Dr. Andrew Ure, the egregious advocate of industrialism, who drew much of his material from the Derbyshire factories of the Strutts and Arkwright, wrote of the latter that a major task was to 'subdue the refractory tempers of work-people accustomed to irregular paroxysms of diligence', and went on to commend 'the science of human nature as it is expounded in the Gospels'.[36] The Strutts endowed chapels. More generally, a certain nexus of attitudes—the security engendered by the doctrine of assurance and the fellowship of the society, the prominent strain of other-worldliness, the respect for authority—made many orthodox Wesleyans (such as Spencer's grandmother and mother, as he described their characters)[37] strongly disinclined to challenge the social order as it was changing everywhere around them. Spencer, like his father and uncle, derived his conscientiousness, his systematic industry, his very restrained taste for pleasure, from the Methodist ethic; but hardly his intellectual restlessness or his scorn for authority.

Discussion of the overall contribution of Methodism to the

process of industrialization in England has been dominated by the argument of Elie Halévy that through its teaching the working classes were held back from revolution.[38] Hobsbawm and Kent have challenged this view,[39] while E. P. Thompson, in a chapter disfigured by an unrestrained malevolence towards Methodism, has essentially restated Halévy's thesis in a modified form. 'Methodism *may* have inhibited revolution', he writes, 'but we can affirm with certainty that its rapid growth during the wars was a component of the psychic processes of counterrevolution.'[40] But the picture was more complex than that; and it is doubtful if it makes for good history to try to tot up all the functions of Methodism in a moral ledger to commend or condemn it for its services to social progress. The difficulty for simplistic views is that, as Thompson says, Methodism served 'simultaneously as the religion of the industrial bourgeoisie . . . and of wide sections of the proletariat'.[41] It will not do either, to explain why the Gadarene rush into false-consciousness on the part of the workers took place (for that is *the* problem for Thompson), to say it was a religion *for* the workers, not *of* them.[42] The intentions of those Tories, John Wesley and Jabez Bunting, were certainly paternalistic; but the effects of their mission were populist. For very large numbers of Methodists, preachers as well as members, and not only drawn from the Primitive Methodists (who had the greatest working-class membership and leadership), were to be found among the political radicals—a local case is Isaac Ludlam, one of the Pentrich rebels of 1817, a local Methodist preacher. Lord Sidmouth's bill of 1811, requiring dissenting preachers to be licensed, was clearly directed against local Methodists among others—'cobblers, tailors, pig-drovers and chimney sweeps'.[43] The same discipline which is said to have made good mill hands out of Methodists also gave them the virtues and skills to be unionists and organizers. The movement depended for its expansion so much on spontaneous initiative from below that discrepancies between the ministers at Conference and the ordinary members in the local churches are to be expected; and even the ministers, as the poll books show, tended to vote Liberal or Radical, and not Tory.[44]

Any explanation of Methodism must make sense of all these things. Methodism, being primarily a 'religious organism', was able to appeal to different kinds of men and to yield various implications for social action. The crucial feature of Methodism was not the politics of its leaders or members but, jointly, its fellowship and its promise of assurance, which had such an appeal, and such an effect on the personality, for men who were undergoing the great anxieties of the Industrial Revolution.

III

Through his father also Spencer was subject to an absolutely contrasting influence. William Spencer was in the early 1830s secretary of the Derby Philosophical Society, which had rooms and a library in the town, opposite the Quaker Meeting House.[45] It had a few dozen members, some scientific apparatus, a collection of fossils and several thousand books, mostly on medicine, 'Natural and experimental philosophy', chemistry and travels. The library was the focus of the society's activity—'a kind of band of Wampum, a chain of Concord, which may hold our society together', said Dr. Erasmus Darwin, Charles Darwin's grandfather, who had founded the D.P.S. in 1783. The Rev. Thomas Mozley, whose father was a member in the 1830s, writes that they were still known as 'Darwinians', and that the tone of the society was 'remarkably enduring, continuous and uniform; few societies could be called so much the same thing for half a century'.[46] A comparison of the 1833 membership with that of 1783 shows that two of the nine founders were still members, as well as three sons or grandsons of founders. There was then, in Mozley's judgment, little that was original or stimulating about the discussions which took place. But what is important for our purpose is that the young Spencer was thus a direct heir to the great tradition of eighteenth-century provincial science and radicalism whose finest bloom had been the Lunar Society of Birmingham. For Dr. Darwin founded the D.P.S. when he moved from Lichfield to Derby in 1782 to recreate some of the atmosphere he had known in Birmingham, 'cut off from the milk of science which flows in such redundant streams from your learned lunations'.

The Lunar Society was not planned or founded, but, like the thriving, unincorporated town itself, grew up as the spontaneous response to needs.[47] Its nucleus was present in 1758 when Benjamin Franklin, on visiting Baskerville the printer at Birmingham, was introduced to Darwin and Matthew Boulton of the Soho Foundry; most of its fourteen members were present in the late 1760s, and it began to break up with the enforced departure of Joseph Priestley after the riots of 1791. The members were nearly all engaged in industrial manufacture, or else were doctors or 'natural philosophers'. Besides Darwin, Boulton and Priestley there was Josiah Wedgwood who transformed the design, technology and organization of pottery production; James Watt, associated with Boulton at Soho; James Keir, a pioneer in glass and chemical manufacture; William Withering, the discoverer of digitalin; Thomas Day and R. L. Edgeworth, influential education reformers; Samuel Galton, a Quaker gunmaker and researcher in optics, the grandfather of Francis Galton; and John Whitehurst of Derby, a leading instrument maker and author of an important book of descriptive geology. At a time when the Royal Society of London was decayed and moribund, these men renewed its founders' view of the close connexion between natural philosophy and the development of art and industry.

Boulton and Darwin illustrate the two sides of the Lunaticks' view of science, which yet never drifted apart. Boulton was a great industrial organizer in the widest sense, the necessary counterpart to the inventor Watt. He lobbied Parliament for patents (a difficult task from Birmingham in those days), developed an extensive and novel sales network, pioneered factory organization and labour relations. More than any other contemporary he had a prophetic philosophy of industrialism. He told Boswell, who visited him at Soho in 1776: 'I sell here, sir, what all the world desires to have, POWER', and foresaw that manufacturing victory over the French displaced the need for any military victory.[48] Despite the radicalism of his innovations he was a Tory in politics, and by religion a Churchman.

Darwin was, in his day, famous equally for his unorthodox, humane and successful medical practice, and for his poetry, most of which was published after he moved to Derby.[49] These bizarre and ingenious verses, celebrating in heroic couplets such topics as the monosexual reproduction of oysters and the formation of potassium nitrate, as well as, in more romantic vein, the beauties of Dovedale, have not retained their original popularity. Though Coleridge said that Darwin's poetry 'nauseated' him, William Cowper admired it and Horace Walpole wrote that 'Dr. Darwin [had] destroyed my admiration for any poetry but his own'.[50] But whatever its aesthetic merit Darwin's poetry shows his characteristic lively inventiveness. His commonplace book, like Leonardo's, is full of sketches for practical devices—steam turbines, canal lifts, copying machines, electrical appliances, and so forth. His view of science was frolicsome. 'What inventions, what wit, what rhetoric, metaphysical, mechanical and pyrotechnical, will be on the wing, bandy'd like a shuttlecock from one to another of your troop of philosophers!' he wrote to Boulton, regretting his absence from a meeting in 1778.[51] The science of the Lunar Society was both playful and practical.

Unlike Boulton or most of the others, who were Quaker, Anglican or Unitarian, Darwin was a Deist. He saw God in nature, but held himself a materialist, like the Unitarian Priestley, and rejected miracles or special creation. Samuel Galton's daughter, the sanctimonious Mrs. Schimmelpenninck, recorded with horror that Darwin used to say that man's material life, and his possession of faculties 'practically to explore and to apply the resources of the world to his use' were realities; but that 'all else is a vain fancy, and as far as being of a God, the existence of a soul, or a world to come, who can know anything about them? . . . these are only the bugbears by which men of sense govern fools'.[52] His poems, particularly *The Temple of Nature: or, The Origin of Society* (1803), and *Zoonomia: or, The Laws of Organic Life* (1794–7), expound his cosmology. An entry in his commonplace-book sums up his Deism:

> All vegetables and animals now existing were originally derived from the smallest microscopic ones, formed by spontaneous vitality; and they have by innumerable reproductions during innumerable centuries of time, gradually acquired the size and strength and excellence of form which they now possess. Such amazing powers were originally impressed on matter and spirit by the great Parent of Parents! Cause of Causes! Ens Entium! . . . A God Dwells Here![53]

Darwin's theological daring contrasts with the more typical view of Whitehurst, maintaining in his geology 'the great analogy between the Mosaic account of the creation and the result of physical reasonings'.[54] But the radical political implications of Darwin's view of religion, and of Lunar science, did not become plain until the 1790s.[55]

In the later decades of the eighteenth century, Derby and its neighbourhood was an equally brilliant cultural focus. 'Derby is no common place', wrote Coleridge in 1797, staying with Jedediah Strutt's daughter, Elizabeth Evans (not to be confused with George Eliot's aunt): 'full of curiosities, the cotton, the silk-mills, Wright the painter and Dr. Darwin, the everything except the Christian'.[56] Darwin apart, Jedediah Strutt (1726–97) was the leading figure of this society. The son of a farmer, he invented a greatly improved stocking-frame, and in partnership with Richard Arkwright, made it the basis of the factory production of stockings. Their factories, up the Derwent at Milford, Belper and Cromford, themselves important engineering novelties, became an attraction for travellers to equal the natural beauties of the Peak. A third member of note was the Rev. James Pilkington, minister of the chapel of which Strutt was the trustee; he was Unitarian, like his close friends Priestley and Wedgwood of the Lunar Society, and the Rev. George Walker, leader of Radical opinion at Nottingham and later President of the Manchester Literary and Philosophical Society.[57]

IV

The role of the Unitarians is remarkable. The lineal descendants, in most cases, of those Puritans who in 1662 had left the Church of England, and had then for several decades suffered persecution and severe civil disabilities, they had, throughout the eighteenth century, become the most radical and tolerant of Christian sects. To Churchmen of all parties, to Wesleyans and to orthodox Dissenters, this 'simple and rational conception of Christianity' (as Walker put it),[58] which denied the divinity of Christ and which Priestley claimed was simply apostolic Christianity purged of the corruption of centuries, seemed little better than atheism. Erasmus Darwin mockingly told Josiah Wedgwood that it was 'a feather bed to catch a falling Christian'.

Excluded from the universities in England, Dissenters were obliged to go to Scotland or Holland, and to found their own Academies.[59] Three of the Lunar Society were Scotsmen, and Adam Smith's just praise of the Scottish universities compared to the English ones echoes Priestley's boast to the Establishment: 'while your universities resemble pools of stagnant water, secured by dams and mounds and offensive to the neighbourhood, ours are like rivers which taking their natural course fertilize a whole country'.[60] He was referring to the syllabuses of the Academies, responsive to the new interests of the age: Locke's *Essay* was the staple, but they included all forms of natural philosophy, history and 'pneumatology' (political economy, ethical and political theory). The Academies, above all Warrington (1757–86) and Hackney (1786–96), were the main source of theological innovation; and the new ministers often found their congregations reluctant to be as radical as they were.[61] Priestley, while a minister at Leeds, 'found many of the lower sort of my own hearers' listening to the Methodists, and wrote his pamphlet, *An Appeal to the Serious Professors of Christianity*, to establish 'liberal principles of religion' against them.

The rationalism of the Unitarians was still *within* their religion; the Priestleys were sincerely pious, and could still maintain that 'unbelievers in general have no conception of the perfect coincidence of Christianity with rational philosophy'. Yet secularization seeped through their sober and moral piety nonetheless. Jedediah Strutt conveys the humble, workaday, implicitly agnostic character of their religion very well, in writing an epitaph for himself:

> With no Ostentation for Religious Tenets and Ceremonies he led a life of honesty and Virtue—and not knowing what would befall him after death, he dyed resignd in full Confidence that if there be a future State of retribution it will be to reward the Virtuous and the good.

Poverty and old age, he felt, were the 'two great calamities' of human life. But

> to improve one's mind in every moral and Divine, as well as every polite and useful, improvement . . . to spend a life of diligence, honesty, sobriety and virtue, to have been the Author of anything great or good whereby mankind are made wiser or better; in the main to have acted agreeable to truth and ones own best reason, and in a firm belief and trust in the existence of God and his providence, is truly to be religious.[62]

In this environment, which so esteemed the creation of useful things and the universal, regular, natural philosophy which made it possible, a Methodist schoolteacher like William Spencer impressed his son with his 'universal consciousness of cause' and 'the absence of the ordinary appeals to supernatural causes'.[63] Rejecting the means offered by Methodism, they sought security instead in a rational providence or a secular necessity, or in their own power to bend nature and society to their purposes.

Hence, perhaps, one source of the political radicalism of the Unitarians. Men are inclined to radical innovation by inconsistencies in their social situation. The Unitarians experienced a marked discrepancy in their being a commercial élite, wealthier, on the average, than any other group, and in towns such as Derby, Birmingham, Leicester and Nottingham, a social élite too; but also, in Priestley's bitter words, 'a sect everywhere spoken against'.[64] In their loyalty to the first two Georges, they had been second to none; but after 1760, as their religious heresy became more marked, they became increasingly more estranged. The revolt of the American colonies, the growing wealth of unrepresented manufacturing districts, their hostility to 'Old Corruption', all pushed the Unitarians to a radical stance. Their connexions with some members of the Whig aristocracy (Priestley was Lord Shelburne's librarian in the early 1770s) became so attenuated that Burke came to refer to Hackney Academy as 'a hotbed of sedition'.[65] The form of their radical critique was determined by their own experience. They had achieved their religious, commercial and scientific successes in spite of the state and the establishment. (Matthew Boulton, Tory though he was, was not alone in maintaining that the prosperity of towns like Leeds, Manchester and Birmingham was due to their not being represented in Parliament, and so free from the expense of elections.[66]) So they demanded liberty: freedom for individuals and associations to pursue their goals, and express their thoughts, untrammelled by obligations and restrictions imposed by an alien Church and State. These were the roots of Spencer's whole political philosophy. Ambiguously linked with it is the demand for equality—sometimes for substantive equality, as in a book by James Pilkington, but more often for equality of opportunity, for the career open to the talents.

The explosion came in 1791. After a dinner in Birmingham to celebrate the French Revolution, which several members of the Lunar Society attended, a mob, crying 'Church and King!' and abetted by the magistrates, rampaged for several days in the town.[67] They burnt houses and Priestley's chapel and drove him from Birmingham. In 1794 he left England for ever, for America where his ideas were honoured All this was noted with alarm in Derby, and the secretary of the D.P.S. wrote a letter to Priestley asking him to

> leave the unfruitful fields of polemical theology, and cultivate that philosophy of which you may be called the father; and which, by inducing the world to think and reason, will silently marshall mankind against delusion, and with greater certainty overturn the empire of superstition.[69]

It was a parting of the ways. Other members protested, and one, a clergyman, wrote, a few years later:

> Destructive principles (adopted by the infidel and propagated by the philosophers) have been disseminated with unexampled diligence, to poison . . . rural life—while the Manufacturer and Mechanic have been called from their important labours and useful occupations to the midnight contemplation of Rebellion and Massacre.[70]

The French Revolution was greeted by many rational Dissenters with a naive, almost apocalyptic, enthusiasm—'the handmaid of pure religion', it seemed to Richard Price, the London Unitarian minister whose writings provoked Edmund Burke's famous attack.[71] Mystical utopianism had been often combined with extreme rationalism in Dissent ever since the Cambridge Platonists, who had been a major influence in the shift from Calvinism to Socinianism. Priestley, like Newton, turned in his declining years from natural philosophy to eschatology, and saw in the times the fulfilment of the prophecies of Daniel.[72] In Derby the Unitarians were enthusiastically reading the prophecies of William Godwin. Elizabeth Evans, Jedediah Strutt's daughter, looked forward to a time 'when the tyrants and the slaves of the earth will be converted into one great alliance of friendship and brotherhood'.[73] How eagerly these prosperous radicals (so strangely united with the artisans of the Corresponding Societies)[74] must have applauded Godwin's judgment: 'With what delight must every well-informed friend of mankind look forward to that auspicious period, the dissolution of political government, of that brute engine, which has been the only perennial cause of the vices of mankind . . . !'[75]

The stubbornness and brutality of the authorities had caused a further radicalization of the Unitarian position. Previously, the Unitarians had maintained that political society was distinct from religious society, and that religious Dissent did not mean political disloyalty. To apply religious tests (taking the sacrament in the parish church) for civil advantages was a corruption of religion, and a denial of just rights to Dissenters—'that firm and generous band in which no traitor to the rights of human nature and of Britain was ever found'; thus George Walker's *The Dissenter's Plea.*[76] Richard Price's famous sermon to the Revolution Society in 1789, *Discourse on the Love of our Country* has the same themes. It amounted to a plea for the final secularization of politics. But it was followed by their moralization: Walker stated simply that politics was 'a branch of morals', and Godwin is permeated by the same moral intoxication.[77] The heightened repression of the 1790s provoked a forthright hostility to the British Government and to government in general. Even the mild and benevolent Priestley wrote that the Dissenters were 'laying gunpowder, grain by grain, under the old building of error and superstition, which a single spark may hereafter inflame so as to produce an instantaneous explosion'.[78]

But this radicalism was contained. 1791 saw the death of Wesley, and in the *Minutes* of 1792 the preachers adopted 'no politics' rule: only thus could they hope to prevent their religious activities being branded as treasonable.[79] Wilberforce's *Practical View of Christianity*, so largely responsible for moulding the evangelical side of 'Victorian' upper and middle-class morality, was published in 1797.[80] Dr. Erasmus Darwin, with his heroic couplets, his illegitimate daughters and his easygoing deism sank into obscurity before the evangelical tide. By the mid-1790s the radical political societies had been harried to dissolution. During the war years the psychic cost of industrialization was paid. Spencer's father grew up in these years, morally an evangelical and a radical in intellect; this combination he bequeathed to his son, and it proved a very potent one. Although John Wesley had opposed everything Erasmus Darwin stood for, their outlooks were synthesized.

VI

In fact it was utilitarianism (in the sense of both banausia and Benthanism) which provided the link. Wesley did not oppose the *utility* of science. What he opposed was the dangerous, and in his eyes frivolous, speculation which was so important an element in

Lunar Science. Like many Puritans in the seventeenth century Wesley tended to display, as Lovejoy has said of Milton, 'an obscurantist utilitarianism hostile to all disinterested speculation'.[81] We find the new narrow attitude in a book dedicated to William Strutt F.R.S. (Jedediah's son), entitled *The Philosophy of Domestic Economy* (1819). Its author, an engineer, before describing the technical novelties of the Strutts' new Derbyshire General Infirmary, simply states that 'The end of all philosophical enquiry is to lessen the number of evils to which we are liable, and to increase the sum of our natural and social enjoyments.'[82] From the model hospital to the model prison, Bentham's Panopticon, is a short step;[83] and in fact Bentham had been corresponding with William Strutt since 1794.[84]

Utilitarianism itself demonstrated great affinity with Methodism on the one side, and Dissent on the other. As long ago as 1781 Bentham had said that a Methodist was 'what I had liked to have been . . . and what I should have been still had I not been what I am'.[85] His utilitarianism, despite the desiccated view of human nature which it exhibits, was driven by an almost religious, and certainly fanatical, passion for social betterment. The ease with which the children of the members of the evangelical Clapham Sect became reforming utilitarians shows that psychological affinity more than compensated for any intellectual discrepancy.[86] What was lost in this very effective alliance was a certain spirit of playful ease which Dickens personified in the circus people in *Hard Times* or George Eliot in her portrayal of 'Old Leisure'. But then it was not this spirit which had wrought the Industrial Revolution, or would triumph over its evils.

Nor, despite the repression, did radicalism perish. Bentham had once been a Tory, but by 1828, in a tone reminiscent of the later Priestley, he is lambasting 'cold, selfish, priest-ridden, lawyer-ridden, squire-ridden, soldier-ridden England'.[87] The Strutts and their kind felt likewise, and they provided the leadership in provincial radicalism. Up to 1832 the radical axis ran from the Unitarian chapels to the working men's political clubs in the taverns. Reports of their activities in Derby underline the paradox of the wealthiest manufacturers leading the radical cause. The Strutts, wrote a friend, 'have fine pianofortes, magnificent organs, splendid houses, most excellent white soups and are, to crown all, right true Jacobins into the bargain'.[88] The 1830s form a crucial watershed. The radicalism in which the middle class and the working class elements had, by and large, run in tandem, began to break up; and with the opening up of the railways the relative autonomy of this radical provincial culture comes to an end. The local radicalism of Derby was united to the metropolitan current when Edward Strutt (1801–80), Jedediah's grandson, went to Cambridge, became M.P. for Derby, and joined the party of Philosophical Radicals in the House.

When we consider the radicalism of this period in the light of the class tensions which later broke it up, we tend to distort its contemporary meaning. For despite the contradiction between the interests of the economic groups involved, its demands did have a cultural unity. Unitarian and Primitive Methodist, manufacturer, greengrocer and artisan, Benthamite and Godwinian, knew who the enemy was. 'No social alliance known in history was so strong as that which then existed between Tories, High Churchmen, landowners, slave-owners and monopolists, . . .' wrote one Derby man of this period, 'At the bottom of [their] theory was the admission that the world was bad; its people were bad; their ways were bad; and the worst of all were those who tried to mend them or to redress social wrongs.'[89] The onslaught was against a cultural ideal, and an intellectual position, as much as against a political order.

Elizabeth Evans, enthusing over Godwin back in 1793, wrote that 'the grand desideratum in Politics is the diffusion of knowledge and morals amongst the poor—This the manufacturer has it in his power considerably to promote and is culpable in the neglect of it. . . .'[90] By the 1820s the movement for popular education—with a particular, utilitarian view of the proper content of education—which was linked with the cause of democracy and a free press, led to the establishment of Mechanics Institutes and the Lancasterian system in education.[91] In 1825 the Derby Mechanics' Institute was founded, its committee almost all artisans and craftsmen, but its patrons the same radical leaders and members of the D.P.S. One of these, the Rev. E. Higginson, of Friargate Chapel, said it was 'designed for the diffusion of useful knowledge among the working classes of the community', and proceeded from 'a desire to improve their mental and moral condition'.[92] In the opening address, Mr. Douglas Fox, a surgeon (a member of the D.P.S. whose children William Spencer tutored), emphasized the unity of all knowledge, and the utility of such knowledge as bore on one's job.[93]

Despite the open hostility shown to the movement by the Church and the Tories, there were contradictions within it. Least contentious was the conviction that working men would benefit from learning natural science; for ignorance was widely seen as the root cause of poverty and vice. Here Thomas Hodgskin and Robert Owen, the avowed precursors of socialism, could agree with Andrew Ure, the apologist of industrialism, and Francis Place. It is only with the advantage of hindsight that it seems strange that the Strutts were equally connected with Owen and with Ure. The disagreements came over what the use of this scientific knowledge should be, and its relation to such subjects as religion and political economy. Hodgskin hoped that 'Mechanics Institutes will teach men the moral as well as the physical sciences . . . [The mechanics] may care nothing about the curious researches of the geologist or the elaborate classification of the botanist, but they will assuredly ascertain *why* they of all classes of society have been involved in poverty and distress.'[94] But others (Place and Ure, for example) believed they would reconcile the working classes to the necessary truths of political economy, and would encourage morality and religion by demonstrating 'the inexhaustible bounty of nature's God'.[95] Ure too criticized their more secularist supporters for neglecting the educational value of evangelical ethics.

They achieved some measure of success. The workers Engels came across, 'with their fustian jackets coming apart, who are better informed on geology, astronomy and other matters than many a member of the middle classes in Germany',[96] had probably acquired their knowledge at Mechanics' Institutes, or perhaps at the Owenite Halls of Science which were infused with the same ethos of rationalism and utilitarianism. And many men who came to lead working-class opinion—G. J. Holyoake or William Lovett for example—owed much to them; for as Holyoake said, 'Science belongs to no party'.[97] James Watt, the artisan whose invention changed the world, was their culture hero. But the majority of working men could not see themselves as so many James Watts. After long hours of work they either wanted mental relaxation (and not to learn about the processes which made their employers wealthy); or they wanted to discuss politics and theology, which the rules usually prevented. In fact, within a few years of their foundation, the working classes came to regard them with apathy. The pursuit of knowledge came to be seen as a means of individual social advancement, rather than to provide 'enlarged views of society' and 'ennobling discussions', as the middle-class founders had hoped.[98] Those who went were the minority intent on a successful rise into the middle class; and in places they were mostly 'not of the class of mechanics, but [were] connected with the higher branches of handicraft trades, or [were] clerks in offices, and in many cases young men connected with liberal professions'.[99]

But the Mechanics' Institutes of the 1820s and 1830s are the most direct fruit of the moral and intellectual culture in which Herbert Spencer grew up. Their ideals and social ambiguities were typical of the culture which produced him—its rationalism, enthusiasm, utilitarianism and radicalism bound in a coherent pattern. The establishment, rooted in Church, monarchy and landed gentry, on the one hand, and an autonomous working-class culture, on the other, were alien to it. For in the Midlands at least, the working class—despite the experiences described by Thompson in *The Making of the English Working Class*—was still ill-developed as a distinct social entity.[100] What we know as 'traditional working-class culture' does not, in most places, go back much beyond 1880. It was in 1875 that G. J. Holyoake, a Birmingham man, involved in working-class politics his whole life, said of fifty years before:

> Now homilies are read to [the workers] against cultivating class feeling. In the days of which I write it was a great point to get them to understand they were a class at all.[101]

Workers and employers, despite at times bitter disputes, shared a common culture and ideal: the self-reliant, industrious and moral craftsman. The same ethic of sobriety and prudence might be invoked both by evangelical preachers and by trade union leaders blaming workers for only supporting the union when their pockets were empty. The members of the Radical Corresponding Societies were of this type; and they were prepared to accept the leadership of men like the Strutts (despite the fact that, as Holyoake put it, 'Unitarians . . . preached in Johnsonian sentences, and used more vowels than any other religionists'),[102] because, in the end, they felt they were essentially *like* them.

Their feeling of identity changed, but only as the character of their social, especially their industrial, experience changed. It is significant that Mechanics' Institutes were so much more popular and successful in Yorkshire than in Lancashire, where the technology of the cotton industry permitted large-scale production much earlier. As late as 1840 hosiery production in Derbyshire, Nottinghamshire and Leicestershire was still domestic in organization; the 'capitalists' were small men, and many had arisen from the ranks of the framework knitters.[102] This society produced manufacturers who were radical, and artisans who read Samuel Smiles. The characteristic culture of the towns of the Midlands persisted fairly intact through the hardest years of the Industrial Revolution; but its contradictions became more evident after 1832, and were even more manifest by the 1840s, when Spencer was politically active. But he was still decisively shaped by it.

3: Anti-Politics of the 1840s

I

To some extent every man is his own sociologist. That is to say, the concepts and mental images through which all men view their social surroundings are not different in kind from those which a sociologist uses in the comparative analysis of society. It is most important to stress this continuity when dealing with the origins of sociology, since what we may regard as technical terms (words like 'class', 'bureaucracy' or 'élite') were often hewn out of a living language of social debate, and carried with them rough theories about the social world. One aim of formal sociology is to refine these concepts so that they can properly be used outside the particular context which gave them birth, for sociology is essentially a comparative subject. The aim of this chapter is to describe the immediate social matrix of Spencer's sociology: the culture of middle-class provincial radicalism between 1832 and 1851. It was not only 'class structure in the social consciousness', to use Ossowski's words, but theories about society held by politically active men, which made a lasting impression on Spencer. There was, as always, a reciprocity between their actions and their theories—though the mental component of this unity is our chief concern. They tended to act as their social theories suggested; and their theories and concepts were not merely (and not most importantly) ideologies, but necessary attempts to make sense of the social world they confronted.

There is an excessive tendency to see such social theories exclusively as class ideologies, projections of their desires for society by different classes. This is a component, of course. But even totally opposed classes face one another in an environment which is overall the same reality for them both; and though they will certainly disagree violently about the unrealized potentialities of that social situation, there will necessarily be extensive areas of agreement too.

Marx was no spokesman for the bourgeois, yet, speaking of class, admitted:

> No credit is due to me for discovering the existence of classes in modern society nor yet the struggle between them. Long before me bourgeois historians had described the historical development of the class struggle and bourgeois economists the economic anatomy of the classes.[1]

At the most basic level Spencer drew from theories which were largely peculiar to the age, but which were shared by different groups within it because they did describe its predominant features. At a higher level he drew from a *radical* culture. It was middle-class radicalism, which was increasingly divergent from working-class radicalism, but the shared elements of radicalism were basic. Since we cannot but look at this radicalism in the light of its subsequent split, we may wish to decide to which class its elements 'properly' belong. Writers like Thompson and Williams are essentially historians, not so much of the times, as of what the times contributed to the socialist tradition.[2] This is legitimate enough, but there is the danger of anachronism. 1832 may have seen the emergence of most of the main socialist themes or the trends which later culminated in a nationwide working-class movement, but it hardly saw 'the English working class' *made*. Despite tensions, and a growing awareness of divergent interests, a joint radicalism was still possible. Only finally, and somewhat reluctantly, was the culture that formed Spencer specifically middle class.

Radicalism was an optimistic anticipation of, or a welcoming response to, industrialism, and goes back to the seventeenth century, its origins in market society and Dissent. The enemy was the traditional conception of state and society, Old Corruption as it had become by the late eighteenth century. Perhaps as a heritage of the Marxist philosophy of history we tend to set the rise of the middle class and its characteristic ideas, and those of the working class in a serial relationship, the one preceding the other. There is a measure of truth in this in so far as developed socialism is a critique of liberalism; but it obscures the way in which two traditions developed parallel to one another, each defining itself against the other, but both committed to a dynamic anti-traditional view of society. Common themes took different emphases.[3] Freedom might rest on property; but was it property in land or capital, or in each man's own labour? Equality might be a good; but was it substantive equality, or equality of opportunity, equality before the law, equal rights to associate and vote? Many writers in the radical tradition—Paine and Godwin for example—came to be invoked by either side when it began to be clear that there were fundamentally opposed collective interests within the anti-traditional camp. By the 1830s even political economy was yielding contradictory implications at different hands, Senior's or Hodgskin's. Radicals were more likely than their opponents to conceive of society in terms of *class*, yet the implications of this concept were, by the 1840s, becoming a sword to divide. But the element of radical thought which most influenced Spencer was the reductionist attitude to politics. Spencer, like Marx, predicted on the basis of current developments, a withering-away of the state. This premiss of the radical view of society (which was an absolute prerequisite for the emergence of sociology) was put succinctly by Thomas Paine:

> Society and government are different in themselves and have different origins. Society is produced by our wants and government by our wickedness. Society is in every state a blessing; government even in its best state but a necessary evil.[4]

—doctrines which found ample confirmation in the political movements of Spencer's youth.

II

Most of the leading agitators for the Reform Act of 1832 were highly dissatisfied with it. Radicalism was now a nationwide movement, and the group of Whig-Radical M.P.s inspired by Benthamism were the parliamentary spearhead of a body of opinion drawing its strength from the Dissenters and the manufacturing districts, in some of which the capitalists and the workers were already in sharp and persistent opposition. The Philosophical Radicals at Westminster were more than the expression of provincial pressures. Their consistent analysis of society, their resolution to put into effect a 'blueprint for large-scale change',[5] and their rather un-English contempt for piecemeal tinkering, were largely derived from their reading of French philosophy, notably that of Saint-Simon; and as J. S. Mill wrote, 'The French *philosophes* of the eighteenth century were the example we sought to imitate.'[6] They were ideological politicians, bent on applying a theory which they believed expressed '*realities*'; for, like the French intellectuals they admired, they considered that 'all political revolutions . . . originate in moral revolutions', and that 'the mental regeneration of Europe must precede its social regeneration'.[7]

J. S. Mill's essays published as *The Spirit of the Age* (1831) put forward, beneath a highly Saint-Simonian colouring, what is essentially the old demand of Dissenting political theory for opportunity for all and the abolition of hereditary advantages or obstacles to self-betterment.[8] There are, argued Mill, two sorts of society: the *natural*, in which 'worldly power and moral influence' go to the 'fittest persons whom the existing state of society affords', and the *transitional*, where power and 'the greatest existing capacity for worldly affairs' are severed. Within the first category there are societies (a) 'in which capacity raises men to power' (i.e. where status is achieved), such as the United States, and (b) those like Scotland of the clans, where power calls forth men's capacity; but the former is more stable since it 'does not contain in itself the seeds of its own destruction'.[9] England is in a transitional stage, and will not enter once more into a natural stage until the landed aristocracy, which was once the proper and natural source of social influence, is forced to relinquish its dominance; for 'the higher classes' have long declined 'in all the higher qualities of mind'.[10] It is simply a matter of 'our institutions [being] adapted to the present state of civilization'.[11] Despite the political failure of the parliamentary activity of the Philosophical Radicals by 1837–8, Mill remained sure of his analysis. The group must align itself with 'the classes who are dissatisfied with their position and who compose the natural Radicals'—i.e. the middle classes, capitalists, Dissenters, 'almost all the skilled employments', and 'the working classes: classes deeply and increasingly discontented'; for, 'what is Radicalism but the claim of pre-eminence for personal qualities over conventional or accidental advantages?'[12]

The Radicals could be united only as long as the aristocracy, the landed interest, the hereditary principle and the establishment, could be seen as the great over-riding enemy. It certainly had been in the days of Priestley and Paine, and certain common political myths still expressed it. The aristocracy was a foreign imposition, 'the Norman yoke', and the law, rigid as it was administered, the supreme Normanism.[13] This was part of the rhetoric of protest for both Paine's most devoted readership, the radical artisans, and members of middle-class radical groups. Cooke Taylor, the 'tame historian' (or rather mythologist) of the Anti-Corn Law League, wrote to Cobden in 1843 of 'the long struggle between the industrial spirit of the Saxon race and the military despotism of the Normans....' But the common myth had more than one meaning: for the artisans it was a claim for political democracy, for their rights as 'true born Englishmen', while for the manufacturers it was a demand for free-trade and their cultural hegemony:

> Every insurrection from 1066 to the present day was more or less designed to set industry free from the trammels which had been imposed on it by feudalism . . . [it is] an invariable rule that free and equitable trade always was a bond of peace and that the spirit of monopoly, particularly when it assumed the shape of territorial aggrandisement, became the frequent source.[14]

In this singling out war as the speciality of the 'Norman' aristocracy the radicals achieved a symbolic unity over divergent class interest.

At this point a brief digression on the nomenclature of class is necessary, since by the 1830s all radicals spoke in terms of it, whether or not they believed in the harmony of middle- and working-class interests. Stratification (the unequal distribution in society of power, wealth, prestige and other good things) is universal in human society. But the word *class* meaning social stratum first occurred in the 1740s, became much more general in the 1790s and was fairly universal by the 1840s.[15] It testifies to the popular realization that industrialism brought a new kind of social stratification. It seems to have originated in the social experience of middle-class provincials, often Dissenters, contrasting themselves with the landed gentry and aristocracy. *Class* meant mobility, both geographical and social, against the stability of *rank, order* and *estate*; it referred to occupation or role rather than to status; it was achieved by one's actions, not inherited by one's birth. Joseph Priestley reflected on the society he knew in Lord Shelburne's salon, and decided that the pitiable dissatisfaction he found there was due to 'the want of necessary employment'; whereas 'the middle classes of life' exhibited more virtue, happiness and politeness because they 'always have some other object besides amusement'—i.e. because they have occupations, not merely rank and wealth.[16] Priestley here claims a cultural superiority for his 'mode of life', and his terminology became universally acceptable as increased social mobility and the determination of status by occupation (and not the opposite) became more general in English society as industrialization proceeded. Another self-made man, Jedediah Strutt, took the same view in a letter to his son where he expressed some admiration for Lord Chesterfield's words on polite behaviour; but he concluded that the nobleman's 'Rules and Precepts . . . are applicable only to those of the same Rank and circumstances', and that his son was simply going to be 'a Tradesman of some emminence [*sic*]'.[17] The same emphasis on occupation and achievement rather than on status and inheritance is found in a letter of Erasmus Darwin, contrasting his own 'professional' fortune, with the 'patrimonial' ones of the other suitors of his second wife.[18] In the provincial towns the terminology of class was used in a polemical way by the Whigs against the landed gentry (especially the term *class-legislation*);[19] and the Tories, sensing its irreconcilability with their own picture of a society held together by obligation and 'the bond of attachment', were still not entirely happy with it in the 1840s.[20]

The new strata, classes, came to be a basis for political action in a way the old orders or ranks had not been. For before the Industrial Revolution politics tended to be the competition of various interest groups and clientages, held together by vertical bonds of deference, loyalty and patronage. The lower orders were outside the political community altogether, and persons in the middling ranks were the clients of the gentry. Classes, however, tended to be marked by horizontal political solidarity—though this was always problematic, and needed to be constantly appealed to—and separated from one another by vertical antagonism.[21] This contrast is an ideal exaggeration, but indicates the real and decisive change which accompanied the introduction of class. The Derby Tory's *cri-de-coeur* quoted in the last chapter[22] is a symptom of this change in social relations which the radicals were eager to forward: it was their intolerable pride and independence which the old élite hated.

The term *class* came to be used in social analysis as well as in social life. (We must make this distinction even while recognizing that analysis is itself part of life.) The economists (Smith, Mill and later Marx) related the three classes to the three sources of livelihood —land (rent), capital (profit), labour (wages). Another distinction erected on social theory is that made by Saint-Simon (and in large part based on his interpretation of the significance of the English industrial revolution) between the '*industriels*' or productive class, and the idlers. The Philosophical Radicals asserted the same distinction: 'the people' or 'the numerous classes' share common interests against the aristocracy.[24] Robert Owen, the clearest possible example of a Saint-Simonian '*industriel*', a factory owner with socialist leanings, contrasted the 'productive' with the 'non-productive' classes, though could also use the phrase 'the labouring classes' in a descriptive sense.[25] Two influential English analysts of social class, J. Wade (1833) and W. A. Mackinnon (1828), illustrates a parallel process among middle-class theorists. Wade links together the middle and working classes, calling them 'the Industrial Orders', and deprecating the stirring-up of class-antagonism; he puts forward what would now be called a functional view of social class and quotes from Plutarch the metaphor of the body politic.[26] Mackinnon's account, less tendentious and much better sociology, also expresses a more distinctively middle-class consciousness.[27] This feeling, as Professor Briggs has shown, grew steadily from the 1790s until it was nakedly proclaimed in open contrast to working-class feeling in the 1840s.[28] The same men who upheld a *concordia ordinum* against the aristocracy appealed to middle-class pride in calling it 'that intelligent and virtuous rank' (James Mill), and 'the glory of the British name' (Brougham). For 'class' was an evocative as well as an expressive term.

The leaders of the Philosophical Radicals were disappointed at the failure of the working class to respond to their call. Chartism, the first uniquely proletarian political movement, followed hard on the heels of the decline of Mill's faction in the late 1830s. No doubt they were sincere in their belief that the working-class interests were essentially in harmony with their programme. But they were politically naive and bad sociologists. Even Francis Place, the former tailor, who led the agitation for the repeal of the Combination Acts in 1824, did so because he thought that trade unions were only kept in being by combinations of employers, and would thereafter die a natural death because, by the laws of political economy, they could not affect wages.[29] He helped draft the People's Charter in 1838, but found the policies and tactics of the Chartist leaders totally abhorrent—particularly their refusal to accept the truths of political economy. The embittered reaction of some middle-class radicals at such 'profound ignorance and necessarily inveterate prejudice', was to argue that mass-enlightenment must precede social advance.[30] And so radicals of various shades of opinion tended to be involved in projects for Lancasterian schools and Mechanics' Institutes which would teach the workers political economy along with natural philosophy. As is shown by the phenomenal success of Harriet Martineau's *Illustrations of Political Economy* (1835), (which Spencer read when he was fifteen, and 'gathered something of a solid kind' from it)[31] the 'dismal science' exercised a remarkable tyranny over social thought. Men might reject its premisses on moral grounds, or in ignorance, but only those who worked from them to draw other conclusions, like Hodgskin, were able to offer a serious alternative radical programme.

Men frustrated in their political programmes, like the Philosophical Radicals, or excluded from the normal channels of political action, like the Chartists, turn away from politics. The former, in failure, blamed 'our diseased social and political system',[32] and eventually found their opportunity as officials and administrators. The latter turned to mass movements, and to theories of anti-politics. The parting of the ways can best be seen when we move back to the provinces. Again we must note the variation from one city to another, and the importance of factors other than class.

III

The reform of the municipal corporations in 1835 inaugurated a new era of provincial radicalism, and the united popular front began to break up. The main dilemma of the radicals was whether to press for the repeal of the Corn Laws, the great symbol of the class-legislation of the aristocracy, or whether to give higher priority to universal suffrage. Its leadership was still provided mainly by the Dissenters, both lay and clerical. The pollbooks suggest that 'no other occupation was so partisan, so militant, so unfloating, as the Dissenting ministers'.[33] One must distinguish between Dissenters as a *religious* pressure group, and Dissenters as a radical, but predominantly middle class or 'shopocrat' social group, for their activities in these capacities did not always coincide. But from the tradition of peculiarly Dissenting political theory they were able to fashion the most coherent case for a system of freedom which included the economic freedoms demanded by Cobden and the Anti-Corn Law League.

'The repeal of the Test and Corporation Acts in 1828', writes Professor Gash, 'was followed by twenty years of greater bitterness between Church and Dissent than had been known since Queen Anne's reign.'[34] Despite the great amelioration of the social position of Dissenters in the first two decades of the century, the mood of the leaders of radical Dissent in the 1840s was intransigent, and the 'voluntaryism' of Edward Miall, the editor of *The Nonconformist* (whose motto was 'The Dissidence of Dissent and Protestantism of the Protestant Religion'), looked back to the harsh, enforced, *laissez-faire* of Joseph Priestley. In this as in other respects the 1840s revived the themes of the 1790s. Back in 1807 the Dissenters had been quite happy to support Whitbread's bill for schools supported by the rates, but withdrew when the Anglicans insisted that this meant Church control. In 1820 a similar bill of Brougham's was likewise defeated; and in 1843 a remarkable petition of four million signatures obliged Graham to withdraw his Factories' Education Bill. (This was the first issue on which the Methodists openly and collectively aligned themselves with Dissent.) Education remained the main cause of dispute between Church and Dissent for the rest of the century.[35] The second major cause of complaint was over the compulsory payment by Dissenters of rates to support the Church, over which there were great meetings in the provincial towns in 1834, and continual agitation in the years following.

Miall put this opposition on a theoretical base, tracing most of society's evils to the Establishment of the Church of England. In 1834 he had become minister of a Congregational church in Leicester, where with the Rev. J. P. Mursell, a Baptist, he was a leading figure of the left-radicals. (The more Cobdenite radicals were led by the Unitarian Biggs, the counterpart of the Strutts.) In this he was stirred by the poverty, the moral destitution and the political discontent of the poorer artisans; and in 1840 he was involved in the defence of a member of his congregation imprisoned for refusing to pay church rates. This issue, the disestablishment of the Church, was the symbol round which Miall's appeal 'to the honest, the thinking, the manly Dissenters of this Kingdom' revolved.[36] He left his ministry and in 1841 founded *The Nonconformist*, to which the young Spencer was an early contributor, and later the British Anti-State Church Association, a body parallel to the others which he supported, the Anti-Corn Law League, and the Complete Suffrage Union. *The Nonconformist*'s themes were simple, and all were repeated in Spencer's later writings—the State Church was the ally of 'aristocratic government' with its 'class legislation'; it was 'the muse and patroness of war'; its education would 'hinder the free development of the youthful mind and produce a race of intellectual dwarfs'.[37] It is small wonder that Matthew Arnold took Miall as a symbol of everything he disliked.[38]

Miall's political radicalism was sincerely felt, but it stemmed from religion. When, supported by Ernest Jones the Chartist, he contested Halifax in 1847, 'he startled the electors by discussing with them spiritual topics',[39] and, realizing the divorce of the working classes from the churches, attributed it to the fact that 'British Christianity is essentially the Christianity developed by a middle-class soil'; it was too 'safe'.[40] In 1848 he went to Paris to see Lamartine, and, his son wrote, 'for a time it seemed as though the very foundations upon which society rests had given way, and kingcraft and priestcraft were to be banished from the world for ever'[41]—we are back with the Unitarians in 1789.

Outside Leicester Miall's main associate was Joseph Sturge of Birmingham, the prosperous Quaker corn-factor and railway promoter closely linked with the tight network of Quaker bankers and ironmasters.[42] Sturge was heir to a Birmingham tradition of harmony between masters and men whose most striking political fruit had been Thomas Attwood's Birmingham Political Union of the 1820s. One can perhaps detect a difference in the way Miall and Sturge speak about class—Miall seems to recognize that the difference between the middle and the working classes is culturally real, but that their interests may and must be brought together, while Sturge, though using similar terms, seems to regard the distinction as politically immaterial. (Attwood had been a Tory, and had usually spoken of the 'industrious classes'; and Sturge's fellow

Quaker, John Bright, unlike his colleague Cobden, always hated the terms 'middle class' and 'working class').[43] Cobden, writing about Bright's election as M.P. for Birmingham in 1857, saw the social structure behind these views:

> The social and political state of [Birmingham] is far more healthy than that of Manchester; and it arises from the fact that the industry of the hardware district is carried on by small manufacturers employing a few men and boys, sometimes only an apprentice or two; whilst the great capitalists in Manchester form an aristocracy individual members of which wield an influence over sometimes two thousand persons. The former state of society is more natural in a moral and political sense. There is a freer intercourse between all classes than in the Lancashire town, where a great and impassable gulf separates the workman from his employer . . . I doubt very much whether such a state of society is favourable to a democratic political movement. . . .[44]

Sturge's argument for complete suffrage was associated with the demand that the state relinquish many of its functions to extra-political activity—perhaps thus the middle classes would find the prospect of working-class control of the polity less frightening. His theory of society was Lockean—'Organized society is a conventional arrangement in which natural rights are exchanged for the advantages of protection'; men 'have the right of claiming from the state that it accomplish the ends for which it was originally constituted', and in order to make these claims men must not depend on public money, since 'political power and personal independence must stand or fall together'.

> The grand *desideratum* of society is that all classes should be guided in their conduct by systematic self-government, rather than by the external restraints of the law. But men never care to obey themselves, until they have learned to respect themselves and until they have received from others the respect to which they are entitled.

Middle class claims that the ignorance and supposed corruptibility of the working class forbid that they should be enfranchised, are countered; and so is the argument that the working classes intend revolution. 'Whilst we attribute to the working man evil *designs* they can charge us . . . with evil *doings*.'[45] Miall added that if things were unchanged 'they have nothing to lose in a general convulsion'.[46] What Marx hoped for was the greatest fear of these middle-class radicals.

The Complete Suffrage Union, founded by Sturge in 1842, was most active in the Midlands—in Birmingham, Nottingham, Leicester and Derby, where Spencer was the local secretary. Sturge's unsuccessful plan at a meeting at Birmingham in December 1842 (attended by John Bright, Miall, Thomas Spencer, Lawrence Heyworth, and fifteen Dissenting clergymen) was to get the 'moral-force' Chartists under William Lovett to form a united front with the Anti-Corn Law League. It was not a vain hope. The Dissenters, after the Radical defeat in the 1841 elections, were in a bitter, sullen mood, and their outlook had much in common with the culture of the 'moral-force' chartists. These were largely skilled artisans and craftsmen, the 'aristocracy of labour', imbued with Owenite rationalism and the moral values of self-help and independence, eager to show themselves worthy of the suffrage and as yet confident in their ability to succeed by swaying public opinion, by 'moral force'.[47] The Industrial Revolution had, as Cole says, on the whole, enlarged their markets and had not yet touched their work processes. William Lovett epitomizes their characteristics: a cabinet-maker from Cornwall, deriving his puritan outlook and his organizing skill from his Methodist background, influenced by Hodgskin at the London Mechanics' Institute, by Owenism and co-operation; believing that the path of working-class advancement lay through co-operation with the middle class, and by its preparation in self-control, education and independence.[48]

To the 'physical-force' Chartists Lovett was a traitor, despite the failure of the 1842 meeting. Here class feeling was quite open. Heyworth's final speech against O'Connor was dismissed with the cry: 'let him go—he is a sample of his class' (loud cheers); and he angrily replied that he was proud of it.[49] The 'physical-force' Chartists were drawn from those sections of the working class, predominantly in the Black Country west of Birmingham, London and Lancashire, who were most isolated socially (a process Engels emphasized in Manchester), or who had been most affected by changes in their work-technology—miners, ironworkers, navvies, casual and general labourers, who were the furthest removed from the common cultural source which was the basic link between men like Lovett and Sturge.[50] Until the development of the Labour movement late in the century such men alternated between political passivity and action of the 'physical-force' type—removed from the chapels, co-operative societies, unions and other forms of organization. Place, replying to Cobden about their possible support for the Anti-Corn Law League, describes the attitudes of this socially isolated mass of workers in London:

> True it is, as they allege, they have been cajoled and then abandoned by the middle class as often as they have acted with them, but their opinions are pushed to extremes, and are mischievous prejudices. They call the middle class 'shopocrats', 'usurers' (all profit being usury), 'money-mongers', 'tyrants and oppressors of the working people', and they link the middle class with the aristocracy under the dignified appellation of 'murderers of society', 'murderers of the people'.[51]

The alliance between radical middle-class Dissenters like Miall and Sturge and the 'moral-force' Chartists, was menaced from another, unexpected, quarter. The agitation for the Factory Acts, and particularly the Ten Hours Act (1847) in the north, had brought about an alliance between the working class, as led by the Chartists, and the *Tories,* who thus found an alternative to simply resisting social change. In the 1840s most adult working people were able to remember the beginnings of the mechanization of their industry, and often their own migration from the countryside; and the most practical of the projects of Fergus O'Connor, the fiery leader of the 'physical-force' Chartists, was the Land-Scheme. Both Chartists and Tories shared a feeling for the loss of roots which urbanization brought about, but, despite certain common intellectual themes in both socialist and traditionalist critiques of Liberal capitalism, they were in general only allies of convenience. 'The Throne, the Altar and the Cottage' was the motto of Richard Oastler the leading advocate of the Ten Hours Bill, and it awoke few echoes in working-class hearts, though his attack on Malthusianism as the theoretical basis of the factory owners' position, was taken up by the socialists.[52] And the Land Scheme in fact appealed most, not to the poorest and most depressed workers, nor to men who really wanted to recreate traditional rural society, but to skilled artisans of the type of William Lovett.[53] O'Connor himself justified it as 'the only means of promoting industry and independence, by affording to each a labour field, and encouraging the grand principle of self-reliance'. This was collective action to enable individualism to work; and similar proposals for allotments or land reform were put forward by Bray, the radical manufacturer of Coventry, by the liberal economist W. T. Thornton, and by Spencer himself in *Social Statics*.[54]

IV

The political failure of Chartism in the 1840s stands against the total success of the parallel middle-class form of anti-politics, the Anti-Corn Law League, with whose object Miall, Sturge and Spencer were in complete agreement. In Richard Cobden it had a leader of singular candour and intelligence. Despite his praise for the class-harmony of Birmingham, the Anti-Corn Law League was the creature of what the Germans called *Manchestertum*. At Manchester 'the great capitalist class formed an excellent basis for the Anti-Corn-Law movement, for they had inexhaustible purses, which they opened freely in a contest where not only their pecuniary interests but their pride as "an order" was at stake'.[55] Cobden exulted in the middle-class basis of the movement—'we of the middle classes—the unprivileged industrial men who live by our capital and labour', who included the 'large class of mechanics who save their forty or fifty pounds'.[56] Despite some support from 'the working classes generally', Cobden wrote, 'we have carried it on by those means by which the middle class usually carries on its movements. We have had our meetings of dissenting ministers [in 1841 seven hundred of them attended a carefully managed conference in Manchester]; we have obtained the co-operation of the ladies; we have resorted to tea parties [!], and have taken those pacific means for carrying out our views which mark us rather as a middle-class set of agitators. . . . We are no political body.' Lecturers toured the country, somewhat like Methodist preachers, and Cobden's account is peppered with terms like 'converts', 'pilgrimage', and 'missionaries'.[57]

What did Cobden mean in thus disclaiming the *political* character of this great class-movement? Firstly, unlike the Chartists, the League had 'a purely economic platform'.[58] He favoured universal suffrage in principle, but kept the League's goal specific since his strength lay in the middle classes, which were, as he wrote to Peel in 1846, 'not given to extreme or violent measures . . . not democratic'.[59] He also believed in a state system of education but did not associate this with the League, since it would alienate Dissent. But the Anti-Corn Law League was anti-political in a more profound sense. Cobden despised 'the emasculating interference of Parliament', and, while ultimately wanting to reform and influence it, worked outside it and even at times undermined public confidence in it, in his direct mobilization of opinion.[60] His movement was an empirical exercise in that theory of politics, tersely expressed by Paine and Godwin, which sees society as the realm of authentic virtue and the polity as something to be avoided or minimized, for the really significant motor lay behind it.

This was *public opinion*—'that sentiment on any given subject which is entertained by the best informed, most intelligent and most moral persons in the community, which is gradually spread and adopted by nearly all persons of any education or proper feeling in a civilized state'—thus W. H. Mackinnon in a neglected *tour-de-force* of social analysis, *On the Rise, Progress and Present State of Public Opinion* (1828).[61] Public opinion was the weapon of the middle class, as the leaders of the people against the aristocracy. It arose, Mackinnon argued, from the economic development of the middle class, which was also the main seat of 'a proper religious feeling'.[62] The growth of European liberalism 'did not in any manner depend upon fortuitous events, on the alteration made by act of parliament, on the concessions or boons of government, as from the requisites for the formation of public opinion being spread through the nation, and the people becoming sufficiently virtuous and civilized to obtain a constitutional form of government, and to secure this blessing when obtained'.[63] The growth of public opinion, then, was a steady continuous process, the effect of causes which were in the end structural and economic;[64] in so far as these requisites changed people's characters, so they were enabled to claim the franchise. Since legal and political *forms* were legitimated by this popular disposition, it made no sense to try to create it by laws. Since it was a steady and persistent process, revolutionary outbursts were evidence, not of an informed public opinion, but of a 'popular clamour', which could not be evidence of a structural change.[65]

So William Strutt of Derby, writing to his son Edward, the future Philosophical Radical, observed that 'all permanent alterations of public opinion are made slowly by degrees, but the red-hot democrats seem to desire revolution more than gradual reform';[66] while J. S.

Mill wrote that 'the people, to be in the best state, should appear to be ready and impatient to break out in outrage, *without actually breaking out*'.[67] Most middle-class radicals were obliged to admit to the Benthamite argument that since every man was the best judge of his own interest (an assumption of the market economy), he also had the right to vote; but they were fearful of some of the possible consequences of universal suffrage. Mackinnon himself was entirely Lockean and Whiggish in his praise of property: 'in a perfectly free country, therefore, it may be assumed that the only legitimate influence is that which arises from property, which acts on mankind by the benefits it is likely to bestow';[68] and even Cobden, who remained radical, in fact advocated a 40/- franchise. They reconciled their principles with their fears by arguing for a progressive reduction of the significance of political power, stripping the state of as many functions as possible, and for allowing the working classes the vote as soon as they had acquired the proper moral and intellectual virtues, which meant those of the middle-class experience. Miall's *The Franchise as the Means of a People's Training* (1851) acknowledges both ideas: having the vote would train the workers for success in extra-political fields, which for one who wanted a reduction of state power, were the really important ones. Many members of the working classes—such as the founders of the Co-operative movement—held these ideas also. So their spokesman G. J. Holyoake, discussing the principles of Co-operation (a theme dear to the heart of John Bright also), stressed that 'the noblest scheme of liberty or set of rules in the world will be dead letters unless men with a passion for the right carry them out'; the working classes must have 'a training in the unknown art of association'.[69] The theorists of public opinion were psychological determinists in the sense that individual dispositions were believed to shape institutions, and not vice versa; and often economic determinists in the sense of maintaining, as did a review in *The Economist* in 1853, that 'unerring natural laws determine the creation and distribution of wealth—that is, of subsistence and of all the products of industry—and determining these, must determine also all the subordinate phenomena of society'.[70] Whether or not they professed the latter, their practice assumed it:[71] men who had acquired wealth by responding to the needs of the market *deserved* to possess political power, for they had thus shown their moral and intellectual worth, and made good their claim to be, as Mill put it in 1831, the 'fittest persons, whom the existing state of society affords'.[72]

Their view of human nature was optimistic (whether or not they shared Owen's opinion about its almost infinite malleability), and this had two related consequences. From their Protestant background they inherited the Augustinian view of the state—that its purpose was to restrain and coerce sinful men (and thus Paine and Godwin saw the state as the expression of human wickedness); but as children of the Enlightenment, albeit mostly churchgoing ones, they abandoned the Augustinian premiss. Since men were either becoming, or were being gradually seen to be, virtuous, the state was potentially functionless. And as more men came to be enlightened, as the middle class was, public opinion, based on 'moral principle and general information',[73] would and should necessarily take over many, if not most, of the former functions of politics; and the mass of the population would acquire the franchise when they really needed it no longer.[74] This is a somewhat 'ideal-typical' presentation of the political thinking of the Dissenters and the middle-class radicals; but these themes re-occur not only in their writings but in those of others who analysed the same society, such as Marx. Their visions of the millennium differed, but all saw a millenium in which the perennial relation of politics and society would be altered. Miall, exulting over the repeal of the Corn Laws, and looking forward to the time when war and slavery would be finally done away with, expressed it thus: 'the reign of opinion will be a sort of intermediate state towards the reign of truth and justice'.[75]

This view of politics and society is personified in George Eliot's *Felix Holt the Radical* (published 1866 but set *c.* 1832). The hero addresses an election gathering of working men in these terms:

> I should like to convince you that votes would never give you political power worth having while things are as they are now, and that if you go the right way to work you may get power sooner without votes. Perhaps all you who hear me are sober men, who try to learn as much of the nature of things as you can, and to try to be as little like fools as possible. . . . The way to get rid of folly is to get rid of vain expectations, and of thoughts that don't agree with the nature of things. The men who have had true thoughts about water, and what it will do when it is turned into steam and under all sorts of circumstances,

have made themselves a great power in the world; they are turning the wheels of engines that will help to change most things. But no engines would have done, if there had been false notions about the way water would act. Now, all the schemes about voting, and districts, and annual Parliaments, and the rest, are engines, and the water or steam —the force that is to work them—must come out of human nature—out of men's passions, feelings, desires. . . . I'll tell you what's the greatest power under heaven, and that is public opinion—the ruling belief in society about what is right, and what is wrong, what is honourable and what is shameful. That's the steam to work the engines. How can political freedom make us better, any more than a religion we don't believe in, if people laugh and wink when they see men abuse and defile it? And while public opinion is what it is—while men have no better beliefs about public duty—while corruption is not felt to be a damning disgrace—while men are not ashamed in Parliament and out of it to make public questions which concern the welfare of millions a mere screen for their own petty private ends—I say, no fresh scheme of voting will mend our condition. . . .[76]

Raymond Williams suggests that the character of Felix Holt does not 'convince', being rather a lay-figure for the expression of George Eliot's apprehensions about working-class enfranchisement and mob violence.[77] Both Williams' judgments may be sound—yet Felix Holt is sociologically better observed than he implies, and some of his opinions are very characteristic of the radical circles which produced Spencer (and George Eliot, for that matter).[79] Felix Holt, a watchmaker and a member of Miall's church, was just the sort of man to have been on the fringes of the 'moral-force' Chartists and the C.S.U.; his simile of the steam and the scientistic analogy are just what the culture of the Mechanics' Institutes would have produced; and the distinction between 'political' and 'social', so far from resting on a prejudice which George Eliot is said to have shared with Carlyle, is the very one which is basic to *all* radical thought.

Yet Felix Holt's opinions do touch on the weakest point in the joint radical outlook. Government was bad and politics did not touch the hard of the matter; but were *all* governments thoroughly bad, and was the simple abolition of politics the best way of securing the goals of radicalism? Spencer and many middle-class radicals thought so, but by the 1840s others were less confident that 'society', left to itself, would satisfy all wants. Neglected hints in the writings of Paine and Godwin (who had been primarily concerned with the critique of government), were developed in the directions of socialism and Owenite co-operation.[79] For government and politics were contrasted with society both because they involved direct, identifiable dictation to people who merely asked to be allowed to get on with their business, and because they represented the interests of one class against the others. This was never stated more simply than by Adam Smith:

> Civil government, so far as it is instituted for the security of property, is in reality instituted for the defence of the rich against the poor, or of those who have some property against those who have none at all.[80]

Society (which often meant in practice the economy)[81] was formed by the satisfaction of the wants of all, and those whom it raised deserved their rewards. But what if it came to seem that the economy itself served a particular, not a general interest? This was emphatically denied by Cobden, Spencer and all those radicals who linked middle and working classes together against the aristocracy. Some radicals demanded a further reduction in the extent of government dictation; but others suggested that, if the true interests of all could be identified, they might be 'organized' and become the object of policy. This would not be government (by definition the tyranny of a minority, or 'class-rule') but *association*. What Paine had called 'a national association acting on the principles of society'[82] was the aim of the Owenite movements of the 1830s and 1840s. Hole's *Lectures on Social Science* (1851), which are a clear statement of the other alternative to the radical dilemma from the one Spencer chose in *Social Statics*, works out the implications in detail: socialism. In Hole's exposition, the antithesis of state and society is rejected, since 'the functions of the state have increased with the wants of society, and the wants of society with the means of gratifying them'; it is only *laissez-faire* which confuses the role of the 'state' under protectionist Toryism and under 'Communism', for government will then be none other than 'Society organized'; and this will become ever more feasible as, with the growth of literacy and the spread of ideas, Society becomes more and more fit to govern itself.[83] But with Hole, as with most Owenites, the legacy of the radical dismissal of politics was still seen in their considerable vagueness about how the desired state of affairs would look; and in their hope that, if only enough people were educated and 'social science' propagated, it would just somehow come about, like the Millennium.[84] (Spencer always took particular exception to the theory, shared by Comte and Mill, that ideas of any sort were the chief motor of social change.)

Felix Holt's speech illustrates another theme prominent in middle-class radical ideology: the contrast of public opinion to the sectional interests and 'class legislation' of Parliament, dominated by what Cobden called 'the two aristocratic parties'.[85] This was maintained despite some very direct appeals to middle-class pride; for middle-class interests were seen as being, in a higher sense, the interests of the nation at large. It recalls the Philosophical Radicals' usage of 'people': 'the manufacturing classes [i.e. like 'industrious classes' a term to unite middle and working class] have no interest opposed to the common good'.[86] J. S. Mill and his associates in the 1830s believed that in the future, in Hamburger's words, 'interest groups, which were sinister, would not exist, nor would there be party conflict', and that 'with the establishment of institutions that allowed for the implementation of the universal interest, politics (which assumes conflict) would be unnecessary'.[87] It is interesting to note that the Benthamites, whose critique of society made them such close allies of the Dissenters and provincial radicals, here espoused a form of anti-politics diametrically opposed to *laissez-faire* and the diffuse reign of opinion. For them 'public opinion' was what the enlightened Benthamite administrator thought; for, as J. S. Mill put it, 'the opinions and feelings of the people are, with their voluntary acquiescence, formed *for* them by the most cultivated minds which the intelligence and morality of the times call into existence'.[88] The provincial radicals were consistent in applying the logic of *laissez-faire* to the polity as well as the economy, and hoped for the end of politics with the end of the state. The metropolitan radicals found politics equally distasteful, but proposed to abolish it by turning the state into an organ of benevolent, disinterested administration. (Their exclusion of the economy from state control was, as Halévy pointed out,[89] quite illogical, but concealed from their provincial allies the precise nature of their anti-politics.)

Despite the single, precise aim of the Anti-Corn Law League, it was part of a great wave of public opinion, possessed of 'a moral and even a religious spirit',[90] which had other cultural objects. The main moralizer of the movement was Bright, 'Rochdale John', who with Cobden saw in the industrial cities of the north the germ of a new civilization. Their ideals were grounded ultimately in a Christian notion of natural rights, made historically feasible, it seemed to them, by the appropriate shaping of character by evangelicalism, or by a purely secular moral enlightenment. Spencer's dichotomy between militant and industrial societies (discussed more fully in Chapter 8) was already commonplace among these provincial radicals. Commerce, wrote Paine, 'is a pacific system, operating to cordialize mankind, by rendering nations as well as individuals useful to each other'.[91] Pacifism, humanitarian opposition to brutal or capital punishment (very marked in Godwin, Hodgskin and Spencer),[92] a distaste for the cultural values of a military aristocracy, anti-imperialism, sympathy for liberal causes and oppressed races, anti-slavery, in sum 'tender-mindedness', were all part of their cultural programme. Cobden must have had men like Bright and Sturge in mind when he said of the repeal in 1846: 'The best effect of all will be that the whole civilized world will become *Quakers* in the practice of peace and mutual forbearance.'[93]

Cobden and Bright were ill-served by their anti-politics of opinion after 1846, and their ideals seemed swamped utterly during the Crimean War. 'The Radicals have cut their throats before Sebastopol . . . the aristocracy have gained immensely since the people took to soldiering', wrote Cobden gloomily in 1856,[94] while Bright used characteristically religious language: 'the world is handed over to Belial in the shape of Emperors, Kings, Lords and soldiers'.[95] But for the young Spencer, planning a work to establish the radical cause by moral prescription and social diagnosis, these disappointments were in the future. What Raymond Williams calls the 'structure of feeling' which informs Spencer's whole work was establishment in these years—it was so diffuse in the provincial culture that he was hardly aware of it, and neglected it in the brief intellectual autobiography, 'The Filiation of Ideas', which he wrote in 1899. The major intellectual influence on him which cleared the way to *Social Statics* came from the Ricardian socialist and individualist, Thomas Hodgskin, who was from 1846 an editor of *The Economist*.

V

It is superficially surprising that Hodgskin, whose 'illustrious disciple' (as the Webbs put it) Karl Marx was, should be an editor of a magazine devoted very largely to justifying the practices and policies of the liberal commercial classes.* *The Economist* was founded in 1843 by a Scottish manufacturer, James Wilson, who had already written a book attacking the Corn Laws.[96] It presented information about stock prices and other commercial business, ran a column on railway news, and reported much political news, both domestic and foreign. Its editorial policy was consistently and thoroughly *laissez-faire*, and it played an important role in diffusing the theoretical basis for *laissez-faire* policies among its readers. The great hero of *The Economist* was Adam Smith; it never ceased regretting the use of the term *political* economy, for it was thoroughly permeated with the anti-political spirit of the decade. As sub-editor from 1848 to 1853 Spencer was not concerned with writing leaders, but with amassing and presenting factual information. He was influenced by, rather than an influence on it—or rather, was simply in accord with it.

The *laissez-faire* arguments of *The Economist* can be seen, with justice, as convenient justification for a certain view of the true interest of the manufacturers. Strikes and trade unions excite a mixture of contempt and blustering condemnation. Strikes are immoral because they coerce individuals and prevent them making free contracts; they are an attempt by one class to subjugate all others; instead the workers 'must hasten [capital] accumulation in order that they may be better paid and all become capitalists'.[97] At the persistence of trade unions it lamented that the operatives 'do not learn from facts and will not learn from words'.[98] A series of letters and articles on the merits of allotments and land-schemes for working men is concluded with the remark that the only right ones are those acquired by workers with their life savings, for 'here THE LABOURER still remains A MAN, and can boast with a

* Editorials and leading articles in *The Economist* are unsigned, and it is perilous to attribute them to authors. Some pieces which Halevy attributes to Hodgskin are so favourable to middle-class interests that it is hard to believe that they were written by the author of *Labour Defended*: whereas there is nothing that seems as if it would have been disagreeable to James Wilson.

reasonable pride that he has something in the world won by his own industry, watched over by his own eyes, and which he can fondly and fairly call his own'.[99] Chadwick's proposals for a Public Health Act excited the strongest denunciation;[100] so did Lord Shaftesbury's 'impracticable philanthropy', and criticisms of political economy from Disraeli, Arnold and Carlyle;[101] even Joseph Sturge, so much lauded in other respects, is castigated for his proposal that there be a public embargo on slave-produced goods.[102] The austere view of *The Economist* was that however noble the motives from which these well-meaning attempts at legislation might spring, they rested on ignorance of the laws of nature, and could have no beneficial consequences.[103] Benevolent societies might be 'the embodiment of physical kindness . . . they have none of the lineaments of *oughtness* about them'; they only made the social sickness worse by tackling symptoms and not causes.

This extreme *laissez-faire* was not at all accompanied by the pessimism and the sense of human powerlessness which is found in the preaching of American social Darwinists like Sumner later in the century, but by a mood of aggressive optimism which made light of social problems. A note of anxiety in the opening number in 1843, when a leader spoke of the conditions of society being 'more and more marked by characters of uncertainty and insecurity', gave way to a mood of serene, even complacent, confidence. 'Progress in Political, Civil and Religious Freedom, the "Great Fact" of the Nineteenth Century', proclaimed an editorial in 1851. *The Economist* rejoiced in the 'vast elevation in the morality of public men', and 'the destruction of Feudalism'; now 'the middle ranks, including all that is educated, sensible, and respectable, are the real rulers of society', but they acted on behalf of 'the greatness of the community—the whole PEOPLE in short'.[104]

Underlying this vision of the middle class leading Great Britain along the path of capital accumulation, peace and freedom for all classes was the image of society as an organism—either actual or potential. James Wilson had already expounded

> the only true theory on national interests—that nothing can possibly be favourable to the whole that is detrimental to a part [here he refers to the detrimental effects of the Corn Laws on the industrious classes, and implies that the aristocracy is not only selfish but mistaken about its own interest] . . . any one part can only prosper in proportion to all

> the others from which it derives its support; and . . . the whole of these parts are so linked together, that no weight or pressure can apply at any one point without bearing less or more on the whole chain of connexion.[105]

An editorial in 1847 indicates the intellectual culture which lay behind this satisfying imagery—natural theology.

> Let one peruse Dr. Paley's eloquent and popular description of the human frame; let him reflect upon the innumerable mechanical and chemical contrivances by which physical strength and animal life are sustained—all regulated by self-acting laws—provided with checks to reprove every abuse, to punish every violation of the laws of nature. . . . Wonderful as is the animal frame, the social frame is infinitely more so.[106]

Thomas Hodgskin (1787–1869), almost certainly the author of this passage, was the son of a Chatham naval storekeeper, and it was his revulsion at the brutality of the naval discipline of his day which initially led him to attack the political order in the name of natural freedom.[107] After Godwin, he is the most anarchistic of radical thinkers, and like him, he derived his social critique from a highly rationalized form of Protestantism. 'Matter, God and Nature appear to me to be three words nearly synonymous', he wrote to his associate Francis Place.[108] Natural theology of this kind is capable of both conservative and extremely radical implications; and it was this commitment to a theoretical model that made *The Economist* under Hodgskin's editorship much more than simply an apology for the manufacturers. One can maintain like Archdeacon Paley that the world as actually existent exhibits the Divine Plan—whatever is, is right: society actually is a harmonious organism. Or, as Hodgskin does, one can regard the harmony of nature as merely potential in the social sphere, and see society, or rather English society with its artificial political controls, as contrasted with nature.

Hodgskin's theoretical approach uses Paley's concepts, gives them a radical slant, and is capable of radical extension far beyond his own position, as Marx showed. There is, argued Hodgskin, a sphere where things are as they should be, and about which one can discover regular laws of operation. This is Nature or God ('I use these terms as one').[109] Actual society might be criticized in so far as it fell short of this harmony—i.e. was 'unnatural'. But before one could engage in criticism one had to have a criterion by which one might *identify* the natural and the artificial in society. Hodgskin took the political economy of Ricardo and Malthus as approximations to a natural science of society. What others have said in criticism of Malthus and Ricardo—that they present an ideal, deductivist model of the economy, timeless and placeless—Hodgskin took as praise. Nothing could be regarded as natural, that is as the subject-matter of science, unless it partook of the unchangeableness which is part of God's nature. So Hodgskin maintains, against Bentham, that

> there can be no science of the regulations of any one government, or of all governments, for they vary, according to no discoverable rule, both of themselves and in relation to the ever altering circumstances of the people for whom they are made. There may be a science of the natural principles by which legislators ought to regulate their conduct, but there can be no science of their decrees. . . . There can be no science except of what is permanent; and nationality not being permanent like the planets, there can be no political science.[110]

Comte's 'science' of sociology was therefore greeted by *The Economist* with derision.[111] The political economists had done good work in plumbing a realm of constants beneath the hopelessly shifting variable of politics and law; but they had stopped too soon. In their analysis of property and capital they had mistaken a transitory legal disposition for part of the natural scheme; the workers were in fact legally deprived of part of the natural fruits of their labour. In this intellectual setting, which gave rise to widespread use of the organic analogy, we find what is virtually Marx's theory of surplus value.

It is unfortunate though understandable that Hodgskin should be called an 'anarchist' (he did advocate that positive—i.e. actual—laws should be progressively done away with until Opinion alone could reign); for the essence of his case was that what is called 'anarchy' would be the prevalence of invariate natural law, and the present corpus of positive laws was in fact a systemless chaos. In 1851 he believed that England was at last on the way to the reign of Opinion which had been predicted so often in the anti-politics of Dissent. The flaw in Hodgskin's case, as it was becoming increasingly clear, was a failure in sociological realism. The social world behind Hodgskin's writing was, as it had been with Paine and Godwin, not a world dominated by factory production, but one of small masters, in which the aim of egalitarian philosophers was to advocate the conditions in which every worker would have an equal chance to use his native ability to become a capitalist. The cost of this anachronism was that what had been intended as a critique of capitalism could be used as a defence of it. The Owenites by contrast, for all their Utopian extravagances, had correctly assessed this essential feature of mature industrial society, and hence show more sociological affinity with such an unabashed advocate of industrial capitalism as Ure. All this is the immediate background to Spencer's first book, *Social Statics*, intended as a decisive vindication of the ideals of the middle-class radicals.

4: Social Statics

I

Spencer's first book is not one that we can read today with much pleasure. It is not the timeless statement of a certain emotional mood, or of a basic philosophical position; it did not have a lasting influence on subsequent legislators and politicians; it is not charmingly written, and contains too many factual loose ends and logical flaws. Yet it is the crucial bridge between the anti-political moralizing of Spencer's early culture and the sociology which he later evolved. It is a pregnant work.

But it is not at once clear *how* it is to be read. It is difficult to categorize in our terms. Sociology it is not: someone once called it that and Spencer retrospectively repudiated the label. In 1850 Spencer had not read Comte properly, and would probably have shared the opinion of the reviewer of Comte in *The Economist*: 'sociology, as explained by M. Comte himself, is little better than despotism both in the church and the state'.[2] It was unfortunate that the title, 'Social Statics', chosen by Spencer, had been already adopted by Comte for one division of his sociology; but Spencer was ignorant of this, and intended no allusion. Nor is it helpful to call *Social Statics* 'social science'. At the time this phrase had quite a precise meaning; and *Social Statics* is implicitly a rebuttal of its claims to be science.[3] 'Social Science' was a term with distinctively Owenite or Saint-Simonian overtones and frequently carried a suggestion of hostility to political economy. In the writings of an Owenite like James Hole 'social science' was held to imply the 'social system' (with the stress on the first word), in contrast to the competitive system.[4] Some argued that it was the task of social science to show how society as a whole might be 'organized' for the achievement of collective tasks, in the manner of a gigantic joint-stock company. Owenite ideas were drawn on very widely, and the

1840s were rich with such schemes.[5] Others, such as the middle-class adherents of the Social Science Association, meant by 'social science' a synthesis of Owenite or social, and economic theories, *laissez-faire* but qualified.[6] Chadwick was the archetype of this sort of social investigator, intent to discover facts useful for the implementation of social policy in such areas as crime, housing, sanitation, factory conditions, poverty, education, labour relations etc. To all this Spencer was unreservedly hostile, as *Social Statics* makes plain.

Its subtitle, *The Conditions Essential to Human Happiness Specified, and the First of them Developed*, reveals the intellectual context in which it was written. It was intended as a critique and a correction of the utilitarian philosophy. Spencer always considered himself a friendly critic of the utilitarians, being in broad sympathy with their social aims, but perhaps alarmed at some of the 'socialist' or statist policies to which their theories were put. If we follow Halévy and see utilitarianism as pulled in contradictory directions, towards enlightened state intervention and towards *laissez-faire*, Spencer wanted to throw all this weight towards the latter. But though Spencer was a friend and associate of J. S. Mill and other utilitarians, his deepest intellectual assumptions were very different; the critique of Bentham in *Social Statics* was intellectually radical.

Yet in a sense it is a conservative, even antiquated work. The core of Spencer's attack on Bentham is his revival of a peculiar form of natural rights, or moral sense, which Bentham had dismissed as 'nonsense on stilts'. Yet 'revival' is perhaps the wrong word, for Spencer was merely the latest representative of a long line of political moralists who grounded their prescriptions ultimately in a divinely implanted moral sense; behind him lay Priestley, Godwin and Hodgskin. A parallel tradition running from Hobbes through Hume to Bentham, grounded public morality on force, self-interest, or mutual need. It is not fortuitous, I think, that these latter thinkers have been markedly men of the court, of London, of the world, removed from that religion which for most men was the focus of community and the evident source of morality. Spencer in fact wanted it both ways—to have his morality scientific, and to make use of the traditional ground of it. *Social Statics* is the only one of his books which is avowedly deist. Greatest happiness is 'the Divine Idea'; the exercise of the faculties is 'God's will and man's duty'; man has 'Divine authority' for claiming freedom.[7] The whole work asserts the necessity of moral absolutism and bids men strive to be perfect. In a mid-nineteenth century work on moral philosophy, with numerous citations of ethnographic and scientific evidence, this has a very archaic ring.

In another sense *Social Statics* is more akin to *The Republic* than to the works of Weber or Radcliffe-Brown, for like Plato its author set himself to answer the question as to how men ought to live:

> Give us a guide, cry men to the philosopher. We would escape from these miseries in which we are entangled. A better state is ever present to our imaginations, and we yearn after it; but all our efforts to realize it are fruitless. We are weary of perpetual failures: tell us by what rule we may attain our desire.[8]

The fundamental purpose of Spencer's whole lifework was to provide a scientific morality; the *Ethics* was the culmination of the whole. Years later, in the *Autobiography*, he stated again that the aim of philosophy was to provide 'a basis for a right rule of life, individual and social'.[9] This ethical purpose was the scaffolding within which the edifice of true sociology was erected; and the scaffolding was demolished by his successors. The sociology is logically independent of the ethics, though genetically consequent on it. The initial question is, therefore: under what conditions does the attempt to establish an ethical system require the support of sociological evidence?

The main overt differences between moral philosophers are in the validity of their reasoning and the soundness of their assumptions. But a richer understanding emerges when we look at the variable functions which their writings perform. To tell men what they ought to aim at, to get men to act in prescribed ways, to provide men with good justifications for acting the way they do, are different tasks which philosophers vary in performing. On the whole moral philosophy's primary role has not been moral innovation, or the discovery of new rules of behaviour, or the enlightenment of those in serious perplexity as to how they should behave. That has been the office of prophets, revolutionaries and of hard men who see the brute necessities of society. In a history of morals pride of place must be taken by the Wesleys and not by the Humes; and Hume, a modest and candid man, recognized this to be so—'generally speaking, errors in religion are dangerous; those in philosophy only ridiculous'. Modern moral philosophy arose, and has always since been rejuvenated, not so much by simple social conflict and divergences of interest (which always call forth ideology, casuistry, and pastoral theology) as by the failure of intellectual authority—the clash of *reasons* and the lack of universal *justification* for the desired behaviour.

The problem was posed because of the secularization which preceded and accompanied the Industrial Revolution. Alasdair MacIntyre has argued that this was an effect of the growth of separate class cultures with urbanization from the late eighteenth century.[10] But in what sense had the social ranks of pre-industrial England shared a common culture and common ways of behaviour? In many ways industrial culture is far more homogeneous than before. What had changed was the unchallenged, deferred-to cultural hegemony of the upper ranks: other classes proclaimed the independent universal worth of their ideals and there was a loss of agreement and self-confidence within the élite. Religious dissension was a major ingredient of this. So J. S. Mill gauged the situation in 1831: 'in an age of transition the divisions among the instructed nullify their authority, and the uninstructed lose their faith in them'.[11] In some quarters the answer seemed to be a new religion. Despite the failure of the exotic Comtism to really catch on in England, Mrs. Humphrey Ward, in her novel *Robert Elsmere* (heavily indebted to the philosophy of T. H. Green) caught a recurrent mood when she wrote:

> The problem of the world at the moment is—*how to find a religion?* Some great conception which shall be once more capable as the old were of welding societies and keeping men's brutish elements in check.[12]

Spencer, not fully aware of how much he assumed the moral residue of evangelicalism, did not feel a new religion was at all needed. He explained in 1879 what he said had been his aim since beginning to write in 1842:

> [His] ultimate purpose, lying behind all proximate purposes, has been that of finding for the principles of right and wrong in conduct at large, a scientific basis. . . . Now that the moral injunctions are losing the authority given by their supposed sacred origin, the secularization of morals is becoming imperative.[13]

The argument was more about the *reasons* for right action than about what right action was.

The traditional reason and justification for any action was that it was in accord with God's Will, and argument began with the citation of scriptural or ecclesiastical authority. How far the use of unaided reason was permitted was a subsidiary focus of debate; but it was generally agreed that reason was a gift of God, and its promptings divine emanations. Natural rights, seen so by the consensus of all reasonable men, were easily equated, in a liberal Protestantism especially, with the Divine Will, and in fact they were most widely published by liberal and modernized Protestants, such as Priestley, Paine and Price (all earnest friends of the French republic), Rousseau, and the founding fathers of the United States of America. Even if one wished to dispense with religion altogether, one could secure the same effects by speaking about 'Nature' exactly as the others spoke about 'God'.

For over a century there had existed a rival, secular, system of ethics and politics. As Macpherson has shown, the central problem of modern ethics—how can one deduce statements of obligation from statements of fact—was realized, and, in his own judgment, surmounted by Hobbes, the founder of secular ethics.[14] In a society where all men were equally subject to the forces of the market, values had a non-subjective, non-supernatural, basis because they were created for everyone by social needs—as long as the market existed. This amounts to a quasi-sociological (quasi- because the sociological assumptions are merely implicit) account of how values are created in a particular society. But since it is only a morality for one kind of society, the possibility of moral criticism of a dominant social order is excluded, and so is any kind of moral change. It is implicit in the method of Hobbes, as also of his disciples Hume and Bentham, that there can only be one kind of scientific morality, and that only one set of social conditions can support one. As Macpherson puts it, the ethics of 'possessive individualism' lose their coherence as the market-society disappears.[15] So Hume believed that 'history's chief use is only to discover the constant and universal principles of human nature'.[16] It was not that different moralities might be demonstrated for different ages as human nature changed; but that one age realized at long last what human nature really was, and could frame a morality to express it.

Hume, often regarded as the first person to have realized that no bridge is possible between scientific, 'is', statements, and moral, 'ought' statements, actually only used his arguments to undermine the validity of moralities which represented obligations as following from divine commands, like the common religion-based morality of his day.[17] Hume's own view was that one could construct a rational morality from 'the constant and universal principles of human nature'—precisely the view which Hume's own argument in the *Treatise* has been thought (correctly in fact, but of course not by Hume) to undermine. Bentham's moral philosophy followed from Hume, though it had a much more precise aim—to enable a fair, clear and rational legal code to be constructed.[18] Law was not to be based on any so-called self-evident truths, such as natural rights, for these, like the religious injunctions whose unreason Hume had shown up, could not be shown to depend on factual propositions. The legislator, in following his guiding utilitarian principle (for which Bentham was largely indebted to Priestley), was to frame laws in accordance with whatever relationships between cause and effect the study of human nature (principally associationist psychology) would reveal. The debate, let us note again, is significant not for the different values that the protagonists adopted, but for the different reasons by which they justified them. Bentham came, in his later years, to share very similar policy views as many of the natural-rights theorists whose logic he denounced; and Burke was to use essentially utilitarian arguments to defend the political system which was the Utilitarians' bugbear. Spencer's defence of natural rights against Bentham concerns us because it obliged him to do sociology.

II

Social Statics opens with a contrast between Bentham's theory, 'the doctrine of expediency' as Spencer terms it, and his own 'doctrine of moral sense'. He acknowledges the rightness of Bentham's utilitarian maxim, but regrets it is too general—men's ideas of happiness are so varied. Furthermore, in all matters of legislation and social policy, it is very hard to adopt just the right means to the desired end. In a way which soon becomes familiar to any reader of Spencer, he then lists a whole series of legislative measures which fail because of unrealistic assessments of cause and effect, and concludes that the most successful legislation is that which repeals existing statutes. At this point Spencer merely suggests that ignorance precludes legislation:

> Considering that man as yet so imperfectly understands *man*—the instrument by which, and the material on which, laws are to act—and that a complete knowledge of the unit—*man* is but a first step to the comprehension of the mass—*society*, it seems obvious enough that to educe from the infinitely ramified complications of universal humanity, a true philosophy of national life, and to found thereon a code of rules for the obtainment of 'greatest happiness' is a task far beyond the ability of any finite mind.[19]

But he soon makes it clear that the lesson of knowledge is that, in the mid-nineteenth century, it is best to have the minimum of government. For government is just a 'probationary' institution, 'begotten by necessity out of evil', and not something to be organized into the perfect morality.[20] Bentham's view of law as the command of the soveriegn is appropriate for one concerned with scientific legislation; Spencer's assertion that 'the triumph of the Anti-Corn-Law League is simply the most marked instance yet of the new style of government—that of opinion, overcoming the old style, that of force',[21] is a generalization from the politics of the 1840s.

Moreover, moral sense and natural rights are not only necessary to *any* morality, but are empirically observable. If one asks a Utilitarian why it is that one man's happiness is as much to be considered as another's, either he cannot answer, or he too makes reference to some form of moral intuition. Moral sense cannot be, as Bentham says it is, an 'anarchical and capricious principle, founded solely upon internal and peculiar feelings'.[22] Moral sense still incurs the charge of vagueness, apparent variability, and difficulty of application, and for the moment Spencer contents himself with a bland assertion of what it is, in a paean of praise to radical opinions. He traces it back to Magna Carta and the early Protestants, and concludes:

> At present it puts on the garb of Anti-State-Church Associations, and shows its presence in manifold societies for the extension of popular power. It builds monuments to political martyrs, agitates for the

> admission of Jews into Parliament, publishes books on the rights of women, petitions against class legislation, threatens to rebel against militia conscriptions, refuses to pay church-rates, repeals oppressive debtor acts, laments over the distresses of Italy, and thrills with sympathy for the Hungarians.[23]

So far Spencer has shown the necessity of some form of moral intuition in all ethical systems; and yet intends to show how his identification of moral sense is scientifically, not merely intuitively, grounded. This is the method of many of Spencer's demonstrations, in sociology as in ethics; first to deduce his conclusion from some kind of first principles or general rule, and then to show how the conclusion is supported by empirical observation.

The introduction concludes with two 'lemmas' (another characteristic little Spencerism) which assert two principles essential to the subsequent argument. First, whereas earlier philosophies 'assume the character of mankind to be constant',[24] a survey of nature shows that all natural phenomena are infinitely variable. Change is the Law of all things, and

> Strange indeed would it be, if, in the midst of this universal mutation, man alone were constant, unchangeable. But it is not so. He also obeys the law of indefinite variation. His circumstances are ever altering; and he is ever adapting himself to them. Between the naked houseless savage, and the Shakespeares and Newtons of a civilized state, lie unnumbered degrees of difference. The contrasts in form, colour and feature, are not greater than the contrasts in their moral and intellectual qualities. That superiority of sight which enables a Bushman to see further with the naked eye than a European with a telescope, is fully paralleled by the European's more perfect intellectual vision. The Calmuck in delicacy of smell, and the red Indian in acuteness of hearing, do not excel the white man more than the white man excels them in moral susceptibility.[25]

It is not at once clear what is the point of the debate about whether human nature is variable or not. Clearly Bentham and others, whom Spencer accused of ignoring this variability, *were aware of* the great variety of actual human desires and conditions. But as Burrow points out,[26] to show that Bentham was aware of it, as Mrs. Mack has done, does not absolve him from the charges that his theories do not account for it and that his prescriptions seem to ignore it. Why this insistence on unity in the face of manifest variety? The practical reason is that an effective guide to conduct in a situation of competing possibilities requires that the range of permitted behaviour be reduced as much as possible, preferably to a single type, which is alone sanctioned by God or nature. Spencer, like Bentham and the others, wants such a clear moral guide, but differs in that he does not think it can be inferred from actual practices, which being varied, merely exemplify the problem:

> If humanity *is* infinitely variable, it cannot be used as a gauge for testing moral truth. When we see that institutions impracticable in one age have flourished in a subsequent one, and that what were once salutary laws and customs have become repugnant; we may shrewdly suspect that the like changes will take place in future.[27]

Yet a long tradition, going back to the Greeks, sees nature not as the phenomena themselves, but as an unchanging constant beneath them. Spencer in fact has a similar concept himself, which however he wants to harmonize with the observable variability. He seems to hold that in a weaker sense all things are equally 'natural' in their circumstances, but also that in a stronger sense only perfection is. We are led back to the logical need for a moral standard that is transcendent—just what moral philosophers since Hobbes had been trying to do without. A right morality must be an ideal one, above what anyone actually does. But 'right principles of action become practicable only as men become perfect; or rather, to put the expressions in proper sequence—man becomes perfect, just in so far as he is able to obey them'. 'Nature' properly refers to the whole process of development to perfection. What to others had been a constant to be discovered beneath tedious and irrelevant variations, was to Spencer virtually a *telos* gradually being achieved. The important difference in Spencer's position was that it obliged him to explain the variations in actual human behaviour systematically, for they alone provided him with the evidence to justify his detailed prescriptions.[29]

Yet despite the implicit relativism of Spencer's rejection of the existence of a unitary human nature in Bentham's sense, he was able to retain clear moral direction by insisting that increasingly it was coming about that what was right for the age was also the absolute dictate of perfection. The second lemma states that 'unable as the imperfect man may be to fulfil the perfect law, there is no other law for him'[30] (an echo of the pre-evolutionary certainties of the *Letters on the Proper Sphere of Government*). But happily the 'perfect law' was coming to be realized as such, and hence could be put into practice:

> . . . rightly understood, the progress from deepest ignorance to highest enlightenment, is a progress from entire unconsciousness of law, to the conviction that law is universal and inevitable. . . .
>
> A belief, as yet fitful and partial, is beginning to spread amongst men, that here also there is an indissoluble bond between cause and consequence, an inexorable destiny, a 'law which altereth not'. Confounded by the multiplied and ever-new aspects of human affairs, it is not perhaps surprising that men should fail duly to recognize the systematic character of the Divine rule. Yet in the moral as in the material world, accumulated evidence is gradually generating the conviction, that events are not at bottom fortuitous; but that they are wrought out in a certain inevitable way by unchanging forces. In all ages there has been some glimmering perception of this truth; and experience is ever giving to that perception increased distinctness. Indeed even now all men do, in one mode or another, testify of such a faith. Every known creed is an assertion of it. . . .[31]

Here speak in unison the voices of the rationalist inveighing against miracles or special intervention, and of the preacher assuring his congregation that, despite all appearances, evil does catch you out and crime does not pay. And Spencer concludes the introduction with a final admonition to submit to the Divine Will giving historical examples of the evil consequences of not doing so: the southern states of America have done wrong to practise slavery, and have consequently been left behind in prosperity by the northern ones. So, 'no matter how seemingly inexpedient, dangerous, injurious even, may be the course which morality points out . . . the highest wisdom is in perfect and fearless submission'.[32]

III

The 'social statics' of the title are the demonstration of the perfect condition of morality, necessary but as yet unrealized, towards which mankind is tending, and the greater part of the book is taken up with showing its implications in different social spheres. The details of this morality are the policies of the extreme *laissez-faire* radicals of the late 1840s. The First Principle of this morality, Spencer asserts, is *a priori*, but can be demonstrated synthetically too. Human happiness is the Divine Will (the *a priori* truth, following from the definition of God), and is a certain state of consciousness produced by certain sensations. These sensations are produced by the use of the faculties; happiness results from the due exercise of all the faculties. The supreme moral value of liberty is easily shown to follow:

> God wills man's happiness. Man's happiness can only be produced by the exercise of his faculties. Then God wills that he should exercise his faculties. But to exercise his faculties he must have liberty to do all this his faculties naturally impel him to do. Then God intends he should have that liberty. Therefore he has a *right* to that liberty.[33]

The only qualification arises from the fact that others have this right too, and the general proposition stands emended as: 'every man may claim the fullest liberty to exercise his faculties compatible with the possession of like liberty by every other man'.

Some instructive casuistry then follows.[35] What if the exercise of one man's faculties causes another pain? Is that right? This depends on whether the active or the passive party has 'abnormally-constituted' feelings (i.e. by a complete circularity of argument, ones that do not accord with the state of perfect morality). For example, if an honest man decides a friend is a rogue, and, having 'certain high instincts to which roguery is repugnant', causes him pain by dropping his acquaintanceship; or if a Protestant in a Roman Catholic country refuses to revere the host, lest 'by showing reverence for what he does revere, tell a virtual lie', and so annoys his Catholic neighbours—in either case the action, though pain-causing, is justified because dishonesty in the one case, and bigoted intolerance in the other, are imperfect feelings. The lack of serious moral perplexity in Spencer's own mind is striking; and so is the logical dependence of his arguments on the potentially sociological fact that human morality really is developing towards the defined perfection as he says it is. How Spencer has derived the content of perfect morality is not really important at all; what matters is whether it can be shown that the human race is moving in the direction of it.

The contrast between mankind's actual moral constitution and the perfect constitution which it is the task of social statics to discover, is constantly used to divert counter-evidence to the latter into positive evidence of the former, that is, into evidence of social change. The problem of sin and suffering, always apt to stick out awkwardly in harmonious systems of natural theology, soon crops up. If the exercise of our faculties leads to happiness, why is it that they may lead us to painful and degrading drunkenness? It is because 'we are as yet imperfectly adapted to our conditions'.[36] Moreover, in the continuous process of self-perfection, it may be right and necessary to have to do painful and irksome things: 'it is self-evident that the ability to work is needful for the production of the greatest happiness; yet the acquirement of this ability by the uncivilized man is so distressing, that only the severest discipline will force him to it'. Pain and strain fulfil the same role for the individual as the state does for the collectivity: they are the price of imperfection, and the finally dispensable causes of perfection and happiness. Spencer's use of this ancient device of Christian theology must have been very persuasive to people who had undergone the great and painful wrench of industrialization, and who in 1851 only needed to be convinced that the sacrifices were worthwhile. He has produced a very indifferent piece of moral philosophy, but an interpretation of social experience which derives all its plausibility from Spencer's identification with the experience and expression of it in the most meaningful language.

Spencer now turns to a 'secondary derivation' of the rights he has established by *a priori* reasoning. The writings of other moralists and philosophers, from Hooker and Filmer to the Benthamites, all testify that an 'instinct of personal rights' does exist—both as a psychological phenomenon, and as a logical requirement of their theories. A notorious difficulty of Bentham's philosophy—the combination of altruistic ethics and individual hedonist psychology[37] (both of which Spencer adopted) is surmounted by developing the argument of Smith's neglected *Theory of Moral Sentiments* that the social sentiment of sympathy is a reflex of self-love: moreover, 'the sentiment of justice is nothing but a sympathetic affection of the instinct of personal rights—a sort of reflex function of it'.[38] Again the example he gives is characteristic. The Quakers have been persecuted and ready to struggle for their freedom; and this has developed in them a sympathy for the rights of others, as witness their role in penal reform and the abolition of slavery. Only as sympathy develops will the perfect morality, which social statics reveals, become practicable; but as it is now being enunciated, and expressed in public opinion, it is becoming increasingly feasible.

The system of rights which Spencer now goes on to set out in detail reveals a liberalism of the most extreme kind. The most striking exception to a list of rights in which the right to property is salient, occurs with regard to land-ownership, and was the only passage in the book which *The Economist*'s reviewer criticized. Private land-ownership is wrong; it originated in military theft and still supports the forces of 'land-owning despotism'.[39] Moreover, it is deducible from 'the law of equal freedom' that 'the theory of the co-heirship of all men to the soil, is consistent with the highest civilization'. Under Spencer's proposals 'separate ownerships would merge into the joint-stock ownership of the public. Instead of being in the possession of individuals, the country would be held by the great corporate body—society'.[40] But Spencer insists that this would not mean socialism; men only have a right to use the land, not a right to the fruits of the land. Socialism would upset the system of merit and reward which the Divine Scheme implies. Property is so crucial to Spencer's thinking that the need for a libel law is discussed as 'Property in Character', and for a law protecting patents, copyrights, etc. as 'Property in Ideas'.

Free speech is obviously dictated by moral sense. Censorship (though advocated by 'old women of both sexes') cannot even be justified by the argument of security. Rather, 'under a sound social regime and its accompanying contentment, nothing is to be feared from the most uncontrolled utterance of thought and feeling'.[41] The rights of women are quite as well grounded as those of men. Their exclusion from equal rights cannot be justified on grounds of their intelligence; and the subordination of women to men is in fact token of a state of barbarism. In a very sensible and humane chapter Spencer argues similarly for children, and criticizes all methods of education other than moral suasion. Force and coercion are utterly opposed to natural equity, and their existence is testimony to the still existing gap between perfect justice and present human capacity.

Having thus sketched out individual rights, Spencer goes on to defend the *liassez-faire* state. The constancy of the Divine Will, and the dictates of moral sense, are again contrasted with the changeableness of 'institutions and social forms'. By now the comparison of actual institutions at different stages of development towards perfection has become a regular feature of the argument. Rousseau's social contract is attacked as a gratuitous historical fiction, and also for making the polity, the result of the contract, eternally binding. Spencer himself views the state as resting on a contract, but one which the individual may repudiate at any time—ideally it is in this respect exactly like a joint-stock company. In a fallen, imperfect condition evil exists, and hence the state exists to counteract it, but it too uses force, which is evil. Spencer even asserts that 'the very existence of majorities and minorities is indicative of a fallen state', for it means that some are oppressing others by coercing them into collective action. But as men come to be perfect, their always-existing abstract right to ignore the state becomes ever more practicable.

As citizenship is voluntary, so it confers equal privileges. On democracy Spencer reproduces exactly the arguments of Sturge and the Complete Suffrage Union. To these who point to the ignorance of the workers, or the danger of the majority's tyranny, he says that the corruption of the existing pseudo-democracy proves nothing against democracy as the moral idea. In fact it will work just as soon as men's characters and notions enable it to work, in particular as self-control and eternal watchfulness, the marks of the free man, become prevalent. Spencer was confident that these character changes were actually taking place:

> Whenever, therefore, a people *calmly* arrives at the conclusion that democratic institutions are right; whenever they *dispassionately* determine that they shall be adopted; or, in other words, whenever the circumstances show that the setting up of such institutions is not an accident, but results from the ascendancy of the aforesaid sentiment; then, and then alone, are such institutions permanently possible.
>
> In the opinion, now so happily prevalent, that the pacific mode of working out political changes is the only efficient one, we have a collateral expression of this truth. . . . It is not that bloodshed vitiates the free institutions it may help to set up; nor is it that when peacefully established such institutions are preserved by virtue of their being so established; but it is that the manner in which the change is wrought

indicates the national character, and proves it to be respectively unfit or fit for the new social form.[42]

A few pages later comes a rapturous description of the radical movement as it seemed to Spencer, an active participant in it:

> Not hunger, nor the anxiety to escape from torture, nor the desire for vengeance, is now the transforming force, but a calm unswerving force to get human liberties recognized. The carrying out of one of these battles of opinion to a successful issue through long delays and discouragements, through ridicule and misrepresentation, implies a perennial source of energy quite different from mere insurrectionary rage. In place of a passing gust of anger, a persistent and ever-strengthening sentiment is here the acting agent. Agitation is its gymnasium. Men in whom it predominates cultivate it in the rest. They address it in speeches; they write articles to it; they convene meetings for its manifestation. It is aroused by denunciations of injustice; it is appealed to in the name of conscience; it is conjured by all that is fair and upright and equitable. . . . After men's minds have been for many years thus exercised and stimulated, a sufficiently intense manifestation of feeling is produced, and then comes the reform. . . .[43]

What is the state then, in the ideal scheme of things? Spencer here uses again a favourite persuasive device—the organic analogy. 'A function to each organ, and each organ to its own function, is the law of all organization'.[44] Just as in economics the most highly developed arrangements show a more developed division of labour, so also the state's function becomes more highly specialized, until it becomes nothing more than a voluntary political organization for mutual protection. For the state to engage in education, or sanitary supervision, or trade-regulation, or succouring the poor, is for it to usurp its proper role, to prevent men from adapting to the environment and so to retard their inevitable perfection. Several chapters justify the position of extreme *laissez-faire* in different fields. The very anti-conservative intent of some of these arguments, particularly that against state education, is to be noted. He rebuts the argument that education for effective democratic citizenship should be undertaken by the state by saying that this implies that the state should be the source of moral values, which further implies a coercive society; and the countries where there is state education—China, France, Prussia—are not noted for liberalism. Moreover, 'a national organization for cultivating the popular mind' would be strongly conservative:

> All institutions have an instinct of self-preservation growing out of the selfishness of those connected with them. Being dependent for their vitality upon the continuance of existing arrangements, they naturally uphold these. Their roots are in the past and the present; never in the future. Change threatens them, modifies them, eventually destroys them; hence to change they are uniformly opposed. On the other hand, education, properly so called, is closely associated with change—is its pioneer—is the never-sleeping agent of revolution—is always fitting men for higher things, and *un*fitting them for things as they are.[45]

Here Spencer is thinking of the ancient universities, and such ideals as Coleridge's 'clerisy' or those that underlay Arnold's *Culture and Anarchy*. This radical philosophy of education is the generalization of the Dissenters' fear of an educational system dominated by the Established Church.[46] The evolutionism that was merely implied when he first expressed these views back in 1842 is now quite explicit. Spencer's liberalism is in 1850 triumphantly optimistic about the potentiality of men freed from the shackles of institutions.[47]

IV

In judging *Social Statics* as a whole, the first question must be to ask whether it achieved its author's aim. Morality, as Spencer saw it, was to be made scientific—i.e. the conclusions were to follow as ineluctably and irrefutably from the premisses as in a scientific demonstration; and it was to be convincing, an effective call to action, to his contemporaries. In an age which values and esteems science, the second result (the conclusion of a practical syllogism), will naturally follow from the first. Yet all philosophers who aim to do more than merely analyse the logic of moral words, recognize the gulf between knowledge and action, and seek to find ways of bridging it. If one senses that mere reasoning does not, somehow, lead to action, but wants it to, one will challenge the boundary between these spheres. In Plato's ethics the result was the principle 'nobody does wrong willingly'[48]—a quasi-logical, quasi-factual assertion, which means that all that philosophy can do is all that anyone can ever do. The failure to act is seen as really a failure to grasp the argument; action is assimilated to reason, will to understanding, psychology to logic. An important consequence of this Platonic tactic is that the question as to why a sound argument does not convince does not become a stepping-off point for psychology, history or social science.

The moralists of the Enlightenment were faced with just the same hiatus, but they bridged it in the other direction, by assimilating reason to action. As Hume put it: 'reason is, and ought only to be, the slave of the passions, and can never pretend to any other office than to serve and obey them'.[49] Hume was here typical of the eighteenth-century Scottish moralists—'men of ideas in a world of action', as Kettler has called them[50]—and prone to justify ideas as a species of action, or as inferior to action. Adam Smith took the same view: understanding is not seen in logical terms, as the filling of an intellectual gap, but as a psychological phenomenon, an antidote to wonder and a 'repose of the imagination'.[51] The same is true of Bentham: logic is dissolved in psychology. Even though it was often the case, as it was particularly with Bentham, that the content of the psychology was more derived, *a priori*, from the requirements of the logic than from the distressing variability of human nature, the decisive intellectual move towards a rudimentary social science had been made. Now all logic could be seen as the structure of a pattern of human action, and the main philosophical task became a sort of moral technology.

This means pragmatism, which, long before Pierce and James, (who did call it 'a new name for some old ways of thinking'),[52] had become the philosophy which was the closest kin to sociology. A pragmatist sees the resolution of theoretical doubt in the appeal to action or practice. If the intrinsic truth of religious doctrine is in doubt, 'true doctrine' in religion can be defined as that which expressed human needs or social functions, which 'works'.[53] True doctrines in philosophy or science are those from which useful, successful, fit consequences follow; the ultimate and only test of validity is to show how any theory of proper behaviour fits the circumstances in which it is to be entertained.

Spencer's argument in *Social Statics* is certainly pragmatic in this sense. The gap between statements of fact and statements of obligation *is*, in the end, unbridgeable; but Spencer managed to secure the same effect as bridging it—providing people with convincing motives for action—by a different technique. A particular, desirable, type of behaviour and social system were shown to be necessary; they were going to come about in the future. Ethical reasoning gives way, in the vital instance, to an invitation to jump on the historical band-waggon, and the persuasiveness of the case comes, therefore, to depend, not on the analysis of moral terms, or on a postulated 'human nature', but the quality of the sociological (as it came to be) demonstration. In a sense *Social Statics*, despite its avowed moral aim and its persistent use of ethnical terms, is not a work of ethics in the modern sense at all. For moral injunction implies that the possibility exists of the subject obeying or not obeying;[54] 'ought' implies 'might not' as well as 'can'—it makes no sense to tell people that they 'ought' to digest their food or to die when their heads are cut off. Yet, in the long run, this is just what Spencer does tell his readers. The ethical problem is not solved but circumvented.

It is evident how close this morality is to a position which Spencer would have indignantly repudiated—*might makes right*. Spencer does indeed attack 'the doctrine of expediency', uphold the practice of living as close as possible to the absolute morality dictated by the moral sense, and insist on what seems totally opposed to any kind of pragmatism. His initial justification of the content of moral sense is almost intuitionist. But the validity of this absolute morality is grounded on historical necessity, and the increasing practical feasibility is shown by—its actual practice! The meek really shall inherit the earth, because meekness, in the historical context, actually is 'fitter' than bellicosity. Look at the industrial successes of peaceful England, and at the social and economic predominance of Quakers like Joseph Sturge! Predatoriness did once have 'a collateral benefit, though in itself so radically bad' when human nature was so ill-developed; but the age in which 'fitness' meant physical might and coercion of one's fellows is long over:

> Let not the reader be alarmed. Let him not fear that these admissions will excuse new invasions and new oppressions. Nor let any one who fancies himself called upon to take Nature's part in this matter, by providing discipline for idle negroes or others, suppose that these dealings of the past will serve for precedents. That phase of civil-

> ization during which forcible supplantings of the weak by the strong, and systems of savage coercion, are on the whole advantageous, is a phase which spontaneously and necessarily gives birth to these things.[55]

> Another illustration this of the perfect economy of Nature. Whilst the injustice of conquests and enslavings is not perceived, they are on the whole beneficial; but as soon as they are felt to be at variance with the moral law, the continuance of them retards adaptation (to the social state, the end-product of history) in one direction, more than it advances it in another: a fact which our new teacher of the old doctrine, that might is right, may profitably consider a little.[56]

Like all the most satisfying essays in pulpit-moralizing, *Social Statics* gives its readers the pleasure of knowing they have taken the course of absolute morality; and hastens to assure them that it is also the most feasible, the most profitable, the 'fittest' in the circumstances. It is an irony that evolutionary ethics, which thus began their career as the instrument of 'the party of humanity', of liberals, pacifists and Dissenters, came to be used, in the 1880s, in support of imperialist 'might is right' policies of the kind which *Social Statics* is particularly directed against. But Spencer was, in his way, no less a worshipper of force—the force of historical necessity—than his opponents.[57] For nearly all Victorian moralists, whatever the content of their morality, were inclined to justify their ethics by a final pragmatic appeal: it works; this is how things are; you really do believe it; it is implicit in your practice; it accords with your real nature; history will prove it so.

The effective tone of *Social Statics* may be described as necessitarian optimism. The optimism follows from the necessity which ensures that the perfect morality—the final adaption of mankind to the social state—must come about. This theme is first presented early in the book as 'the evanescence of evil', still very much in the dress of natural theology:

> All evil results from the non-adaptation of constitution to conditions. This is true of everything that lives. . . . No matter what the special nature of the evil, it is invariably referable to the one generic cause—want of congruity between the faculties and their spheres of action. . . . Equally true is it that evil perpetually tends to disappear. In virtue of an essential principle of life, this non-adaptation of an organism to its conditions is ever being rectified: and modification of one or both, continues until the adaptation is complete.[58]

This process is the realization of the Divine Idea. Hence:

> Progress . . . is not an accident, but a necessity. Instead of civilization being artificial, it is a part of nature; all of a piece with the development of the embryo or the unfolding of a flower. The modifications mankind have undergone, and are still undergoing, result from a law underlying the whole organic creation; and provided the human race continues, and the constitution of things remains the same, those modifications must end in completeness. As surely as the tree becomes bulky when it stands alone, and slender if one of a group . . . as surely as a blacksmith's arm grows large, and the skin of a labourer's hand thick . . . so surely must the human faculties be moulded into complete fitness for the social state; so surely must the things we call evil and immortality disappear; so surely must man become perfect.[59]

All the essential elements of social evolution are present here—progress, necessity, adaptation, continual modification until perfection is reached—and they are recapitulated in the closing stages of the book. 'The course of civilization could not possibly have been other than it has been';[60] it is useless to ask why perfection was not established at once—the fact of the matter is that we are becoming perfect as fast as is possible. Only if men had had 'some utterly different mental constitutions could the process of civilization have been altered'.[61] The mechanics of the divine scheme are different from how Paley had seen them, but the effect is the same: 'Civilization no longer appears to be a regular unfolding after a specific plan; but seems rather a development of men's latent capabilities under the action of favourable circumstances; which . . . were certain some time or other to occur.'[62]

The surest way to ground one's values is to show that their realization is determined. But there is only a narrow partition between a confident determinism and an indolent fatalism which if acted upon would falsify the predictions. Spencer always was, as George Eliot wrote, 'very sensitive on the point of being supposed to teach an enervating fatalism'.[63] He may have maintained that 'in teaching a uniform unquestioning obedience does an entirely abstract philosophy become one with all true religion',[64] but this submission did not mean with him, as any more than it did for the Calvinists who were his intellectual forbears, an attitude of passivism or surrender, but an aggressive confidence that his will was also the will of God. Spencer's determinism was quite different from the fatalism expressed by his American disciple Youmans, who on being asked what could be done to alleviate social evils, replied:

> Nothing! You and I can do nothing at all. It's all a matter of evolution. We can only wait for evolution. Perhaps in four or five thousand years evolution may have carried men beyond this state of things. But we can do nothing.[65]

But determinism only turns to fatalism when events make the determined historical sequence lose its plausibility; and in 1850 Spencer was still confident. Spencer gave up active radical politics not because of a conviction that circumstances were too strong from them, but because he felt that their success was so certain that his individual effort was hardly needed. *Social Statics* is as much the exultant cry of success, as it is a blow for victory.

So he addresses 'the candid reader', who might feel that the time is not yet ripe for the final putting-into-effect of perfect morality, in these terms:

> Let him but duly realize the fact that opinion is the agency through which character adapts external arrangements to itself—that *his* opinion rightly forms part of this agency—is a unit of force, constituting, with other such units, the general power which works out social changes—and he will then perceive that he may properly give full utterance to his *innermost conviction*; leaving it to produce what effect it may. It is not for nothing that he has in him these sympathies with some principles and repugnance to others. He, with all his capacities, and desires, and beliefs, is not an accident, but a product of the time. Influences that have acted upon preceding generations; influences that have been brought to bear upon him; the education that disciplined his childhood; together with the circumstances in which he has since lived; have conspired to make him what he is. And the result thus wrought out in him has a purpose. He must remember that whilst he is a child of the past, he is the parent of the future. . . . He, like every other man, may properly consider himself as an agent through whom nature works; and when nature gives birth in him to a certain belief, she thereby authorizes him to profess and act out that belief.[66]

V

In its ethics as well as in its arguments, *Social Statics* shows itself an integral part of a cultural tradition massively influenced by Calvin. Since sociologists have been so fascinated by Calvinism and have made it their special pleasure to trace many features of modernity back to it, often to repeated protests from historians, it may seem obsessional to re-introduce the theme here, in showing how the origins of sociology itself were shaped by Calvinism. Yet it is true that Spencer and a number of other writers who shared his Dissenting origins and his deist/secularist opinions based their detailed historical and psychological theories on a necessitarian optimism which was demonstrably a transformation of Calvinist themes. It is understandable enough that just as predestination had been the response of some men to radical social change in an earlier period, so a secular determinism was one response to equally disturbing changes in a later one. Spencer's necessitarian scheme of evolution, and his general concern with certitude cannot be grasped otherwise.

Any account of Calvinism must begin with Calvin's conception of God. 'No theology was ever more theocentric. All is of God. . . . Calvinist theology is informed throughout with an adoring sense of the transcendence, the sole and absolute causality, of God, before whose infinite majesty, incomprehensible essence, boundless power and eternal duration, man is utterly insignificant, save to illustrate the operation of God's grace in redemption'.[67] Calvinism is the most extremely transcendental form of Christianity, the remotest from immanentist, pantheistic conceptions of all nature as enchanted and God as coterminous with nature. All traditional religions, whether primitive or folk versions of world religions, are immanentist to a strong degree, for the worshipper's ability to cajole or coerce the gods to intervene in the physical world on his behalf, depends on the 'enchantment' of the world, the actual embodiment of God in manipulable material things.[68] Petitionary prayer and sacraments are, in Christianity, the product of a balance between immanentist and transcendental conceptions of God.

The Calvinist conception of God, in thus stressing the world's profanity, had certain implications for the scientific study of nature. For the passionate Calvinist, intent on the worship of God and the scrutiny of the Scriptures to know His will, profane nature hardly seemed worth man's serious attention. But the revolutionary implications of this total abstraction of value from existing natural phenomena were shown in a completely unsentimental attitude towards them. Only God was sacred and mysterious: there could be no barrier to the systematic investigation of the structure of nature, or to the wholesale alteration of it according to one's purposes—if, that is, one had a mind to. In practical terms this came to mean that, when Calvinists did come to investigate nature, the analysis of secondary, empirical, causes could go ahead uncluttered by repeated magical or irrational intrusions of the supernatural. God was a great First Cause, the author of the whole chain of secondary causes, and only He was inscrutable. So Hill writes of Ralegh that he 'does not show God directly intervening to smite the sinner; he shows the ineluctable working out of cause and the effect at the human level . . . [he] secularized history not by denying God the first cause, but by concentrating his vision on secondary causes and insisting that they are sufficient in themselves for historical explanation'.[69]

But as science develops a transformation takes place, that is both a development and an inversion of the original. Scientists come to value the study of nature in itself, and to rejoice in it as good; and since God is the first cause of it, it can be seen as proof and exemplar of the Creator's nature. Calvinism leads to science, and science on to natural theology, which was the more attractive after 1660 because it was a way of establishing religious truths that was satisfactory to all theological parties. Many of the religious scientists of the Royal Society circle whom Merton refers to were natural theologians.[70] But though Calvinism helped the emergence of natural theology, there is a deep antipathy. (It is significant that the modern champion of Calvin, the neo-orthodox Karl Barth, made natural theology and liberal religion his central target.) Why is this? Because natural theology amounts to seeing God in terms of His creation; the attributes of nature are assessed and evaluated by human reason, and are then predicated of God. The final result, which we see in figures like Harriet Martineau and Thomas Hodgskin (whose doctrines were formed by a continuous evolution from those of the Calvinist Presbyterians of 1662), is a total pantheism, the logical opposite of the Calvinist transcendentalism. The insidious slide back to immanentism could only be avoided by carefully maintaining that God controlled the universe 'not as its Soul, but as its Lord, exercising an absolute sovereignty . . . not as over his own body but as over his own work; and acting it according to his pleasure, without suffering any thing from it'.[71] Hodgskin maintained that God and Nature were one, and Harriet Martineau asserted of Nature what Calvin asserted of God, that it simply *is* something one must subject oneself to. Natural theology, which says that nature and God are distinct, standing in the relation of watch and watchmaker, but that nature reveals God's character, provided the bridge between them.

'There is no safe dwelling-place between the house of Calvin and that of Socinus.'[72] It is true; and more remarkably, a Methodist and a Unitarian would agree it is true. But nonetheless the stages between are significant. The major crisis came in the late seventeenth century, an age which put a high premium on toleration, internal peace, and material advancement: men felt the times were good. The doctrine of original sin came under attack, with the crucial repercussions on the political theory of the state that I have described. The *horrible decretum*, the extreme of Calvinist rationality, came under criticism. God was good; how then could he have predestined some men to external perdition, and deprived all of free will? The Cambridge Platonists, who were members of the Church of England, led the attack, which soon set off the process which took the Presbyterians from Calvinism through Arianism to Unitarianism. They considered the Calvinist God as not divine but diabolical, and were 'concerned . . . to prevent the separation of divine and human values by asserting the priority of moral ideas over the will of God'.[73] The choice seemed to be between God's omnipotence and His goodness—or the abandonment of much of the scriptural tradition. Partly the debate concerned the meaning of the word 'good'. The Calvinist upheld a tautology: God is good, because 'good' means whatever He does or reveals. There is no criterion of goodness outside God by which He might be judged; and what is good for men is revealed in the Scriptures. The Platonists derived the meaning of 'good' independently, in fact from whatever sorts of actions we men customarily called 'good', and said that God could not be 'good' unless he acted in accord with these criteria. Like the natural theology with which it was associated, the religious ethics of the Cambridge Platonists took mundane standards and reasoned from them to God.

Then it was ex-Calvinists—Pierre Bayle and David Hume (or rather Philo in the *Dialogues concerning Natural Religion*)—who employed irony and Calvinistic reasoning to puncture the facile natural theology:

> Observe too, says Philo, the curious artifices of Nature, in order to imbitter the life of every living being. The stronger prey upon the weaker, and keep them in perpetual terror and anxiety. The weaker too, in their turn, often prey upon the stronger, and vex and molest them without relaxation.[74]

There is too 'the inaccurate workmanship of all the springs and principles of the great machine of nature'.[75] To the natural theologian Hume says that if Nature does express God's will, and if we accept human criteria of goodness, then God must be either evil or incompetent, or else Nature furnishes no evidence of His character. Only the orthodox Calvinist, or the Manichaean (as Bayle pretended to be) could withstand this reasoning. Whatever God does must be good, is the Calvinist's reply, and His ultimate purposes must remain inscrutable. Natural theology, which remained a temptation for Calvinists, could only be rescued by introducing a time-scale, so that the observable imperfections of creation could be interpreted as a step towards future perfection. (And here, the argument of *Social Statics* at once comes to mind.)

So far nothing has been said concerning the emotional impact of Calvinism, which means, very largely, the psychological causes and consequences of the denial of free will and the belief that men were predestined to salvation or damnation. Much modern speculation about the emotional meaning of this doctrine has been as ill-founded in empirical evidence as the writings of those eighteenth-century Arminians and Calvinists who argued whether free-will or predestination was the ally of morality. Weber (and ever more markedly Weber's interpreters) said that predestination stimulated worldly acquisition because of the *insecurity* it fostered in Calvinists—a point which is essential to his argument, but which, however plausible, is not well based, and is rather contradicted by the evident confidence of many early Calvinists.[76] It is also commonplace to see a contradiction between a belief in predestination or determinism, and an active resolve to modify the world. But whatever logic may say, these traits are frequently combined.[77]

In actual practice, for the early Calvinists and the most committed ones, predestination was not a cause of insecurity but an expression of supreme self-confidence. Though the doctrine said that nobody could *know* they were saved, Calvin, Knox and others did have that conviction and said that the Christian had the duty to believe it—an easy matter for those who already did. Their contemporaries did not imagine predestination led to a passive acceptance: 'predestination is the root of Puritanism, and Puritanism is the root of all rebellion and disobedient intractableness, and all schism and sauciness';[78] and later, in the 1660s, the 'proud, factious' spirit of the regicides was attributed to their belief in predestination.[79] Jonathan Edwards, America's greatest Calvinist, saw a congruence between Locke's theory of the passivity of the mind and the Calvinist doctrine of the inability of man to earn salvation: but, says Perry Miller, 'the empirical passivity became for Edwards . . . not an invitation to lethargy but a programme of action'.[80]

The evidence for the anxiety-inducing character of Calvinism comes mostly from people who were brought up in the belief and later turned away from it; and it is clear that it was not in the first place the notions of predestination or necessity as such which alarmed them, but the Calvinist doctrines of sin and damnation. They simply did not have the self-confidence which originally produced predestination, and without which it was unbearable; nor could they believe God capable of actions which were not humanly 'good'. But they might be very happy to have their hopes for human perfection underpinned by a doctrine of divine necessity. Robert Boyle rejected predestination but applied all Calvin's logic to paint a totally deterministic, if benevolent, picture of God as Clockmaker, and the world 'a rare Clock where all things are so skillfully contrived that the Engine, being once set a' Moving, all things proceed according to the Artificer's first design'.[81] It is neither an acceptance nor rejection of Calvin, but a critical transformation of his theology. David Hartley, the founder of associationist psychology, declined to enter the Church because of scruples about eternal punishment, and became a necessitarian, seeing man's gradual perfection as an ordained secular necessity.[82] Joseph Priestley, having experienced as a child great distress because he feared God had forsaken him, progressed all the way from the strictest Calvinism, via Arianism and Socinianism, to full-blown Unitarianism, adopting on the way Hartley's doctrine of necessity which, he says, improved his innate 'disposition to piety'. It seems to have only been 'the gloomy notions' of Calvinism which he rejected; for he was 'constantly in the habit of viewing the hand of God in all things', and saw God 'punishing . . . as a wise and kindly parent . . . to fit us for the highest state of happiness of which our natures are ultimately capable'.[83] Free will was out of the question, a thoroughly meaningless and incoherent concept.

Hartley and Priestley were a direct influence on the loose group of early nineteenth-century necessitarians, radical dissidents of Dissent, such as Harriet Martineau, George Combe the phrenologist, Charles Bray the Coventry manufacturer and George Eliot's chief guide to free-thinking, and H. T. Buckle.[84] All were acquaintances, as well as intellectual allies of Spencer. All reacted against their childhood religion, rather more than Spencer did. Harriet Martineau lost her religious faith through comparative religion on a visit to the Holy Land, Buckle his on a visit to Italy.[85] Bray developed moral objections to orthodoxy and Combe turned away from the terrible sermons on Election and the 'terrors of eternal perdition' preached by the Kirk.[86] They all found comfort and assurance in a secular necessitarianism which they justified by citing the statistical work of Quetelet, showing the regularities underlying such 'free' actions as murders and marriages,[87] and by quoting the arguments against freedom of the will which had been put with unmatched lucidity and force by Jonathan Edwards.[88] Buckle goes through the motions of examining Arminianism and Calvinism to reject both, but the only objections he can bring against Calvinism are that it is morally objectionable, and that is is bound up with 'providential interference'.[89]

All were confident secular progressives, eager to use science to better the human condition. All of them, like Spencer, adopted phrenology as revealing determinate laws which would revolutionize education and the treatment of criminals, where they consequently emphasized cure rather than punishment, and moral rather than physical methods of correction. For the doctrine of Necessity showed that 'a man could in no case have acted differently from the manner in which he did act, supposing the state of his mind and the circumstances in which he was placed, to be the same'.[90] Buckle put it thus: 'When we perform an action, we perform it in consequence of some motive or motives, . . . those motives are the results of some antecedents; . . . and if we were acquainted with the whole of the antecedents . . . we could with unerring certainty predict the whole of their immediate results.'[91] Phrenology was for a time a convincing statement of the content of the necessary and determinate laws of mind, and could be used 'to develop Man's nature to its full and true proportions'.[92] Morality, that 'transcendental physiology' (a very phrenological phrase which Spencer used in *Social Statics*)[93] was not undermined by necessity, but demanded it; for all moral exhortation assumed constant relations between cause and effect, which was just what the necessitarians asserted. The doctrine of necessity could survive the collapse of systems like phrenology (which Buckle, Spencer and Harriet Martineau were quick to abandon).

But the emotional implications of necessity were equally significant. At a time of dramatic social change, exhilarating and terrifying as the seventeenth century had been, marked by the weakening of old authority and the claims of the newly powerful, necessitarianism provided (or expressed) a secular *certitudo salutis*. It is appropriate that ex-Calvinists worked out this rationale for confidence; but this 'neo-Calvinism' was essentially a product of a similar social soil as the old. At the most basic level it meant a lifting of personal anxiety. Harriet Martineau stopped worrying about whether her salvation depended on God's decree or her own weak will when she came to believe in 'eternal and irreversible laws, working in every department of the universe, without any interference from any random will, human or divine'.[94] For her, necessity meant a total immanentism in which she need fear nothing in nature or society because she saw herself as totally identified with them. Charles Bray remained closer to an older view when he wrote that his rule of life was 'to follow Nature reverently, to accept the inevitable, after doing our best, sure that under all the circumstances and in the long run God knew what was good for us'.[95] But both justifications express the same feeling.

Predestination and determinism are the 'natural' doctrines for those who, in a situation of general anxiety and disagreement, feel that they *know*. Though primarily the expression of confidence, they are also suited for the communication of a leader's or an élite's confidence to a following; and hence for the creation of parties or bodies of opinion. It is this, as Michael Walzer has shown, which accounts for the striking psychological similarities between the Calvinist Elect and modern revolutionary parties. It is only those who are brought up to hold determinist beliefs and come to find their content implausible (as did many Calvinists in the late seventeenth century), who derive confidence from a *rejection* of determinism. Examples of this abound too. William James, brought up in the austere traditions of New England Calvinism, attributed a great feeling of release and self-confidence to his abandonment of these beliefs for a philosophy stressing chance, free-will and personal decision.[96] James Mill's secular predestination was of the most cheerful and optimistic kind—indeed absurdly so—but his son still wrote:

> During the latter stages of my dejection the doctrine of what is called philosophical necessity weighed on my existence like an incubus. I felt as if I was scientifically proved to be the helpless slave of antecedent circumstances; as if my character and that of all others had been formed for us by agencies beyond our control and was wholly out of our own power.[97]

The very thing which underpins the predestinarian's confidence—the belief that he and his will are merely the dependencies of a great force with which he identifies—becomes the source of crisis when, for whatever social or psychological reasons, men find that their desires no longer coincide with what their predecessors 'demonstrated' to be ineluctable. The rejection of determinism, sacred or secular, is made by men who feel they have no right to certainty but genuinely and openly seek answers to their problems; and in social circumstances where order can be taken for granted because there is a higher tolerance of certain kinds of disagreement and uncertainty. Such conditions developed in England in the late seventeenth and the late nineteenth centuries as the tensions of the Puritan and Industrial Revolutions subsided.

The young Spencer was a confident man in a society where many were fearful—of the social dissolution that the decay of religious faith might bring, of what the working class would do if there were universal suffrage, of where urbanisation and the growth of industry might lead, of the loss of so many customary procedures and social landmarks. General determinist beliefs, and a particular determined scheme of secular providence were therefore highly congenial to him.[98] Where the members of a society no longer share basic existential premisses (such as are provided by an established religion), moral argument proper becomes difficult, since it usually concerns the applications of the basic tenets. So the advocate of a morality, such as Spencer was, will find it easier to 'explain' his code by using historical and scientific arguments (since they can, in principle, compel assent as moral or ethical ones do not) to show how it is necessary. He may not be believed, but a by-product of his tactic will be a sociology of morals.

5: From Certainty to the Unknowable

I

Though a sociological programme is adumbrated in *Social Statics*, over twenty years were to elapse before Spencer turned to the systematic fulfilment of that promise with *The Study of Sociology* in 1873. The years between were occupied with the creation of the evolutionary edifice within which the sociology rests—a task requiring, among other things, some sort of epistemology and the establishment of a viable psychology. These writings may well be considered in a variety of ways—in the light of the Victorian debate about science and religion, or as metaphysics, or as a chapter in the growth of modern psychology.[1] My aim is more restricted: to see them as part of the bridge from his early political moralizing to his mature sociology, and as a further outcome of that crisis of confidence in thought which is so marked in the origins of sociology. Three groups of writings need to be considered in particular:

(*a*) The essay 'The Universal Postulate' (1853) out of which grew *The Principles of Psychology* (1855) which preceded the Synthetic Philosophy but was later greatly enlarged and incorporated into it.

(*b*) Various essays on the development and classification of the sciences which took Spencer into an extended polemic with the ghost of Auguste Comte.

(*c*) The book which thrilled his contemporaries the most and which seems to us the most dated, *First Principles* (1862), which laid down the basis for the rest of the Synthetic Philosophy.

Social Statics reads like the work of a man who was so confident of the historical fitness and necessity of his position that he would never bother a moment over the grounds of his certainty. Such feelings of confidence are virtually self-authenticating; with a theory of their necessary causation they seem unassailable. But the quest for certainty which seems so settled at the level of social action with which *Social Statics* deals tends to re-appear at the level of thought. Doubts about ethical certainty are replaced by epistemological ones: 'How can we attain certainty in what we call knowledge?' With Spencer, as with other nineteenth-century social theorists, the attempted solution of ethical problems, individual or social, raises deeper questions about the validity of particular 'knowledge' or of knowledge in general. A partial scepticism, directed at a particular area of knowledge, itself suggest the way it is easiest met: by attempting to assimilate the questioned type of knowledge to the implicitly unquestioned. More disturbing is a total scepticism which may be, in its own terms, unanswerable. To the question 'What are your grounds for being certain of anything?' there are, however, two possible responses. One is the pleading of inescapability ('I can do no other'), followed up, not by the reasons which *a fortiori* cannot be given, but by the causes of things being as they are. The seeker after philosophical certitude has not then got an answer to his question, but a programmatic psychology instead.[2] A second, or supplementary, tactic, will be to probe the questioner's implied criterion of certainty, and to scale it down, suggesting that for most purposes lesser degrees of certainty are adequate,[3] and even that it need not matter that certainty is not to be had.

Spencer adopted all these responses in some measure. The certainty which we have of logical truths is reduced to biologically inescapable pressures; a psychology of the reasoning processes and a theory of scientific development are offered in place of logical justification; and finally his readers are told that the ultimate reality is in any case unknowable. When I say Spencer was led to psychology by an unanswerable epistemological problem, I do not mean that he had no psychological opinions before. His earliest psychology was phrenology, on which he had written heterodox articles; and as Dr. R. M. Young has shown, it was phrenology which provided the language of 'faculties' by which he justified *laissez-faire* in *Social Statics*. But, on his own admission, Spencer was led to write the *Psychology* by trying to find 'the test of truth' between J. S. Mill and William Whewell. It is only from the viewpoint of the immanent development of psychology that it is possible to say that 'the connexion between this part of his work and the rest is very tenuous indeed'.[4] It was only when, once launched on psychology, he became properly acquainted with Mill's associationism, that he began to criticize it in the light of some of the assumptions of the phrenology whose detailed doctrines he had abandoned, and to move towards the evolutionary psychology whose importance and originality Young demonstrates. But it was while seeking the Indies of an epistemological foundation that Spencer opened up the America of the empirical analysis of thought.

We can regret that in this area Spencer did not go further. In the *Psychology* his main achievement was to produce a 'psychology of knowledge', and his writings on science put forward a kind of sociology of knowledge. Only with the help of an 'embryology' of science, he wrote, was it possible to understand the nature of science.[5] But his attempt to solve problems of logic and epistemology through psychology falls far short of his attack on ethical problems through sociology, though the two processes are exactly parallel. The transition to sociology, the science of human action, was complete: its counterpart, a science of belief-systems or culture, was only completed in its psychological component. But we know he realized the need of it, for in the prospectus for the Synthetic Philosophy issued in 1860, he planned several volumes on the development of language, thought, morals and aesthetics, 'associated developments which aid, and are aided by, social evolution'.[6] This was never finished though the essay 'Of Laws in General, and the Order of their Discovery' was intended to be a part of it.[7]

II

Not long after the completion of *Social Statics*, Spencer wrote to his father that he had 'been much absorbed of late in metaphysics, and [believed he had] made a great discovery'.[8] Almost certainly this was what Spencer considered to be the solution of the dispute between J. S. Mill and the Rev. William Whewell concerning the basis of logical certainty.[9] Superficially, it is surprising that Spencer should modify Mill ('whose agreement I should value more than that of any other thinker', he wrote)[10] in the direction of Whewell, since Whewell was persistently associated with causes that Mill and Spencer joined in opposing. He was for conservative, even reactionary policies in Church, State and University; he did not accept the Darwinian theory since he clung to natural theology; he regarded the fundamental axioms of science as emanations of the Divine Mind; and because he stressed that experience was not sufficient to account for the progress of science, he was stamped as an intuitionist. Mill saw their controversy very much in terms of black and white. Intuitionism was condemned as:

> The great intellectual support of false doctrines and bad institutions . . . a philosophy which discourages the explanation of feelings and moral facts by circumstances and association, and professes to treat them as ultimate elements of human nature, a philosophy which is addicted to holding up favourite doctrines as intuitive truths, and deems intuition to be the voice of Nature and of God, speaking with an authority higher than that of our reason.[11]

Mill believed passionately that all that we can call knowledge—even down to the basic axioms of mathematics and logic—proceeds solely from experience; and aimed in his *Logic* to present formal methods of inductive proof, so that they might be used in further scientific investigation. In the sixth book he sketched out how these would apply to psychology, 'ethology' (i.e. the science of character formation), and sociology. (Needless to say, despite many imitators, this methodology before the fact has proved at best useless in the encouragement of sociology.) Whewell's aim was quite different:

> . . . to learn the best methods of discovering truth, *by examining how truths, now universally recognized, have really been discovered.*[12]

A leading contemporary philosopher of science has summed up the difference between them thus:

> [Whewell's] philosophy gives us a realistic epistemology, metaphysics and logic, in the sharpest possible contrast to the philosophy of science of J. S. Mill . . . [who] takes logic as he finds it, and then constructs a philosophy of how science ought to be, were this the only logic possible. Whewell takes the methods of science as his datum, and tries to extract from them their rationale.[13]

This difference of purpose led to the same words being understood in different ways. 'Induction', for example, meant for Mill an ideal process of reasoning which led to proof, whereas for Whewell it was rather the actual historical path of a science's progress.[14] Whewell's criticism of Mill's four methods of proof was not that they were false, but that they did not explain the actual origination of any scientific theory (though copiously illustrated with data for which Mill professed thanks to Whewell) and certainly could not be recipes for further discovery. There was also disagreement over 'necessary' truths, by which Whewell meant, not truths that were in essence opposed to contingent truths, but ones which are so basic to thought that a thinker cannot clearly conceive their contraries. 'Necessity' lay not in the truths themselves, but in the manner of their being thought. For Whewell, the enquiry was not for what *logical* conditions had to be fulfilled before a proposition could be considered 'proved', but for the *historical* and *psychological* conditions under which men find a proposition irresistible.

But why did Mill and others consider Whewell's position so anti-empiricist? Partly it was because he emphasized (correctly, it seems to us) the active role of the mind in supplying 'right conceptions . . . to bind the facts together',[15] rather than, as in most 'inductivist' accounts, the passive receptivity of the mind to the impressions of external nature; for these conceptions could not themselves be provided by experience, even though experience called them forth. But the chief cause of Mill's hostility was the further thesis that these necessary truths or 'fundamental ideas', which become so for us as they are firmly established as part of the mental equipment through which we apprehend nature, were pre-existent in the mind of God, and progressively intuited by man, 'not derived from experience, but . . . only [to] be exercised on it and realized through it'.[16]

It was not the seeming intuitionism of Whewell's position which attracted Spencer (despite the intuitionist aspect of *Social Statics*) but the peculiar character of the certainty which it promised. Mill's static logic could only offer guarantees of truth that were easy, as a matter of psychological fact, to doubt. What Spencer wanted, and got from Whewell, was a starting point which was not subject to doubt, being inescapable. Other theories are treated with some impatience. Descartes' *Cogito* assumes the criteria of logical inference; Berkeleian idealism and Humean scepticism both assume the truth of what they seek to call in doubt; Kant, to escape scepticism, asserts things impossible to believe, that space and time are merely subjective forms of thought; Fichte, Schelling and Hegel (one fears, unread) are despatched in a sentence. The starting-point must be 'not any substantive proposition believed, but some canon of belief itself'. For 'belief' must not be treated as cognitively inferior to knowledge. It is the form in which all facts are presented to us, and may remain indestructible when whatever gave rise to it may be doubted. In the final analysis 'our logical justification [for a belief] and the inexorable necessity we are under of holding it'[17] come to the same thing.

> Mean what we may by the word truth, we have no choice but to hold that *a belief which is proved by the inconceivableness of its negation to invariably exist, is true.* We have seen that this is the assumption on which every conclusion whatever ultivately rests. We have no other guarantee for any axiom; we have no other guarantee for any step in a demonstration. Hence, as being taken for granted in every act of the understanding, it must be regarded as the Universal Postulate.[18]

Necessity and contingent truths, as in Whewell's account, differ only in degree, not in kind. The Law of the Excluded Middle is 'simply a generalization of the universal experience that some mental states are directly destructive of other states',[19] just as we cannot conceive it to be dark when we look at the sun. The only difference between what we call 'necessary' truths, and absolutely certain contingent ones, is that with the latter the conviction of the inconceivability of their negation is present on only some occasions. Although Spencer sometimes contrasts logic and psychology (as when he writes 'our immediate object is not logic but the nature of the reasoning process'),[20] his general procedure is to reduce logic to psychology: 'a syllogism represents an act of thought'.[21] But a test of the relative validity of complex beliefs is provided by the Postulate: those that use it the least, because they are less decomposable, are the surest. Reasoning is 'the formation of a coherent series of states of consciousness',[22] a struggle between alternative patterns of coherence; but consciousness itself is imperative, not to be verified or falsified but accounted for. 'Here, then, rises before us a definite course of enquiry'—not to formulate canons of sound reasoning, it turns out, but to 'examine the cohesions among the elements of consciousness, taken as a whole',[23] to show how in fact complex reasoning develops from unquestioning and irresistible responses to the source of impressions.

The certainty Spencer wants is not that of an infallible technique to prevent us falling into intellectual error. He knows that this is impossible, because knowledge is progressive and science corrects itself. It does not worry him that the Universal Postulate, 'in common with any test, is liable to yield untrue results, either from incapacity or from carelessness in those who use it'.[24] He does claim for the Postulate that its use will help people to discover those propositions which are relatively better grounded than others, but so do other tests. The need for the Postulate arises not so much from the problem of partial scepticism and uncertainty, as from a kind of diffuse uncertainty, at a time of unparalleled success in the use of thought to practical ends, about whether the cosmos was playing a ghastly trick on man. Whereas some thinkers reject the everyday world, with its obvious partial uncertainties and delusions, for a realler and more certain world of hidden permanencies, Spencer takes the inescapable realities of the mundane, biological joys and terrors, as a touchstone for the more elaborate creations of abstract thought. Science is to be accepted as true because it depends, in the end, on commonsense beliefs, of which we simply have to say, that we cannot do otherwise. Hence Spencer opens his essay, 'The Genesis of Science' (1854) by saying there is no sharp distinction between commonsense and science, which is merely its refinement;[25] and dismisses 'every metaphysical doctrine at variance with ordinary credence'.[26]

Spencer's pragmatism is evident here too. The attitude of Spencer and Whewell differs from Mill's in that they take knowledge as it is, as something which manifestly works, something to be known more in its effects than in its justification. Whewell's description of the law of gravity as 'a simple and ultimate truth in which the mind can acquiesce and repose' recalls Adam Smith's account of the understanding as a 'repose of the imagination', and prefigures pragmatism proper.[27] Prior logical justification, the complete antithesis to pragmatism, is alien to Spencer's whole approach, which leads both to what later became known as operationalism in scientific method, and to the analysis of things in terms of their functions. The relation of Durkheim's sociology to philosophical problems follows identical lines. In *The Elementary Forms of the Religious Life* Durkheim claimed to have found a solution to the age-old debate between realism and nominalism about whether categories are experimental or innate and given; but instead of doing so, he produced a functional account of how concepts have their uniquely *compelling* hold over man because they are social properties.[28] The American pragmatists, Wright, Peirce and James, were both massively influenced by Spencer and defined themselves against him. But Chauncey Wright's remark, 'The most profitable study is . . . a study of other minds—seeing how others see, rather than the dissection of mere propositions',[29] captures perfectly the attitude which took Spencer, with Whewell, from epistemology to psychology.

Spencer shared entirely Mill's moral horror of anything that smacked of innate essences or intuitions, Kantian or theological, but was able to rescue the associationist psychology—as it came down to Mill from Hartley—at its weakest point. This was, as Young observes, its inability to explain species or individual differences, which the phrenological school claimed to do. As Spencer wrote:

> If, at birth, there exists nothing but a passive receptivity of impressions, why should not a horse be as educable as a man? Or, should it be said that language makes the difference, then why should not the cat and dog, out of the same household experience, arrive at equal degrees and kinds of intelligence?[30]

Mill combined associationist psychology with philosophical empiricism; and in order to preserve them Spencer picked up Whewell's and the phrenologists' criticisms, which were curiously parallel, the former stressing non-experiential conception, the latter innate or racial character, as factors which interact with direct experience. Spencer saved and extended Mill's tradition, however, by representing these 'innate' factors as the result of past experiences. Why is there such a difference between a Newton and the Papuans in their response to the surroundings? Past experience becomes 'organized' (i.e. physically constituted), so that the individual, besides responding to new stimuli as the associationists had said, already has in his nervous system certain pre-established relations corresponding to ones in the environment.[31] What were, from the individual's standpoint, *a priori* axioms, inconceivable otherwise, were yet derived from experience and *a posteriori* 'for the series of individuals of which he forms a part'.[32] What Whewell had claimed as evidence of mankind's divinely created nature were in fact merely 'the net result of our experiences up to the present time'. Forms of thought may thus be likened to reflex actions which are also the result of experiences far back in the development of 'the race of organisms forming [the individual's] ancestry'.[33] The pattern of the whole course of mental evolution is set by the gradual adjustment of the internal relations of consciousness to the structure of the external world. He concludes the first edition of the *Psychology* with a firm statement of the empiricist faith:

> . . . were the inner relations to any extent determined by some other agency . . . there would be an arrest of that grand progression which is now bearing Humanity onwards to perfection.[34]

III

When we compare Spencer's *Psychology*[35] with any modern textbook on that subject, we are at once struck by the absolutely dominating place in it that is occupied by the explanation of the conscious operations of thought. Yet this is set within a naturalistic framework of explanation which presents thinking as being only different in degree from feeling, and as a response to the environment which should be compared with those of the lowest animals and the humblest plants. For although Spencer agreed that the 'essential truth' of psychology was the associationist tenet that 'the method of composition remains the same throughout the entire fabric of mind',[36] in his hands psychology is evolutionary, not static, and in principle closely allied with physiology. The second edition was more biological and more sociological than the first.

The starting point for an exposition of Spencer's *Psychology* follows directly from his epistemological solution: that whatever we cannot conceive otherwise is certain and 'necessary' for us. This complex, irresistible mass of sensations 'implies a fundamental experience on which (it) must rest'.[37] The subject experiences an object, some force outside himself, and this impression is 'the primordial, the universal, the ever present constituent of consciousness'. The complex notion of Force (which is perhaps the key term in Spencer's evolutionary synthesis) is merely a generalization of the resistance to other, outer forces; and the experience of resistance is fundamental to all forms of life. In fact 'cognition of resistance is finally resolved into that of muscular tension [which elsewhere he calls 'something of the same order as that which we call a nervous shock',[38] such as a micro-organism experiences if an alien substance is introduced into its environment] . . . and this forms the raw material of thought in all its forms'.[39] How Mind, or the conscious response to external force, differs from spontaneous responses, Spencer cannot say, except by truisms such that Mind is what is affected by the object known;[40] but he does oppose Hume's view that 'Mind' is just a collective name for impressions and ideas. Mind is only to be known in its operations and responses. Spencer emphasizes the close correspondence between Mind and Matter (or the world as object), but denies with some irritation the charge that this makes him a materialist.[41] For the antithesis of subject (Mind) and object (Matter) cannot be surmounted; there is no formula by which one can be reduced to the other. Spencer charges all forms of idealism and solipsism, his chief philosophical targets, with ignoring that self-consciousness in fact can be seen to develop only in response to the external force of other objects; it is by these that the subject comes to recognize itself. The very words that such philosophers use 'turn traitors', since 'language has . . . been throughout its development moulded to express all things under the fundamental relation of subject and object . . . and if detached from this fundamental relation . . . becomes as absolutely impotent as an amputated limb in empty space'.[42] So there only remains the empirical question of comparing and analysing the various responses of the organism to the environment, forms of resistence among which are thought and science.

All vital processes are to be seen as a correspondence between the organism and its environment; death is the total cessation of correspondence. Definitions of life were then felt to be of more scientific importance than now, and Spencer's bears his authentic stamp: 'a definite combination of heterogeneous changes, both simultaneous and successive . . . in correspondence with external coexistences and sequences'.[43] Spencer's tendency to dissolve categorical distinctions into gradations even leads him to say that the degree of life varies with the degree and complexity of correspondence: a man is thus more 'alive' than a hydra, and by the same token, a civilized man should be more 'alive' than a savage. Correspondence is more complex as it deals with more of the coexistent environment beyond the immediate vicinity, and as the contact between the organism and the environment gets less and less direct—from touch, which is only a direct means of correspondence with the immediate environment, to sight which is an indirect contact with a more remote realm of objects. Correspondence may extend in time as it extends in space; and the 'primordial irritability' of the organism increases in speciality (in that, as it differentiates internally, external impressions come to have specialized significances) and also in generality (in that different impressions through time come to be classed together). In all these ways the correspondence comes to be more complex, and these developments are functionally interdependent—complexity in one dimension presupposes complexity in another. The mechanism by which the development of correspondence takes place is provided by the stimulus of pleasures and pains, as in classic associationism; all behaviour consists of habit and learning; and the ultimate arbiter is the struggle for survival in Nature. (This is much clearer in the Second Edition, where Darwin's influence is evident, but it sits quite easily on the treatment of it in the First Edition.)

Amid the general blurring of categorical distinctions there is one distinction which remained basic and indispensable in Spencer's system, though it re-appears in various guises. Whereas, speaking of Perception and Reasoning (which tend to be sharply distinguished in philosophical systems like the Kantian, that contrast empirical truths with logically necessary ones), he says that 'the divisions we make between the various mental processes have merely a superficial truth',[44] he does uphold a fundamental distinction between sensation/perception, impressibility/activity, sensation/emotion, all of them variations of the object/subject distinction.[45] The distinction is a structural one, between phenomena which are peripherally initiated, the mere responses to external stimuli, and those which are centrally initiated, the 'active' response of the organism, drawing also upon its own resources.

The basis of intelligence, says Spencer, is classifying like with like, and since there is no radical difference between conscious and instinctual responses, the latter too may be seen as involving a form of assessment of what states of the environment are like or unlike others. There are three basic sorts of likeness—sameness in space occupied (coextension), sameness in time of perception (coexistence), and sameness in attributes (connature); of these coextension is fundamental, and from it develops the notions of linearity and hence measurement. As correspondence increases, so does the ability to classify in an ever-increasing variety of ways; and always to know something is to achieve 'the assimilation of it to its past kindred'.[46] Vital processes range from those in which stimuli are dealt with simultaneously, as in respiration or digestion, and those in which the stimuli are dealt with serially. The tendency to seriality is never complete, but the highest forms of correspondence, such as thought, approximate to it. At the same time processes which are at first automatic become deliberate. Memory, which Spencer admits it is hard to see as correspondence, arises 'when the connexions among the psychical states cease to be perfectly automatic'; it 'pertains to that class of psychical states which are in process of being organized'.[47] Reason and Feelings arise with Memory—involving representations of pleasures and pains—at the point when the growing complexity of correspondence prevents spontaneous and automatic responses. The transition from spontaneous to deliberate action is partly a general feature of progress. Reason is merely the conscious pursuit of methods already adopted by living organisms and their extension to greater effectiveness. Spencer conceived of his own argument in a similar way; to seek out and generalize processes of thought which were already being pursued with some success, to make explicit principles which were assumed by the practice of scientists. In his essay 'Of Laws in General', making the point that general opinion is gradually adopting his view that all the manifestations of the Universe are expressible in one grand law, he says that 'not out of a conscious regard for these reasons [which he has given], but from a habit of thought which these reasons formulate and justify, all minds have been advancing towards a belief in the constancy of surrounding coexistences and sequences'.[48] But while deliberateness is here seen as a mark of a higher type of thought, the conversion of deliberately worked-out sequences into automatic or spontaneous responses, or their 'organization' so that they become second nature, is seen as a further progress. The growth of a system of symbols which facilitate semi-spontaneous responses to elaborate stimuli is a mark of higher development. Instances of the 'organization' of learned traits may be found in the way in which a man learns to tie slowly and deliberately, and then gradually finds himself able to do it 'automatically'; and also in the forms of thought, 'which being the constant and infinitely-repeated elements of all thought . . . must become the automatic elements of all thought —the elements of thought which it is impossible to get rid of'.[49] Spencer regarded any human achievement as very precarious until it had been 'organized' in this way; and what is organizable is not knowledge or theories but powers or capacities for action, including mental action. The 'forms of thought' are not knowledge, but patterns of action.

The concluding part of the Second Edition was intended as an introduction to the analysis of Social Evolution which was to follow. It soon moves from considering, in summary, the development of conceptions to 'the language of the emotions' and thence to the chief motor of change, moral sentiments. 'Intellectual evolution,' writes Spencer, 'as it goes on in the human race along with social evolution of which it is at once a cause and a consequence, is . . . under all its aspects, a progress in representativeness of thought.'[50] A 'presentative' feeling is one that is a direct, synchronic copy of its stimulus; feelings become 'representative' as they express much more distant stimuli, and so involve recollection, imagination and elaborate inference. These properties are not things *in addition to* the stimulus, but how we describe a richer and fuller correspondence with the external realm. The world of objects provides a potentially infinite source of stimuli, but the character of the correspondence to them varies with the development of the subject; for ethnographic evidence shows, says Spencer, that 'the minds of the inferior human races cannot respond to relations of even moderate complexity'.[51] The savage and the child both differ from the synthetic philosopher in that their powers of representation are limited.

In primitive societies there is little capacity for developing general law from specific truths, since thought is so unrepresentative.[52] Whereas 'those having well-developed nervous systems will display a relatively marked premeditation—an habitual representation of more various possibilities of cause, and conduct, and consequence— a greater tendency to suspense of judgments and an easier modification of judgments that have been formed', the intellect of the savage is 'sudden in its inferences, incapable of balancing evidence and adhering obstinately to first impressions'.[53] But though mental capacities are here portrayed as relatively fixed, the residue of generations of adaptation by ancestors, elsewhere they seem merely untrained but actually existent potentialities. For he says that the women of his own day differ from men in the same way that savages do, similar in kind but less in degree, being fixed in their ideas and quick to draw conclusions; and that the 'higher quadrumana' are in many respects quite as rational as schoolboys![54]

The final, and most important consequences of representativeness, is that it permits the growth of sociality, sympathy and altruism. Many animals, Spencer concedes, show domestic affection and herd-instincts, but these feelings are merely presentative. Sympathy is a representation of human likeness which depends for its effective growth on the growth of 'the language of the emotions'—symbols by which feeling may be aroused and communicated. 'Only when the struggle for existence has ceased to go on under the form of war, can these highest sentiments attain their full development';[55] hence only in his own day, with the displacement of militancy by industrialism, was there a decisive shift towards altruism and the 'growth of feelings adjusted to a fundamental unchanging condition of social welfare'.[56] Radical humanitarianism and the Doctrine of Utility were its fruits. Spencer had thus powerfully underpinned the argument of *Social Statics*, and prepared the way for the *Sociology*.

IV

And so we come to *First Principles*, which was intended to put forward the most general laws in nature to take in the more particular truths of the different sciences, and which can therefore be seen in Spencerian terms as the pinnacle of representativeness in correspondence to the environment. It is the consummation of Spencer's essays of the 1850s on the embryology and classification of the sciences. Spencer became involved in a long drawn out polemic with the Comteans partly based on the very substantial differences between them, and partly on Spencer's justified but nonetheless rather paranoid concern to establish the independence of his thought from Comte.[57] Comte's classification of the sciences was assailed on both logical and historical grounds. It is significant that when Spencer came to engage in philosophy, and not the metaphilosophy of the *Psychology*, logical classifications of science turn out to be distinct from genetic or historical classifications. For to Spencer 'philosophy' was not any kind of meta-science, as tends to be assumed today, but simply 'knowledge of the highest degree of generality'.[58]

Comte's hierarchy of the sciences—mathematics, astronomy, physics, chemistry, physiology, sociology—is criticized first for being *serial*. In fact, argues Spencer, the various sciences have not developed serially, one after the other, but in co-ordination; a steady generalization of observations to laws has accompanied a particularization of subject-matter, resulting in a division of labour between the sciences. The root of Comte's error is his supposition that 'as thought is serial, Nature is serial'.[59] But just because men must arrange their thoughts in sequence (and Spencer has already said in the *Psychology* that conscious responses have a tendency to seriality), it does not follow that 'Nature has consulted the convenience of book-making'. Spencer's point against Comte seem to me to be sound; but it does assume that we must put the order of Nature, and the proper development of thought, in opposition, which is against the tenor of Spencer's whole approach. His own explanation of the order in which types of natural phenomena are reduced to law is quite in line with his *Psychology*. It depends on the frequency and vividness with which the relevant relations are experienced; and these depend on (*a*) how far the phenomena involve personal welfare directly, (*b*) how conspicuous they are, (*c*) how absolutely frequent the particular relations are, (*d*) how relatively frequent they seem to the observer, (*e*) how simple they are (which Comte had taken to be all) and (*f*) how concrete they are. In all departments of thought, truths which fulfil these conditions are discovered first. The consummation comes when the search for ever more general laws covers all concrete phenomena, and when it is realized that 'progress in the discovery of laws itself conforms to law'.[60] So *First Principles* which was aimed to effect the former, is closely associated with the essays on science which attempt the latter.

Spencer also produced his own logical classification of the sciences (though unlike Comte's it was not identical with his scheme for the development of thought). Science is divided into two branches: (*a*) abstract, 'which treats of the forms in which phenomena are known to us', including logic and mathematics, and (*b*), 'which treats of the phenomena themselves', subdivided into (i) abstract-concrete, which treats of things in their elements such as mechanics, physics and chemistry, and (ii) concrete, which treats of things in their totalities such as geology, biology, psychology and sociology.[61] Comte's error lay in confusing 'abstract' and 'general'. Whereas Comte saw a highly complex but particular and concrete science, his own sociology, as completing the hierarchy, Spencer saw his own synthetic philosophy in this role, since it dealt in most general terms with the concrete phenomena which are sciences's basic subject-matter. His treatment of the abstract propositions of mathematics was unsatisfactory. For, though absent from *First Principles* they could not be any less *a priori* or 'laws of consciousness' than the irrestible metaphysics which First Principles expounded. But the general aim of Spencer's classification was the same as Comte's had been: to provide both logical and pragmatic or historical justification for what he saw as his own major achievement.

V

What Spencer has to say of a substantive nature about evolution in *First Principles* will be considered in the next chapter. Here I simply wish to discuss how the search for certainty with which he started out in the *Psychology* reached a most paradoxical conclusion, in the doctrine of the Unknowable. This was intended as the final resolution of the struggle between science and religion which was then at its height. The antagonism built up from two sources: evolutionary science, from Lyell's *Geology* (1830) and the *Vestiges of Creation* (1843) with gradually heightening tension through the 50s to the publication of *The Origin of Species* (1859), followed a year later by the famous debate between T. H. Huxley and Bishop Wilberforce; and German Biblical criticism, which had already destroyed George Eliot's faith, and had led to H. L. Mansel's Bampton Lectures, preached to a clerical Oxford in 1858 and published as *The Limits of Religious Thought* (1859). Orthodox religious opinion was equally horrified by *Essays and Reviews* (1860), in which liberal clergymen suggested how Christian teaching would need to be revised in the light of both sources of criticism.[63] *First Principles* (1862) was seen by both author and public as a contribution to this debate.

The breezy deism of *Social Statics* had given way by a gentle and painless declination to a simple agnosticism which was still, despite

Spencer's continued opposition to the 'theological party', conciliatory towards religion. *First Principles* opens with the typically pragmatist position that there is a modicum of truth in most erroneous beliefs. Just as Durkheim came to do after him, Spencer insisted that 'the diverse forms of religious belief . . . have all a basis in some ultimate fact . . . to suppose that these multiform conceptions should be one and all *absolutely* groundless, discredits too profoundly that average human intelligence from which all our individual intelligences are inherited'.[64] Since science is simply 'a higher development of common knowledge' to gainsay it would be folly; what is needed is a higher abstract truth which can unite the basic insights of science and religion.

Spencer's answer, as William James noted, is very largely to be found in Mansel's *Limits of Religious Thought*.[65] (Spencer, who was rather reluctant to admit intellectual debts, barely acknowledges any here; and it is true, as with most of Spencer's borrowings, that it does seem to fit naturally into the earlier development of his thought.) Mansel's intention was to defend religion from rationalist criticism by arguing that the object of reason could not be God, absolute and infinite, but merely relative and finite things, which in theology were religious *evidences* (but not doctrines) and 'the nature of the human mind in its relation to religion'.[66] Reason aims to make all human experience subject to its criticism; but there is a realm which is necessary even to the exercise of reason which is beyond the scope of reason. The principle of causality, and the concept of the infinite, are unjustifiable and incomprehensible by reason, which yet requires them. Reason cannot offer a critique of things beyond its scope, and hence the constructions of 'rational theology' (a contradiction in terms, it seemed to Mansel) are nothing but 'Babels of Reason' and 'barren vague meaningless abstractions in which men babble about nothing under the name of the Infinite'.[67] At the centre of Mansel's attack was 'the fundamental vice of Rationalism itself—that of explaining away what we are unable to comprehend'.[68]

Mansel recalls Tertullian in setting the core of religion beyond rational defence and criticism, and insisting that *therefore* it should be believed. Faith is snatched from the jaws of scepticism; theology is denied any claim to be a science. Within this setting Mansel preserves a traditional view of the truths of religion. In addition he argues that traditional practices and conceptions—of God as a person, of prayer, of confession and repentance—are rooted in basic human needs or mental affections, and 'the deep wants of our human nature'. To think of God as a person *is*, as far as our present minds can reason, inconsistent with Him being infinite, but we *must* (as a matter of psychological fact, implicitly recognized by theology) believe it. This is not a speculative but a regulative truth, 'intended not to satisfy our reason but to guide our practice; not to tell us what God is in his absolute nature, but how He wills that we should think of Him in our present finite state'.[69] Mansel's pragmatic defence of religion is very close to William James'; and his conception of man as practical is closely allied with that relativism about truth which is so signal a feature of sociology's treatment of all belief systems. 'Action and not knowledge is man's destiny and duty in this life,' he writes; 'to assert that a representation is *untrue* because it is relative to the mind of the receiver is to overlook the fact that truth itself is nothing more than a relation.'[70]

The influence of Mansel, like the earlier influence of Whewell, took Spencer away from the position of J. S. Mill. Mansel had derived his philosophical position from Sir William Hamilton's doctrine of the Unconditioned which moved Mill, in opposition, to state his own philosophy. Mill thought Mansel's Bampton Lectures 'detestable . . . absolutely loathsome',[71] and found much in both Spencer's *Psychology* and *First Principles* which alarmed him, yet considered him 'on the whole an ally in spite of his universal postulate', because of his empiricism.[72] But he was right when he said that Spencer's relativism was much more marked in *First Principles*: 'he expresses himself almost as though he thought there is no objective standard of truth at all'.[73] Here lay the widening gulf between Mill and Spencer. Mill was committed to the search for objective standards of truth, and for methods of proof. Spencer's relativism took him to the sociological analysis of institutions and thought, and to a form of operationalism in scientific method which is first clearly put forward in *First Principles*: 'The fundamental intuitions that are essential to the process of thinking must be temporarily accepted as unquestionable; leaving the assumption of their unquestionableness to be justified by results.'[74]

About the Unknowable, as might be expected, there is little to be said. All dogmatic religious positions, whether forms of atheism,

theism or pantheism, are inconsistent and unacceptable but contain the basic truth that beyond the phenomena that we know is an Unknowable Power. Comprehension, as the *Psychology* had shown, involves a relation between the internal subject and the external object; and since the Absolute cannot be relative, it is not comprehensible and nothing can be said about it. That an Unknowable exists both science and religion agree, and the value of religion is that 'from the beginning [it] has had the all-essential office of preventing men from being wholly absorbed in the relative or immediate, and of awakening them to a consciousness of something beyond it'.[75] Both religion and science have been false to truth in attempting to dogmatize about this necessary area of ignorance. Spencer's answer to the charge that he has emptied religion of all content carries no conviction.[76] There is a point at which Mansel and Spencer seem to draw different conclusions about religion from their shared belief in the incomprehensibility of the absolute: Spencer attacks anthropomorphism in religion as 'the impiety of the pious',[77] while Mansel had attacked anti-anthropomorphist theologians for presuming to 'twist and torture the divine image on the rack of human philosophy and call its mangled relics by the high-sounding titles of the Absolute and the Infinite'.[78] But there is really nothing for them to engage in rational argument about; for Mansel, like any other religious thinker who protects the kernel of his own existing faith from rational criticism and offers a pragmatic justification of religion in general, offers his listeners a simple existential choice—either they find it in them to accept the proferred religion, or they do not.[79] Spencer did not. The Unknowable might be contemplated, but it was wholly without attributes, and those positivists who saw in it something analogous to the Humanity which was the object of Comtean religion were mistaken.[80] If the Unknowable functioned as a kind of sheet-anchor of certainty, an ultimate assurance that there was *something* beyond the phenomena of science, it was merely because of human frailty. For Spencer had moved from looking for a rock-like source of certitude, to the view that all the certainty which it was possible to have (and that was wholly relative) was all that people should need.

6: Evolution

I

Spencer's theory of evolution was intended to cover all types of natural process—the development of species, the organic evolution of every animal, the maturation of the embryo, the evolution of the solar system—besides social development. But it must not be supposed that therefore his idea of social evolution was simply the inappropriate transference of biological concepts to sociology. The commonest misrepresentation of Spencer is that he applied Darwinism to the study of society; and even those who are well aware of Spencer's independence, as Professor Marvin Harris is, may vastly overrate the biologism of his theory of social evolution.[1] (That what was called 'Social Darwinism' often derived largely from Spencer is another matter. But it seems that the social sciences have derived very little from Darwinism proper.[2]) Evolutionary views were adopted by Spencer in the early 1840s, and, somewhat disconnectedly, are expressed in his writing on sociological and biological topics through the 1850s.[3] What was lacking was their synthesis into a general Law of Evolution—a feat whose necessity was proclaimed in his essay 'Progress: Its Law and Cause' (1857), and achieved in *First Principles* (1862). Little of what had gone before was abandoned, and thereafter there was (indeed there could be) little development. Apparent shifts of emphasis are due less to any change in Spencer's general conception of evolution than to the exigencies of convincing explanation in one or another of its parts. A theory as ambitious and all-embracing as Spencer's is sure to result in persistent tension between the parts and the whole. But he still wanted to preserve the whole. The only major exception (which, significantly, did not affect the general theory) was that he became more pessimistic about man's imminent attainment of the social state, and so shifted to regarding present character-change as a very slow process.

Why did this 'architectonic instinct' so tyrannize over Spencer?

Why was it so essential that all processes of change whether 'astronomic, geologic, organic, ethnologic, social', should be manifestations of one 'fundamental necessity', the discovery of which was the chief goal of philosophy?[4] The master-aim was 'to interpret this Law of Progress, in its multiform manifestations, as the necessary consequence of some universal principle'. The underlying reasons for Spencer's belief in the unity of Evolution were metaphysical. The basic division for him was between those who believed unthinkingly in special creation or divine intervention, and those who adopted 'the doctrine of the universality of natural causation' and 'its inevitable corollary the doctrine that the Universe and all things in it have reached their present forms through successive stages physically necessitated'.[5] Furthermore, since all explanatory theories indicate basic similarities shared by subjects which differ in more superficial respects, there could be no *a priori* reason for not supposing that the basic, underlying causes of all processes of change were not identical. Whether the basic causes were truistic as explanations of phenomena, was less important than the demonstration that all things were, in the last analysis, the outcome of the same natural forces. Spencer's approach was unlike that of his biological contemporaries (and, I should hope, of his sociological epigoni) in that he did not start off from a phenomenon to be explained, but from ethical and metaphysical positions to be established. Consequently he was an evolutionist long before Lyell, Huxley and Darwin. Huxley wrote:

> [Apart from one other biologist] the only person known to me whose knowledge and capacity compelled respect and who was, at the same time a thorough-going evolutionist, was Mr. Herbert Spencer. . . . Many and prolonged were the battles we fought on this topic. But even my friend's rare dialectical skill and copiousness of apt illustration could not drive me from my agnostic position. I took my stand upon two grounds:—Firstly, that up to that time, the evidence in favour of transmutation was wholly insufficient; and secondly, that no suggestion respecting the causes of transmutation assumed, which has been made, was in any way adequate to explain the phenomena. Looking back at the state of knowledge at that time, I really do not see that any other conclusion was justifiable.[6]

Spencer even called his own adherence to evolution a 'profession of faith'.[7]

There was also a particular need for a unitary Evolution, arising from the social-ethical side. Once the traditional and religious sources of morality had been discredited, ethical systems were best legitimized by being hitched to science. The arguments of *Social Statics*, set in a theory of necessary historical progress, would be clinched if this process were shown to be merely a segment of cosmic evolution. This need not mean that natural processes are predicated of society and that history is biologized. No: the same effect—the legitimation of ethics—is as easily secured by projecting the desired historical processes on to biology, and claiming that hence, being shown scientific, they are legitimate. If there is an analogy between natural and social-historic processes, the analogy, like all analogies, can be worked either way; and either way the distinction between nature and society is dissolved. This is all that needs to be done for it to seem that agreeable moral conclusions may be deduced from science.

II

When Spencer became an evolutionist in the early 1840s, he combined two ideas which were at the time generally regarded in scientific circles as irreconcilable: uniformitarianism, and the theory of descent or the 'development hypothesis'.[8] Like Lyell he was unable to 'accept any doctrine which implied a breach in the uniform course of natural causation'[9] and believed that the formations of the past must be explained by causes still operative in the present. The opposing geological doctrine, catastrophism, held that slow, steady processes like erosion and sedimentation were not sufficient to account for rock formations, and that recourse must be had to more dramatic forces, 'catastrophes'. Although by the 1840s the two schools were in fact moving towards one another, their antagonism was sustained by what both sides took to be the religious implications of the debate. Lyell and the uniformitarians, writing 'to sink the diluvialists and . . . all the theological sophists'[10] (who included Whewell), aimed to clear natural theology out of science; while their opponents were partial to floods and volcanoes because they did seem more like 'acts of God' than the processes Lyell emphasized. The superficially surprising hostility of uniformitarians to the theory of descent was due to its use by the less orthodox natural theologians, such as the German *Naturphilosophen* and Robert Chambers. The latter's *Vestiges of Creation* (1844), a very popular book, learned but amateurish, full of errors, was equally objectionable to the orthodoxly religious and the professional scientists, among whom it probably acted to delay the eventual acceptance of evolution. It is necessary to distinguish two sorts of natural theology: the orthodox, whose chief example was Paley, who saw all species as exhibiting the direct results of the Creator's once-for-all design; and the unorthodox, such as the developmentalists, who saw the development of species as an immanent process, the progressive realization, by natural means, of God's original plans for the completion of nature. The latter, despite their deism, rejected the argument from design in its classic form. As Paley's target, Erasmus Darwin, had put it in *Zoonomia*: 'the world plainly resembles more an animal or vegetable, than it does a watch or knitting loom'.[11]

Uniformitarianism, meaning the rejection of anything resembling miraculous intervention in natural process, was the core of Spencer's scientific creed. The evolution preached by Chambers seemed indefensible because of its teleological imputation of a divinely planned 'impulse' to evolve in animals.[12] But he saw the possibility of a non-teleological mechanism of progress in Lamarck's theory of evolution by adaptation to the demands of the environment, as Lyell had expounded it in order to reject it. Whether Lamarckianism is to be seen as a real precursor of Darwinism, or else, as Gillispie describes it, 'a medley of dying echoes all of a piece with Thales and Lucretius',[13] cannot be discussed here. But it is hard not to think that in his rapid adoption of Lamarck's ideas Spencer was not only seizing on a theory of biological evolution which lends itself well to sociological use, but was reverting to an older source of evolutionary influence—that of Erasmus Darwin, mediated through his father and the other 'Darwinians' of the Derby Philosophical Society. There is, I think, much more reason, both internal and biographical, to suppose that Spencer was more subject to Erasmus Darwin's influence than Charles Darwin was.

Lamarck kept the essence of eighteenth-century evolution while getting very largely rid of the teleological elements found in Diderot, Erasmus Darwin and the German proponents of *Naturphilosophie*. Whereas the teleological evolution of the eighteenth century had regarded organisms as if they were men, striving to improve themselves and to realize their natures, Spencer, developing Lamarck's emphasis on the role of the environment, tended to reverse the process. In *Social Statics* especially, he presents the self-betterment of mankind as being beyond their own control, just as the adaptation of organisms to their physical environment is, and hence infallible and inevitable. But nonetheless Spencer is very ambivalent about teleology. He expels it from the front door of the evolutionary palace, because otherwise he cannot claim the legitimacy of science: Erasmus Darwin, the author of the *Vestiges*, and even Lamarck are reprimanded because

> they imply the belief that organic progress is a result of some in-dwelling tendency to develop, supernaturally impressed on living matter at the outset—some ever-acting constructive force, which, independently of other forces, moulds organisms into higher and higher forms.[14]

Spencer is here writing up the teleology of these thinkers in to a form in which it could be refuted.

But he is still obliged to smuggle teleology in by back ways since, because he wants to demonstrate history's inevitable path to perfection, he needs a guarantee of direction in evolution. This cannot be provided by adaptation, since that provides no account of how the environment may change. Hence he writes that only if man had 'some utterly different mental constitution could the process of civilization have been altered'; and the inconsistency is evident when he says that 'civilization no longer appears to be a regular unfolding after a specific plan; but seems rather a development of man's *latent capabilities* under the action of favourable circumstances'.[15] (The same confusion is evident in Spencer's biology, since he repeatedly failed to distinguish between processes like the development of the embryo, where the outcome is genetically programmed at the outset, and ones like the evolution of a species or the socialization of infants, where the form of the outcome is in no sense innately determined right from the beginning.[16]) It is neither necessary nor really possible to say that Spencer's belief in natural causation was primary, and in teleological evolution secondary.[17] For he had set himself the task of harmonizing incompatibles. In his quest for scientific morality he had to walk the tight-rope between a teleology which would yield moral guidance but threatened to let in God, and a natural causation which was blind and amoral. He was in fact much closer than he thought to the eighteenth-century evolutionists, of whom Gillispie has justly written that they wanted 'things from biology which science cannot give without ceasing to be science, and becoming moral or social philosophy'.[18]

After accepting the fact and suggesting the mechanism of evolution, the next step was to characterize its process. Here again the effect of reading was to confirm and bring to the fore themes which were already present. Now it was European biologists, especially K. E. von Baer, who stimulated the idea that evolution *was* differentiation.[19] Von Baer, a member of the *Naturphilosophie* school, teleological but anti-miraculous, was a careful anatomist, who noticed two seemingly related facts: (*a*) that animals, on the basis of the fossil record and comparative anatomy, could be placed in an ascending order of development, being the more complex the higher they were, and (*b*) that the embryo, in its development from single cell to whole animal, also became progressively complex through division and differentiation, and that there was a parallel between the hierarchy of species and the stages of growth of the individual animal. Many other biologists were much less cautious than von Baer in placing great significance on the law that 'ontogeny recapitulates phylogeny' (i.e. the individual organism, as an embryo, goes through forms which are recapitulations of earlier stages in the evolution of its species). Although, whatever the parallels, the two processes are decisively different in that the outcome of ontogeny is initially determined as that of phylogeny is not, von Baer's discoveries were a powerful support for organic evolution on a Lamarckian or Darwinian model. And they added extra plausibility to the sociological version of 'ontogeny recapitulates phylogeny'—the theory, amply evidenced in Spencer's *Psychology*, that more than an analogy exists between the social development of a child into an adult, and the evolution of the savage into the civilized man. (This notion, summed up in the description of savagery as 'the childhood of the human race', had a much more ancient pedigree than the novel biology which seemed to confirm it.[20]) All these processes, it seemed to Spencer, could be characterized in the same way, and strengthened the case for a general law of evolution.

So, he wrote triumphantly in 1857:

> We believe we have shown beyond question, that that which the German physiologists have found to be the law of organic development, is the law of all development. The advance from the simple to the complex, through a process of successive differentiations, is seen alike in the earliest changes of the Universe to which we can reason our way back; and in the earliest changes which we can inductively establish; it is seen in the geologic and climatic evolution of the Earth, and of every single organism on its surface; it is seen in the evolution of Humanity, whether contemplated in the civilized individual, or in the aggregation of races; it is seen in the evolution of Society in respect alike of its political, its religious, and its economical organization; and it is seen in the evolution of all those endless concrete and abstract products of human activity which constitute the environment of our daily life. From the remotest past which Science can fathom, up to the novelties of yesterday, that in which Progress essentially consists, is the transformation of the homogeneous into the heterogeneous.[21]

This truth was further ground down and polished up until finally in *First Principles* it stood thus:

> Evolution is definable as a change from an incoherent homogeneity to a coherent heterogeneity, accompanying the dissipation of motion and the integration of matter.[22]

But why is there this tendency to differentiate? To this Spencer gave varyingly specific answers. An initial problem was to link the process, differentiation, with the mechanism. To the first question of why differentiation is adaptive, the answer was suggested by a social science, political economy, which had already made its mark on biology as the phrase 'la division du travail biologique', noted by Spencer in the French biologist Milne-Edwards, attests. As Adam Smith had classically shown, the division of labour greatly enhances the productive power of labour—and hence, in a situation of scarcity, the adaptiveness of those who adopt it.

This is most clearly shown in an essay of 1852, 'A Theory of Population, deduced from the General Law of Animal Fertility', famous because in it Spencer coined the phrase 'survival of the fittest', and because he seems to have come within a stone's throw of anticipating Darwin and Wallace in seeing in Malthus the clue to organic evolution by natural selection.[23] But for all the apparent biologism of the theory of social progress (which most commentators have taken at face value), the major influences are, first and unacknowledged, Adam Smith, and then Malthus.

Spencer's overall aim is to show that 'faith in the essential beneficence of things,[24] is rationally grounded, even granted a tendency for population to outstrip food supply. There is, he argues, a rough equilibrium between any animal population and its food supply. But the evolution of animal species is due to their tendency at times to over-increase their numbers, upsetting the precarious balance. (In seeing population pressure as the prime agent of progress, Spencer reverts to the grandfathers of sociology, the Scottish moralists.) The explanation is prompted by the observable fact that in the animal kingdom there is an *inverse* relation between brain size and fertility. Without specifying any biological mechanism whatever, Spencer proposes that a change in the one will induce a change in the other. If a species increases excessively, there will be a struggle to survive; and only those which are more intelligent than the average, or which become so under pressure, will succeed. Thus the quality of the stock will improve over time. And since the more intelligent the less fertile, their descendants, while making better use of the environment, will also be less likely to overbreed. Hence a self-correcting mechanism is built into population, which secures evolution as a by-product.

This holds for society as well as for nature. 'The wants of their redundant numbers constitute the only stimulus mankind have for a greater production of the necessities of life.'[25] Population pressure forces men to efficient, sociable habits to make the best use of their environment:

> To get more produce from the acre, the farmer must study chemistry, must adopt new mechanical appliances and must, by the multiplication of tools and processes, cultivate both his own powers and the powers of his labourers. To meet the requirements of the market the manufacturer is perpetually improving his old machines and inventing new ones; and by the premium of high wages incites artizans to acquire greater skill. . . .[26]

From the beginning pressure of population has been the proximate

> cause of progress. . . . It forced men into the social state; made social organization inevitable; and has developed the social sentiments . . . it is daily pressing us into closer contact and more mutually dependent relationships.[27]

Differentiation, specialization, the division of labour, come about because they are more adaptive.[28] They also presume a higher degree of functional interdependence, which in society means the development of sociality and altruism, as was emphasized in the *Psychology*. It is a Godwinian revenge on Malthus, Malthus turned on his head: from being the great obstacle to human perfection, the principle of population becomes its prerequisite and guarantee.[29]

The economic division of labour is a paradigm of all other kinds of differentiation whether within such units as organisms, planets, societies and cultures, or between them—as in the increasing variety of species. Now whereas adaptive efficiency can explain internal specialization, it can hardly explain variety. The explanation of this turns out to be 'the ultimate cause' which Spencer said was still needed beyond all observable 'proximate causes'. Even in the *Biology* 'only when the process of evolution of organisms is affiliated on the process of evolution in general can it be truly said to be explained'; it was yet necessary 'to reconcile the facts with the universal laws of the redistribution of matter and motion'.[30]

Although Spencer later saw evolution as being a special kind of change, a theoretically worked-out version of progress, in his essay of 1857 he seems to have seen evolution as equivalent to change, 'and hence, in some characteristic of changes in general, the desired solution will probably be found'.[31] The 'fundamental necessity' behind the tendency of change to heterogeneity is the law that 'every active force produces more than one change—every cause produces more than one effect'. Whether we consider the results of the cooling of the earth, or the effects of a disease on the body, or of an invention on society, there is a built-in tendency to ever greater complexity. The more complex the recipient of an impression, the more varied still will be its effects—so that the tendency to variety is ever-increasing. A marvellously detailed and eloquent passage describes the effects of the steam engine on modern society, and concludes:

> Illustrations to the same effect might be definitely accumulated.

That every influence brought to bear upon society works multiplied effects; and that increase of heterogeneity is due to this multiplication of effects; may be seen in the history of every trade, every custom, every belief. But it is needless to give additional evidence of this.[32]

But still the demonstration of why evolution means differentiation had not achieved the desired deductive form—that is, not until 'there came the perception that the condition of homogeneity is an unstable condition . . . [and] the theorem passed into the region of physical science'.[33] Stimulated by recent work in physics which had led to the discovery of the conservation of energy (or force), Spencer gave his theory its final shape as 'a question of causes and effects reduced to their simple forms—a question of molar and molecular forces and energies—a question of the never-ending redistribution of matter and motion considered under its most general aspect'. It is unclear whether Spencer regarded his basic propositions about force as *a priori* laws of thought—as seems most likely—or in some way inferences from physics. For while acknowledging the stimulus of physics, he also denied that the 'Persistence of Force' was simply another name for the conservation of energy, though the basic intuited image seems very similar. As in the *Psychology*, the key concept, uniting mind, matter and motion, was Force, the basic element of consciousness, the 'ultimate of ultimates', which 'can be regarded only as a conditioned effect of the Unconditioned Cause—as the relative reality indicating to us an Absolute Reality by which it is immediately produced'.[34] So we are back with the result of the initial search for certainty, the Unknowable. The desire for certainty had also led to the quest for unified knowledge, or true philosophy, which could only be guaranteed by the arcane metaphysics expounded in *First Principles*. Only thus was Spencer able to conclude:

It may seem to some extent a coincidence that the same law of metamorphosis holds throughout all [Evolution's] divisions. But when we recognize these divisions as mere conventional groupings, made to facilitate the arrangement and acquisition of knowledge—when we remember that the different existences with which they severally deal are component parts of one Cosmos; we see at once that there are not several kinds of Evolution having certain traits in common, but one Evolution going on everywhere after the same manner.[35]

III

This brief summary of the main elements of Spencer's theory of evolution indicates how different were its objectives and achievements from Darwin's, and consequently how misguided it is to see Spencer as a generalizer of the Darwinian theory and so necessarily a corruptor of a proper theory of *social* evolution. But Spencer immediately accepted Darwin's theory (and such new elements as natural selection) when it came out, and Darwin for his part seems to have accepted Spencer's general theory of evolution as providing an appropriate overall framework for his own ideas. At any rate Darwin wrote to Spencer, thanking him for sending a volume of his *Essays:*

> Your remarks on the general argument of the so-called development theory seem to me admirable. I am at present preparing an Abstract of a larger work on the changes of species; but I treat the work simply, and not from a general point of view. Otherwise in my opinion your argument could not have been improved on, and might have been quoted by me with great advantage.[36]

This was kind of Darwin; but nonetheless Spencer's theory was very different from Darwin's, and in this section I wish to contrast the two theories in greater detail.

Darwin's theory is much more modest than Spencer's and his original contribution is summed up in the phrase 'natural selection'. His great achievement was to indicate the principal, universal mechanism (and his followers, especially August Weismann, insisted the *only* mechanism) by which the transformation of species can take place. The general sequence or hierarchy of organic species was already known, and Darwin gave no account of why the variegated totality of species was as it was, and could suggest nothing as to the path of the future development of the evolutionary tree. Darwin's was not a theory to explain why some particular species had emerged in terms of particular causal antecedents, but one which put forward a mechanism that was operative for any conceivable species in any conceivable environment. If the numbers of natural species tend to outstrip their food supply (as Malthus had said), and if (as any farmer or stockbreeder knew) there is a tendency, within the species, for purely spontaneous variations to occur, some of which will be more favourable to survival in certain environments, then there will be a tendency for those animals possessing these accidentally favourable characters to survive and pass them on to their descendants. Thus the species can be modified; and given enough time (which was Lyell's main contribution to Darwinism), and a geographical spread, new and distinct species might emerge.

There is no *necessary* direction in Darwin's evolution, no *necessity* for any particular criterion of 'fitness' to triumph or for particular forms to become predominant; nor is there any reason for more complex animals to develop or for the variety of species to increase. 'I believe . . . in no law of necessary development,' stated Darwin simply.[37] The theory of natural selection can say none of these things because the content, or path, of evolution in substantive detail is determined by the demands of the environment, whose characteristics are taken for granted, or vary randomly as far as the theory is concerned. That for long periods of time the earth's environment has favoured particular kinds of animal, so that evolution has in fact possessed direction, is not within the scope of Darwin's theory, which cannot therefore be bent to the purposes of those who, like Spencer, *are* concerned with producing a *determinate* account of the content or process of evolution.[38] The difference between them may be summed up thus: Darwin's theory accounted for the secular transformation of each species by the mechanism of natural selection, while Spencer's attempted to explain the total configuration of nature, physical, organic and social, as well as its necessary process.

Spencer readily accepted natural selection (indeed, he regretted that in his essay of 1852 he had not seen it, though coming so close), and made some use of it.[39] But it is a great exaggeration to give it pivotal importance in the construction of his social theory, as Abrams does;[40] and it is mistaken to say he changed his Lamarckism for Darwinism ('a substitution which helped rather than hindered his argument', says R. C. K. Ensor[41])—he did not do so, and it would not have helped him if he had. Spencer fought a long rear-guard action in biology to defend the Lamarckian principle of the inheritance of acquired characteristics, since he did not think that natural selection was adequate by itself to explain organic evolution. (It must be remembered that until the development of genetics the details of how and why mutations are produced remained extremely vague.) Spencer maintained to the end that the direct impression of the environment on the organism, at all levels of development, and the transmission to posterity of the features thus acquired, must account for a great deal of evolution.[42]

Quite apart from the biological issues raised by the debate over use-inheritance, there was a general reason why Spencer was unwilling to abandon Lamarckism—it would have driven a wedge between biological and sociocultural or 'superorganic' evolution, and so nullified the major premiss of the entire Synthetic Philosophy. For the transmission of environmentally-induced traits to the next generation is just what does happen in culture[43]—it is a truism to say it—and to have denied it in biology would, by destroying the unity of all evolution, have weakened the necessity of social evolution. It is therefore equally fair to criticize Spencer for writing culturized or historicized biology, as it is for 'biologized history' as Harris does.[44]

Spencer's Lamarckism is indispensable to his concept of race, where he is liable to be seriously misunderstood by those who accept modern biology. Since we operate with certain clear-cut distinctions, so well established that we take them for granted, between natural and cultural process, or between positivistic, scientific demonstration and the establishment of ethical or aesthetic values, we tend to misunderstand the thought of those who did not find these opposites incompatible and tried to bridge them. In discussing the differences between individuals' behaviour we sharply contrast the influence of learned, modifiable, cultural factors and innate, biological, 'racial' ones, which for most purposes we have to take as given, since they change very slowly in accord with Darwinian evolution. Anyone who regards differences between ethnic groups in such things as moral values, scientific and artistic creativity, social patterns etc. as stemming from relatively unchangeable genetically-grounded differences between groups of men stands condemned morally and intellectually as a racist. Harris, who evidently derives a certain sombre satisfaction from pointing out the racism of much nineteenth-century anthropology, writes that 'it is Spencer . . . and not Darwin who bears the greatest share of the onus of having crippled the explanatory power of cultural evolutionary theory by merging and mixing it with racial determinism'.[45] He goes on that Spencer's 'fundamental error' (it is a big claim) was to overrate the importance of the factor of heredity, and that his method was to explain 'sociocultural difference in terms of biological selection'.[46]

It is true that the 'character' which Spencer saw as the determinant of society and culture was, in some vague way, physically grounded and directly inheritable. But this does not make him an anti-environmentalist in the sense that a racist is when he denies that nurture, training and environment can make any difference to someone who is racially inferior. As we have seen in the case of the *Psychology*, Spencer often likens the responses of savages to those of women and children in general—who can hardly be 'racially' inferior to men.

Spencer's confusions on this topic result from his being unable either to reconcile, or to choose between two traditions both of which he was heir to: environmentalist and hereditarian. The former descends from Locke with associationist psychology and the optimistic and perfectionist philosophy of the Enlightenment: Hartley, Helvétius (who held that every child, properly educated, could be a Newton), Godwin, Priestley, Hodgskin and Owen belong to it. It provided much-needed ammunition for the middle-class and Dissenting assault upon hereditary privilege, and is expressed in their educational philosophies. Owen summed it up in saying that 'any general character, from the best to the worst, from the most ignorant to the most enlightened, may be given to any community, even to the world at large, by the application of the proper means'.[47] Men are made by their environment. 'Human nature' and 'innate ability', without being denied altogether, become unimportant residual categories. Stress is laid on the changeable, rather than the constant features of humanity, as it is by Spencer in *Social Statics*.

The hereditarian view is to be found, not merely in conservative and pessimistic philosophies, but in the writings of scientists well aware of the persistence of traits in individuals and species. It was therefore an important element in phrenology, especially in its continental form, and seemed obvious to ethnologists confronting the differences both physical and 'cultural' (though that was neither their word nor their concept) between races. James Hunt, of the London Anthropological Society,[48] and Francis Galton, author of

Hereditary Genius and a book about the Damaras which Spencer drew on for his *Psychology*, came down strongly for nature against nurture. But it is impossible for a Lamarckian to decide between the two viewpoints, or to establish how significant either factor is, for race or disposition, being the effect of past environmental influences, can itself be changed—in time, though there is no theory to suggest how quickly change can take place. British phrenology came to be an indeterminate compromise between the mapping of innate dispositions and attempted character-change through education. Owenism was combined with phrenology, and with a Lamarckian type of evolution.[49]

On Spencer's stated assumptions he could take up a position at any point between a near-Owenite one, and a near-Galtonian one. His only fundamental quarrel with an Owenite would be that the environment which affects character is not, as Owen said, 'to a great extent at the command and under the control of those who have influence in the affairs of men'. His agreement with Galton could only be over the practical unchangeability of a particular race or character in the near future, since Galton's eugenics rested on the rejection of Spencer's environmentalism.[50] With Spencer, as with most other nineteenth-century anthropologists, talk of 'racial temperament' went with belief in Lamarckism. Such an elastic doctrine, which permitted what Stocking calls a 'bland and blind shuttling' between race and environment, was both ideologically useful and scientifically unhelpful.[51] Without abandoning any theory Spencer shifted from the radical optimism of his early writings, where he shows himself convinced of the variability of human nature and sceptical of the fixity of species, sure that the final consummation of history was just round the corner, a strong associationist and environmentalist, to a pessimism and practical conservatism which played down the present action of the environment in favour of the sum of past environmental influence, 'organized' as character or race. The modern separation of cultural progress from racial or biological evolution depends on the rejection of Lamarckism in biology. Only then is real racism possible, with 'race' treated as an independent variable with regard to culture.

Nobody saw Spencer's environmentalism more clearly than T. H. Huxley:

> You appear to me to suppose that external conditions modify machinery [meaning 'organs' generally here] as if by transferring a flour-mill into a forest you could make it into a saw-mill.[52]

The way to the modern conception of culture, sharply distinguished from race, was opened by the forceful statement of the sole efficacity of natural selection in biology by Weismann, later greatly strengthened by Mendelian genetics. Spencer's unsuccessful rearguard action from 1886 to 1889 in defence of the inheritance of acquired characteristics (which was, it must be emphasized, a serious piece of biology) was as much required by his conception of sociology as it was a contribution to a debate in biology.

IV

Natural selection implies the struggle for survival, and Spencer has been widely regarded, in his own day as well as in ours, as favouring a merciless competition between individuals to take place in society. Marvin Harris offers a fair stereotype of this view of Spencer. His 'idiom is pregnant with struggle-for-survivalism'; 'the most direct Spencerian paradigm' is the struggle of man against man, not man against nature; 'condemnation of co-operativism' is a marked feature of his social theory. Spencer's opposition to the state provision of social welfare is well known. The social background to struggle-for-survivalism seems clear enough. 'The milieu in question,' Harris goes on, 'was remarkable for the intensity and geographical expanse of its international wars, its internecine political struggles. . . . It would seem undeniable that the wedding between racism and the doctrine of struggle was in part an excrescence of this class and national warfare.'[53] But this account of nineteenth-century history is fanciful. No period in British history was freer from continental wars, or wars which impinged on the popular consciousness than the period 1815–1914 within which Spencer's entire life-span fell. Wars were small, sporadic and remote; and Spencer was utterly opposed to wars of the kind which occurred with greater frequency from the 1880s in the phase of colonial expansion. Why someone with such pronounced peace-loving sentiments should espouse the views Harris attributes to Spencer is altogether obscure. As for the class struggle, Spencer belonged to a party which persistently and with some success deprecated it largely by denying its reality. The import of real Social Darwinist writings such as Ammon's and Lapouge's is quite alien to Spencer's.[54] It is significant that Prince Peter Kropotkin, pacifist and anarchist, though his social ideals differed markedly from Spencer's, only quoted Spencer in support of his own views. There are passages in *Mutual Aid* which would not have been out of place in *Social Statics*.[55]

Spencer's position is quite distinct from Darwin's even where he is thought to have most nearly anticipated him, in the 1852 essay on population. Here he argued that since population tends to outstrip food-supply, there is a struggle to survive, and those who fail to adapt must therefore perish, and 'it unavoidably follows that those left behind to continue the race must be those in whom the power of self-preservation is the greatest—must be the select of their generation'.[56] But the mechanism of adaptation is Lamarckian: animals confront challenging circumstances and must adjust to them if they can, the successful passing on their organic achievements to their descendants. There is no *logical* necessity for competition of animal against animal, or man against man, for in principle all might improve themselves; and if this doesn't apply in the case of animals, it does in the case of man, where adaptation, forced by the struggle for survival, results in co-operation and the division of labour. Spencer compares England's response to population pressure with Ireland's (in a manner strikingly foreshadowing T. S. Ashton),[57] and says Ireland's catastrophe was due to her failure to adapt—the struggle being not against England, but against nature. In various places he says that it is only at the lower stages of evolution that adaptation by some will entail the deaths of others.[58] The prime criterion of a high state of social evolution is that adaptation is not competitive but co-operative; and the end-product of history will be a society where the pursuit by individuals of their own goals will not be detrimental to others. 'Modifications of nature, in one way or another produced, are inheritable.'[59] A distinctive character like the national character of the Americans, may be built up over an indeterminate period of time.

> Since, in common with every other creature, Man is modifiable—since his modifications, like those of every other creature, are ultimately determined by surrounding conditions; and it is continually thrust on men's attention . . . [that] faculties and powers of all orders, while

they grow by exercise, dwindle when not used; and that alterations of nature descend to posterity.[60]

The Lamarckian character of the struggle for survival in Spencer is fundamental. The reason why welfare-statism is counter to the principles of evolution is not that the weakest *must* be made to go to the wall in order for improvement of the race to occur by natural selection, but that welfare measures will prevent people adapting themselves through their own efforts so that their improvements become 'organic' in the race. For the character of a whole society depends on the characters of all its constituent units aggregated together. Pain, unhappiness and discomfort are the signs of imperfect adaptation; 'there must exist in our midst an immense amount of misery which is a normal result of misconduct and ought not to be dissociated from it'.[61] To remove the symptoms of ill-adaptation by welfare legislation would prevent evolution by removing the incentive for each individual to adapt himself more fully to the social state. Spencer's Lamarckian view of the mechanism of evolution is worth quoting at some length:

While, however, each society, and each successive phase of each society presents conditions more or less special, to which the natures of citizens adapt themselves; there are certain general conditions which, in every society, must be fulfilled to a considerable extent before it can hold together, and which must be fulfilled completely before social life can be complete. . . . It is needful that [any citizen] shall perform such function or share of function as is of value equivalent at least to what he consumes; and . . . that, both in discharging his function and in pursuing his pleasure, he shall leave others similarly free to discharge their functions and pursue their pleasures. . . . Now, under one of its chief aspects, civilization is a process of developing in citizens a nature capable of fulfilling these all-essential conditions . . . [and] the course of civilization shows us a clearer recognition and a better enforcement of these essential conditions [and] a moulding of humanity into correspondence with them. . . .

From the biological laws we have been contemplating, it is, on the one hand, an inevitable corollery that if these conditions are maintained, human nature will slowly adapt itself to them: while, on the other hand, it is an inevitable corollary that by no other discipline than subjection to these conditions, can fitness to the social state be produced. Enforce these conditions, and by so much there will be a cessation of the adaptive changes. Abolish these conditions, and after

> the consequent social dissolution, there will commence (unless they are re-established) an adaptation to the conditions thus resulting—those of savage life. These are conditions from which there is no escape, if Man is subject to the laws of life in common with living things in general.[62]

The last section of this passage indicates that Spencer did not see life of civilized man, at least, as a *bellum omnium contra omnes*. But there was a streak in Spencer which was 'Darwinian' in this crude and specific sense. Once the theory of natural selection was out, and accepted as a factor of evolution, it could not be ignored, even though it was *logically* dispensable for a Lamarckian; and its ideological utility for a man of strong *laissez-faire* views was undeniable. The argument is used most explicitly in the following passages from *The Study of Sociology* (1873), much more than in *The Man versus the State* (1884). Even here Lamarckism is not entirely absent:

> Besides an habitual neglect of the fact that the quality of a society is physically lowered by the artificial preservation of its feeblest members, there is an habitual neglect of the fact that the quality of a society is lowered morally and intellectually by the artificial preservation of those who are least able to take care of themselves. . . .
>
> Fostering the good-for-nothing at the expense of the good, is an extreme cruelty. It is a deliberate storing-up of miseries for future generations. There is no greater curse to prosperity than that of bequeathing them an increasing population of imbeciles and idlers and criminals. To aid the bad in multiplying is, in effect, the same as maliciously providing for our descendants a multitude of enemies. It may be doubted whether the maudlin philanthropy which, looking only at direct mitigations, persistently ignores indirect mischiefs, does not inflict a greater total of misery than the extremest selfishness inflicts. Refusing to consider the remote influences of his incontinent generosity, the thoughtless giver stands but a degree above the drunkard who thinks only of today's pleasure and ignores tomorrow's pain, or the spendthrift who seeks immediate delights at the cost of ultimate poverty.[63]

But the main application of the Darwinian struggle of nature is to the *early* stages of social evolution, for Spencer believed (as I shall discuss at greater length in Chapter 8) that there was a secular trend from militancy to industrialism, and, as he put it in the

Psychology, from egotism to altruism. His candid admission of the past benefits of brutality and violence in the consolidation of societies and the elimination of 'inferior races', did not lead him to advocate such policies for the civilized; and when imperial wars were justified and practised in this way, Spencer called them 'barbarous' and 'cannibal', and saw them not as a means of advance, but as a symptom of regression. For he remained a pacifist-inclined critic of the public-school educated establishment—'those educated in the religion of enmity—those who during boyhood, when the instincts of the savage are dominant, have revelled in the congenial ideas and sentiments which classic poems and histories yield so abundantly, and have become confirmed in the belief that war is virtuous and peace ignoble'. Spencer admits the force of the struggle of nature, but in applying it to society relativizes it:

> Though, during barbarism and the earlier stages of civilization, war has the effect of exterminating the weaker societies, and of weeding out the weaker members of the stronger societies, and thus in both ways furthering the development of those valuable powers, bodily and mental, which war brings into play, yet during the later stages of civilization, the second of these actions is reversed. . . .
>
> Such advantages . . . as the race receives from the discipline of war, are exceeded by the disadvantages . . . which result after a certain stage of progress is reached. Severe and bloody as the process is, the killing-off of inferior races and inferior individuals, leaves a balance of benefit to mankind during phases of progress in which the moral development is low, and there are no quick sympathies to be seared by the infliction of pain and death. But as there arise higher societies, implying individual characters fitted for closer co-operation, the destructive activities exercised by such higher societies have injurious re-active effects on the moral natures of their members—injurious effects which outweigh the benefits resulting from extirpation of inferior races.[64]

What Spencer does not seem to realize is that by this relativization he destroys the footing from which it is possible to advocate a distinct ethical position, as he did in *Social Statics*. For though we know that he thinks it both absolutely wrong and (which comes to the same thing) inappropriate for a civilized society for there to be perpetual war and aggression, all he is now justified in saying is that in savage societies war is 'natural' and prevalent, and that where war *is* prevalent, society must be described as savage. Without his fully recognizing it, there is now a disjunction of social philosophy and sociology.

The last major controversy of Spencer's life, which caused him much distress since it brought about a temporary breach of his friendship with T. H. Huxley, concerned the ethical implications of evolution. It may be seen as the final tribulation of a peace-loving Lamarckian in a relentlessly Darwinian age, and involved the restatement of the arguments deployed in the use-inheritance debate. In 1888 Huxley published an article 'The Struggle for Existence in Human Society', with Spencer in mind whom he said would be put 'in a white rage' with him because of it;[65] and its thesis was presented again, in fuller form, in May 1893, in his famous lecture 'Evolution and Ethics', at once a summation and a repudiation of evolutionary thought.[66] His aim was to discredit certain positions—notably *laissez-faire* opposition to extending the role of the state, and the celebration of the benefits of struggle between individuals and nations—which were being justified by an appeal to evolutionary biology. He makes it seem that ruthless struggle follows from Spencer's premisses—though he must have known what Spencer thought of war. Huxley's argument was that the proper mechanism of social development may not be inferred from cosmic processes, for it rather resembles a process of horticulture, a deliberate intervention in nature and not an abject submission to it. It is not denied 'that, at its origin, human society was as much a product of organic necessity as that of the bees',[67] or that 'men in society are undoubtedly subject to the cosmic process'; but nonetheless 'the ethical progress of society depends, not on imitating the cosmic process, still less in running away from it'.[68] This was a rejection of an earlier faith, which Spencer still tenuously upheld, in the morality of nature. Huxley now maintained:

> . . . the practice of that which is ethically best—what we call goodness or virtue—involves a course of conduct which, in all respects, is opposed to that which leads to success in the cosmic struggle for existence. In place of ruthless self-assertion it demands self-restraint; in place of thrusting aside or treading down all competitors, it requires that the individual shall not merely respect, but help his fellows; its influence is directed, not so much to the survival of the fittest, as to the fitting of as many as possible to survive. . . . Laws and moral precepts are directed to the end of curbing the cosmic

process and reminding the individual of his duty to the community, to the protection and influence of which he owes, if not existence itself, at least the life of something better than a brutal savage.

It is from neglect of these plain considerations that the fanatical individualism of our time attempts to apply the analogy of cosmic nature to society.[69]

The leading exponent of 'fanatical individualism' and 'reasoned savagery' was Spencer. The issues between him and Huxley were complex. The main area of ethical disagreement was over *laissez-faire,* which Huxley saw as resting on the main theoretical disagreement—over the applicability of biological concepts to social ethics. But as we have seen, evolutionary ethics does not mean for Spencer that behaviour appropriate and 'natural' for savages or animals is also so for civilized men. Spencer maintains that co-operative and altruistic behaviour is sanctioned *by evolution* for contemporary society. He was even, in a letter to Huxley in 1888, prepared to speak of the 'non-moral character of Nature—immoral indeed, I rather think . . . for 99 hundredths of the time life had existed on the earth (or one should say 999 thousandths) the success has been confined to those beings which, from a human point of view, would be called criminal'.[70] Huxley felt Spencer's view of the unity of evolution was unjustifiable because he, Huxley, saw evolution in exclusively Darwinian terms—which meant natural selection—and had recently debated this with Spencer. But since Spencer remained a Lamarckian, to whom adaptation, in any manner, is the shared feature of all kinds of evolution, he could regard natural selection as a passing phase of evolution, and consequently other modes of adaptation as not being any the less evolutionary for not being natural selection. He stated his unchanged view of the controversy thus:

Practically [Huxley's] view is a surrender of the general doctrine of evolution in so far as its higher applications are concerned, and is pervaded by the ridiculous assumption that, in its application to the organic world, it is limited to the struggle for existence among individuals under its ferocious aspects, and has nothing to do with the development of social organization, or the modifications of the human mind that take place in the course of that organization. . . . The position he takes, that we have to struggle against or correct the cosmic process, involves the assumption that there exists something in us

> which is not a product of the cosmic process, and is practically a going-back to the old theological notions, which put Man and Nature in antithesis. Any rational, comprehensive view of evolution involves that, in the course of social evolution, the human mind is disciplined into that from which itself puts a check upon that part of the cosmic process which consists in the unqualified struggle for existence.[71]

To the last then for Spencer, evolution is one. That this conception of evolution is biologically inappropriate, does not deprive it of sociological value. To the validity of social evolution, therefore, we now turn.

V

What might be of scientific value in the theory of social evolution falls into two categories—mechanism (i.e. how change takes place) and process (i.e. what change consists in). The theory purports to show how a certain state of affairs, established as good by independent moral arguments and also by being shown to be ultimately necessary, is progressively being realized in the course of time; and that its realization cannot fail because it is in accordance with mechanisms which are operative throughout all nature. The process is a continuous differentiation of social institutions, and, at a psychological level, a development of altruistic natures in men, until the end-state of history is reached—a heterogeneous society in which men will rejoice in being highly and subtly dependent on one another, will be morally capable of this interdependence and will find no discrepancy between it and the free fulfilment of their own natures. The mechanism to ensure this happy outcome is adaptation, which operates at the higher levels of development through the medium of consciousness, but is basically the same at all levels of nature.

Put thus in general terms the theory seems clear and straightforward. But it is not, and contains more ambiguities than complexities, particularly over the matter of adaptation. As a mechanism of change adaptation is only appropriate for something that is not a real totality, but a part which must be referred to a whole. For Spencer the totality is the cosmos, whose ultimate mechanism is therefore not adaptation but immanent principles such as the

Persistence of Force. To this extent Spencer is less sociological than Marx, for whom the totality was society, and Durkheim, who insisted that the social was only to be explained by the social. For adaptation must be *to* something.

The simplest sort of adaptation is that in the 'Theory of Population', where population pressure, taken as an extra-social, biological tendency forces men to adapt to their material environment by devising new methods of production. This has the advantage that the tendency of evolution always seems the same, and that, granted the (false) assumption that population increase is a biological fact independent of social causation, no circularity is involved in the explanation. It is not clear how far this mechanism is basic to other sorts of adaptation (such as that 'to the social state'), but it is never repudiated and occasionally reintroduced, in a somewhat *ad hoc* manner, in the later volumes of the *Principles of Sociology*.

All other sorts of adaptation are inadequate in some way. A society may be forced to become warlike because of the presence of other hostile societies: 'Certain conditions, manifest *a priori*, have to be fulfilled by a society fitted for preserving itself in the presence of antagonistic societies'.[72] This may be true for any single society but it does not explain why societies should be antagonistic at all. Spencer sometimes speaks of 'societies' evolving, sometimes of 'Society'.[73] But, true to his methodological individualism (of which more in Chapter 7), Spencer will maintain that societies are determined by the character of their members, and that with evolution men progressively shed their selfish violence for altruistic pacifism. This process, loosely described in *Social Statics* and merely elaborated in later works, is called 'Adaptation to the Social State'.

It is really a misnomer to call this adaptation. For the social state is certainly not environment, something external to society, for it seems to be what we could now call the structural prerequisites of an ideal society, the supposed end-product of history. The use of the word 'adaptation' to cover both this long-term continual approximation of mankind to an unrealized perfection *and* the perpetual adjustment to variable present conditions in Lamarckian biology is very misleading. Spencer's usage is not quite consistent here, since he also speaks of man becoming adapted to a less than perfect state of society, in a manner much closer to the adaptation, or ecological *modus vivendi*, of organisms in an environment in biology. But in speaking of 'adaptation to the social state' Spencer has implicitly shifted from treating society as a part to treating it as a totality. This has a great advantage for anyone whose ethical purposes require that a consistent direction be demonstrated in history. To take society as part, as adaptation implies, is to make its progress contingent on persistently favourable conditions in the non-social environment. That is not static, but evolving according to principles of its own, and it is hard to show convincingly that the differentiation of the cosmos must cause man to become more altruistic and societies more industrial. But adaptation to the social state is essentially a secular process which is immanent in society itself, and like all such processes conceals teleology—the psychological telos of a human nature with a potential, and the sociological telos of an unrealized perfect society which seems to be drawing the human race towards itself through history.[74]

In his early, optimistic phase Spencer explained social changes as coming about because they made society more coherent, solid, efficient, ordered etc.—qualities which imply a fairly consistent picture of what *specific* things are adaptive. For unless adaptation has a specific content and implies particular standards of fitness and efficiency, adaptation is a quite vacuous concept: from explaining the occurrence of *x* because it is adaptive (which implies a theory of the conditions of existence) there is a shift to upholding the tautology that 'adaptation' is the name given to *anything* that happens, irrespective of content. Where everything is thus 'explained', nothing is. If Spencer were not claiming to have a determinate theory of all history, there would be no difficulty when things happened which were not adaptive by specified criteria. If differentiation and the division of labour occur because they are adaptive (i.e. efficient), why does the opposite sometimes occur? Spencer could not deny that it often did. Why was it that, as Richard Potter told him, 'some businesses grow diverse and complicated, others get simpler and more uniform, others again go into the Bankruptcy courts';[75] or why, since they are so maladaptive, do 'indeterminate heterogeneity' and 'loss of clearness of function', come about, the result of socialist movements, and 'agitation, growing into revolutionary meetings, fuses ranks that are usually separated'?[76] A less ambitious theorist than Spencer, who felt no obligation to prove the overall directedness of change, could easily drop the word 'adaptation' and try to specify the conditions under which one set of phenomena occur, and other conditions under which other sets occur.

But Spencer's brief did not allow him to do this. What had initially seemed a great merit in the adaptive mechanism—that, being specific and determinate, it only permitted movement in one direction, like a fixed ratchet on a toothed wheel, so that progress was predestined—came to be a great hindrance to saving the theory when evidence of regression could not be denied. For Spencer was later prepared to admit that human society can regress, and even that it is 'highly probable that regression has been as frequent as progression'—as witness survivals like the elaborate ruins in central Java, or the complicated marriage-rules of the lowest Australian savages.[77] But *why* societies should regress at all in view of the persuasive determinate theory of progress, remains a problem which is only palliated by a *deus ex machina* from *First Principles*, the Law of Rhythm, 'deduced' from the persistence of force. All things throb, oscillate and pulse, so that exceptions to the rule of progressive unidirectional adaptation, such as the re-emergence of warlike sentiments in civilized society or a return to homogeneity, are only apparent. Towards the end of the *Sociology*, after lamenting the rise of opposing factors to those he happily saw predominant with *Social Statics* in 1850, Spencer says that 'rhythm everywhere results from antagonistic forces' and implicitly abandons adaptation for a kind of immanent dialectic.[79] But he still feels that 'the study of Sociology is useless if from an account of what has been, we cannot infer what is to be . . . there is no such thing as a science of society unless its generalizations concerning past days yield enlightenment to our thought concerning days to come, and consequent guidance to our acts';[80] and manages to conclude the whole work with the hope that the pendulum must turn and mankind continue its course of adaptation to the social state.

But though adaptation as a necessary and universal mechanism of change does not work, being either false, or tautologous, or indeterminate, it does not follow that all the given instances of 'adaptation' are worthless, or that the characterization of the process of evolution as differentiation is thereby invalidated. For although differentiation in society does not appear to be determinate as an overall process—and certainly does not follow from Spencer's metaphysics (a word which can be taken here in its most literal sense)—it does remain true that what anyone would be likely to call 'social development' *is*, by and large, a process of differentiation. Spencer deserves high credit for seeing this and documenting it so amply, in the volumes of the *Sociology*. The definition he gives of a primitive society could be little improved on today: 'While rudimentary, a society is all warrior, all hunter, all hut-builder, all tool-maker: every part fulfils for itself all needs.'[81] The effects of differentiation of the economic from the political sphere, or of the moral from the religious, are traced out in great subtlety. The theme of differentiation as a key to understanding social change was taken up again very profitably (without acknowledgement to Spencer) by Smelser in the 1950s, and is prominent in the most fruitful contributions, notably Eisenstadt's, to the current debate on social evolution, stimulated very largely by problems of development in the Third World.[82]

Differentiation, too, suggested to Spencer an image for the whole evolutionary achievement. It was to be considered not as a *chain*, as in the old image of the great chain of being or, applied to society, as a series of sequential stages which all societies must pass through, but as a *tree*, since 'this conception of divergent and redivergent branches implies the conception of increasing multiformity or heterogeneity—one thing giving rise to many things'.[83] That this image holds true for societies as well as organisms, and for between them as well as for social groupings within them, is clear from the opening to the final volume of the *Sociology* where he says 'social progress is not linear but divergent and redivergent' and speaks of species and genera of societies.[84] It is important to emphasize this point since Spencer, like other nineteenth-century writers, has been accused of being a 'unilinearist'—that is, of holding that there is laid down one path, or series of stages through which all societies must pass in their development.[85] Unilinearism (which moderns pride themselves on not falling into) was associated with an ascending scale of moral preference, whether the subject was religion (where, with Tylor, the final stage was scientific deism) or family patterns (where, for Morgan, the final stage was Victorian monogamy). Indeed, if evolution is to be set to ethical purposes, a unilinear scale of moral preference is virtually unavoidable, and Spencer makes it quite clear that he has one. The embarrassment of a rigid unilinearism is that it is so easily disproved by events or by careful historical research. And so the image of the tree, while already an ingredient of Spencer's thought at a time when his view of the progressive, continuous attainment of moral perfection was strongest, was used to loosen the determinacy of the fixed forward march of history at a time when unilinearism was embarrassing. For it remained true that the various social 'species' could be ranked on a moral scale, and that the factors which were morally neutral and gave rise to the appearance of species, were less important than those which were arranged in stages. So Spencer practises unilinearism and disavows it, like many of his successors. Such a posture is forced on people whose ethical purposes require them to see history as a determinate whole but who wish to enjoy freedom of choice or are forced to recognize indeterminacy.

VI[86]

The data for the generalizations of social evolution are particular ethnographic and historical facts. Spencer cites an impressive number of source books, and employed specialists to compile tabulated lists of data in the *Descriptive Sociology*. In an obvious sense social evolution is easily the most time-oriented style of sociology, and many writers, Collingwood and Toulmin among them,[87] have seen the dominance of evolutionary modes of thought as a sign of the conquest of science by history. Up to a point this is doubtless so; but it must not blind us to a profoundly anti-historical bias in social evolution. For in one respect evolution was not so much a victory of the historical style of explanation as a denaturing, or rather naturalizing, of the proper study of society and history.

Spencer's attitude to history was mostly dismissive and to historians nearly always dismissive and contemptuous. At the time when his reading in biology was crystallizing the concept of differentiation, he wrote to his friend Edward Lott in these terms:

> My position, stated briefly, is that until you have got a true theory of humanity, you cannot interpret history; and when you have got a true theory of humanity *you do not want history*. You can draw no inference from the facts and alleged facts of history without your conceptions of human nature entering into that inference; and unless your conceptions of human nature are true your inference will be vicious.

> But if your conceptions of human nature be true, you need none of the inferences drawn from history for your guidance. If you ask how is one to get a true theory of humanity, I reply—study it in the facts you see around you and in the general laws of life. For myself, looking as I do at humanity as the highest result yet of the evolution of life on the earth, I prefer to take in the whole series of phenomena from the beginning as far as they are ascertainable. I too am a lover of history: but it is the history of the Cosmos as a whole.[88]

When Spencer wrote this, his uniformitarian convictions were still unshaken: that all history has one direction and all sections of it resemble all others, both in process and mechanism. But this belief is only seemingly empirically grounded, for the moralist in Spencer needs it as an ideal standard of development by which to pronounce abnormal or improper certain unwanted historical trends. Nature, in fact, is used to discipline history. Later, when preparing sociology, his attitude was somewhat more moderate:

> I take but little interest in what are called histories [he writes in recollection of a visit to Pompeii in 1868], but am interested only in Sociology, which stands related to these so-called histories much as a vast building stands related to the heaps of stones and bricks around it.[89]

It is of the nature of building that the builder need use only those stones and bricks which are useful for the realization of his blueprints, and may throw the rest away. The sight of the courtyard arrangement of the houses at Pompeii made Spencer think, not of the facts of Roman history, but of similar house structures among Pueblo Indians, of feudal castles, medieval inns, South African kraals, and ultimately of the pre-requisites of a military type of society.

Spencer's animus against history has complex origins. But as Kenneth Bock has shown,[90] his ambition for scientific history, alias the natural science of society, alias sociology, has a pedigree running back to Thucydides, whose programme to plumb beneath superficial appearances to basic causes, was inspired by Hippocratic medicine.[91] According to this scientific conception of history, science studies the realm of nature, which though it superficially includes all phenomena equally, basically only consists of certain fixed essences and potentials. Not all phenomena therefore are equally natural and the fit material for science, but only those which lead to this half-ridden (and only to be revealed in time) world of real nature. Now although Spencer stressed the variety of 'human nature' and even encompassed a great deal of it in his explanatory system, he still divided historical data into basic facts and incidental ones which could be discounted; and this distinction lay in the facts themselves, not in the selection of them by the thinker according to his theoretical purposes.

In *The Study of Sociology* Spencer takes the historians, J. A. Froude and Charles Kingsley in particular, to task and puts forward the first real theoretical justification for sociology in English. He criticizes their argument that social science is not possible because man has free will or, as Kingsley put it, a 'mysterious power of breaking the laws of his own being'.[92] For all historians make constant reference to human nature and as citizens show by their belief in legislation that implicitly they do accept 'that there is a natural sequence among social actions, and that as the sequence is natural results may be foreseen'.[93] Nor does it follow that since biographical facts about individuals may be quite unpredictable, aggregate facts about society should be. The obsessions of historians with political, military and court history, all with heavy patriotic bias, are related to what Spencer sees as their conservative attitudes, tied to the ruling classes, with outmoded philosophies, ignorant of the natural science which would undermine their position. In the cases of Kingsley, Seeley, J. R. Green and Stubbs, all professors at Oxford or Cambridge in the second half of the century, there was substance in these attacks.[94] They returned his scorn: Stubbs, while Canon of St. Paul's, solemnly burnt a volume of Spencer.[95]

The true position is that 'what Biography is to Anthropology [by which Spencer means 'Science of Man' or comparative human physiology and psychology], History is to Sociology—History, I mean, as commonly conceived'.[96] It is not surprising that historians should think determinate history, or sociology, is impossible because they make it out of inessential and unimportant elements. For psychology deals with the nature of man, and sociology with the nature of the social aggregate, and 'I say the *nature*, meaning of course, the essential traits, and not including the incidental'.[97] The old Thucydidean dichotomy between the superficial and essential is reaffirmed:

> . . . the denial of a Social Science has arisen from the confusing of two essentially-different classes of phenomena which societies present—the one class, almost ignored by historians, constituting the subject-matter of Social Science, and the other class, almost exclusively occupying them, admitting of scientific co-ordination in a very small degree, if at all.[98]

> [In both individuals and societies] there lie underneath the phenomena of conduct, not forming subject-matter for science, certain vital phenomena, which do form subject-matter for science. Just as in the man there are structures and functions which make possible the doings his biographer tells of, so in the nation the structures and functions its historian tells of; and in both cases it is with these structures and functions, in their origin, development and decline, that science is concerned.[99]

The studied ignorance of these 'vital phenomena', considers Spencer, results in a puerile style of historiography which has become predominant in those seminaries of the governing classes, the ancient universities. Of these he writes sarcastically:

> The supreme value of knowledge respecting the genealogies of kings, and the fates of dynasties, and the quarrels of courts, is beyond question. Whether or not the plot for the murder of Amy Robsart was contrived by Leicester himself, with Queen Elizabeth as an accomplice; and whether or not the account of the Gowrie conspiracy, as given by King James, was true, are obviously doubts to be decided before there can be formed any rational conclusions respecting the development of our political institutions.[100]

> . . . the ordinary historian . . . thinking of little else but the doings of kings, court-intrigues, international quarrels, victories and defeats, concerning all which no definite forecasts are possible, asserts there is no social science: overlooking the mutually dependent structures which have been quietly unfolding while the transactions he writes about have been taking place.[101]

It cannot be denied that Spencer's criticisms of the content of historiography were salutary and well-deserved, or that his definition of the object of sociology—the 'order among those structural and functional changes which societies pass through'[102]—is as good now as when he wrote it. History as practised today is far more 'sociological' in Spencer's sense, and seems to be becoming more so. At least up to a point we tend to think important those sorts of things that Spencer did. But in successfully establishing sociology Spencer also set it on an anti-historical course that can in the end only be self-defeating.

The trouble initially lay in the unexceptionable assertion that human behaviour is subject to law and hence material for science. This began as the simple conviction of a uniformitarian, and led directly to a search for laws. But the raw material is recalcitrant. One may then either (*a*) decide that human behaviour is not law-governed after all, at least in the sense in which organic life is (out of the question for Spencer); or (*b*) one may divide the phenomena into essential and incidental, not allow any possible counter-evidence to the thesis to be considered as essential, thus depriving exceptions to established substantive laws of full ontological status and so virtually rendering the thesis tautological; or (*c*) one may take the thesis as empirical but irrefutable by claiming it as axiomatic to rational thought. The third option is assumed by today's social science methodology. It bids us look for determinate relations between things without hinting what form any laws might or must take. Whereas the second option rests confidently on the knowledge of determinate laws, the third assures us that we must and do remain very largely in ignorance of determinate relationships.

Spencer takes the second option. He not only believes human actions are subject to law, but that history as a whole is subject to a law of development, which is the gratuitous assumption of a particular substantive law. Consequently one can only derive laws of change by looking at evolution over long periods of time:

> In society living, growing, changing, every new factor becomes a permanent force: modifying more or less the direction of movement determined by the aggregate of forces. Never simple and direct, but, by the co-operation of so many causes, made irregular, involved and always rhythmical, the course of social change cannot be judged of in its general direction by inspecting any small portion of it. . . . You must compare positions at great distances from one another in time, before you can tell rightly whither things are tending.[103]

Since these gradual structural and evolutionary changes are the real stuff of science, the real material for laws, what doesn't fit the evolutionary trend must be dismissed as incidental. A dangerous distinction is set up between events, the particular doings of men, on the one hand, and the stuff of social change, on the other, to which they are epiphenomenal. The evolution of social structures and functions thus becomes 'reified'—which was just what Spencer the moralist needed, since 'law' was to be as much an injunction as an explanatory generalization. The distinction is untenable, however, because events are the primary evidence for establishing what institutions and social structure are. Where is it believed that a uniform evolutionary law runs through history, and has been determined, detailed data of all kinds are dispensable: for either they fit the law, in which case they are superfluous, or they do not, in which case they are incidental. Either way, as Spencer put it, '*you do not want history*': sociology is no sooner begun than it is completed. So in 1897, quite unrattled by contrary political developments, he wrote to the Director of the newly founded London School of Economics:

> . . . through the prospectus you send me there obviously runs the idea that political science is to be based upon an exhaustive accumulation of details of all orders, derived from all sources—parliamentary papers, reports of commissions, and all the details of administration from various countries and colonies. I hold, contrariwise, that political science is smothered in such a mass of details, the data for true conclusions being relatively broad and accessible.[104]

It is not surprising that he concluded that the L.S.E. would be 'an appliance not for the diffusion of political *science* but for the diffusion of political *quackery*'. This stubborn know-nothingism is the hardest of Spencer's foibles to forgive.

The distinction between essential and incidental is closely related to one between general and particular, which from Spencer's time to our own has bedevilled sociological theory. A common notion is that history concerns the particular and sociology the general—a distinction that has commended itself to many historians and sociologists, but one that is not borne out by their practice. In history, as Spencer observed, all sorts of general categories, covering laws, assumptions about likely behaviour and so forth, are used and by use roughly tested. In sociology (if that is defined as the explanation of social behaviour) the real object is not the creation of the most sweeping theories—and the current distinction between 'theorists' and 'empiricists' is quite absurd and harmful—but the explanation of (necessarily particular) instances of behaviour. We don't want theories *qua* generalizations but *qua* explanations of the particular. *That* is the touchstone of truth; and if so, there should be no fundamental distinction between sociology and history. 'But sociology is a science', it will be chorussed with Spencer, 'What about prediction?' But prediction is not a matter of mechanically applying some supposedly universally-true equation. Apart from the intricate hanging-together of unique, historically-unrepeatable variables which is how sociological situations usually are, the application of a general theory always involves identifying it in the particular situation, to establish it if it is relevant at all. For we can never have any automatic guarantee that anything will ever be repeated. This would only be the case if we were prepared to say, with Spencer, that the end is contained in the beginning of history, that there is a discoverable organic pattern, or cosmic programme, called evolution. The corollary would be that the purpose of social science would be not partial and limited prediction in order to control, but knowledge in order to submit intelligently to what must be, a secular parallel to the Calvinist's humble intent to know God's providential Will.

Spencer's conception of the sociologist's task is, as it should be, closely related to his conception of social evolution. Despite being 'very sensitive on the point of being supposed to teach an enervating fatalism'[105] Spencer had no real sense of either the historical actor, or the sociologist, intervening or participating in the flow of events. For him the pattern of evolution was what it was, by him revealed for the first time in its true nature. It was not to be bent. There was little leeway for any 'extra-evolutionary' action. He argued against applied sociology because it could not change things:

> A true theory of social progress is not a cause of movement but simply oil to the movement—serves simply to remove friction. The force producing the movement is the aggregate of men's instincts and sentiments, and these are not to be changed by a theory.[106]

This helpless utterance does not follow from a belief in scientific determinism as such, but from believing that he had discovered actual substantive determinate laws covering in one sweep the whole of history. The price of that hubris is indeed fatalism.

The belief in the incidentality of historical actors to the evolutionary process led Spencer, in his analysis of social change, to speak in the impersonal terms of mechanism and function rather than in terms of motive and cause. It is only when explaining the very beginning of superorganic evolution that Spencer really employs causes and origins. Once social evolution is off the ground, and unsocial men are gradually getting more adapted to the social state, causal explanations give place to functional ones. It is ironic that Spencer only attempted a historical form of explanation, as in his account of the beginnings of primitive religion, when the results had to be conjectural and worthless because of the absence of any direct evidence! This section of the *Sociology* is right at the beginning, strangely separated from his evolutionary account of institutions by that part which deals of social evolution and the organic analogy in general terms.[107] Spencer's virtual creation of functionalism (which I shall discuss in the next chapter) has been of enormous importance and benefit in sociology; but it did lead him to attribute the occurrence of things not to their creator's intentions but to their function—what they contribute to adaptation to the environment. This means virtually that they happen because the evolutionary scheme as a whole requires that they should happen. Functionalist language, as became clearer after Spencer's death, is highly suited to the delineation of the interconnexions and feed-backs of multiple factors in any existing social situation; but as soon as it is divorced from evolution of Spencer's type, it provides us with no means of explaining change by reference to its agents, men evaluating and acting.

Some change, it is true, does happen without men either willing it or being aware of it except as *faits accomplis* (the economic history of the classical world is full of examples), and the unintended consequence of deliberate actions ('latent functions', in the patch-work terminology of modern functionalism) are extremely significant, as Spencer reiterates. But, as Max Weber spelled out for us, social action, *qua* the doings of men, only becomes meaningful and specially comprehensible to us when it is made to make sense in terms of the purposes of its agents. In the first instance, it is these, rather than its consequences for adaptation, which provide the explanation of behaviour, and so must be central to sociology. The permanent debts which we owe to Spencer for the theory of evolution are considerable, but in this vital respect it must be judged a failure.

7: The Organic Analogy

I

Evolution, as Professor Nisbet has observed, is the portrayal of history as growth. That this is an analogy, a figurative way of speaking, is clearer in the accompanying portrayal of society as an organism. The early sociologists, like all men engaged in novel activity, edged forward to new topics with instruments and assumptions with which they were already familiar; and so it is as important to probe the similes, metaphors, imagery and analogies in which they tried to convey their insights as it is to look at their causal explanations and predictions. Though they tried to be explicit and systematic in their use of what we now call models, they were prone to mix their metaphors, to switch from one image to another, and to use different assumptions in their concrete analysis from those they elaborated in their self-conscious methodologies. The two main sources of imagery are the living, especially the human body and the instrument or machine, the inert creation of a living intelligence. The organic analogy is probably as old as social thought itself, but for Spencer it meant two things: the rejection of a rival analogy, the machine, to the support of *laissez-faire*, and an emphasis on the interdependence of parts, to the creation of functionalism.

It is sometimes suggested that metaphors and models are things that any science can and should come to do without.[2] Certainly it is the case that they are much less prevalent in areas where the phenomena are well understood and where there is an agreed focus of interest. Here it is possible to say confidently 'everything is what it is, and not another thing', and to regard the prevalent classifications as expressing the nature of things. But analogy, or the setting alongside of objects or terms which differ in some respects and are alike in some others, will be inevitable until our knowledge of the construction and intrinsic classification of nature is finally complete. But it will always be unavoidable where the phenomena are not in themselves sufficiently discretely grouped for there to be one unambiguous system of classification, and where one set of names and definitions will not suffice for anything we may want to say about them. Such is the case with the subject matter of the social sciences; and it permits another reason for the permanency of metaphor and analogy—the fact that classifications cross-cut because they may depend, not merely upon the characteristics of things in themselves, but upon how men may choose to regard them, *quite legitimately*, in terms of their purposes. One man's meat is another man's poison, so to speak, or society is one man's organism and another man's machine. One feature of the positivist tradition is to deny the 'man-given' character of classification, and hence to discredit any metaphor or analogy at all. This was Spencer's view, and Spencer's own use of metaphors might be criticized on the same grounds.[3] But, I shall suggest, Spencer's metaphors may be defended on grounds that he should have repudiated.

Argument about the proper and the improper uses of analogy means examining, in any particular case, whether the claimed similarities really are such.[4] For analogies are constantly used, not simply to expound an unknown and complex relationship by means of a known and simple one, or else to assert an actual identity of some kind beneath superficially different external features (at which point the analogue is replaced by an abstract model), but to invite others to regard some aspects of actuality otherwise. This persuasive use of analogy plays on everyone's need to see likenesses between things, and thus to order the world's apparent chaos; and a small degree of likeness is expected to be the token of a larger degree of it. But this use of analogy is often a symptom of other decisive differences between the things; for if the likeness or identity were uppermost in people's minds (leading perhaps to a common designation), there would be no need for an analogical appeal to be made.

The perpetually shifting language of social theory is especially liable to this. Consider one of the most ancient and popular analogies, that between the state, its sovereign and his subjects, on the one hand, and the family, its paterfamilias and his children, on the other. In societies with a segmentary lineage system, like the

Tiv and the Luo, or the archaic Greece which Aristotle could look back to, there was little, if any distinction between these two sets of terms; the language of kinship was the language of politics; and the minimal lineage was the smallest sub-unit of, and essentially the same in nature as, the total society.[5] The heyday of the analogy between the state and the family came in the sixteenth and seventeenth centuries, and culminated in Sir Robert Filmer's conservative treatise *Patriarcha*, published at a time when the king was being regarded progressively less and less like a father.[6] In interpreting Filmer, one may perhaps note that society was much more dominated by the family than it is now,[7] and regard the analogy as needed to convey 'the idea of two free wills inescapably linked together', the king with the commonwealth as the father with his family. But Filmer wanted to change people's minds: to get people who weren't doing so already to love and obey the king as if he was their father, for *really* he was. The very need for the analogy testifies to the unfamilylike character of society.

The additional danger (or potential) in the use of analogies is that the terms can easily be reversed and worked the other way. Whereas most Victorian social theorists insisted that the family was very unlike the state,[8] and perhaps merely hoped that the state might, or said that it should, resemble the family, Freud asserted that the family, so long sentimentalized as a haven from society, was in fact like the industrial state—relations within it were marked by competition, domination, subordination, authority and manipulation.[9] Since Freud does not see the peculiar nature of the family as a consequence of industrial society, the analogy only serves to elucidate a truth (and, perhaps, enabled Freud to recognize that truth).

But it is harder to assess Spencer's organic analogy. It is used to advocate moral viewpoints, and to approach an object of study which stands at a considerable 'cognitive distance' and to illuminate an underlying structure of greater simplicity. There are paradoxes too. The organic analogy is widely considered to imply collectivist political theory and holistic methods of analysis, while its rival, the mechanistic analogy, sustains individualism and atomism. Raymond Williams' judgment that 'it is . . . perhaps one of the most important facts about English social thinking in the nineteenth century that there grew up, in opposition to a *laissez-faire* society, this organic conception, stressing interrelation and interdependence' is echoed by many sociologists.[10] What are we to make of Spencer, then, who was both the extremest *laissez-faire* liberal, and the most systematic exponent of the organic analogy? We must start by noting what images and metaphors are used to what effect, leaving till later the possibly meaningless question of whether Spencer was 'fundamentally' an organicist and holist rather than a mechanicist and individualist.

It is helpful first to ask if the implications of organism and mechanism are really as obvious as they seem to those who use them. The word 'organic' itself suggests by its etymology and history, how many cross-references may be made between living things and machines.[11] One must note too that not only does the analogue of the living body commend whatever is compared to it, but that the very word 'organic' carries its own cachet. Its promiscuous application, with a very low cognitive content, by such early critics of industrialism as Carlyle and Ruskin, and by such contemporary writers as Leavis and Mumford, has left it barely more than a commendatory noise, a word incapable of critical use. The counter-word is 'mechanical'. Yet the word *organon* itself originally meant, if not quite machine, then tool or instrument, intended for uses devised by an external mind, and only later applied to bodily organs, with its cognate *organismos* meaning 'a living thing'. At the same time the Greeks took a generally 'organismic' or vitalist view of the universe, explaining its motion and organization by reference to its immanent soul.[12] The Greeks lacked any conception of a personalized Creator God, which is a prerequisite of the Renaissance view, that the universe is inert, God's machine, the work of that Invisible Hand. So any theory of the 'organic' character of society has to grapple with the fact that the analogue itself was itself generally likened to the rival analogue, the machine, one stage further back.

The clearest difference between organisms and machines is that the former are the result of growth, and can still grow, whereas the latter are not. But what follows from this about society, especially during a period of rapid and drastic social change? If society is organic, our attention might be directed to those features of social change which were as unintended by anyone as the effects of physical growth—and this would be valuable since anyone's first impulse is to look at motives and intended consequences. But if emphasized strongly, it might suggest that since the course of change was fairly unplannable, it did not make sense for us to form large-scale social goals and to try to bring them about. And if, in addition, the natural processes to which social processes were thus assimilated, were seen as themselves the working out of immanent principles of growth, men could stop worrying about things, since the outcome of social growth would as little need to be interfered with as the maturation of an embryo. For it is possible to make the point about the spontaneous or automatic character of society either by organic/immanentist metaphors or by mechanistic/transcendental ones. As a counterpart to natural growth, and with the same effect, Spencer employs the ideas of homeostasis or equilibrium—native to mechanics and naturalized in political economy.[13] One may mix one's metaphors as much as one likes, since different analogues may resemble the subject in different ways. The charge of inconsistency can only stick when one has moved from using analogies to point up particular features to elaborating an abstract model to link them together. What is intended by likening the 'self-acting' (or as we should say, automatic) character alike of the economy,[14] of modern machines, and of the lower physcial functions of the body, is clear enough.

The organic analogy for society has often seemed to be pre-empted by political conservatives, the direct opponents of liberals like Spencer.[15] They mean that since a society is essentially the product of natural growth any social arrangements that are suddenly created are less proper than those of long standing. It is hard to see much of cognitive, as distinct from evaluative, significance in this argument. It might be combined with organicism of Spencer's type (as it was by Sumner for example); but it is an argument, not against government intervention, but against any sort of rapid social change. Usually it is combined with the oldest and naivest of organic arguments, that as men have brains, societies must have governments to tell the other organs of society what to do.

Radicals and interventionists may agree with the conservatives in their moral response to capitalist industrialism, but they share the liberals' view that to stress society's growth inhibits *planned* change. If society is a mechanism, however, it can, and should, only express the purposes of its human creators. Whereas a social organicist might present human purposes as the product of a growth process, a necessary part of the changing entity, but not a significant independent variable, a mechanicist can see them as contingent, the extra-social starting-point of society-building, only open to be criticized on the grounds of feasibility. Bentham detested the organic analogy;[16] and his Fabian and socialist successors show by their phrase 'social engineering' (piecemeal or otherwise) their technocratic leanings. The same imagery of blueprints and building materials is much beloved by the modernizing élites of developing countries today.[17]

Here we see that the core difference between these rival conceptions of society is just the same as that between the immanent and transcendental solutions to the problem of God's relation to the cosmos: namely, is mind to be regarded as within, as part of, as acted upon, or as outside, other than, and acting upon, the social structure. The dilemma, and the two analogies, are not fated to be superseded in time by a *true* model which will better express how society really is, as Stark and Buckley suggest. We will, hopefully, gradually acquire better models for society (or rather for different societies); but the organic/mechanical dilemma will continue to be with us because it expresses, not *merely* the necessary nature of things (and that, it is agreed, deficiently), but a contingent attitude towards society. Both conceptions are true, or rather appropriate, in their context. Spencer of course wanted to suggest, by means of the organic analogy, that a proper observer's attitude was fixed by the character of the subject-matter. If, as most people do at some time and as governments have to do, we think and act as reformers and manipulators of society, the mechanistic analogy is inescapable; yet informed action requires prior social analysis in which the actor must see himself and others, their purposes and their situations, as the product of a process which may justly be likened to growth in that the determining forces are independent of his will. The practice of sociology in a social context will continue to involve both.

In its dynamic aspect the analogy is used loosely, to establish a half-truth about social process. Metaphor gives way to a rudimentary model, however, to which the strictures of Deutsch and Buckley do apply, when the organic analogy is used statically, as an instrument for the perception of society as it is in itself. But here too the implications of organism and mechanism become merged. Consider Ure, extolling and describing 'The Factory System':

This title, in its strictest sense, involves the idea of a vast automaton composed of various mechanical and intellectual organs, acting in uninterrupted concert for the production of a common effect, all of them being subordinated to a self-regulated moving force. [The factory-system is defined as] the distribution of the different members of the apparatus into one co-operative body, in impelling each organ with its appropriate delicacy and speed, and, above all, in training human beings to . . . identify themselves with the unvarying regularity of the complex automaton.[18]

So far the mechanical metaphors are predominant. But later Ure says there are three principles of manufacture or, 'organic systems, the mechanical, the moral and the commercial, which may not ineptly be compared to the muscular, the nervous and the sanguiferous systems of an animal'.[19] The three organs are the operatives, the masters and the state (i.e. the London money market and the investors), and 'three powers concur to their vitality'—labour to move, science to direct, and capital to sustain. When the whole are in harmony, they form a body qualified to discharge its manifold functions by an intrinsic self-governing agency like those of organic life. Government regulation of industry is wrong, Ure concludes, since 'like love, its workings must be free as air . . . [and it] has the same principles of vigorous growth as the mountain pine'.[20]

Systematic arrangement and co-ordination of specialized parts into a unified whole—the same may be seen in both animals and complex machines. Both *organism* (which usually refers to single living things) and *organization* (which refers to inanimate, collective, abstract things) carry this general meaning. The division of labour can be seen in both, and so it provides, for Spencer and for others, a bridge between the analogues. But the form of social criticism will still tend to vary. If the division of labour is seen mechanistically, it will have to be criticized for failing to fulfil the manufacturer's purposes; if organically, it will be criticized as pathological in terms of general natural principles.

Much social controversy in the nineteenth century did not concern the appropriate analogy for society but rather whether existing society fitted the organic analogy. For writers like Kingsley and Carlyle, whose views were often such as Spencer used *his* organic analogy against, were quite as likely as Spencer to damn measures they disapproved of as mere 'machinery'.[21] When the critics of industrialism opposed Spencer's ideals in the name of an *organic* society what was at stake was a theory of social integration. The conservatives contrasted what they took to be traditional society, its ranks or estates each with their rights and duties, status and function, united by a sense of mutual obligation and responsibility and by a shared religion, with the discordant, conflict-ridden, selfish, utilitarian society of their own day, its classes animated only by brutish self-interest, bound together by compulsion and by what Carlyle christened the 'cash-nexus'.[22] This critique was taken over by radicals, whether revolutionary socialists like Marx or Christian Socialists like Charles Kingsley, whose *Alton Locke* was described by one liberal reviewer as 'the usual jumble between the fourteenth century and the nineteenth'.[23] The political economists' claim that under the unregulated liberal economy private selfishness naturally led to public benefit seemed an obvious and impudent lie. If society was to be 'organic' once more, there would need to be moral bonds and an active moral agency to uphold them. The bodies proposed, from Hegel's bureaucracy to Coleridge's 'clerisy' or Comte's Church of Humanity, were in intention universal institutions, above class and special interests. In their opinion of these, radicals and liberals tended to converge: Marx said that in medieval society they had merely masked class-interest and would continue to do so as long as there were classes, and Spencer that industrial society *was* organic in a more fundamental way than medieval society had ever been, and that such bodies could not make it more so.

Spencer's liberal view (roughly, that all societies are organic, but that industrial society is the most), must now be considered in detail.

II

It was not his reading of K. E. von Baer and other continental biologists which drew Spencer to his use of organic analogies, though it greatly sharpened his conceptions. Spencer thought that Coleridge's essay on the idea of life might have been influential, but the natural theology and the vitalism of Erasmus Darwin and other evolutionists in his intellectual background clearly inclined him to speak about nature and society with a single vocabulary. His use of organic metaphors in *Social Statics* is unsystematic and casual; nor does it exclude other metaphors. He can speak in terms drawn from physics, and go on: 'changing the illustration and regarding society as an organism . . .'[24] The following seems intended simply as a striking illustration:

> In an animal organism the soft parts determine the forms of the hard ones; and it is equally true that in the social organism the seemingly fixed framework of laws and institutions is moulded by the seemingly forceless thing—character. Social arrangements are the bones to that body, of which the national morality is the life.[25]

A little later the same conclusion is supported by a simile from engineering: an institution is like a building in that it depends on 'the strength of the materials' rather than on 'the ingenuity of its design'.[26] Spencer can hardly have intended this analogy to be taken very far, for he always scorned the 'futile contrivances of man' by the side of 'the admirable silent-working mechanisms of nature'.[27] But the mechanical images were absorbed into the organic analogy, which was then used against 'social engineering' of any kind.

Spencer's essays of the 1850s, whether political and moralistic like 'Representative Government' (1857) or 'Over-Legislation' (1853), or scientific and analytic like 'A Theory of Population' (1852), 'Manners and Fashion' (1854) and 'Progress, its Law and Cause '(1857), make continual reference to 'the social organism', and the essay of that name (1860), produced about the time when Spencer was working out his general scheme for *The System of Synthetic Philosophy*, unfolds the analogy in detail. Revised and more subtle versions appear in *The Study of Sociology* (1873), and in Part 2 of *The Principles of Sociology* (1876); and the leading concepts of *structure* and *function* are used throughout the subsequent empirical analysis.

The main theme of 'The Social Organism', is that 'society is a growth and not a manufacture'.[28] In Spencer's judgment this truth was coming more and more to displace the traditional view that social organization is the result of Divine Providence, working as 'a skilled mechanic', or as a 'master builder', 'artificer', or 'strategist'.[29] This basic motif of natural theology is finally discredited by pointing to its congruity with primitive cosmological ideas. Cognate views—that society is the artefact of lawgivers, great men, or legislatures—are also rejected. Instead, he insists, the main features of social organization 'are neither supernatural, nor are determined by the wills of individual men . . . but are consequent on general natural causes'. It is impossible for any individual to step outside the ever-growing social organism; individuals may be said to be 'imbedded' in the social structure.[30] 'The Great Man Theory of History', then upheld by Kingsley and especially Carlyle, received knocks at Spencer's hands from which it has hardly recovered. The 'biographical view of affairs', says Spencer, is allied to a taste for common gossip, and 'if you want roughly to estimate anyone's mental calibre, you cannot do it better than by observing the ratio of generalities to personalities in his talk'.[31] Generally, the will of a 'great man', like a law or statute, is only effective when it really is not needed—when it expresses a state of the popular character. In fact social systems arise 'under the pressure of human wants and activities'; for 'the true sources [of legislative enactments] lie deeper than the acts of legislators'.[32] But is this an argument against having legislators at all, or merely against historians taking them to be an important independent variable in history? Spencer evidently intends both, but his argument is only valid for the latter.

Sometimes Spencer emphasizes the impotence of politicians to affect society, sometimes the damage they may do. In addition he says that the social organism is so complicated anyway that they cannot know how to effect their wishes:

> Wonderfully constructed as it is—mutually dependent as are its members for the satisfaction of their wants—affected as each unit of it is by his fellows, not only as to his safety and prosperity, but in his health, his temper, his culture; the social organism cannot be dealt with in any one part, without all other parts being influenced in ways that cannot be foreseen.[33]

> That connexions among social phenomena should be so little understood need not surprise us if we note the ideas which prevail respecting the connexions among much simpler phenomena. . . . How abundant are the proofs that human nature is difficult to manipulate; that methods apparently the most rational disappoint expectations; and that the best results frequently result from what common sense thinks unpractical. . . . Is it not probable that as in Biology so in Sociology,

the accumulation of more facts, the more critical comparison of them, and the drawing of conclusions on scientific methods, will be accompanied by increasing doubt about the benefits to be secured, and increasing fear of the mischiefs to be worked? Is it not probable that what in the individual organism is improperly, though conveniently called the *vis medicatrix naturae*, may be found to have its analogue in the social organism?[34]

My general purpose . . . has been that of showing how utterly beyond the conceptions of common-sense . . . are the workings out of sociological processes . . . such that even those who have carried out to the utmost 'the scientific use of the imagination' would never have anticipated them. . . . My more special purpose has been that of showing how marvellous are the results indirectly and unintentionally achieved by the co-operation of men who are severally pursuing their private ends.[35]

This Smithian picture of the self-regulating economy does not logically entail the necessary ignorance of complex causes and effects which is for Spencer the proximate justification of *laissez-faire*.[36] The British government, he goes on, familiar with the classics but ignorant of social science, [37] cannot know 'the mutual dependence of the many functions which taken together make up the social life' but yet, by telling people what to believe by means of the State Church, by relieving distress caused by improvidence, by controlling books in state-schools, and by censoring literature, 'they aim to control and direct the entire national life. . . . If some social process does not seem to them to be going on fast enough, they stimulate it; where the growth is not in the mode or the direction which they think most desirable, they alter it; and so they seek to realize some undefined ideal community.'[38]

This normative role of the organic analogy, to promote *laissez-faire* in Spencer's own society, makes it hard for it to be applied to earlier societies in which lawgivers and controlling governments were much in evidence. Can one argue that the Solon- and Lycurgus-figures of the past were either superfluous or harmful in their own day, as they would be, if Carlyle had his way, in the present? Spencer wants the future to differ from the past, but a naturalistic argument expressing what seem to be constant truths of human society inhibits the explanation of variation. In fact he has two distinct societal models, made explicit in the militant/industrial distinction. There are (*a*) societies where the laws *express* the natures of citizens and consequently are virtually superfluous—which is, in fact, stated as a general proposition; and (*b*) societies in which laws and great men play an exactly opposite role, serving not to express the social nature but to *evoke* it because it is of itself lacking—and here, interventionary actions are normal and, apparently, not to be taken as infringements of the organic character of society. Spencer shifts from maintaining that all societies are alike in this respect, and only differ in that the present generation is coming to realize their eternal nature, to maintaining that they differ in respect of the role played by law and political coercion; or rather, that though all societies may be organic, industrial society is the most so.

The militant/industrial dichotomy is assumed too in an implicit classification of actions into those which infringe the 'society is an organism (*qua* growth)' thesis, and those which do not. Some, such as the actions of tradesmen making contracts, buyers and sellers of labour and goods, technical innovators, middlemen, artisans, organizers of voluntary associations of all kinds, linked together in very complicated ways, *are* the social organism growing; while others, such as the actions of national legislators, political rulers and overall social improvers like Sir Edwin Chadwick, are the token of an attempt to treat society as if it were not an organism but an artefact. The classification is quite clear, but not its rationale. For 'growth' is not defined in the metaphorical context of society, merely contrasted with another, rejected, analogue, 'manufacture'. There is no clear indication of where the line is to be drawn between 'growth-actions' and 'manufacture-actions'.

Spencer does not seem to notice that, if what he says about the superfluity of lawgivers is true, his own preachings must be superfluous also. His ethical purposes would have been better served by a non-evolutionary theory of the 'health' or 'sickness' of societies which would not have involved him in the logical circularities of evolutionary necessitarianism.[39] But then he would not have been able to explain social differences. As it has turned out, the chief use of the organic analogy has not been in social ethics, where it means all things to all men, nor in the explanation of social change. It has produced, not a theory of society, but a language of social analysis, useful in comparison because so unspecific.

III

In his essay of 1860 Spencer's eiconic imagination seems to have been struck by the total overall vision of society as an organism. Different aspects of the analogy are closely intermingled in his account, though he does attempt to list the similarities and differences. That the basic concept of 'growth' has serious ambiguities he did not seem to notice; or perhaps, because these ambiguities are essential to his persuasive use of the analogy, he ignored them. The similarities are: (*a*) both commence as small aggregates and increase in mass; (*b*) both develop a more complex structure as they grow; (*c*) in both, as they grow, the functionally distinct parts get more interdependent; and (*d*) the life of both is independent of, and longer than, the life of any of their units. The differences, of which only the fourth, with its awkward implications, so often pointed out, for *laissez-faire*, is ever made use of by Spencer, are: (*a*) that societies have no external forms; (*b*) that the units of societies are not contiguous with one another in a mass; (*c*) that the units of the social organism are spatially mobile; and (*d*) that all the units of a society are endowed with consciousness, but only one part of an organism.[40]

There is a certain incompatibility, if not inconsistency, between Spencer's awareness of the proper logical bounds of the comparison, and the evident pleasure he took in picturesque and striking parallels. It is helpful, and not at all tendentious, to compare the undifferentiated and fragmented social structure of Bushmen to the protozoa, or those peoples who break off segments when they become too large for their territory with the hydra. The point of comparing the ruling class, the trading or distributive classes, and the masses, to the mucous, vascular and serous systems of the liver-fluke is less clear. But dubious biology is added to pedestrian sociology when the coalescence of the Anglo-Saxon kingdoms into England is likened to the formation of crustaceans. (Spencer had the odd theory that insects and crustaceans were composite animals, their segments representing independent units joined together.) And when he writes, 'Blood vessels acquire distinct walls; roads are fenced and gravelled';[41] or describes two French engineering *Écoles* as 'a double gland . . . to secrete engineering faculty for public use',[42] the effect is merely ridiculous. But beneath the grotesque resemblances there may lurk a common structural feature which has only been fully worked out since Spencer's death. Some critics of Spencer have laughed at the parallels he drew between 'internuncial agencies' in animals and societies;[43] but this is just the theme which is central to cybernetics and modern systems theory, the most recent major source of imagery for sociology.

In soberer mood Spencer states that a society is like an organism, rather than an inorganic body, because of 'the parallelism of principle in the arrangement of components'.[44] The proper use of the analogy involves 'ignoring the variable outer components and relations, and looking for the invariable inner components and relations', in order to perceive 'likeness between things which externally are quite unlike—perhaps so utterly unlike that, by an unanalytical intelligence, they cannot be conceived to have any resemblance whatever'.[45] Years later, in the *Autobiography*, Spencer defended his use of the analogy as follows:

> [There must be] an analytical process of stripping off whatever the two things had not in common. And then, when the nakedness of the essential relations in each permitted comparison of them, it became manifest that the fundamental analogy was determined by the operation of the same cause in each: this cause being the mutual dependence of parts.[46]

The method stated here is hard to fault. He offers an 'emphatic repudiation of the belief that there is any special analogy between the social organism and the human organism', and concludes:

> Though, in foregoing chapters, comparisons of social structures and functions to structures and functions in the human body, have in many cases been made, they have been made only because structures and functions in the human body furnish the most familiar illustrations of structures and functions in general. . . . Community in the fundamental principles of organization is thus the only community asserted.[47]

I think it is fair to say that Spencer was trying to pass from the material model, the organism, a structure of physical processes, to the formal model, a set of symbols and the rules governing their use.[48] His search for what he called 'the general law of organization' was the first step on the path to what is now called general systems theory.[49] What followed from the abstract model of organization could then be empirically verified, with a triumphant flourish as he loved to do. (Appropriately, he was also prepared to use the social analogy in elucidating organic structures in biology.[50])

But in practice he was not satisfied with the austerities of formal model-building. It is clear, despite his disclaimers, that he wanted to establish the analogy in its own right since ethical and political conclusions depended on it. There was too, I think, a pure metaphysical delight in attempting to go *behind* the structural parallels to the arcane natural laws expounded in *First Principles*. But what Medawar says of complementarities like male/female, positive/negative, etc., also applies to the basic notion of co-ordinated structure which is at the bottom of the organic analogy: 'the similarity between them is not the taxonomic key to some other deeper affinity, and our recognizing its existence marks the end, not the inauguration of a train of thought'.[51] From the viewpoint of sociology Spencer's inclination to cosmogony is harmless; not so his habit of stepping beyond his avowed principles for the use of analogy, to infer things from other, unlike, aspects of the analogue.

Spencer described the concrete internal structure of societies in two different ways, which he is not entirely successful in uniting. The first is twofold, and is based on a particularly favoured analogue, the coelenterata. The lowest coelenterata are composed of an ectoderm 'directly exposed to the surrounding medium with its inhabitants', concerned with catching food and warding off enemies, and an endoderm, concerned with digestion and sustentation.[52] Likewise in societies there develops a distinction between rulers and ruled, the political and the economic, the centrally co-ordinated and the automatic. Significantly this is the model he enlarged upon when he wants to make his point against state intervention, as in the essay 'Specialized Administration'. It is closely related to the militant/industrial dichotomy. Internal, industrial functions, he argues, require automatic decentralized control, while external functions need the opposite. Societies are divided into those in which the external or the internal system predominates.[53] Industrial society, to be true to the structure revealed by analogy, cannot therefore have a strong central control. (Here Spencer was opposing that persuasive version of the organic analogy which said that since the most complex animals had the largest brains, so the most complex societies needed the most active governments.)

In the *Principles of Sociology* the social structure is seen in terms of three systems—the sustaining or industrial system, the distributing system (communications and commerce), and the regulating or political system, all compared at great length to their organismic analogues.[54] It must be said there is little of scientific value in all the detailed correspondences. The three-organ scheme is similar to Ure's in *The Philosophy of Manufactures* but differs in detail, and it is not always clear why one function is put in one system rather than another. The dichotomous model, and the alleged growing ascendency of the internal and automatic over the external and deliberate, leads Spencer to argue for a progressive decline in the important of the regulating system, or rather for the diffuse performance of regulative functions. Thus, arguing in the chapter on the regulating system that industrial organization becomes independent of state control, he says that there grows up another regulating system to adjust functions to needs—the banking and credit systems (= the vacso-motor system in the individual): 'volition . . . cannot alter these local supplies of blood; and legislation . . . ceasing to make the mischievous perturbations it once did in the movement of capital, now leaves it almost entirely alone'.[55] Spencer's argument would have been more persuasive here, if, instead of taking *structure* as his key-concept and saying that some structures disappear or become redundant, he had concentrated on function and developed the idea that the functional requisites of a society may be fulfilled by other means.

Because sociology is so permanently indebted to Spencer for the regular use of such concepts as *system*, *equilibrium*, *institution* and above all *structure* and *function*, some significant differences in his use of them are liable to be overlooked. This is particularly so with *structure* and *function*, which he discussed at especial length and really are the warp and weft of his evolutionary analysis of institutions. 'Order among those structural and functional changes which societies pass through' is what sociology is about.[56] As societies/organisms grow there is an 'increase in structure' by differentiation, and parallel with it, a differentiation of function.[57] These differentiated actions are called 'functions', because evolution does not merely bring about differences, but reciprocally acting differences, each one making the others possible in endless circular causation: 'the changed actions of the parts are mutually dependent'.[58] This is the main respect in which speaking about function is not a mere rephrasing of what he has had to say about structure:

> If organization consists in such a construction of the whole that its parts can carry on mutually dependent actions, then in proportion as organization is high there must go a dependence of each part upon the rest so great that separation is fatal; and conversely.[59]

The word *function* is much less problematic than *structure*, to which, the above remarks notwithstanding, Spencer usually allots priority. Function is unproblematic because, despite its use in mathematical, as well as biological or sociological contexts, it is not metaphorical. A function is simply what something does: 'the function of A' is what A does: 'A's function for B' is what A does for B, or the effect which A has on B. This underlies all its uses, and Spencer's earliest use of it is quite unforced: 'the sentiment of justice is nothing but a sympathetic affection of the instinct of personal rights—a sort of reflex function of it'.[60] Its use in a sociological context is entirely appropriate.

It is otherwise with *structure*, which is metaphorical, both in biology, and more markedly, in sociology too. In biology it is part of a mechanistic analogy; and the biology which Spencer employs is very largely anatomy—which treats of the structures of organisms largely independent of their functions, as if they were machines at rest.[61] But while it is both possible and useful to speak about organisms in this way, it is a severe hindrance to realistic sociology—for what we call 'social structure' is merely a regular pattern of the way things are done by people—in fact functions. Structure, we may say 'is an abstract construct, not something distinct from the ongoing inter-active process, but rather a temporary, accommodative representation of it at any one time'.[62] The rigid distinction Spencer maintained between structure and function is nowhere more clearly seen than in the folio volumes of the *Descriptive Sociology*, where the structures and the functions of each society are detailed in columns on pages opposite one another. So the modern usage of social *structure* is different from Spencer's: we say societies have different structures, but not 'in societies . . . increase of mass is habitually accompanied by *increase* of structure' (my italics)—a literal, physical, usage that resembles Tylor's use of the term *culture*.[63] Spencer lacked any concept of *role* which in modern sociology relates function to structure.[64] The drawbacks of his literal-minded conception of structure are not due to Spencer's ideological leanings but to his ill-developed vocabulary, bound by alien imagery. His own change-directed, individualist, anarchist, preferences led him to regret the development of structure (or organization as he synonomously called it) as a hindrance to change, yet he believed that functional changes, the responses to changed conditions, would be ephemeral unless they became 'organic', or 'organized' in the social or individual constitution. So Spencer was a somewhat reluctant 'structuralist':

> That with social organisms, as with individual organisms, structure up to a certain point it needful for growth is obvious. That in the one case, as in the other, continued growth implies un-building and re-building of structure, which therefore becomes in so far an impediment, seems also obvious. Whether it is true in the one case (society), as in the other (organisms), that completion of structure involves arrest of growth, and fixes the society to the type it has then reached, is a question to be considered.

Yet in *The Principles of Sociology* there is so much functional analysis of an entirely modern kind that it is hard to understand why so many latter-day functionalists (though not Radcliffe-Brown) should have supposed that in promoting the new 'structural-functionalism' that they were rebelling against Spencer the evolutionary-functionalist.[65] The essence of this method is to explain institutions not in terms of the motives and purposes, either of the actors whose actions compose the institutions, or of the creators of the institutions, but in terms of the functions they fulfil, that is of their effects or consequences for the whole system of which they form a part within the environment to which they are adapted. Any such definition of function as 'what contributes to the maintenance of the system in recognizably its present form' would fail to satisfy Spencer because this would ignore the environment, whether physical or social, to which adaptation will never be complete, at least not until the end-point of evolution comes. There therefore is a built-in propensity to change. There is a *tendency* to equilibrium between external and internal factors; but since this equilibrium can only be perfect when men are entirely 'adapted to the social state', there is very little point in saying as a criticism of Spencer that it leads to an unawareness of change or conflict.[66] Comte was criticized by Spencer for having a division of sociology called social *statics* on the grounds that no society is exclusively at rest.[67] When Spencer speaks of 'equilibrium', he sometimes (as in the 'Theory of Population', or in some of the functionalist analyses of the *Sociology*) refers to a single time and place, but very often to the whole sweep of evolution as one giant process of equilibration. In any case, he is always aware of how conditional equilibrium is, and how liable to upset; and his institutional analysis is full of phrases like 'While there go on changes of this kind . . .', 'if continued militancy makes . . .', 'if conditions favour the growth of . . .', 'while if the surrounding circumstances and mode of life are such as to . . .'[68] His functionalism, in fact, is inseparable from his evolution.

Nevertheless his treatment of many topics is quite simply functionalist in the modern sense—especially when he casts a disenchanted ex-Quaker's eye on social rituals, ceremonies and symbols in Part IV of the *Sociology* and in Chapter 9 of Part VI, entitled 'An Ecclesiastical System as a Social Bond', which largely anticipates Durkheim's theory of religion. It is in areas where individual actions lead to overall social effects without these being willed as such—where the *laissez-faire* economy might suggest a model for primitive religion—that his methods are most successful. His functionalist account of polygamy in Part III of the *Sociology* may be taken as typical.

§304: Polygamy is very widespread among primitive peoples. It is not, as is commonly thought, due to a surplus of women, and tends to be the preserve of the wealthy in the population. §305: There are economic reasons for it, and it comes to be a mark of 'social status'. Although it may be 'initiated . . . by unrestrained sexual instincts among savage men' [here the causal/psychological explanation widely taken as Spencer's typical argument] it has 'very generally been fostered by the same causes that have established control'. §306: It gives greater coherence to the family structure. §307: Polygmy prevails where men are killed off in war: it strengthens the male line, and along with ancestor worship 'serves in another way to consolidate society'. It prevents surplus women being uncared-for but causes dissensions among wives. It restricts the 'higher emotions' because under it women

> tend to be regarded as chattels. §308: Within polygamous systems a distinction between wives and concubines, and between chief and other wives tends to develop; it survives longest among royal houses and the 'governing organization which everywhere and always displays a more archaic condition than other parts of the social organization'.

That much of this is speculative, and some of it wrong, does not alter the fact that the method is functionalist. The close kinship of functionalism in sociology with a pragmatic philosophy is again evident. Things are judged in terms of their consequences in the social context where we find them; social science assists the pragmatic moralist or epistemologist by showing the correspondence between an institution and its setting through the use of functionalist methods.

IV

It is now possible to return to an issue broached at the beginning of this chapter. Is there an inconsistency between Spencer's functionalism and his use of the organic analogy, on the one hand, and his methodological individualism and political liberalism on the other? Is it really the case as Bramson says, that 'the idea of a liberal-individualist sociology is somewhat contradictory'?[69] Spencer surpasses even the high standards of liberalism set by Popper and Hayek, the great champions of methodological individualism, yet his reliance on the organic analogy, and the holism which is implicit in functionalism, is frequently said to be 'intimately connected with hostility towards the liberal political individualism of the Western tradition'.[70] Those who would approve of Spencer's politics would not, it seems, approve of his choice of imagery, and *vice-versa*; and perhaps everyone would find an inconsistency in the holistic functionalism which he often actually employed, and the methodological individualism which he professed. This latter is the real problem.

There is no serious difficulty over his combination of the organic analogy with political individualism, even though the analogy has often seemed to be pre-empted by conservatives and radicals who have wanted a strong state—English Hegelians and racial Darwinists, fascists and certain kinds of socialist, Ruskin, Kingsley and Carlyle, French positivists, Catholic reactionaries like Bonald and Maistre.

But it is extreme to say, as Andreski does, that Spencer's view of 'society from the point of organic analogy, . . . lent no support whatsoever to his individualistic liberalism, and . . . should have led him to espouse some form of authoritarianism, whether of socialist or conservative variety'.[71] As we have seen, an analogue has like features and unlike ones—it is up to the theorist to indicate which ones he has in mind, and to justify them as the expression of a fundamental structure shared with the explicandum. Organic analogies are especially fertile in contrary implications, and since it is a mark of analogies that they do break down in the end, it is a truism to say that his political views (which were justified by one aspect of the analogy) and other aspects of the analogy can each only be kept intact at the expense of the other.[72]

The debate about methodological individualism in history and the social sciences has been largely conducted by philosophers of science, and despite its potential relevance for the practice of social analysis has in recent years been of little real moment for sociologists. Although things were different in Durkheim's time, neither side today seems to want to change sociological practice, but to score a philosophical victory by showing that actual modes of explanation fit their method. As Gellner says, the individualists claim that the holists' actual practice belies the holist arguments; and the holists claim contrariwise of the individualists. Broadly speaking, methodological individualists claim that all valid statements in the social sciences are reducible to statements about individuals and the circumstances which confront them, while the holists insist that explanation must refer to social laws as well, and agree with Durkheim's injunction to 'consider social facts as things',[73] not decomposable into the interactions of individuals.

Historically the holists have been inclined to combine two positions: (*a*) society cannot be understood by seeing it as the result of individual choices and dispositions, for the individual is shaped by inherited and traditional forces over which he has no control, and (*b*) the rights of individuals should if necessary be subordinated to the needs of the whole, since that is the natural and proper dispensation for man and society. Comte's view that society is 'no more decomposable into *individuals* than a geometric surface is into lines, or a line into points' can be taken either as methodological advice or political exhortation.[74] The argument took the form of a social pathology. Since it was demonstrable that individual characters *were* shaped by society, it was natural that this was so. Hence the social condition was diseased, and men in general would suffer even as individuals, if individuals were somehow detached from social pressures and obligations. What individualism proposed was chimerical; or rather it amounted to a dissolution of society. As for happiness, individuals might be as deluded about that as about their own medical symptoms. Sociocracy would no more permit the luxury of individuals' errors about ethics than it would their mistaken ideas about physiology.

Spencer like Comte linked methodology and ethics, but to the elevation of the individual:

> Society exists for the benefit of its members; not its members for the benefit of society . . . the claims of the body politic are nothing in themselves, and become something only in so far as they embody the claims of its component individuals.[75]

At a superficial reading Spencer's methodology seems clear. It follows exactly the recommendations of Mill's *Logic*, with ethology (though Spencer does not use the word) or an analysis of character, coming between psychology and sociology. Social institutions are to be explained by reference to the characters of the individuals who work them:

> There is no way of coming at a true theory of society but by enquiring into the nature of its component individuals.[76]

Later the same point is made about nature in general; what holds of crystallography holds of biology—'given the nature of the units and the nature of the aggregate they form is predetermined'—and of sociology also:

> Given the structures and consequent instincts of the individuals as we find them, and the community they form will inevitably present certain traits; and no community having such traits can be formed out of individuals having other structures and instincts . . . there must everywhere be a *consensus* between the special structures and actions of [a society] and the special structures and actions of [the men who compose it].[77]

The ethical implications which Spencer drew from his methodological individualism are perfectly clear. The socialists, he claimed, showed by their eagerness for legislation 'unwavering faith in a social alchemy which out of ignoble natures will get noble actions'. Spencer believed that:

> The welfare of a society and the justice of its arrangements are at bottom dependent on the characters of its members; and . . . improvement in neither can take place without that improvement in character which results from carrying on peaceful industry under the restraints imposed by an orderly social life.[78]

Spencer's exaltation of the potentiality of the individual reads like the photographic negative of Durkheim's conception of morality. He speaks of 'the familiar fact that the corporate conscience is ever inferior to the individual conscience—that a body of men will commit a joint act, that which every individual of them would shrink from, did he feel personally responsible'.[79]

Political individualism seemed to imply an atomistic method, and this psychologism. But since Spencer believed in the inheritance of acquired characteristics, character was as much a dependent as an independent variable. In an essay 'The Comparative Psychology of Men' (1875) he sketched out a programme for the study of character as sociologically as well as biologically variable. So far from emphasizing the indelible and determining character of race, as Galton and the racial anthropologists did, he claimed to be trying to bring about:

> . . . a salutary consciousness of the remoter effects produced by institutions upon character; and [to] check the grave mischiefs which ignorant legislation now causes . . . to rationalize our perverse methods of education; and so to raise intellectual power and moral nature.[80]

The reciprocal relationship of individual and society is fully recognized:

> The individual citizen [is] embedded in the social organism as one of its units, moulded by its influence and aiding reciprocally to remould it.[81]

> The cardinal truth, difficult adequately to appreciate, is that while the forms and laws of each society are the consolidated products of the emotions and ideas of those who lived through the past, they are made operative by the subordination of existing emotions and ideas to them.[82]

In summing up 'The Scope of Sociology' Spencer said it covered kinship, politics and the relations between the political and the productive structures; with social control and the relations between political, ecclesiastical and ceremonial institutions; and with social possessions like knowledge and language (here he quotes Tylor but does not speak of 'culture'). The final aim of sociology is to show the consensus of institutions, and 'so to grasp the vast heterogeneous aggregate as to see how each group is at each stage determined partly by its own antecedents and partly by the past and present actions of the rest upon it'.[83]

There seems to be a serious incoherence between Spencer's professed methodology (to which his political ideals seemed to commit him) and his actual procedures. I shall try to show that Spencer was confronting an important and as yet unresolved dilemma in sociological explanation which he misconstrued as involving the choice between individualism and holism. Durkheim prolonged the confusion when, in the course of putting his own view forward, he (fairly) paraphrased Spencer thus:

> [Spencer] admits, it is true, that once it is formed society reacts on individuals. But it does not follow that society itself has the power of directly engendering the smallest social fact; from this point of view *it exerts an effect only by the intermediation of the changes it effects in the individual*. It is, then, always in human nature, whether original or acquired, that everything is based. (my italics).[84]

Here the only obscurity, and it amounts to a mystification, is Durkheim's own contrasted view—that society somehow 'engenders social facts' quite apart from any effects on or through individuals. What he intends as a critical paraphrase of Spencer is in fact an account of the proper relationship between individual and social causation. Social facts are to be explained by references to other social facts (so far Durkheim's rule is acceptable); but this can only be done through individuals as the ever-present intervening variable.

It is here that the real difficulties begin. The disagreement concerns the relative importance, in social causation, to be attached to social structure on one hand and culture as it is expressed in personality, on the other. Do structural changes cause consequent, rather than require precedent, changes in 'character', or is the reverse true, either generally or in particular cases? In a discussion about, let us say, rural development in India, 'structuralists'[85] will argue that change will come about through land-reforms, coercion or financial inducements of the right kind, technical innovation, modifications in the political system or the methods of tax-collection, etc., in order that the peasants may confront a different system within which to operate; while those of the culture-and-personality school[86] will see the main drawbacks in the peasants' characters and attitudes, in the absence of 'need-achievement', the conservative influence of traditional religion, etc., and will require changes to be made in these, perhaps by mass-education, before change can come about.

Durkheim's account of Spencer, as I have quoted it above, can be applied to both these views. Both assert that the individuals are the intervening variable between social fact and social fact but they conceive of the relevant features of individuals differently. Those who stress the importance of culture imply that human nature, though variable, is not readily malleable through institutional changes ('machinery' as Spencer would say); for culture, embodied in religious and ethical systems and transmitted by socialization, can normally only change slowly. On this view individuals' behaviour changes as the culture which directs them does. The objection to this view is that what would seem to be considerable social changes—the French Revolution for example—have taken place so quickly that it is quite implausible to attribute them to such slowly operative factors.[87] In the opposing view, the individual is seen as a *social actor*, whose attributes do not merely consist of a personality, but of roles and statuses in a system of social relations, and of types of knowledge not very directly expressed in personality, and of very general propensities to respond to particular threats and inducements. Here the individual's attributes and behaviour can be modified without immediate modifications of personality, and hence the social structure can be too, for it is none other than the general pattern formed by individuals acting. The existence of personality need not be denied and should not be reduced to what people actually do;[88] but it is to be seen as permitting a range of possible behaviours and as one constraint among others on the individual's behaviour.

Spencer, like the culture-and-personality school (which, appropriately enough, is strongest in the USA, where Spencer's individualist creed found its best audience), sees the society as a large-scale model of its typical personality: innovating entrepreneurial societies are animated by 'creative' personalities. It is more understandable that Spencer should have held this view than his contemporary, unwitting followers, since his biological notions of character formation made him suppose that all attributes of an individual had to get 'organized' in his constitution in order to be effective. 'Mere' acquired knowledge, or tenure of a social position (for, as I have said, he lacked a concept of role), he discounted as serious determinants of behaviour.

Just how much of a constraint culture is upon social change is a matter that is still undecided, and should not be settled by a philosophical fiat.[89] If the analytical distinction is justified, sociology should abandon the search for an empirical answer that is universally true, and try instead to establish the conditions under which culture is a powerful determinant of behaviour, and when it is not. It is likely to be less true of today's underdeveloped countries, which are the focus for the contemporary debate, than of a country like England whose industrialization was the unplanned outcome of many centuries' preparation. In this context *laissez-faire* and the belief that institutions are only made possible by men's characters were mutually supporting. Spencer's methodological individualism is saved by his acute awareness of human variability from that profoundly anti-sociological individualism which we see in Malinowski, Freud and Pareto: where the object of sociology becomes the discovery of psychological constants, whether they be called 'needs', 'drives' or 'residues'. If the organic analogy gave rise to a universal grammar for sociology, Spencer's analysis of real social change lay in his distinction between militancy and industrialism.

8: Militancy and Industrialism

I

Spencer's account of social development has two aspects. One, differentiation, is characteristic of evolution in general. The other is peculiar to social evolution, and is an elaboration of what had become a commonplace in societal contrasts since the mid-eighteenth century, the distinction between military (or 'militant' as Spencer usually said) and industrial societies. The contrast referred, in the first instance, to changes observed by contemporaries as European society, above all Great Britain, underwent industrialization; but it was extrapolated by Spencer to cover the course of general human development from the crudest savagery to the acme of civilization which the radicals felt they could glimpse in the 1850s. His overall view of social evolution was therefore built up from two sides—general natural principles and his perception of England's recent social experience. It followed from the principle of the uniformity of natural processes that the small segment of human history which initially gave rise to the militant industrial distinction must have the same direction as the whole span of human evolution and development. The empirical obstacles which such a view necessarily confronts gave rise (particularly in the light of social development from the 1860s) to increasingly desperate and inadequate theoretical shifts. And from the wreckage of Spencer's theory comes the awareness that historical generalizations and ideal types are different things.

It is best to begin from the social experience which Spencer shared with other members of his provincial, dissenting culture. In presenting the industrial revolution as their own cultural victory over a military aristocracy the spokesmen for industrialism were both analysing a power-shift that was in fact occurring and striking an ideological blow for their complete victory.

In the late eighteenth century there was gaining currency a new view of a traditional topic—the relationship between the civil and the military in society.[1] The older view is to be found in Machiavelli and was dominant up to the end of the seventeenth century, appropriate to a world of chronic political disorder and fragile sovereignties. It regards military excellence as the requisite of civil virtues, and not their enemy, and considers that citizen-soldiers and good laws together make the best armies and the happiest states; those disciplines, techniques and aptitudes which make for military competence are readily transferable to the civil sphere. This was still the view of Adam Smith, who feared that the liberal-commercial society which he saw developing (and for which he has often mistakenly taken to be the wholehearted apologist) would decay through neglect of the austere but necessary civil-cum-military virtues.[2] Ferguson too was apprehensive about what he called 'Relaxations in the National Spirit incident to Polished Nations'.[3] But they did make a sociological distinction between warlike and patriotic societies and ones dominated by commerce, freedom and perhaps softness.

In the other view the distinction has become a contradiction. Societies may be classified as whether the civil or the military predominates; the violence and autocracy which distinguish military rule are inimical to decent government and all the arts of peace; an army is at best a regrettable necessity whose influence within the polity must be carefully minimized. By Spencer's day the militant/industrial distinction had become a richly embroidered common-place in those liberal-radical, provincial, dissenting circles where he was nurtured.[4] In the propaganda of the Anti-Corn Law League a valid societal typology was most blended with the successful self-advertisement of a party as standing for a society that would be pacific, anti-hierarchical, industrial, libertarian, that would en-courage the natural desire of individuals to excel and strive, and ensure that virtue was rewarded, but would at the same time facilitate voluntary co-operation. We must consider first the logic of the two ideals, and then the actual societies and social experiences which were claimed to be their embodiments. The choice of these two ideals, militancy and industrialism, was almost entirely the work of those who considered themselves to be of the peaceful and industrial party. They had a continuity and coherence from the radicalism of Priestley and Paine in the late 1780s until the third quarter of the nineteenth century, but were most proclaimed in the 1830s and 1840s. The division of opinion over the Governor Eyre controversy in 1865–7 was one of the last clear expressions of it. By the late 1870s, for a variety of reasons, it was difficult to see in the dichotomy a real social division.

The surest evidence for the dichotomy lay in their experience of the industrial society which they were creating. The benefits of industry were possible because a feudal aristocracy had been displaced from power. As Harriet Martineau saw it (1838), feudalism was marked by the rule and admiration of force, the dominance of the past, by a sharp division of the population into rulers and ruled, by a typical character that was imperious, vain, superstitious, contemptuous, lavish, 'vain of rank and personal distinction'.[5] Such a society could still be seen in Spain and was furthest removed from the northern states of America which were widely regarded as the model for the future.[6] The northern U.S.A. was at this time, though rapidly becoming less so, part of the same moral Community as English Dissent. Priestley and Paine were mid-Atlantic figures, and Dissenting leaders of opinion saw America as a fuller embodiment of their social ideals than England, and their works were eagerly read. (Spencer was almost the last in a line.) By contrast, 'the opposite state of society, which has begun to be realized' produces trade, equality, the rise of the lower classes, the growth of mutual respect, and 'the value of men for their intrinsic qualifications is discovered'. Here she echoes Mill's demand in *The Spirit of the Age* for competence to take the place of inherited right; and implying that the absence of hierarchy is entailed by this she is less percipient than Saint-Simon who argued in like terms. For there is also a populist strain, a professed admiration for the disagreements of open debate and frank opinion, which might run counter to expert judgment, and was seen to distinguish England from France. So Harriet Martineau, the great popularizer of *laissez-faire* economics, was still proud to compare 'the English artizan discussing with his brother-workman the politics of the town, or carrying home to his wife some fresh hopes of the interference of parliament about labour and wages' with 'the French peasant returning from the field in total ignorance of what has taken place in the capital of late'.[7] The 'idiocy of rural life' (as Marx called it) was something which Cobden too saw as disappearing in the industrial society.[8] The abilities of ordinary men, moral rather than intellectual, are celebrated most by Samuel Smiles, who attributed the railways, the wonder of the age, not to 'the invention of one man, but of a nation of engineers', and of course rejoiced that 'leading engineers—not, like Stephenson, self-taught men, but regular professionals' pronounced impossible an engineering feat which Stephenson performed.[9]

The railways were the proof of the supreme worth of the social organization which had produced them, and were contrasted with the useless monuments of despotic regimes. The great pyramids, or Napoleon's military road over the Simplon, were nothing to the Leeds and Derby Railway:

> and whilst the Egyptian work was executed by a powerful monarch concentrating upon it the labour and capital of a great nation, the English railway was constructed in the face of every conceivable obstruction and difficulty by a company of private individuals out of their own resources without the aid of Government or the contribution of one farthing of public funds.[10]

As France differed from England, so did Turkey more so, in industrial backwardness and despotic government. Cobden pictured Constantinople as it might one day be:

> Let us conjure up the thousands of miles of railroads, carrying to the very extremities of the empire—not the sanguinary satrap but the merchandise and busy traders of a free state; conveying—not the firman of a ferocious Sultan armed with death to the trembling slaves, but the millions of newspapers and letters which stimulate the enterprise and excite the patriotism of an enlightened people.[11]

The same images are evoked by Mackinnon, far less radical than Cobden, when in defence of property rights, he notes that in Turkey political power is so dominant over property that a 'bashaw' (a favourite contemporary sobriquet for administrative authority) may bastinado and pillage a man ten times wealthier than himself (which to Mackinnon was the ultimate scandal).[12]

Internal despotism was associated with external aggression. In her *History of England during the Thirty Years Peace* (1849) Harriet Martineau smugly recorded national development since 1815, seeing *laissez-faire* at home the natural counterpart to a pacific foreign policy, of which prosperity was the fruit. Our notions of buccaneer capitalism and of the ruthlessness of business are owed to a later period, when industrial 'empires' were described in Darwinian language. Andrew Ure was sincere in thinking industry the ally of peace when he wrote:

> Nations, convinced at length that war is always a losing game, have converted their swords and muskets into factory implements and now contend with each other in the bloodless but still formidable strife of trade. They no longer send troops to fight on distant fields but fabrics to drive before them those of their old adversaries in arms, and to take possession of a foreign mart.[13]

Ure would have agreed with Buckle's argument that Adam Smith, in proving the futility of wars to secure long-term economic benefits, had done more for human happiness 'than has been effected by the united abilities of all the statesmen and legislators of whom history has preserved an authentic account'. Hence 'the commercial spirit, which formerly was often warlike, is now invariable pacific'.[14]

But Buckle's explanation goes much further than this. His main concern is with the progress of intellectual culture, which he relates to the decline of militarism and the rise of the middle classes. Here England is contrasted with Russia, where 'there is as yet no middle rank, and consequently the thoughtful and pacific habits which spring from the middle ranks have no existence'; but 'in our country a love of war as a national taste [is] utterly extinct; and this vast result has been effected not by moral teachings, nor by the dictates of moral instinct; but by the simple fact that in the progress of civilization there have been found certain classes of society which have an interest in the preservation of peace, and whose united authority is sufficient to control those other classes whose interest lies in the prosecution of war'.[15] Together the military (i.e. aristocratic) and the ecclesiastical spirit decline—Buckle, like almost all those who used the militant/industrial dichotomy, was highly critical of the Established Church. Technical innovation has always fostered the decline of militancy, argues Buckle: steam power obviously, through increasing international trade, and even gunpowder, which in causing the rise of professional armies removed the citizens from fighting and rendered them peaceable. (Here Machiavelli is decisively reversed.)

Spencer is sometimes said to have taken the militant/industrial dichotomy from the French sources of sociology, Comte and Saint-Simon.[16] Saint-Simonianism did have an influence on English social thought (often through Comtean positivism), on Owen and early socialism, and more strikingly on Mill, Harriet Martineau and G. H. Lewes.[17] Nonetheless the dichotomy is much more deeply rooted in the direct experience of English provincial Dissent, is rather different in its content and meaning from Saint-Simon's and was largely an interpretation by Saint-Simon of English and American society as he found them. Saint-Simon, who had been in America during the revolutionary war, was both an earnest admirer of the 'first new nation', and a persistent anglophile, an eager student of the first industrial society. His military/industrial distinction dates from this period, and is essentially a contrast of old France and Anglo-America or France as it might be. After 1815 there is a shift of values. The need for a restoration of the religious principle culminates in 'le nouveau christianisme', and the social ideal, while still emphasizing work, peace, and competence, becomes a technocracy—a conflictless, undemocratic hierarchy, ruled by industrialists, bankers, managers, experts. 'Error' is no more to be permitted in social theory than it would be in chemistry. Equipped with this vision of the future, the Saint-Simonians, Rodrigues, Enfantin and the Pereires set about the large-scale industrialization of France during the Second Empire, when the banks and the government were to play the role of the entrepreneurs of England and America. Saint-Simon refused to draw Buckle's conclusion, that England was industrial because there 'the government has been most quiescent and the people most active'.[18]

The inventors of the militant/industrial dichotomy were themselves closely involved with the transformation of society. They linked together the obvious fruits of industrialism (or rather some of them, especially the technology and its potentialities), with the real or supposed attributes of the groups to which they belonged (provincial towns, Dissenting congregations, etc.) and some of the circumstances which enabled industrialism, in the case of England, to come about. Argument was to come when later developments were to suggest incompatibilities within these various features, and when other circumstances were to imply that some of the features of the industrial model are not incompatible with the militant model. When, in the 1870s, it no longer seemed that competence and efficiency were indissolubly linked with total freedom from state-management, and government began to recruit professionals for administration, or when Germany showed how industrialization might be piloted by a military élite, social theory had to abandon the dichotomy. It is a paradox that the dichotomy was probably last used, as a moral classification that underlay all his work, by Veblen (who derived it from Spencer); for Veblen has also provided the acutest analysis of that effective synthesis of archaic militancy and modern industrialism by imperial Germany.[19]

II

Spencer's peculiarity was that he took a two-stage characterization of recent history and turned it into a pattern for general social evolution. The general outlines are visible in *Social Statics*, the view of character is clearly presented in the *Psychology*, and the thesis is documented at great length in the *Principles of Sociology*. It has frequently been remarked, and sometimes regretted, that Spencer devoted so much space to anthropological material, as if this was largely irrelevant to his main ethical purpose.[20] But since his major premiss was the uniformity of historical change (admission of exceptions was wrung from him when they were too evident to be denied), it was quite relevant to support his thesis about the social meaning of industrialization by data about savages, who were in general taken as even less industrial and more militant, than the feudal aristocracy. The wider the militant-to-industrial theory held, the more likely was it to be true in the case of nineteenth-century England, and, as will be seen, Spencer's notions of the primitive character were largely derived from middle-class views of the behaviour of groups—their contemporaries, the newly urbanized working class and the landed aristocracy—which they felt was incompatible with industry.

The great classical systems of sociology all need to place, within the total pattern of history, both contemporary, early industrial society and the ideal society of the future. There are two chief ways of doing this. Liberals like Spencer, who are more aware of the superiority in all fields of contemporary society over all societies of the past, will see history in terms of a temporal continuum between two poles. The ideal society of the future will resemble the past in every way less than the present does, and will be a prolongation of changes already begun. The primitive, the traditional, the militant are the reverse of the ideal.

By contrast, those who are fundamentally critical of the society they live in, as Marx was of capitalist society and Comte of post-Napoleonic France, tend to adopt a three-stage vision of human history, with the present as the second stage or the transition to the third, and the third as a reversion to the first in certain important respects. A two-stage or single-continuum model does not fit the moral purposes of either the conservative or the revolutionary. But they are likely to differ in what they think the future society will recover from the past. In Comte's scheme—theological, metaphysical, positive—future society would see again the revival of shared moral values, order and hierarchy.[21] Science would replace theology, and scientific sociocrats priests, but the Middle Ages was the prototype of the future.

Marx, unlike some other socialists, had no sympathy at all for the Middle Ages, but he too presented the end-product of history as resembling the beginning. For behind the six stages of primitive, slave, feudal, capitalist, socialist and communist society is a simpler tripartite scheme, in which the third stage abolishes the alienation of the second stage, class-society, to restore the moral condition of the first. For despite Marx's frequent assertion that man makes his own character, he did have a primitivist *Anthropologie* or theory of human nature which presented the division of labour, social differentiation, inequality, stratification and specialization—all the things which distinguish class-society from primitive society—as responsible for alienation. The future society, whose main difference from primitive society would be that man's conquest of nature would be so complete that total plenitude would reign, was to be a primitivist utopia in which men would be able 'to do one thing today and another tomorrow, to hunt in the morning, fish in the afternoon, rear cattle in the evening, criticize after dinner . . . without ever becoming hunter, fisherman, shepherd or critic'.[22] When one feels that man's present condition is profoundly wrong, one will see in those people who are most different a model of how men ought to be; and if one is inclined to optimism one will search the present for contradictions out of which the perfect society will emerge. So the schemes of conservatives like Comte and radicals like Marx, despite their sense of historical progression and their eagerness for the future, see the future as a recovery of things lost, and the course of history as reversionary in important moral (though not technological) features.

Spencer never criticized society from a primitivist ideal. His basic position (which he never outright rejected though the facts forced him to admit other contradictory ones) was that underlying the gradual development of industrialism was a shift in men's characters from the egoism of the savage to the altruism of the forward spirits of the modern age. The way forward lay in the completion of these changes. This portrayal of the primitive is very detailed. The moral attributes are more important than the intellectual ones. Primitives are above all unsociable, and consequently unreliable and inconstant in their passions and affections; they are prone to follow immediate individual impulses and find it difficult to stick to long-term co-operative projects:

> That 'wavering and inconstant disposition' which commonly makes it 'impossible to put any dependence on their promises', negatives that trust in mutual obligations on which social progress largely depends. Governed as he is by despotic emotions that successively depose one another, instead of by a council of the emotions in which they all take part, the primitive man has an explosive, chaotic, incalculable behaviour, which makes combined action very difficult. . . . Sociality, strong in the civilized man, is less strong in the savage man. Among the lowest types the social groups are very small, and the bonds holding their units together are relatively feeble.[23]

This is most clearly shown in the domestic relations of primitives. Spencer shows little understanding of primitive kinship systems, and rejects Maine's theory of the patriarchal clan as the original social unit.[24] He attributes to the Digger Indians, who are 'very few degrees removed from the ourang-outang' an 'entire lack of social organization'.[25] The earliest sexual relations, says Spencer, inclined to promiscuity; they were casual and unsettled, for there were 'no guides save the passions of the moment'.[26] Naturally, where 'the wills of the stronger, unchecked by political restraints, unguided by moral sentiments, determine all behaviour', women have low status, and there is little tenderness between the sexes:[27] 'a savage makes his wife a slave, and usually treats her brutally'.[28]

Improvidence and irregularity are secondary effects of this basic un-sociality:

> The immediate desire, be it for personal gratification or for the applause which generosity brings, excludes fear of future evils; while pains and pleasures to come, not being vividly conceived, there is no adequate spur to exertion, but a light-hearted, careless absorption in the present.[29]

> Primitive men, improvident in all ways, never devised and instituted a usage with a view to a foreseen distant benefit: they do not make laws, they fall into customs.[30]

The activity of primitives is highly spasmodic, since it is the result of passing fancies rather than long-term goals. There is a distaste for monotonous work, and production only develops slowly, because of their 'defect of emotional nature, shown . . . by inability to sacrifice present to future'.[31] This emotional inconstancy, which must be mastered if social evolution is to occur, is one of the respects in which savages resemble children. Its counterpart is an extreme conservatism and reluctance to innovate, which is partly grounded in the supposed physiology of their nervous systems and is partly dependent on, and responsible for, their subservience to 'ecclesiasticism' and ceremonial. 'Adhering tenaciously to all his elders taught him, the primitive man only deviates into novelty through unintended modifications.'[32] The primitive is so unsocial that he must be held in a social pattern by constraints, which thus oblige him to be conservative. 'Ecclesiasticism, embodying in its primitive form the rule of the dead over the living, and sanctifying in its more advanced forms the authority of the past over the present, has for its function to preserve in force the organized product of earlier experiences versus the modifying effects of more recent experiences.'[33] Conservatism is therefore as much the result of institutions needed to socialize the primitive character as it is an intrinsic part of that character. Ceremony or ritual, the mark of conservatism, is both the expression of the militant type of society, and the force which educates 'the anti-social nature into a form fitted for social life'.[34]

It does not require much evidence or logic to demolish this conceptualization of the primitive, and the materials for a naive exposure of its errors are even to be found in Spencer himself. He was aware that this portrait was deducible *a priori* from the arguments of the *Psychology*, yet still claimed the ethnographic evidence, on the whole, supported it *a posteriori*. We can say we know it had to, and that it blinded Spencer to the difficulties of valid generalization. Yet he knew the dangers:

> To what extent the facts justify this *a priori* inference, it is not easy to say: the evidence is very difficult to disentangle and to generalize. Many causes conspire to mislead us. We assume that there will be tolerable uniformity in the manifestations of character in each race; but it is not so. Both the individuals and the grops udiffer considerably. . . . We assume that the traits shown will be similar on successive occasions, which they are not: the behaviour to one traveller is unlike the behaviour to another; probably because their own behaviours were unlike. Very generally, too, the displays of character by an aboriginal race revisited are determined by the treatment received from previous visitors; being changed from friendliness to enmity by painful experiences.[35]

He quotes some of the extremely variable estimates of character given for different peoples, from the peaceful Bodo and Dhimals to the ferocious Fijians and Dahomeans, and even asserts that 'there does not exist a necessary connexion between the social types classified as civilized and those higher sentiments we commonly associate with civilization'.[36] But because it follows from uniformitarianism and methodological individualism that primitive 'character' must differ in some *systematic* way from civilized character, Spencer feels that if we 'average the evidence'[37] (i.e., in fact, if the counter-examples are disregarded) we will still have a real generalization. It is disarming of him to write:

> The evidence, then, does not allow us to infer, as we should naturally have done, that advance in the forms of the sexual relations and advance in social evolution, are constantly and uniformly connected.[38]

But this does not inhibit him from continuing as follows:

> Nevertheless, on contemplating the facts in their *ensemble*, we see that progress towards higher social types is joined with progress

> towards higher types of the sexual relations. Comparison of the extremes makes this unquestionable.

The complexity of Australian Aboriginal kinship systems, of which Spencer was uncomfortably aware, is treated not as counter-evidence to his general theory, but as evidence that they must have retrogressed from a higher state.[39]

What, then, is the origin of Spencer's image of the primitive, that is so clear, and presents in all its features such a *Gestalt*, that it so easily consumes all contrary evidence? Spencer gives us a clue when, speaking of the conservatism of primitives, he writes:

> . . . even on contrasting different classes in the same society, it is observable that the least developed are the most averse to change. Among the common people an improved method is difficult to introduce; and even a new kind of food is usually disliked.[40]

He was right in an important respect. The common people of the early nineteenth century, those ex-farm labourers who swelled the towns and manned the industries, were not eager for the changes in living and working conditions which innovating entrepreneurs forced on them. The entrepreneurs, aware that in many respects public opinion was against them, pictured themselves as heroic moral innovators and were persistently critical of the irregular, pre-industrial work-habits of the working class. Ure, their leading spokesman, spoke of their drive 'to subdue the refractory tempers of work-people accustomed to irregular paroxysms of diligence';[41] for most men were reluctant to exchange the work rhythms of agriculture for the unyielding regularity of factory production.[42] Spencer saw these characteristics writ large in the savage and praised even priests for their evolutionary contribution:

> No developed social life would have been possible in the absence of the capacity for continuous labour; and out of the idle improvident savage there could not have been evolved the industrious citizen, without a long continued and a rigorous coercion.[43]

Nobody, whether supporter or opponent of the industrial system, denied that evangelicalism had a hand in contributing this to the moulding of the industrial work-force.

Then again the working masses were repeatedly censured for improvidence, lack of foresight, propensity to consume wages on useless ritual or drink, and so forth. Smiles, for example, urged manufacturers to 'actively aid their workmen in the formation of prudent habits, by establishing saving banks . . . by encouraging the formation of provident clubs and building societies, of provision and clothing clubs. . . .'[44] Spencer's characterization of his own ancestors, those Dissenting paragons of anti-primitivist virtue, reveals the same ethic. He commends their 'relinquishment of present satisfactions with the view of obtaining future satisfactions' and their practice of 'that prudence which by denial seeks terrestrial welfare'.[45] Significantly one of the instances of this prudence which Spencer cites is their late age of marriage—a focus of Cobbett's traditionalist attack on Malthus.[46] The notion of the primitive as lacking the moral requisites for co-operative life is a striking reminder of a problem that confronted the founders of the co-operative movement and the trades unions, attempting to create coherent and viable institutions among an atomized working population, alienated in the towns from their traditional forms of community and for years prevented by their employers from organization. The views of Holyoake, Lovett and Applegarth blended with those of Smiles, Cobden and Spencer in the co-operative movement of the fifties and sixties.

Finally, it must be noted that Spencer's view of the primitive as shaped by militancy (rather than simply in himself) also contains elements of the middle-class critique of aristocracy—in his attachment to ceremonial, expressive pomp, titles, callousness and brutality. Spencer has not been alone in observing similarities in the manners and tastes of the English aristocracy and working class, or between the conservative and socialist critiques of the industrialism which the middle-class entrepreneur had created. To this we shall return.

III

Militancy and industrialism, however, are not just to be seen as the outcomes of a gradually evolving race or character, but as diametrically opposed forms of organization which arise in response to environmental pressures. In quasi-biological terms militancy is marked by the predominance of externally directed organs, industrialism of internally directed ones. It is the same twofold division which was seen as the only categorical distinction in the *Psychology*: and one effect of conceiving social organization as being like individual organization is to breach the often professed methodological individualism. Individual character is seen as very closely related to social organization, however, and Spencer is always readily to proclaim it the decisive variable. By the time he wrote Volume I of the *Sociology* (1876) he was much less optimistic about the steady improvement of character and the consequent decline of militancy (though his premisses still demanded them), and tended to take the militant/industrial distinction as non-evolutionary, one which partially cross-cuts a more evolutionary classification into 'societies compounded and recompounded in various degrees . . . and [ones] which, differing in their stages of culture, have their structures elaborated to different extents'.[47] Increasingly Spencer came to fear the resurgence of militancy in his own society, and he admitted that there were instances of industrialism 'in its rudimentary form—the form which it assumes where culture has made but little progress' among the simplest societies, such as the Indian hill-tribes.[48] While 'militant' always denotes what the word implies, 'industrial' comes to mean certain structural and cultural attributes which Spencer, along with other radical liberals, had once believed inseparable from the developing industrial society of his day.

A society is founded on co-operation; co-operation 'is at once that which cannot exist without a society and that for which a society exists'.[49] The two basic reasons for co-operation, which are usually combined but of which either may predominate, are biological—food finding and self-protection. There are two types of co-operation to secure these goals most effectively: spontaneous co-operation to help individuals secure individual goals, which ultimately gives rise to the economic division of labour, and deliberate co-operation to secure collective goals, which gives rise to political bodies. What distinguishes militant and industrial societies is the basic form of their co-operation, whether deliberate or spontaneous, though nearly all actual or extinct societies have been transitional.

'The militant type is one in which the army is the nation mobilized, while the nation is the quiescent army, and which, therefore, acquires a structure common to army and nation.'[50] Efficient fighting requires clear collective goals and a centralized control to coordinate men to achieve them, which is then transferred to civil tasks. The community tends to have 'precise gradations of rank . . . and complete submission of each rank to the ranks above it'.[51] The lives of its members are regulated in sundry respects—by sumptuary laws, censorship, injunctions and prohibitions of every kind in accord with the policies of the authorities. Most serious of all 'is the theory concerning the relation between the State and the individual, with its accompanying sentiment', namely 'the belief that its members exist for the benefit of the whole and not the whole for the benefit of its members'.[52] In sum:

> As the soldier's will is so suspended that he becomes in everything the agent of his officer's will; so is the will of the citizen in all transactions, private and public, overruled by that of the government. . . . The social structure adapted for dealing with surrounding hostile societies is under a centralized regulating system, to which all the parts are completely subject; just as in the individual organism the outer organs are completely subject to the chief nervous centre.[53]

Since the central features of these types is the mode of co-operation, (and the type is usually identified empirically by whether the social character seems peaceful or warlike) Spencer has to admit of the industrial type that it may 'coexist with but very moderate productive activities', and that 'there may be, and often is, great industry in societies framed on the militant type'.[54] But nonetheless the paradigm of industrial co-operation is provided by the sorts of relations which hold in trading transactions, between employers and workmen, or buyers and sellers. The essence is voluntary co-operation as the judgments and interest of the participant individuals dictate, so that in industrial societies there is 'an unchecked power of forming associations' that rule themselves on democratic principles. There is a minimum of collective or corporate tasks for whose attainment individuals are disciplined, but all tasks are left to be performed by voluntary associations. In a climate of peace, forbearance and democracy, the overriding social philosophy is 'that the combined actions of the social aggregate have for their end to maintain the conditions under which individual lives may be satisfactorily carried on'. Spencer sees a parallel between the decentralized regulation of the sustaining system in the animal organism, and the decentralization of decision making, ultimately to the perfect democracy of the pure market society, in industrialism. Although Spencer readily admitted the necessity and the past benefits of war as the great consolidator of kingdoms and of militancy as an effective system for the disciplining of the unruly, selfish savage,[55] his own moral preferences were wholly with industrialism, and he identified the policies which he opposed in his own day—protectionism, imperial expansion, the state provision of social services, regulation of the economy or dictation of educational syllabuses, socialism, the development of an enlarged professional civil service—as uniformly militant. It was late in the day, and with little success, that he turned from condemnation of them to an attempt to explain their growth.

Militancy and industrialism are exemplified in a series of paired opposites: status *vs.* contract, vertical ranking *vs.* functional role, tradition *vs.* innovation, the ritual and ceremonial *vs.* the matter-of-fact, the figurative *vs.* the literal, subordination *vs.* equality, guilds and the command economy *vs.* the free market, deliberation *vs.* spontaneity, and so forth. It is the most elaborate version of a dichotomy which dominated classical sociology and can perhaps be best summed up as a contrast between a dynamic economic realm and a static political realm. Since these were felt to be irreconcilable one could only gain at the expense of the other; any historical shift had to be from one to the other—either way was possible, but the most likely and certainly the overall trend was towards industrialism. Attempts to reconcile the two were unsuccessful: Comte's motto 'Order and Progress', which refers to the two realms, acknowledged both, but in details he plumped for order, a modernized version of traditionalism. Spencer's Utopia of industrialism is strangely un-Utopian (since Utopias must be changeless) in that he wanted to make change and innovation permanent.[56] That is quite possible, but not on early nineteenth-century premisses. The past appeared to show that the attributes of militancy—its real merits as a means of creating and maintaining social aggregates—prevented it from responding to social needs and pressures and made it intrinsically conservative. Institutions always resist change, he claims: the church opposes legislation affecting its discipline, the army the abolition of the purchase-system, and the legal profession any form of law-reform.[57] Their members, and place-holders and bureaucrats in general, were always eager to preserve and extend their sphere of control. So different from ourselves in this, Spencer considered it utterly out of the question that the polity could preside over a programme of economic and social transformation. Why should those in positions of power want to innovate except when forced to wage war against outsiders? Innovation meant the upsetting of existing patterns of status, and so could not originate from the politically powerful.

Durkheim criticized Spencer's analysis of contract in industrial society on the grounds that a contract could not create a social bond since it presupposed that the contractors already shared certain common values and assumptions; hence even industrial society was fundamentally united by non-rational bonds of a type Spencer had largely confined to pre-industrial militant forms of society. Durkheim is here asserting that certain of Spencer's 'militant' features positively co-exist with industrial ones in the *same* social setting. Spencer, in his treatment of religion and ceremonial, argued that militancy had to have done its work before industrialism could develop. Industrial society presupposed these things only in its past; in themselves they were anti-industrial. Spencer's functional analysis of religion is often very 'Durkheimian';[58] but its place in his theory is quite different, since it is used to point up a *difference* between types of society, not a fundamental feature of Society in general. The convergence between militancy and industrialism in the late nineteenth century led to a qualified revival of primitivism, stripped of its eschatological significance, in order to state social constants. So Durkheim described the religion of Australian Aborigines as 'better adapted than any other to lead to an understanding of the religious nature of man, that is to say, to show us an essential and permanent aspect of humanity'.[59] It would even be relevant to the task of filling what Durkheim felt to be the moral vacuum in the French Third Republic. And Toennies, with an obvious moral preference for the pre-industrial *Gemeinschaft* whose disappearance he was analysing, still wrote that 'the force of *Gemeinschaft* persists, though with diminishing strength, even in the period of *Gesellschaft* [contractual society] and remains the reality of social life'.[60]

Militant society is marked by undifferentiated roles and sharply segregated ranks. This is an extrapolation of one of the assumptions of the theory which is contained in the early language of class: it stressed a man's occupation or role in the division of labour, rather than his rank in a system of honour. Empirically a role (say landowner) might be attached to a rank (say baronet); with industrialism the role was regarded as of greater importance than the rank. What tended to be denied (and this is the most serious defect in Spencer's analysis of social structure) was that it could be a persistent and necessary feature of society that ranking, prestige and power tend to be attached to functions and roles. What is valuable in Spencer's approach is that the 'vertical' dimension of rank is *analytically* distinguished from the 'horizontal' one of function, which is effectively concealed in the most widely-used current definition of role (Linton's) as simply 'the dynamic aspect of status'. Only with the analytic distinction is it possible to explain the way in which particular occupational roles vary in status attributes, and (which is another aspect of the same matter) the variable ways in which wealth, political power and social prestige may determine one another.

Spencer's treatment of social class (about which he is not wholly consistent) shows the ill-effects of the permanent disjunction of rank and role to which the militant/industrial dichotomy led him. The element of power in class-relationships tends to be underplayed (for it is in places acknowledged) and quite unaccounted for. In militant society power and status relationships are predominant, and differences of wealth are said to 'originally follow differences of power'.[61] Some highly Veblenesque analyses of wealth and status are presented.[62] (It is significant that Veblen, so often regarded as a kind of native American Marx, explained conspicuous waste and consumption as alien to industrialism, the survivals of earlier military society—a prime Spencerism.) Spencer admits there may be antagonisms between classes in industrial society, but these are seen in purely functional terms, competing for capital in the same way that stomach, head and legs may compete for blood supply. The 'classes' are not employers and workers but different industries:

> . . . in a society, not only individuals but classes, local and general, severally appropriate from the total stock of commodities as much as they can . . . and their several abilities to appropriate normally depend upon their several states of activity. If less iron is wanted for export or home consumption, furnaces are blown out, men are discharged, and there flows towards the district a diminished stream of the things required for nutrition, causing arrest of growth and if continued, even decay. When a cotton famine entails greater need for woollens, the increased activity of the factories producing them, while it leads to the

drawing in of more raw material and sending out of more manufactured goods, determines towards the cloth districts augmented supplied of all kinds—men, money, consumable commodities, and there results enlargement of old factories and building of new ones.[63]

Here the rise and fall of particular 'classes' is not determined by any sort of hierarchial power relationship but by that form of voting by the consumer known as demand. The Industrial Revolution had merely shown that the relationships between wealth and political power, or role and rank, were variable. Spencer argued that they were inversely related, and that the rise of one meant the demise of the other. Like Marx, he believed that power-relations and politics were transitory; but he did not accept Marx's further conclusion that this meant the disappearance of the division of labour too.

It is sometimes said, for example by Ossowski,[64] that Spencer's (or the modern 'functionalist') view of class is merely a revival of the traditional hierarchical concept of the body politic. It is not so. The traditionalists justify hierarchy by a largely symbolic or imaginary division of labour (e.g. fighting, praying, working), whereas on Spencer's model hierarchy is totally unjustifiable, since he denies there should be any carry-over from function to status, except perhaps on the basis of uninstitutionalized esteem. The only ideological use of Spencer's model (and it *has* proved quite useful in this regard) is to make it seem, in a highly differentiated society, that power-relationships don't exist.[65] The ranks of militant society, as he sees it, cut across function, since a prime criterion of little-developed societies is just their lack of role-differentiation. Political, legal, military and ecclesiastical functions are blended, and their differentiation is a step towards industrialism, when status will yield to contract entirely. It is precisely because, whereas division of labour is rational, rank is intrinsically irrational, though under militant conditions necessary, that ritual is so necessary to sustain it. All forms of ceremonial are essentially methods of underwriting political and military leadership and subordination; they 'are naturally initiated by the relation of conqueror and conquered . . . and they develop along with the militant type of society'.[66] Spencer hoped in his youth for the complete collapse of irrational social conventions. He demanded 'a protestantism in social usages' and regretted that 'in rules of living a West-end clique is our Pope; and we are all papists with but a mere sprinkling of heretics'.[67] But though ceremonial may be 'natural' in a narrow sense, in a wider one its results are to be contrasted with the 'natural products of social life'. Data from 52 peoples, in an early exercise in statistical correlation (one of the fruits of the *Descriptive Sociology*), are used to show how bodily mutilation is highly associated with a compound political structure and marked hierarchy. Fashions to distinguish legal statuses, special modes of speech and address, patterns of visiting and present-giving (here a very Maussian account of the social functions of the gift) are all prominent symptoms of militancy, and must pass when their evolutionary role in promoting social cohesion is complete. The modern decline of ceremony (Spencer greatly prided himself on his own punctilious flouting of conventions) is most marked among Quakers, those exemplars of what industrial man should be. Spencer, we must remember, still saw the British aristocracy at the pinnacle of a system of deference whose tenacity Bagehot observed and Cobden deplored.[68] So it was left to Veblen, citizen of a nation which boasted no *ancien régime*, to document the continued role of ceremonial in industrial society.

The same is so of religion. For a long time ecclesiastical and political hierarchies display 'a unity of nature consequent on their common origin', and ecclesiastical religion has always provided a moral supplement to the discipline of militancy.[69] Religion, having its origin in ancestor-worship (of which Spencer gives a good account), 'stands for the principle of social continuity . . . embodying in its primitive form the rule of the dead over the living, and sanctifying in its more advanced forms the authority of the past over the present, has for its function to preserve in force the organized product of earlier experiences versus the modifying effects of recent experiences'.[70] But it seemed to Spencer that the positive contribution of ecclesiasticism had been made, and that it might in his day be dispensed with:

> Priests habitually enforce conduct which in one way or another furthers preservation of the society; yet preservation of the society is so often fostered by conduct entirely unlike that which we now call moral, that priestly influence serves in many cases to degrade rather than to elevate.[71]

Hence with the advent of religion based on voluntary association, the power of a state church, whose bishops belong to leading naval and military families, is steadily weakened. Its most persistent critics are dissenters, 'derived from classes engaged in one or another form of industrial activity'.[72] The functions of institutional religion, like those of the state, were restricted by Spencer to a special type of society, now largely in the past. The future would see a proliferation of sects yet 'approximation to a unity of creed in essentials'. Moral duty and wonder at the 'Infinite and Eternal Energy' of Nature would be its substance.[73]

The various things whose conservative functions Spencer had stressed, flourishing with militancy when the social aggregate is unstable, both without and within, and declining with social maturity and industrialism, have it in common that they are *institutions*—set, established procedures which shape, rather than are shaped by, individuals. Spencer had very little feeling for the antiquity of social creations like the colleges, churches, traditions and local communities which provided emotional bearings for most nineteenth-century English critics of industrialism—men who despite, or because of, their conservatism, are cited as ancestors of modern socialism like Carlyle, Ruskin, Kingsley, F. D. Maurice, Arnold, Beesly and Harrison, Coleridge and William Morris. These thinkers have contributed a soft, nostalgic strain to modern British socialist thought, quite distinct from the toughmindedness of Marxism. They wanted change only to recreate institutions and a society whose model was the idealized community of the past, which, like all Utopias, they took to be changeless. Marx might share their moral assessment of capitalism, but not their social ideal; for he, like Spencer and like Veblen, saw the dynamic of social change in economic processes forever outrunning their institutional super-structures and pictured a largely anti-institutional Utopia.

Against institutions Spencer set the spontaneous pressures and groupings by which individuals satisfy their felt needs, in an unhampered and perpetual process of innovation which is typically the mark of industrial society and economic 'institutions' (in a very loose sense). There are guilds, slavery, serfdom and other militant methods of regulating industry, but these are regarded as essentially alien to efficient industrial life which should, above all, be *spontaneous*, and hence highly flexible.

> . . . with the cessation of those needs that initiate and preserve the militant type of structure, and with the establishment of contract as

> the universal relation under which efforts are combined for mutual advantage, social organization loses its rigidity. No longer determined by the principle of inheritance, places and occupations are now determined by the principle of efficiency; and changes of structure follow when men, not bound to prescribed functions, acquire the functions for which they have proved themselves most fit. Easily modified in its arrangements, the industrial type of society is therefore one which adapts itself with facility to new requirements.[75]

Spencer often says of social processes in general what is fully true only of market economic processes, as when he calls social structures 'the aggregate results of the desires of individuals who are severally seeking satisfaction'.[76] When preaching *laissez-faire* in one of his less relativistic veins, he states it as a 'law of social evolution' that things are done in the order of their need: men do *X* before *Y*, because at the time they need *X* most. In a trivial sense this could be true of anything, even of the rise of the institutions of militancy. But Spencer uses this law to criticize a governmental decision to fulfil need *Y* which is not being fulfilled spontaneously; this can only be done, he says, by the diversion of resources from the prior need *X*. Hence, always leave well alone, since 'no man or men by inspecting society can *see* what it needs most; society must be left to *feel* what it most needs. . . . Until a requirement is spontaneously filled, it should not be fulfilled at all.'[77] In the fields of banking and science, it is positively beneficial to have had no institutional encouragement, for that would have stultified adaptability and spontaneity.[78] Hence America is the most developed instance of industrialism, the least weighed down by the tradition, control, and 'torpidity of paternally-governed' societies.[79] It is summed up in this panegyric of industrialism:

> It is not to the State that we owe the multitudinous useful inventions from the spade to the telephone, it was not the State which made possible extended navigation by a developed astronomy; it was not the State which made the discoveries in physics, chemistry, and the rest which guide modern manufacturers; it was not the State which devised the machinery for producing fabrics of every kind, for transferring man and things from place to place, and for ministering in a thousand ways to our comforts. The world-wide transactions conducted in merchants' offices, the rush of traffic filling our streets, the retail distributing system which brings everything within easy reach and

> delivers the necessities of daily life at our doors, are not of government origin. All these are the results of the spontaneous activities of citizens, separate or grouped.[80]

Here the commonplaces of vulgar political economy, imbibed no doubt from boyhood readings of Harriet Martineau and reinforced by his years with *The Economist*, are allied with a hopeful and vigorous conviction that progress depends on innovation, and innovation on popular demand and voluntary association. Such a vision came most easily to men like Spencer and his forerunners Paine, Priestley and Godwin, who as Dissenters were already estranged from the traditional institutions of English society. Their Utopias were solidly based on those features which had made for the success of the industrial transformation by which they were emancipated. What is sociologically precluded by the militant/industrial distinction which summed up their view of events are the possibilities that innovation might itself be institutionalized, and that the trappings of militancy might be set to the purposes of industrialism.

IV

Ideals are not the same as ideology. Spencer's writings, particularly in America, seemed to yield consistent ideological support for untrammelled capitalism of the buccaneering type. Here by 'ideology' is meant the instrumental use of ideas to justify policies dictated by practical interests. Spencer is seen as 'the favourite philosopher of the successful railway man and stock-jobber',[81] and 'a sort of tutelary genius to big business'.[82] S. E. Finer sees *The Man versus the State*, whose author had once been an engineer, as a manifesto of Tory and protectionist railway engineers: 'the social philosophy of the whole profession—civil engineering and social buccaneering'.[83] Much of what was taken by capitalists as a justification for their own activities was only applied by Spencer to the militant phase of society, when law and fashion are in fact determined by 'the strong men, the successful men, the men of will, intelligence and originality who have got to the top'; but this would change 'when human nature has grown into conformity with the social state'.[84]

In fact Spencer was in no way the apologist of capitalist interests (least of all of such enormous industrial empires such as Carnegie's

—despite Carnegie's admiration for him). Spencer's writings are not ideological in this sense; but they do contain ideals—ideals which reveal deep misgivings about industrial capitalism. Not surprisingly these were ignored totally by his business admirers. Like nearly all ideals which are voiced in criticism of industrial society, these stem from a certain pre-industrial matrix—though one which (and this is the awkward and interesting thing) stimulated the emergence of industrialism.

Spencer, like Harriet Martineau,[85] saw in his own day wealth displace birth as the chief determinant of social influence; and like her he looked forward to a time when mental qualities would displace wealth. The first opinion is common throughout the middle classes; the second is peculiar to middle-class *intellectuals,* writers, publicists, freelance interpreters of the age to itself, and is shared by theorists who disagreed on almost everything else about the future organization of society. Its appeal to them is clear enough. But Spencer is very elusive:

> Were this the fit place [he writes in Part II of the *Sociology*], some pages might be added respecting a possible future social type differing as much from the industrial as this does from the militant—a type, which, having a sustaining system more fully developed than any we know at present, will use the products of industry neither for maintaining a militant organization nor exclusively for material aggrandizement; but will devote them to the carrying on of higher activities. . . . The contrast between the industrial type and the type likely to be evolved from it is indicated by the inversion of the belief that life is for work into the belief that work is for life. But we . . . cannot enter upon speculations respecting societies that may be. Merely naming as a sign, the multiplication of institutions and appliances for intellectual and aesthetic culture and for kindred activities not of a directly life-sustaining kind, but of a kind having gratification for their immediate purpose, I can here say no more.[86]

This vision of Utopia is intriguingly similar to that of another solitary literary man of bourgeois origin—Karl Marx—not only in its dialectical view of historical progress, but in its assumption (which runs rather counter to much of Spencer's writing) that the fundamental characteristic of past human activity, that its purpose is to sustain life in an environment, can be transcended, and that men might at last *play,* devote themselves to expressive activities. Men will in the end reap the rewards for the harsh external restraints of militancy, and the tight internal controls of industrialism. Spencer implies the same ideals for human activity as did Marx's bitter diatribe against *homo oeconomicus*:

> The less you eat, drink and buy books, go to the theatre or dances, or to the public-house, and the less you think, love, theorize, sing, paint, fence, the more you will be able to save and the greater will become your treasures which neither moth nor rust will corrupt—your capital. The less you are, the less you express your life, the greater is your alienated life and the greater is the saving of your alienated being.[87]

More remarkably still, in the concluding part of the *Sociology* (1897) the encomiast of industrial private enterprise, who had praised the division of labour because it made use of the existing, and ever-increasing variability of human character, after comparing the life of a factory operative with that of a cottager, admitted 'that this industrial development has proved extremely detrimental to the operative'.[88] His work-life is monotonous, his faculties are either overused or disused, and he is not really free to contract at will: 'this liberty amounts in practice to little more than the ability to exchange one slavery for another, since, fit only for his particular occupation, he rarely has an opportunity of doing anything more than decide in what mill he will pass the greater part of his dreary days'. This is a confession by a middle-class radical that the means —industrialism—which in the 1840s and 1850s was put forward for the attainment of real universal freedom and satisfaction, were inadequate to that end. Spencer's conclusion is a despairing and inadequate return to earlier remedies—a real tiredness and failure of imagination. (It must also be said that even today the only answer given to the problem of tedious, choiceless, 'alienating' work is to hope that with increased productivity there may be more leisure. Interesting work, for the bulk of the population, seems an unattainable ideal.) He observes that 'in the course of social progress parts . . . are sacrificed for the benefits of the society as a whole'; whereas in earlier days men were killed in war, now there was a 'mortality entailed by the commercial struggle', and 'in either case men are used up for the benefit of posterity; and so long as they go on multiplying in excess of the means of subsistence, there appears no remedy'. To thus hark back to Malthus, quite inappropriately, is a total abandonment of the optimism of the 1850s; and to see commerce as *resembling* war in competitiveness (rather than to stress the *differences* in the character of the competition) is a decisive break from his earlier attitudes, but one that was a commonplace by the 1890s.[89]

In the next chapter I will consider in detail how history revenged itself on Spencer—how cumulatively from the 1860s events showed that his ideals, which he had initially justified by an appeal to history, were becoming less and less realizable. Here the task is to demonstrate the sociological origins and assumptions of those ideals. Spencer's earlier writings are similar to those of the 1890s in their moral aspirations; but they are also hopeful. An essay of 1859 entitled 'The Morals of Trade', dwells at length on the 'sins' and 'demoralization', at all levels of the commercial world, caused by the 'pressure of competition' among people of imperfect character. He denounces adulterations of goods, selling short, dishonest salesmanship, misrepresentation of goods, false circulars and trade descriptions, fraudulent directors—all the sorts of things, in fact, which co-operative trading set out to overcome.[90] 'Trade is essentially corrupt', writes this so-called Social Darwinist; 'It has been said that the law of the animal creation is—"Eat and be eaten"; and of our trading community it may similarly be said—cheat and be cheated. A system of keen competition carried on, as it is, without adequate moral restraint is very much a system of commercial cannibalism.' But, says Spencer, things are improving, owing to 'purified public opinion', and 'the evolution of something that stands for a social *self-consciousness*—a self-consciousness in each citizen, of the state of the aggregate of citizens'. The root of the present state of affairs is the 'organic conviction' that regards wealth as the sole thing to be admired, 'this idolatry which worships the symbol (wealth) apart from the thing admired (noble character)'. But it is a sign of moral change that the wealthy (he has the manufacturing wealthy in mind) devote their wealth to 'furthering the material and mental progress of the masses'. Here, one feels, a few Strutts are made to go a very long way.

An identical complaint that wealth, the means, has been taken for culture, the end of life, was voiced by Samuel Smiles, accorded equal place with Spencer as a publicist for individualist *laissez-faire* capitalism:

> The love of gold threatens to drive everything before it. The pursuit of money has become the settled custom of the country. Many are so absorbed by it that every other well-being is either lost sight of or altogether undervalued. . . . In their pursuit of riches the English are gradually losing sight of their higher characteristics.[91]

What were the ideals which both men felt had been betrayed by the commercial classes in the pursuit of wealth? And why is it that these arch-'individualists' make such trenchant criticisms of a social order that prided itself on its 'entrepreneurial ethic'? The real nature of their dilemma is concealed if we fail to go beyond the slogans of 'individualism' *vs.* 'socialism' and 'co-operation' *vs.* 'competition' under which a series of political debates were conducted in the nineteenth century.[92] 'Individualism' was used to justify the creation of enormous industrial corporations, and 'socialism' was used by many who wanted to preserve and enlarge the sphere within which men could count as individuals. Men like Smiles and Spencer who praised the merits of individual striving and competition repeatedly stressed the value of voluntary association and co-operation;[93] and G. J. Holyoake, a co-operator of Owenite descent (who spoke of 'the Sodom of competition' and 'the unrest of pitiless competition more devastating than that of the sea'), defined co-operation as 'the organization of self-help' and as 'self-defensive Individualism, made attractive by amity, strengthened by interest and rendered effective by association'.[94] Underlying both sides was a social ideal which came to be felt progressively irreconcilable with English society as the century wore on and the scale of industrial organization increased.

The ideal was a community (or association) in which self-respecting and worthy individuals could share their resources for the common good and in which every particular individual could participate directly in the running of what concerned him. That Spencer shared this ideal is clear from a splendid and original analysis of the functioning of railway companies (of which he had an insider's knowledge)—'Railway Morals and Railway Policy' (1854).

English industrialization was remarkable in that it was almost entirely carried through by private partnerships.[95] There was a corresponding belief that successful enterprise demanded close surveillance of all activity by the owner-managers.[96] The railways were the first large-scale joint-stock companies permitted (by an

Act in 1844, extended to limited liability in 1856),[97] and for the first time emerged a phenomenon which came to be of the greatest importance for the structure of advanced industrial society—the divorce of management or control, and ownership or share-holding.[98] Spencer was well aware of this, and his response is significant. The 'democracy', or the control of their property by owners, is largely illusory, he says; board elections are quite insubstantial; despite the railway mania's excesses shareholders trust their directors, who lead them into all sorts of foolish and extravagant schemes, unnecessary branch lines, irrational competition between rival companies, and so forth. The reason is that the typical shareholder is ignorant and timid:

> Executors who do not like to take steps involving much responsibility; trustees fearful of interfering with the property under their care, lest possible loss should entail a lawsuit; widows who have never in their lives acted for themselves in any affair of moment; maiden ladies, alike nervous and innocent of all business knowledge; clergymen whose daily discipline has been little calculated to make them acute men of the world; retired tradesmen whose retail transactions have given them small ability for grasping large considerations; servants possessed of accumulated savings and cramped notions; with sundry others of like helpless character—all of them rendered more or less conservative by ignorance or timidity, and proportionately inclined to support those in authority.[99]

The proprietors have different interests from the directors, who often don't own many shares, but profit from expansion because they own land near the line, or industries, mines and harbours served by it, or because of other interests. The directors always have their way because, unlike the proprietors, they are 'in constant communication and have every facility for combined action'.[100] The root of the trouble is that those who own have not got control over their own interests. This is a consequence of the great scale of operation, far vaster than the ideal enterprise, the private partnership. Spencer's solution is to insist that the contract by which a proprietor invests money for a particular line should be limited, so that lines cannot be extended except unanimously. A proprietor should not be compelled to accept a new line or sell out. The goal of policy should be not to allow companies any life beyond what has been initially stipulated. The ideal is typical of Spencer, and the proposals typically unworkable in advanced industrial society.

This is co-operation of those who own property. Elsewhere co-operation is conceived of more widely, as a free association of workers. The essentials are that people should reap the just rewards of their labour, should be self-respecting and responsible, have a full and equal share in decision-making, and be free of 'dictation and authoritative classing'. Under the present wage-system, he says, 'the marks of *status* do not entirely disappear' for the worker 'is temporarily in the position of a slave and his onlooker stands in the position of a slave driver'.[101] It is illuminating to contrast his position with that of Marx, who like Spencer saw in the development of the joint-stock company and the divorce of ownership and management the end of a social era—in fact as a step towards the socialization of production.[102] But Spencer is more astute than Marx, and indeed anticipates much later criticism of Marx, in not regarding the abolition of manager-ownership as meaning the end of wage slavery. 'Authoritative classing' will last as long as some men have the right to tell others what to do. As for socialism, that is a species of militancy whose rule is 'do your task and take your rations', and whose motto 'to each according to his *needs*' will sever the natural and proper relations between *merit* and reward.[103] He holds out hope for an industrial system, difficult to envisage, in which workers merely contract to do work without coming under a capitalist's control. It reads like nothing so much as the domestic system of hosiery production practised in Nottingham and Derby in his youth. But towards the co-operative movement (not merely the system of shops) he is favourable, and even wrote in 1897, in the face of a trend towards militancy, that 'could a great spread of co-operative production be counted upon, some hope of arrest [of militancy] might be entertained'.[104]

Spencer's ideals are of a peculiar kind, anachronistic (in the sense of making totally unrealistic social assumptions) but traceable back to a time and place well *before* the ideological battle-lines of mature industrial society were drawn. Surveying the development of political ideals, and their related sociological assumptions, from the securely established positions of right and left, we find it hard to explain, for example, the similarities between Spencer (with his *laissez-faire* a man of the right, it must seem) and Holyoake (with his praise for Owen and co-operatives, a man of the left). How could Spencer call socialism 'the new Toryism',[105] or Holyoake state that

Lassalle, Marx, Comte and Disraeli, 'have all sung in varying tunes the same song'?[106] Both left and right have drawn sustenance from a common source, an ideal which was coherent only in a particular kind of society; with social change the elements of the ideal lost their coherence and were severally inherited by the left and the right, in new patterns of coherence.

The society presupposed by the ideal was small, permitting the worth of each member to be assessed by his fellows. It therefore excluded the large towns and factories of industrial society. But though it existed in pre-industrial society it was the least traditional part of it. For it was typically a *Gesellschaft*, a voluntary association, like the dissenting congregation, the private partnership in industry, the group of friends drawn together in pursuit of a common interest, Its rule was not that element which the socialist and the traditional 'organic' ideal have in common—'to each according to his need'—because this would have destroyed the primary value of individual independence. It was important not to reward or encourage laziness or fecklessness, for this would undermine the bonds of society, self- and mutual respect. The members were to decide of themselves to participate; membership were not 'of right', but was conditional upon the possession of suitable personal characteristics (e.g. religious commitment, not being a burden on one's fellows, knowledge or interest of a particular kind). Emulation and superiority in esteem were not excluded, but hierarchy and ascriptive status of all kinds were, and hence within the bosom of traditional society, with its orders and deference, such associations were anti-traditional. 'Idiocy' was excluded: for since the ideal was that all members should participate, all should be equally well-informed. Public opinion, not the judgment of an authority, was the prime agent of social control. The ideal was fostered by parish-education and the lay-control of the Kirk in Scotland (where Smiles was born); and in England wherever artisans, Dissenters and townsmen grew up in the interstices of traditional landed society and resolved to run their own affairs.

There was disagreement about the 'ground rules' of such a society. Men needed some prerequisites to enable them to be independent; but when did the provision of prerequisites amount to the undermining of independent self-reliance? Ultimately, by gradual extension of social benefits the ideal could become indistinguishable from a socialism which provides according to need rather than judged merit. But the ideal of independence required only a minimum of initial provision before individuals could be expected to prove their worth. Family was assumed, the agency which prepared the individual to face the cool winds of society and the co-operation of independent men. Spencer saw the family as reversing the moral rule of society—providing according to need, but in order to train in merit—and criticized socialism for applying family ethics to society. Most supporters of the ideal—Smiles, Cobden, Holyoake, but not Spencer—believed universal primary education should be provided too. And in a society in which land-ownership carried so much direct social power and influence, it was widely held necessary, to secure the conditions for independence, to grant equal rights to land, and to eliminate land as a buttress of social hierarchy.[107] Hence Spencer's 'land-nationalization' scheme which otherwise seems so out of place in his system. Other kinds of property did not seem, as land did, to be a source of unequal social power and a hindrance to independence. Only when they did, with the growth of large-scale industry, was their nationalization proposed, for most of the early 'socialists' only wanted to nationalize land.

It was not a rural ideal (except in the U.S.A.), nor, despite appeals to the Anglo-Saxons or occasional praise of the Medieval village-community, a traditionalist one. It was distinctly populist (in the American, not the Russian sense), the ideal of townsmen within a traditional society rapidly moving towards industrialism.[108] Even where it was adopted by industrial workers, such as the Chartists or Spencean philanthropists and involved land settlements, the model for the community was not the deferential, pseudo-paternalist village of recent memory but rather an urban type of society transferred to a rural setting. We find it in Paineite and Spencean radicals; among Dissenters of all sorts; among co-operators and trade-unionists; among the most radical of the entrepreneurial middle class such as Smiles and Cobden; among many founders of Utopian communities. Above all it underlies Spencer's ethic of co-operative individualism and is the basic model for what he called 'industrialism'.

So the competing social ideals of the period of industrialization, which might be called independence and paternalism, are rooted in pre-industrial social relations. The irony of history is that the ideal which sustained many of the early pioneers of industrialism created a social system in which its prerequisites were obliterated.[109] Though it survived as an ideal well into the late nineteenth century, once large-scale industry had emerged it could only be the source of social illusions. The evolution of the market, one of its concomitants, had a similar trajectory. Free market competition assumes a large number of fairly equal producers none of whom can dominate the market; but the efficient working of the market mechanism should by itself lead to a progressive reduction in the number of producers until the market evaporates into monopoly and cartels. The ideal of independence, like the perfect market, destroyed itself in time. Socialism only came of age when large-scale industry destroyed the old ideal's coherence. Its elements were divided up between the two heirs, who also divided the inheritance of the rival paternalist ideal; and there came into being the distinguishing marks of left and right. The left took participatory democracy and welfare provision according to need; while the justness of institutional inequalities of power and wealth, and the reduction of the sphere of government have become the property of what we are pleased to call 'conservatism'.

9: History's Revenge

I

The obsolescence which overtook Spencer's ideas at the end of the century raises two related questions. Firstly, what was it in the changing society of Britain that destroyed the coherence of Spencer's social philosophy by making its sociological assumptions irrelevant? The 1890s saw a new look in sociology, with Weber, Durkheim and others (often unbeknown to one another) opening up new themes and concerns. This period is properly considered a turning-point in sociology's history, and, more contentiously, as the beginning of modern sociology. The second question is how and why this new sociology was so different from the older evolutionary style.

Spencer was desperately aware of the emergence of phenomena, from as early as the late 1860s, that were contrary to his ideals: the growth of a professional civil service with ever-widening scope, compulsory primary education, the halting beginnings of a welfare state and new conceptions of the positive role of the state, and later the revival of working-class militancy, demands for the re-imposition of tariffs, imperial preference, accelerated acquisition of colonies, rearmament, jingoism. His confusion and discredit were compounded because he had tried to ground his ideals in determinate social theory. As their vision of the future fades, social evolutionists first stretch their theories, affecting to rejoice fair-mindedly in admitting exceptions and even claiming that their theories allow for them. For Spencer there was the 'Law of Rhythm' to invoke.[1] At the beginning of *The Man versus the State* (1884), asking why an unpredicted shift to 'militancy' was occurring, he wrote:

> Unaccountable as at first sight this unconscious change of policy seems, we shall find it has arisen quite naturally. Given the unanalytical thought ordinarily brought to bear on political matters, and under existing conditions, nothing else was to be expected.[2]

That is: if people had had the right ideas, they would not have given increased functions to the state—an explanation quite at variance with Spencer's usual theory that social formations are *not* the result of ideas, even wrong ones. One excuse he didn't use was that employed by Marx in similar circumstances: that he never intended his theory to be taken 'mechanistically'.[3] Sociologists *do* aim at determinancy: a theory is only such if it states a determinate relationship between variables. But as the inevitable exceptions pile up, the once-vaunted determinacy drains away and what were born as theories die as models.

During the years of the so-called 'Great Depression' (1876–96) there was a marked general loss of confidence in liberal thought. It no longer seemed that peace, commercial prosperity and liberalism of the *laissez-faire* variety were indispensible allies to one another. As Germany and the United States industrialized, Great Britain's industrial hegemony began to slip. Free trade had been suited to the first and for a long time the only industrial nation; but others found it essential to create tariff barriers to protect their infant industries. The process of technical and industrial competition between nations began to lead to imperialism. Then too Britain began in many spheres to pay the penalty for her industrial pioneering by obsolete equipment and organization. The financial operations of the City of London and the export of capital increased in importance at the expense of manufacturing; and in a variety of ways the centre of gravity of British life shifted from the provinces, where it had been for a century, to London once more.[4]

It became clear that there was a residue of problems at home which would not yield to *laissez-faire* and hopes of higher productivity and/or improved morality. Even the economists began to examine the timeless truths of their most British science, and social philosophers, since *laissez-faire* liberalism seemed to lead nowhere, began to seek new inspiration in French and especially German thought. Comte and Hegel each acquired fresh English followers. It is widely said that from the late 1860s the dominant tone of English social philosophy shifted from *laissez-faire* to 'collectivism'.[5] But the reality is more complicated. Most social doctrines do not simply express a condition of society but are an instrument in social policy, perhaps even a 'myth'.[6] Certainly *laissez-faire*, through political economy and the utilitarian philosophy, so dominated the social thought of the early and mid-nineteenth century that its opponents were faced with an uphill task in combating it. In the hands of Cobden, Spencer and others, it was the chief weapon against the aristocracy and the landed interest, and any traditionalist conceptions of the state and the economy. At the repeal of the Corn Laws they envisaged a future in which the principles of *laissez-faire* would be further extended. Yet the 1840s were already seeing important measures of a 'collectivist' kind—over factory conditions and public health. For several decades, indeed, 'collectivist' and '*laissez-faire*' measures proceeded apace alongside one another, but it was not until the 1860s and 1870s that it came to be felt that a new era of 'collectivism' was coming into being.

In the *laissez-faire* climate collectivist measures were enacted piecemeal in response to the various new demands of industrial society, and initially were often justified as means to enable individual initiative and self-help to flourish. Thus Finer writes of Sir Edwin Chadwick's labours for the New Poor Law, and legislation for factory regulation and municipal sanitation, that 'his activity was a ruthless and bureaucratic attempt to keep the ring clear for individual initiative wherever customs or vested interests stood in the way'.[7] Economic arguments were to remain individualist long after social philosophy and welfare had gone over to collective or statist ideals (as the case of T. H. Green shows).[8] The first steps towards 'collectivism' were either humanitarian, designed to alleviate particularly intolerable areas of distress, as with the Ten Hours Bill and other early measures supported by Tory radicals on traditional paternalist grounds; or were a direct response, in a utilitarian and expedient spirit, to practical problems created by the simple vastness and complexity of industrial organization. In both areas there was a steady advance from the inspectorates set up in the 1830s to a more positive regulation by the government and its departments. The railway companies, much vaster than other companies, required parliamentary bills, and, while remaining outside full public control, were increasingly subject to the rulings of the Railway Department of the Board of Trade (after 1851).[9] More importantly perhaps, they showed how very complex organizations could be, indeed *had* to be run, as planned enterprises. Later in the century it was businessmen like Joseph Chamberlain who proposed that public services of all sorts should be municipally owned, and could be as efficient as any large 'private' enterprise.[10] Birmingham should not be any different to run than a large engineering factory. Chadwick had argued that public services were much more efficient under a single control than under private partnerships, such as the six private companies which provided London's water in 1849. Here the argument was simply that things could be run much more efficiently in this way.

There was innovation in means before the ends of liberalism were challenged. Yet in the *laissez-faire* radicalism, Spencer's ideals, which had been the midwife of industrial society the ends and the means were closely intertwined. In the creation of industrial society it had seemed that such desirable goals as individual liberty and self-responsibility, efficiency and the satisfaction of mass needs, and the bringing of the mass of the people into the political community, were, granted the character of traditional society, solely and uniquely associated with the freeing of private initiative from the dead hand of state control in order that needs might be spontaneously met. This was the system of natural liberty. Moreover, industrial society was so utterly novel that it could not have been planned and engineered in its totality by any single agency, least of all a traditional political élite. As a whole the new system did arise spontaneously. But this did not mean that industrialism might not be planned and executed by an élite in a country *imitatively* industrializing itself, like imperial Germany, which, as we shall see, came to exercise great fascination even on British social theorists. Nor did it mean that the diminution of state-power was a condition for the continuance of industrialism, or for the curing of its (as it seemed to Spencer) incidental ills. What was called 'collectivism' was at first merely a conscious and deliberate pursuit of policies, and a systematization of procedures which had come about by spontaneous means.

The role of Benthamites, whether conscious disciples or those who unconsciously followed utilitarian principles, was crucial in the new developments. Although utilitarianism had seemed in the first half of the century indissolubly linked with the *laissez-faire* of political economy, as it was so propounded by James Mill, to excite the scorn of Carlyle and Dickens, this was a marriage of convenience. Political economy had then seemed the best means to the greatest happiness, and 'collectivism' might therefore seem to be a rejection of utilitarianism. But the Benthamites did not want the abolition of government so much as the establishment of expert, disinterested, efficient, uncorrupt, impartial government, seeking the general happiness far above sectional interests. Their legislative ideal was the *Code Napoléon*. Finer has said of Chadwick, the leading mid-century Benthamite, that 'as an administrator he might typify Prussia'.[11] They esteemed expert, professional opinion, and were the chief supporters of the National Association for the Promotion of Social Science (an 'absurdly self-titled' body, it seemed to Spencer),[12] which took an essentially managerial or technocratic approach to social problems, and saw 'social science' as an adjunct to legislation. These attitudes, with the addition of a positive socialist element, later found expression in the Fabian Society.[13]

An important element in the rise of collectivism was the growth, owing to the enormous expansion of technical and administrative tasks, of the professional, as against the entrepreneurial, middle class.[14] In Chadwick's day professionals were the main agents of the silent expansion of government, and eventually became, in the Fabian Society, the prime advocates for it. The new fields of professionalism—in the Civil Service, science, technology, teaching, management particularly—had emerged piecemeal with industrialization. The new professionals had initially distinguished themselves from the old professions—law, medicine, the Church—which had tended to be Tory in sympathy, long unreformed and implicated in the coils of 'Old Corruption'. But in the middle and late nineteenth century the new professions began to organize themselves, setting up institutions to defend professional standards and cultivate a professional ethos, and to claim unique expertise and even monopoly over their special fields. At the same time the old professions began to reform themselves. The antithesis between efficiency and competence, and professional monopoly, which had been natural when the new social functions were being forged, broke down when the new procedures began themselves to be institutionalized. Spencer never adjusted himself to the fact of the new professionalism, and always thought of professional monopoly and 'expertise' in terms of the corrupt old professions. When T. H. Huxley, alarmed at the prowess of organized German technical education, began to work for a new professionalism in English science, he was led to a sharp attack on the 'administrative nihilism' which Spencer stood for.[15] The professional middle class, as the manpower of the new inspectorates, institutes and bureaucracies, had everything to gain from collectivism, whose strongest opponents were found in the entrepreneurial middle class and their spokesmen. Yet even here, with the larger scale of industry, there was a growth of specialized management, and manufacturers like Chamberlain and Mundella were prominent advocates of aspects of collectivism.[16] Here, opposition to collectivism, where it was not just a lament for the passing of old, small-scale social conditions, was shifting from the old liberalism to the new conservatism. Spencer did not fully understand these developments, and wrote to Youmans that his counterblast to collectivism, *The Man versus the State*, meant that 'oddly enough I am patted on the back by the conservatives, which is a new experience for me'.[17]

Spencer felt a sense of betrayal when he saw members of the Liberal Party leading the movement towards collectivism. *The Man versus the State*, in terms of political theory, is a reassertion that true liberalism must involve the negative concept of liberty, being a freeing of men from restraints, not the fostering of happiness by the imposition of further restraints. 'Most of those who now pass as Liberals', he wrote with men like T. H. Green in mind, 'are Tories of a new type.'[18] The new trend could only be seen as a reversion from industrialism to militancy, from a social order like 'a body of producers or distributors' to one like 'an army formed of conscripts'. One trend which seemed to him particularly regressive was the growth of collective bargaining, with the trade unions negotiating on behalf of a mass of members and claiming to speak for all the operatives in a trade. A. J. Mundella's Act of 1872 on industrial arbitration struck Spencer, as it also struck Dicey, as a shift back from 'contract' to 'status'.

Despite the great differences, which seemed of little account to Spencer, between the ideals of the new collectivists and those of the old Tories, the new age did see the reintroduction of themes and ideals which radicals had hitherto shunned. The earlier conservatives, whom Spencer saw unambiguously as the foes of his ideals, in one way or another criticized capitalism and liberalism in the light of traditional society, its ideals or supposed attributes. Groups like the Christian socialists, the provincial Tory radicals or Young England were on the losing side. Marx, who did not just oppose, but sought to transcend liberalism, wrote their epitaph: 'the holy water with which the priest consecrates the heart-burnings of the aristocrat'.[19] What alliance there was between such Tories and the Benthamite professionals against the strict *laissez-faire* liberals in the middle years of the century stemmed from convenience more than from conviction.

But by the 1870s men who did not desire to preserve or restore society to its former condition, mostly Liberals closely involved in industry or the professions, were seeking to use arguments hitherto employed only by conservatives. In *Culture and Anarchy* (1869) Matthew Arnold both attacked the 'philistinism' of middle class, especially dissenting, opinion and provided inspiration for a system of universal education. For him the Established Church was the paradigm for an institution of nation-wide culture, not the reactionary oppressor of minority groups, much like Coleridge's 'clerisy', a sort of updated clergy as the guardian of the nation's shared intellectual, spiritual and cultural values. Arnold joined hands with advanced Liberals like A. J. Mundella whose Act establishing compulsory education, to the great disgust of Spencer and the Dissenters, became law in 1870. The same period, the late 60s and 70s, saw the development of the first self-conscious 'collectivist' school of thought among Liberal intellectuals—the English positivists under Harrison, Congreve and Beesly.[20] Comtean positivism had had its admirers ever since Mill, Lewes and Harriet Martineau had publicized it around 1850, but had little resonance as a social doctrine until *laissez-faire* liberalism (which Comte, half-technocrat and half-medievalist, hated) had run out of steam. Positivism's technocracy appealed to the new professionals; it expressed paternalist concern for the working classes, and several positivists forged links with labour leaders; the Religion of Humanity, with Catholicism as its model, offered a less negative social policy than Cobdenite liberalism.

Though positivism in the narrow sense was expressed in too alien (and in detail, too silly) a system to attract widespread support, it was a straw in the wind. The advanced liberalism of T. H. Green, Fabian socialism and the various strands of social imperialism took up one or another of its themes. Individuals, such as Beatrice Webb, paused at positivism on their way to the more permanent solution of socialism. The positivism of the 1870s was, in England, a solvent of ideological themes, which eased the search for a rationalization of the silent departures from *laissez-faire* which a mature industrial society was demanding. The appeal of technocracy and professionalism was what linked the positivism of the 1870s with Fabianism, just as it had drawn the utilitarians in the 1830s to Saint-Simonism.[21] A dash of the Middle Ages came to be as common in socialism, despite Marx, as in positivism. Apart from William Morris, Beatrice Webb could describe the Fabian social ideal of a tutelary state as 'straight out of the nobler aspect of the medieval manor'.[22] Both conservatives like Ruskin and socialists advocated welfare provision according to *need*, in direct opposition to Spencer's and the liberal position.

The intellectual coping-stone of collectivism was a new theory of political obligation and the positive function of the state. For providing this T. H. Green and Bosanquet turned to the justifier of the Prussian state, Hegel, who pictured the state as the repository of national culture.[23] Hegel had argued for the state bureaucracy as an agency which counteracted the class-conflict of civil society and protected the weaker members. The Fabians, civil servants to the core, adopted this position in their advocacy of state socialism, blandly ignoring Marx's criticism of Hegel on this very point, that a bureaucracy must represent one of the class-interests it was supposed to counteract.[24] In Britain, they maintained, there need be no antagonism between state and society, or between state socialism and social democracy. Other writers, such as D. G. Ritchie, saw Spencer as the main opponent and sought to rebut his charge that the new radicals were no different from the old Tories.[25] Much of Ritchie's case against Spencer concerns that unprofitable subject: what 'really' follows from the organic analogy. What is acceptable in Spencer, Ritchie, like many others, attributed to Comte; and as before, methodological must be attacked with political individualism.

Spencer deplored the revival of idealist metaphysics under Hegel's influence. He wrote to Alexander Bain in 1902 regretting 'the fate which has overtaken *Mind* . . . turned into an organ for German Idealism . . . this old world nonsense': it was hardly surprising, he considered, that their 'incredible dogmas' needed to be supported by 'Unthinkable propositions'.[26]

II

The political philosophies which gave a positive and ennobling function to the state were also highly convenient for imperialist use. It might be debated to the end of time just how much imperialism was a 'necessary' outcome of capitalism. J. A. Hobson, driven by sociological realism from the Cobdenite position, put forward the thesis, later incorporated by Lenin into his own explanation of the non-advent of the proletarian revolution, that imperialism was a direct consequence of the nature of the capitalist economy.[27] Since wages were so low, Hobson argued, industry was faced with a steadily diminishing rate of returns in the home market and so turned to overseas markets in competition with other industrial powers. Imperialism was only to be avoided by drastic measures at home to raise the purchasing power of the masses—which meant structural changes in the economy. Hobson shared with the Cobdenites a dislike of imperialism, but unlike them did not believe in a natural affinity between capitalism in any form and a pacific, internationalist foreign policy. Spencer's ideal of international peace was shared by the Marxists (who saw all wars as capitalist wars), by Cobdenite liberals such as John Bright (who still upheld the old antithesis of militancy and industrialism), by organized labour (to whom Bright's arguments probably still meant more than Marx's), and by a sprinkling of left-liberals such as Hobson, Graham Wallas and L. T. Hobhouse. These parties were against Empire and Protection. Others who called themselves socialist, such as the Webbs, Shaw and the majority of the Fabians, were for both.

So Spencer had a good case in seeing collectivism at home and imperialism abroad as a single nexus of 'social imperialism' as Bernard Semmel has called it.[28] As I have said, he did not really understand its 'necessity', or explain it in terms of the dynamic of historical development, as Hobson did. Yet he sought actively to oppose it. It called forth the same responses as the Crimean War or the Jamaican atrocities had done.

In 1881–2, when the Empire was being extended in India and Egypt, he wrote to John Bright asking his support for gathering together 'the large amount of diffused opinion against our aggressive policy' in an Anti-Aggression League.[29] But despite the verbal support of many eminent men it came to nothing. Spencer became more pessimistic about 'our Christian creed and our pagan doings, our professed philanthropy and our actual savagery'[30] as imperialism pursued its course. He argued that colonial aggrandisement was disastrous since any commercial advantages would not outweigh the cost of conquest and administration, that it would lead to an arms race and ultimately conscription from which the working classes would suffer most, and cause general demoralization because it fostered 'those sentiments which, joined with development of militant organization, end in destruction of free institutions and despotism'. By the 1890s his tone was apocalyptic:

> Now that the white savages of Europe are overrunning the dark savages everywhere—now that the European nations are vying with one another in political burglaries—now that we have entered upon an era of social cannibalism in which the strong nations are devouring the weaker—now that national interests, national prestige, pluck and so forth are alone thought of, and equity has dropped utterly out of thought, while rectitude is scorned as 'unctuous', it is useless to resist the wave of barbarism. There is a bad time coming, and civilized mankind will morally be uncivilized before civilization can again advance.[31]

The rush to acquire colonies seemed to Spencer an aberration, albeit one whose internal characteristics, granted its existence, were readily expressible by the model of militant society. Yet he had an astute grasp of the trend of events, as he showed in his correspondence with leading Japanese diplomats and politicians. He wrote to Kentaro Kaneko (whom he also got elected to the Athenaeum) giving advice about foreign policy and a new constitution.[32] On both scores his advice was very sound. 'Japanese policy should be that of keeping Americans and Europeans as much as possible at arm's length', lest they seize a territorial foothold which, Spencer said, would inevitably lead to annexation; don't allow Europeans to participate in coastal trade or have mining concessions; forbid intermarriage; pursue a conservative policy to avoid social dissolution. At a time when Europeans tended to believe that the best thing that might happen to an Asiatic country was for it to become a European colony, it is not surprising that *The Times* considered this 'advice as narrow, as much imbued with antipathy to real progress, as ever came from a self-sufficient, short-sighted Mandarin, bred in contempt and hatred of barbarians'.[33] Marxists opposed imperialism for a similar reason as social imperialists such as Chamberlain and the Webbs supported it—it was a form of heightened nationalism in which the working class was bound in more closely with the propertied classes either through sentiment ('false consciousness') or through actual social benefits ('bribes') à la Bismarck. The mechanism of social imperialism was perfectly comprehensible in terms of Spencer's sociology: hostility between nations was functionally related to solidarity within the nation. This was what militancy meant. Though Spencer's ethics were the opposite of Ruskin's, he would have agreed with Ruskin's social diagnosis, when, in advocating a society where every child would have the *right* to housing, food, clothing and education, Ruskin said this would mean that 'the government must have an authority over the people of which we now do not so much as dream'.[34] Welfare-statism, state socialism, patriotism, imperialism, protectionism were distinct objectives which yet seemed to point to the others. So Chamberlain, whose early interests were in efficient municipal management and protectionism, which had a peculiar relevance for Birmingham industries, shifted, over the period 1880–95, from the liberal distaste for colonial expansion to a fervent imperialism.[35]

The cruellest irony was that imperialism was most widely justified by an appeal to 'Social Darwinism', a heterogeneous body of doctrines, themes and symbols which had virtually become the ideological *lingua franca* of the age.[36] Spencer, of course, was taken to be a leading Social Darwinist. The merit of Darwinism was that, apart from the notion of struggle, it was almost all form and no substance. In particular there was no substantial proposition as to the criteria of fitness, or to the units of struggle, whether individuals, classes, nations or races. Social Darwinism is most readily associated with the competition of individuals, as in the work of bourgeois political economists like Malthus, bourgeois social philosophers like Spencer and bourgeois biologists like Darwin. The social influence of Darwinism has mostly been studied in this form.[37] But elsewhere a different social moral was drawn. In Emile Zola's novel *Germinal* (1885), the young strike-leader Etienne says that the workers will triumph in the struggle because they are stronger than the effete bourgeois; not so, replies Souvarine the anarchist, for the lesson of

Darwin is that there will always be an aristocracy to rule the masses.[38]

The socialist Darwin was just one version of the collectivist Darwin, the principle mutation of the bourgeois individualist Darwin. In Germany there was a long debate between Haeckel and Virchow over the relationship of Darwinism to socialism;[39] and a synthesis of the two, or even a presumption that Darwinism *implied* socialism was very prevalent. Marx's view (expressed in a letter as early as 1860) that Darwin 'contains the basis in natural history for our view' is well known, as is his desire to dedicate a volume of *Capital* to Darwin.[40] Engels associated socialism and Darwinism even more strongly. An Italian socialist and member of the Second International, Enrico Ferri, even argued that Marxism was the natural culmination of the theories of Darwin and Spencer.[41] The only social group which could find no way of accommodating Darwinism, since their social image totally excluded a sanctification of struggle in society, was real conservative traditionalists of whose ideologies Roman Catholic social philosophy is a typical instance. Despite their eclectic use of some traditionalist themes, social imperialists found collectivist variants of Darwinism ideally suited to their purposes.

By another irony initial attempts to take tooth-and-claw struggle *out* of individualist Darwinism furnished material for collectivist Darwinism. In *Mutual Aid*, Kropotkin was concerned to show how group sympathies, and the deliberate restriction of competition, had been important facts in evolution.[42] Instances ranged from the swarming of bees to that institution beloved of anarchists and Russian populists, the ancient Slavonic *mir* or village-community. As I have said, Kropotkin's view of the mechanism of evolution was more Spencerian than Darwinian; but once natural selection had completely ousted the possibility of non-exterminating improvement through use-inheritance, it came to be argued that mutual aid worked to strengthen groups in their *competition* with other groups. What might be called the dialectic of struggle and solidarity, so well entrenched in the Marxist view of social evolution, came to occupy the central position in collectivist Darwinism. Now it was commonplace to emphasize the necessary role of struggle in nation-building. Bagehot's *Physics and Politics* (1869) contains a lucid statement of the argument. But whereas Spencer gave militancy a crucial role in the formation of early society, the collectivist

Darwinists insisted that these processes continued to be operative, and needed to be forcefully re-emphasized.

There were class-variants, nation-variants and race-variants (the last two often synthesized) of the same theme, which tended to use identical arguments. Ferri is an influential example of the first. In *Socialism and Positive Science* (*Darwin, Spencer, Marx*) he rejected the argument of T. H. Huxley and those socialists who said the struggle for survival did not apply to civilized society: it does, even though, as Spencer and Kropotkin have shown, it assumed a less 'violent and muscular' character.[43] But the philosophical individualism of Spencer and the liberals is rejected, for, as Darwin has shown, 'the species—that is to say the social aggregate—is the great, the living and eternal reality of life'.[44] In the core of the book, a chapter entitled 'Class Struggle and the Struggle between the Species', Ferri compares the socialist conception to 'the grand drama of the struggle for life among the species', while the liberal-capitalist one is merely 'the savage and insignificant fight of one individual with another'.[45] He concludes by praising the 'heroic nationalism' which has given Italy and Germany independence and which, with socialism, would build them into nations. His language is replete with biological words like 'hypertrophy', 'hygiene' and 'pathology'.

In Britain the working-class labourites, being still left-liberal in outlook, tended to avoid collectivist Darwinism, which was the natural idiom of social imperialism. Here nation and race were stressed. Perhaps the most popular serious book of the age was Benjamin Kidd's *Social Evolution* (1894), said by Halévy to have gone through nineteen editions in four years.[46] Kidd shared with the neo-Hegelians the idea that the state was the source of morality and that it was fitting for individual interests to be subject to it. (This, to Spencer, was simply immoral). Kidd was fundamentally opposed to internationalism—whether of the Marxist or the liberal variety. He had a number of traditional pieties, particularly religion, whose office was to get men to subordinate their present, individual desires to remote, collective ones. Once again, theories which Spencer had related to an earlier, militant phase of social evolution were by others advocated as ever-present truths.

The organicism of Kidd stressed the superiority of the social whole rather than the functional division of labour. But for the collectivist social Darwinians biology furnished a rich fund of suggestive imagery (nations fighting and surviving, or being sick or healthy, with the centre regulating all the organs, etc.) rather than the precisely specified analogy which Spencer had used. The extremes of biologism were found where the racist influence of Francis Galton, that versatile genius, was strongest. In Galton's judgment, no social determinants were half as significant as race and heredity, and nations were to be conceived of as genetic stocks. So the chief business of a government should be to improve the national genetic composition. This was 'a hard doctrine for democracy', said Galton, 'but the safety of the state lies in its acceptance'. It was painful for Spencer to see how a scientist and a friend (especially one of provincial, Quaker descent) could express sentiments—'One able leader, inspirer and controller of men, is worth thousands of everyday workers to the race'—which once would have been the mark of opponents of science and humanity, like Carlyle and Sir Fitzjames Stephen.[47] Wars were inevitable, a means to the genetic improvement of the human race at large. Eugenics as a national policy was easier to combine with *laissez-faire* of Spencer's variety than with socialism (though Karl Pearson managed to effect a marriage, and many Fabians flirted with it), but the necessary racial competition between nations was well tailored for justifying imperialism. In a more collectivist mode, it was argued that social welfare policies and protection of home industries, would make the social organism 'healthier' and fitter for the international struggle for survival. The consequently increased power of the state was another nail in the coffin of *laissez-faire*. While it was clear to Spencer, in terms of his social models, why these various tendencies of the 1890s were so mutually supporting, it remained inexplicable, in terms of his theory, why the overall shift had occurred.

III

The sociology of the 1890s has been the subject of two major studies by Professors T. Parsons and H. S. Hughes.[48] It was, significantly, a continental creation, not a British one. The difficulties for sociology in England were partly institutional and partly intellectual. The colossal achievement of Spencer, bound to an impossible political philosophy for a developed industrial society, had become a stumbling-block. Abrams' verdict on Spencer's influence in his native country is just:

> Confronted with Spencer's conception of sociology, many British intellectuals of the 1880s felt themselves drowning in their own thought world. Comte and Le Play were the straws they clutched at. Modern British sociology was built, more than anything else, as a defence against Spencer. It is in this sense that his influence was decisive.[49]

Even where Spencer's influence was both positive and acknowledged, as in the functionalist anthropology of Radcliffe-Brown, it was largely indirect through Emile Durkheim.

Both Parsons and Hughes see the original achievement of the 1890s as a decisive rejection of positivist modes of thought. Yet this formulation raises almost as many problems as it solves. If positivism means 'the application in sociology of the methods of the natural sciences', there may be as many variants of it as there are conceptions of what science is. To some even Comte and Spencer may seem to have been very unsuccessful as positivists. If positivism is defined more clearly as materialism, mechanism, behaviourism or determinism, it is doubtful if these labels usefully stick on Spencer, or can be used to distinguish him from later writers. He denied being a materialist, as many so-called materialists do;[50] someone so attached to organic imagery can hardly be called a mechanicist; he frequently asserts that in explaining behaviour the sociologist should not ignore subjective conditions;[51] and, while certainly a determinist, was not more of one than many of his successors.

Stuart Hughes frequently stresses the kinship of the new style of thought which superseded Spencer with William James' pragmatism: a suspicion of intellectualist explanations, an emphasis on the practical character of thought, an operationalist treatment of theories and concepts. Yet, as I have indicated at various points in this study, these orientations are equally true of Spencer (or, for that matter, of Adam Smith and Marx). They are in part demands for looseness, for a liberation from the confines of particular determinate theories; and as such are not so much the special characteristic of *this* wave of innovation as of innovation in general. Spencer made these criticisms of the rigid utilitarian philosophy and psychology (as Marx of the

Hegelian), and was criticized in his turn. As long as theory aims at being a closed, determinate system of variables, criticism may take this form. But it does not explain the content of the innovation. Even here Parsons often exaggerates the change, as in his references of Spencer's treatment of religion. Spencer's theory is both inadequate and inferior to Durkheim's, but the differences are more of degree than of kind.

Despite their points of agreement, Parsons and Hughes set about explaining the change in rather different ways. Hughes sees the age as 'the period in which the subjective attitude of the observer of society first thrust itself forward in peremptory fashion', resulting in 'an enormous heightening of intellectual self-consciousness—a wholesale re-examination of the presuppositions of social thought itself'.[52] There is much truth in this sophisticated cultural history. But why? Somewhat imprecise references to social disorders, to 'old practices and institutions no longer conforming to social realities' and to a 'sense of demise of an old society'[53] do not really go far enough. All these things could equally well be said of the Britain which produced Smith and the political economists, Paine and Burke, Godwin and Malthus, the romantic poets, Bentham, Mill and Spencer, George Eliot and Dickens. Hughes says a great deal about the way in which the new intellectual wave, figures like Bergson and Proust as well as the sociologists, saw the world, but little about that world itself. Yet it was this which gave the sociologists at least a new subject matter and, with it, new occasion for theorizing.

The same lacuna is to be found in Parsons' *The Structure of Social Action*, declared by its author to be 'an attempted empirical verification, in a particular case, of a theory of the process by which scientific thought develops'.[54] Explicitly, the theory advanced states that there is a long-term shift, in the writings considered, to the 'voluntaristic theory of action', which is objectively superior to earlier positivist theories of action. More implicitly, Parsons only considers seriously two sorts of factors as determinative of thought: ideology, related to social class; and 'the general process of "immanent" development of science itself', achieved, as in all science, by the mutual influence of theories and observations.[55] The former is discounted here, because the political values of Weber, Pareto and Durkheim were so divergent (though in fact perhaps not as much as he says). So the sociology of the 1890s outlines a general theory of society, worked out through particular empirical studies, that is a permanent improvement, scientifically truer, than previous theories going back beyond Spencer to Hobbes. It is at least partially true that Durkheim, say, chose his detailed studies as being critical for a general theory of society to rival Spencer's and Hobbes'. But what is ignored is that Spencer and Durkheim were theorizing very largely, not about Society but about different societies; and Durkheim and Hobbes even more so. For each new sociological generation's writing is shaped primarily by what social features distinguish their age from previous ones. If we ask why Durkheim wrote about the causes of suicide and the religion of Australian aborigines, or why Weber and Pareto made so much of their respective concepts of bureaucracy and élite, we should not look first at the deficiencies of the then current, but immanently developing, 'theory of Society', but the novel features of their own societies, so different from that which had produced Spencer and provided Marx with so much of his subject matter. The influence of this is worth considering, as it rarely is, in greater detail.

The new sociology was obsessed with the problem of social order and rediscovered the centrality of politics in the social system. Talcott Parsons is well aware of this and under his influence it has become common for it to be said that *the* problem of sociology is the problem of order.[56] But it was so re-emphasized because of the fragile, problematic nature of social and political order, and because of the difficulty of reconciling order and liberal ideals, in Germany, France and Italy in the late nineteenth century. It was not so much innate defects in liberal and Marxian sociology, as the fact that they did not apply well to certain societies. Similar themes may be traced through the whole group, but the new preoccupations are seen most starkly in Max Weber.

The circumstances of German industrialization were vastly different from Great Britain's. Whereas Britain's, being first, unanticipated and spontaneous, had been long drawn out, pushed through by middle-class entrepreneurs who had been largely hostile to the old political élite, in a political unit of unquestioned national coherence, employing relatively simple technology and small-scale methods of organization, Germany's was the first successful imitative industrialization—being undertaken under the patronage of the political élite, in defence of national interests, in a country lately united by force of arms, employing relatively advanced technology and large units of production, at great speed and compression.[57] The presuppositions of earlier theories of industrialism were upset. The German experience displayed, in Spencer's terms, a combination of militancy and industrialism. Referring to Spencer, a modern liberal, Ralf Dahrendorf, asks why the liberal qualities were so lacking in Germany. 'Not even industrialization managed, in Germany, to upset a traditional outlook in which the whole is placed above the parts, the state above the citizen, or a rigidly controlled society above the lively diversity of the market, the state above society. Wherever one would hope for the word 'rational' the other one 'national' appears instead as an argument for policy decisions. Instead of developing it, industrialization in Germany swallowed the liberal principle.'[58] Where the state, dominated by a landed and military aristocracy, was the biggest entrepreneur, the bourgeoisie, the historical bearer of liberal values, was weak and 'its aspirations were individual desires for recognition rather than the solidary demands of a new political class'.[59] No Paines, Cobdens, Spencers here! The state under Bismarck prevented true civility, that nexus of independent and self-restrained attitudes that Spencer called the industrial character, because it treated its subjects 'like children of the patriarchial family'.[60] Even at its best it was benevolent but severe, that is, authoritarian.

The Marxian analysis of capitalism ran into difficulties too. It was not possible to treat the state and political power as emanations of the classes of civil society and economic power in a society where, as Golo Mann says of Bismarck's Germany, 'the government was not the executive committee of the nation, in essence identical with it, but a power apart which might negotiate with it'.[61] Bismarck had for decades held himself aloof from all parties, National Liberals (Weber's father's party), the Centre, the Social Democrats, even the Conservatives, giving concessions (such as the policy of social benefits for the workers which so impressed the Fabians) and shifting his alliances as State policy dictated. In so doing he relied on the bureaucratic traditions of Prussia. It was not simply that these survived but, as Veblen saw,[62] that they were refurbished because they were so convenient for the direction of the State's planned industrialization and the containment of its social tensions.

For such an autonomous state-controlling bureaucracy was really alien to the Rhineland, the chief industrial area and the cradle of German liberalism. In the early nineteenth century Marx the Rhinelander had criticized the Prussian Hegel's view that the bureaucracy both could and should be a counterpoise to the open class struggles of 'civil society'.[63] Marx drew on political economy and the experience of England and France to argue that a bureaucracy could not be other than an expression of the forces in civil society; to argue that it was, he insisted, was to deny the *social* character of man and his institutions. There is little point in trying to decide whether Marx or Hegel was 'right', *tout court*, on this issue; for the societies which each took as his model were different. But Imperial Germany does provide evidence for the Hegelian implication that power need not rest on property, and that, in important ways, there is an irreducible element in bureaucratic or political institutions. Weber's theory of bureaucracy, and the writings of Pareto, Mosca and Michels on élites focus on newly perceived inadequacies in the concept of social class, seen as an economically determined phenomenon.

The rejection of economic determinism, correctly seen by Parsons and others as a central theme in Weber's work, did not come about simply because its intrinsic theoretical inadequacy was obvious but because it is much less true of imitative than of spontaneous industrialization. For, as I have discussed in Chapter 4, it was an important ingredient, expressing a real feature of the English Industrial Revolution, in the liberal creed.[64] In Spencer it took the form of the theory than in industrial society it is the economy as it spontaneously satisfied needs through the market which is the leading, dynamic sector of society. Such could not appear the case where the polity took the leading role in the industrial transformation. Appropriately enough, it was not in his famous historical study of the Protestant ethic that Weber first claimed a decisive role for ideas and culture in social change, but in his early study of agrarian migration in East Prussia.[65] Moreover, the migration of German peasants constituted a problem because of the national policies of the *Machtstaat*, or 'power-state' to which Weber was loyal.[66]

Weber was genuinely attached to the rational, individualist and civil values of classic liberalism. Yet liberalism comes easiest when nationhood is unproblematic, and when the problems of nation building, usually an illiberal and violent process, are safely in the past.[67] Nationalism was not the problem for Marx, and he misunderstood its force, while Spencer took it for granted. Many of the moral concerns of the sociologists of the 1890s may be profitably seen as those of liberals in circumstances when liberalism was, or was seen to be, difficult to work. The pleasure which Pareto took in exposing hypocritical liberal pieties derived, at least in part, from his failure to get the Italian government to adopt liberal economic policies, and reflected a profound disillusionment with liberal ideals.[68] Durkheim was more hopeful about the prospects for a liberal society with full individual's rights for every citizen, though he rejected what he called 'the narrow utilitarianism and utilitarian egoism of Spencer'.[69] But this was liberalism for a more troubled society than England—the French Third Republic which had been beaten by Germany with the loss of two provinces (including Alsace, Durkheim's homeland) and had endured the brief but bloody agony of the Paris Commune in 1871. The Dreyfus affair of 1898, in which Durkheim had taken a public stand, exposed the raw nerves of bitterly opposed parties. Industrialization begets tensions which a strong and united élite, by appealing to national traditions, may contain; but France's public traditions, founded by the great Revolution and by Napoleon, were not accepted by many leading bodies of opinion, and different factions—bourgeois republican, Royalist (Orleanist or Legitimist), Bonapartist, Socialist, Catholic and anti-clerical—had different views of what 'France' properly was. Durkheim's sociology has a remarkable unity of moral purpose, marked throughout by the fear of *anomie* and the desire to establish a *conscience collective* suitable for industrial society. Durkheim's sociology is much closer to Spencer's than Weber's is, as France resembled England more than Imperial Germany, and took over many Spencerian elements. But whereas Spencer had been able to assume the solution of basic problems of national legitimacy and public norms, Durkheim had seen them as highly problematic. The norms which Spencer took as the enduring psychological residue of past militant political and religious discipline, Durkheim saw in perpetual dependence on institutional arrangements. Here, very properly, modern sociology has taken its cue from Durkheim.

IV

Sociological theory was not only struck by a new subject matter but by new conceptions about the relationship between sociology as an activity and the mainstream of social life. Weber, the most original and far-sighted of his generation, not only insisted, against the Marxists, on the important role of ideas in society *qua* object of study, but worked out the methodological implications of a relatively new view, which contrasts sharply with Spencer's, about the place of the sociologist's ideas in social life. It is here, rather than to society as subject-matter, that what Parsons calls 'voluntarism' properly applies.

Spencer did not think that men's ideas and theories, whether his own or others', were of much independent force as causative factors in social change. Most clearly in *Social Statics* he argued that men only envisaged things when the basic forces of evolutionary adaptation were on the point of bringing them to pass. Marx's relegation of thought to 'superstructure' makes a similar point against Hegel. Spencer's depreciation of reason is not remotely akin to the irrationalism, in the sense of injunctions to worship the dark gods of one's instincts, that became prevalent in some quarters in the late nineteenth century.[70] Why did he and Marx consider theory so 'weak'? It was, I suggest, an appropriate response to a period of history in which events in their totality were in fact more truly unpredictable than they have been before or since. To consider theory 'powerful', in the sense that social arrangements and the course of social change happen as they were previously intended to in the schemes and theories of the intellectual élite, is hardly possible in a society like England in the period 1750–1850, where social developments, through the result of an infinitude of tiny plans, absolutely outstripped the power of any intellect to predict them. The most striking instance of this is that Adam Smith's *Wealth of Nations*, published in 1776, a handbook of what lay behind the Industrial Revolution if ever there was one, betrays no sign that its author thought that there was anything revolutionary or irreversible about the change that Europe was beginning to undergo.[71]

Theory can only be really credited with power in traditional or post-industrial societies. In traditional or ideally stable societies there is a mutual adjustment between theory and things which permits intellectuals (priests or teachers in some sort of establishment) to claim with plausibility, even when it is not quite true, that things are as theory intends them to be. An incidental effect is that the role of the intellectuals themselves is magnified. Theory tends to regain the prestige it loses during industrialization in technologically advanced societies. For these societies depend on what has now become possible in very many fields: great skill at predicting trends which are or are decided to be considered as inevitable, and at realizing social goals by the application of the proper techniques. Amitai Etzioni's *The Active Society* is a detailed attempt to analyse this situation. Again, as in medieval Europe and as Saint-Simon predicted, the intelligentsia form an establishment—scientists, technicians, experts of various kinds. But the most percipient thinkers of the transitional period were free-booters, sceptical alike of institutions and of the potency of 'theory'.

Where events outstrip the power of theory to predict or plan them, what is the function of theory? It becomes a kind of theodicy, with the function, if not the prime purpose (which may be prediction or ethical demonstration), of reconciling men to the necessity of things. At a time of unprecedented, seemingly uncontrolled and terrifying change, Spencer reassured the bewildered by interpreting the transition that men had experienced and setting it within a longer arc of change covering all nature.

At the end of the century evolutionary theories, Spencer's above all, lost their power to convince very suddenly because history played them false: their predictions, stages and continua just did not fit events any more. Sociology's inability to function as theodicy permitted it to be of use for limited prediction in order to control. This use had already been envisaged by Comte ('*Savoir pour prévoir, prévoir pour pouvoir*'), but it is difficult for the evolutionary sanctification of desired ends to be combined with the open-ended assessment of feasible means. The latter requires that the ends be considered as contingent and that theory have the role of effecting change, not reconciling men to it. The end of the century saw therefore a revived discussion of the place of ends or values in sociology. The issues were sidestepped by evolution since it attempted to establish values without moral argument by showing how a particular set would inevitably come about. Durkheim, who shared the Enlightenment desire for a rational, science-based ethic, reverted to an archaic and pre-evolutionary method: by using the language of pathology to suggest that 'normal' and 'sick' states of society could be demonstrated.[72] For the Fabians Sidney Webb asserted that 'the conditions of social health are . . . a matter for scientific investigation'.[73] Unlike Durkheim and S. Webb, Weber saw that there was a problem, and, in the context of a society for applied research, attempted a solution.[74]

The argument over values involves various distinct themes, not all of which are relevant to the issue that was debated at the end of the nineteenth century. Without being exhaustive one might note these five:

(*a*) Should sociologists practise moral indifference towards the world? This is an impossible question, since indifference is a moral stance. But since it does not follow from other of the possible meanings of ethical neutrality, it can be disregarded.

(*b*) Is it not the case that science, like all other activities, *presupposes* certain moral values, such as respect for the evidence, liberal climates of discussion etc.? This is true, but peripheral to the central issue.

(*c*) Does not the scientist, in his analysis of the data or his selection of problems, rely on guiding principles of relevance and significance, which are values? Again true, but peripheral.

(*d*) Does one admit the possibility of bias and prejudice arising from one's moral values, and seek to counteract them?

(*e*) Is it, or is it not, possible to deduce moral principles from factual premisses? If science is a matter of inferences and deductions from facts, it cannot, of itself, yield moral values, and where it seems to do so, cannot be purely science.

Only the last two are central to the matter as discussed by Weber. Spencer was fully aware of the dangers of moral prejudice (*d*), but still aspired to establish a system of rational ethics (*e*). 'Pull to pieces a man's Theory of Things,' he wrote in *Social Statics*, 'and you will find it based upon facts collected at the suggestion of his desires. A fiery passion consumes all evidences opposed to its gratification and fusing together those that serve its purpose, casts them into weapons by which to achieve its end.'[75] Several successive chapters of *The Study of Sociology* consider in turns political, religious and class sources of vicious bias in sociology. This sounds very salutary advice, and is only surprising because of what we would judge to be Spencer's flagrant and repeated breaches of it. But though biased selection of evidence may always give a case undeserved support, the establishment of values through their evolutionary inevitability may *in principle* avoid it completely. When Spencer's evolutionary scheme fell through and its author was incidentally convicted of bias, it came to be asserted, or rather reasserted, that moral conclusions could not rest solely on scientific reasoning.

The philosophical argument against Spencer in England was formulated by Henry Sidgwick in an essay 'The Relation of Ethics to Sociology' (1899), from which it probably passed to the attack on Spencer for committing the 'naturalistic fallacy' by G. E. Moore in *Principia Ethica* (1909), a book that is often taken to be the beginning of modern British moral philosophy. Sidgwick examines Spencer's attempt to reduce ethics to sociology by means of the laws of evolution. After presenting the '*ought* can't be deduced from *is*' argument, he criticizes Spencer thus:

> As this wide and quasi-architectonic use of sociological conception leads to a mistaken attempt to get the ideal out of the actual, so the converse influence of ethics on sociology leads to equally mistaken attempts to get the ideal into the actual—i.e. to predict a future state of society in harmony with ethical ideas without any adequate support in scientific induction from the known facts of past social evolution.[76]

Sidgwick here confuses common bias and the naturalistic fallacy. Complaints that Spencer committed the latter may apply to parts of *The Data of Ethics* or the brief 'intuitionist' sections of *Social Statics* but hardly touch the power of a well-founded evolutionary argument, that the contingently desirable will necessarily come about. The predictions turned out wrong, and no doubt this was because of Spencer's bias: he predicted what he wanted to see. But to preach that naturalism is a philosophical error does not provide an antidote to simple self-deception. The answer to that is not to forswear values but to pay more attention to facts.

Neither moral evaluation nor sociological argument can be kept wholly untouched by the other. But this was not intended by Weber when he employed the Kantian argument for the autonomy of ethics in support of his plea for a value-free sociology. For this did not derive merely from a desire for a sociology uncontaminated by prejudice, but from a new conception of the function of sociological theory. So far from value-freedom meaning that the social sciences should strive to be useless or detached from what men value, it came at a time when they were being increasingly used as means to ameliorate social conditions, to effect social ends. In England a position similar to Weber's was first achieved by the economists, who were always remote from evolution.[77] In being value-neutral sociology would be like other sciences, whose utility as means depends on theory being a representation of actuality, and not the presentation of a 'reality' which is in fact a projection of the theorist's desires. Where sociology has a technological function, it must take values or ends, for the purpose of the study, as contingent, and not seek to validate them as such by evolutionary necessity. In the end it was technology that killed evolution.

10: Sociology and its History

I

After Spencer's dethronement, it must have seemed most improbable that social evolution could be revived. But in the last decade it has been, chiefly in the hope that, suitably renovated, it could provide a framework for an important contemporary focus of sociological research: problems involved in the development and industrialization of the Third World. Before evaluating this revival it is necessary to consider some of the leading features of the orthodox sociology of the first half of this century, which has been responsible both for the burial and the resurrection of Spencer. In fact, evolution's revival is not as radical a break as it looks, just as the innovations of the 1890s were not such a shift of approach as was supposed. The enduring thread has been positivism: a continuous, often inappropriate desire that sociology should be as other sciences are supposed to be. Its most persistent effect has been to reject history and to drive a wedge between history and sociology—subjects which, like it or not, still have the same subject-matter.

Sociology was made a reasonably unified and coherent subject by the Americans, who welded together very diverse streams: the heritage of Spencer, much modified and criticized; the great tradition of empirical research on urban, racial and social problem areas begun by Park, Thomas and their disciples at Chicago; the native social psychology of Cooley and Mead which later fused the insights of Durkheim and Freud to produce the first really satisfactory theory relating individual and society; the absorption of much material from Pareto, Weber and other continental European sociologists, and from the British social anthropologists, by Parsons, Merton, Homans and others. By the 1940s all this was being synthesized into a mainstream of 'theory' to which most ongoing research was related. Many of its definitions are still widely accepted: that the fundamental problem of sociology is the problem of order, that functionalism is its particular method, that with the development of proper methods of controlling its data sociology would fulfil its scientific promise, that social institutions can be classified by their functions in a general theory of society. Under these convictions much excellent work was done, especially in the U.S.A., despite continuous guilty laments that it didn't look as if the *science* of sociology was coming into being very quickly.

But for an era of sociology which regarded itself as such a total improvement on its imperfectly remembered past, a great deal was left out. Social philosophy, and serious attempts to discuss the changing relationship between sociological research and political or moral values, were regarded as pre-scientific concerns—except by such white blackbirds as the Russian-born Sorokin and Morris Ginsberg, for years the only British sociologist of wide reputation. Partly this was because—despite the ironies of a congenital outsider like Veblen—values could virtually be taken for granted in the liberal, progressive, Social Gospel to New Deal ethos of American sociology.

Another blank area lay in the analysis of social conflict. It was not that sociologists were unaware of its existence, for there were a great many studies of delinquency and deviation from the norms and values which were seen as the basic feature of a society. But there was for years an ignorance and neglect of Marx and an unwillingness to look at areas such as industrial unrest or class struggle except to stress the temporary and soluble nature of conflicts, granted wisdom and goodwill all round. It could not be denied that in other unhappy lands revolutions occurred (Sorokin even wrote a book on the sociology of revolution in 1925); but America, since she manifestly existed as a society, and since, almost by definition, societies rest on value-consensus, demanded analysis in functional, consensual terms. For a while 'structural-functionalism' was virtually coextensive with sociological theory. The so-called 'conflict school' never existed. It is a figment of the writers of textbooks on theory, looking for some way to bracket together a number of distinct approaches which were unhappy with the synthesis:[1] Marxism (which has only been revived as a style of sociology in the last decade or so), writers influenced by Simmel such as Coser and Gluckman, and rather Weberian critics like Dahrendorf and Lockwood.

A third, related, aspect of this phase was the neglect of history, which though significant and typical, does not follow from functionalism as such. Its origins are various. There was the influence of Malinowski and Radcliffe-Brown, in recoil from the excesses of conjectural history in social anthropology, who argued, very properly, that the only way of studying societies with no recorded history was to analyse institutions in terms of the functions they performed in the current working of society. Radcliffe-Brown's admission of the need for studying society diachronically was perfunctory;[2] and Malinowski's analysis of social change was trite.[3] But their functional concepts entered American sociology, and the heritage of Spencer was wholly purged of evolutionism. Then there was the notion that, since sociology was becoming a cumulative science, its subject matter 'human behaviour' not only could be studied adequately in the present, but ought to be. Scientific method required that the subject-matter be 'created' under controlled experimental conditions, if at all possible. Hence the great development of attitude studies based on questionnaires. History was not only dispensable, but undesirable since it contained loose, unrepeatable, unverifiable and, worst of all, incommensurable variables. Lloyd Warner's 'Yankee City' studies of class and other topics, which deliberately ignored history in the interests of 'science', was the outcome of both these traditions, the anthropological and the sternly positivist.[4] To this day sociologists may be found apologizing for pursuing the usual methods of historical research by claiming that really they are replicating laboratory conditions in another way.

A final, and I suspect the fundamental reason, for the ahistorical character of most modern sociology, lay in its dominance by Americans rather than by Europeans. It is not that America has not produced excellent and numerous historians to brood on the 'Manifest Destiny' of that unique nation's origins and growth. She has. But until very recently the contact between historians and sociologists has not been close.[5] For American society cast sociologists into a very particular role. Despite the influences, which historians such as Perry Miller have traced, of the early Puritan and colonial culture and institutions on modern America, the U.S.A. had a deliberately revolutionary charter. There was no *ancien régime*: that had been another society. European sociology was inescapably time-oriented, because the problem for sociologists of France and

England alike had been to comprehend how their society had passed *through* the industrial and democratic revolutions. Though American sociologists were very much concerned with the effects of social change—urbanization and its attendant problems, immigrants and their Americanization—they were not really asking 'How and why is society changing?' but rather how was their society, indeed Society as such, possible, granted the mobility and heterogeneity of its elements. Their question, 'What makes a society and how are individuals related to it?' induces men to look for constants, rather than historical variables.

Their search for constants, general propositions about society, is evident even in the Spencerian Sumner's *Folkways* (1906), beneath the shifting mass of variable customs. It is manifest in all the early social psychology—work on socialization, primary groups and social control; and in the enormous mass of work on small groups by Bales, Homans and others, in which the unavoidably specific and historical variables of culture and power are carefully held constant.[6] It prepared American sociology for the reception of Durkheim, who was similarly more interested in constants than variables; and above all of Pareto. The chief source of American Paretianism was the biologist L. J. Henderson's seminar on Pareto at Harvard in the late 1920s and early 1930s, attended by, among others, Parsons and Homans.[7] Two aspects of Pareto's work are especially relevant here. Firstly his notion of what a theoretical system is, strongly influenced by mechanical and chemical models; and secondly his theory that underlying the superficial accounts people give of their actions ('derivations') are a limited number of motivations, which vary a little but much less than the derivations, called 'residues', which are the real determinants of action. Many of the 'values' (with overt reference to Weber) which are discussed in works of American sociology are in fact much more akin to Paretian residues: dispositions to act which are so enduring within a system that they have the force of constants.[8] In this the Americans were much closer than they thought to Spencer (now at the nadir of his reputation). For they, like him, had found that the sheer variability of social phenomena in all their historical specificity affronts the requirements for 'scientific' theory. So the really important things must be at some deeper level than the phenomena. Parsons' *The Social System* (1951), which attempts to itemize the various functional requisites for any and every social system or subsystem, is the culmination of this era.

For years lipservice had been paid to the idea of a 'theory of social change', and the functional systems were claimed to be steps towards one. But despite the 'pattern variables' (mostly derived from aspects of the old evolutionary continua like militancy/industrialism or *Gemeinschaft/Gesellschaft*) which were built into the Parsonian system to account for ranges of variation, the effect of the whole was to deny or ignore them.[9] Although several studies of social change were made by Parsons' pupils in the fifties to show that the system did have 'heuristic value' in the study of change, it is hard not to think that where these studies were good history, it was in spite of, and not because of the theoretical impedimenta.[10] By this time sociologists were losing sight of their proper goal: they were asking questions not about the doings of men but about the ambiguities of theory, and a theory so lax that it could hardly specify what human actions it referred to. The period ended with a diffuse sense of crisis in sociology, despite its institutional strength in America and other countries, even Great Britain. The crisis was twofold: internally, the failure of sociological theory as conceived to live up to its promise, and, externally, the rise of world problems, such as racial conflict and development, which demanded sociological attention but which the sociology of fifty years, shy of history and embarrassed at its own connexion with moral values, seemed unable to cope with.

II

The responses to the crisis have been manifold and discordant: more rigorous quantification, further use of models from mathematics and cybernetics, new schemes for grounded theory, a revival of historical sociology, impassioned calls for political commitment, sweeping claims for new basic approaches (ethnomethodology, structuralism and others), new areas of research, more neo-Marxism and even neo-evolutionism, extending to a revival of interest in Spencer. As to the last, it is wholly understandable that sociologists seeking to explain, predict or guide social change should turn again to the greater classical theories of change, those of nineteenth-century evolution. For the attempts of the developing countries to industrialize provide a subject-matter both intrinsically demanding and socially imperative. It raises in an acute form fundamental questions about the relation of sociology to its past, and between social research and social values. I shall argue that this revival of evolution, in the context of development, is misguided in the light of our acknowledged purposes, heuristically unproductive, intrinsically unsound, and based upon a mistaken attitude towards past sociology.

Evolution revived first where it had least died out—in cultural anthropology in the late forties and early fifties. Marxist anthropologists and archaeologists, V. Gordon Childe most notably, had never really abandoned it.[11] Outside Marxism, however, it was the Americans White and Steward who opened neo-evolutionary theorizing, in opposition to the Boasian, anti-evolutionary orthodoxy of American anthropology.[12] The subject-matter was the cultures of primitive peoples, particularly as codified in the Human Relations Area Files at Yale (where, as a matter of fact, Sumner and Keller had kept the traditions of Spencer's *Descriptive Sociology* greenest), that is in a form ideally suited for aggregate statistical treatment. Their basic postulate is that cultures can be ranked in a cumulative scale 'as the amount of energy harnessed per capita per year is increased, or as the efficiency of the instrumental means of putting the energy to work is increased'.[13] There are disagreements within the school over the path of evolution, about how such undeniably cumulative aspects are related to the less quantifiable aspects. But all evolutionary anthropologists, no matter how 'multilinearist' they are, share this same goal: to map the paths traced in the 'evolution' of particular cultures and, by statistics and comparisons, to lay down certain typical routes which have been followed—e.g. by showing that the existence of some institutions presupposes the prior development of certain others. Insofar as this is just a systematic ordering of historical facts (information about cultures recorded at a particular point in time), it is a perfectly legitimate activity. Presumably the evolutionary conclusions will get increasingly complex and multilinear as study proceeds. I can see no reason why, when the subject-matter is cultures thus frozen in the Human Relations Area Files, a large number of 'evolutionary' sequences might not be discovered.

But the full blast of neo-evolutionism, despite its debts to anthropology, came in the early sixties, in the study of development.

Two books were its harbingers: in sociology N. J. Smelser's *Social Change in the Industrial Revolution* (1959), whose key-concept, though applied to material classified in the Parsonian manner, was differentiation—thoroughly, though unacknowledgedly Spencerian; and in economics W. W. Rostow's *The Stages of Economic Growth* (1960), whose subtitle, *A Non-Communist Manifesto*, immediately challenges comparison with the nineteenth century. By 1966 Parsons had so far revised the abrupt dismissal of Spencer with which he had opened his first book in 1937, as to advocate the systematic revival of evolution, and even to reprimand the classic evolutionists for not having gone far enough in the assimilation of society and nature. For, he claims, his work 'belongs to a movement in contemporary social science which aspires to emulate the much grander Renaissance by doing more than merely reviving old ideas'.[14] Neo-evolution comes in two varieties. There is a looser sort, very widely diffused in writing on development, fallen-into rather than willed, with evolutionary assumptions, styles of argument and phraseology often no more than implicit in the detailed discussions of topics;[15] and there is a stricter sort, which labours self-consciously to build a new theory of social evolution which can be used to predict necessary social change. This trend is recognized to be enough of a movement to have attracted at least two symposia or books of readings devoted to the revival of evolution in the context of development, on which there is now such a mass of detailed field studies.[16]

I have pointed out elsewhere the almost identical assumptions that the new evolution shares with the old, despite Parsons' claims to originality and the use of new techniques of scalar analysis.[17] Evolution proposes that, with society as with nature, there is a discoverable natural order of change and universal mechanisms of change which, if they are known, will reveal the proper path into the future. Parsons himself has, from a survey of the histories of industrial nations, elaborated a sequence of stages, the 'evolutionary universals', the going-through of which constitutes evolution; and others claim to have verified it.[18] But this theory only emerges from truism to falsity or vagueness. It is obvious that literacy (at least for a minority) and a market economy (to some extent) are pre-requisites for the development of a complex society; and it is plausible to claim (though more vaguely and contentiously) that universalistic norms and what Parsons calls 'democratic association' (actually something more like political mobilization or the involvement of the masses by some means in the political community) are necessary for industrialization. But the variations between industrial nations are still enormous, and their paths to industrialism vary even more. That old trick of evolution—to dismiss the ungeneralizable as superficial—may be worked; but only at the cost of disregarding what most causes us to theorize about developing countries—their own particular problems. Even if it were the case, which it is not, that in the great majority of instances there was one characteristic pattern of development (which is the most that the currently fashionable empirical 'verifications' of evolutionary schemes can do),[19] we could never be sure in advance that it would apply in each particular case without analysing each in its turn to establish the theory's applicability; but if this is done properly, the evolutionary scheme is superfluous—at the very best. For our proper object is not the establishment of evolutionary schemes in themselves—those that survive criticism are always poor, uninformative things—but the use of general schemes and typologies heuristically, to employ an over-used word in its exact sense, that is to help us find things out.

We can derive very little help from social evolution in what we really wish to know: how to solve particular problems in bringing about higher rates of productivity, national integration, the relief of hatreds and social tensions, effective land reforms, the encouragement of particular kinds of social activity, the control of population increase, and the combination of all these factors in the best sequence, granted the present situation in each developing country. If there is a lesson of history in the grand evolutionist sense, it is only that the actual course of events by which nations achieve that condition we call 'industrial society' does not repeat itself very closely; and hence that the future must be a field for intelligent discrimination, not the application of evolutionary nostrums. The sociology of development has two starting points: the actual situation of any developing country and the plans and ideals which are entertained for its future. The latter may be revised because they may be criticized on the grounds of their feasibility, side-costs etc.[20] The evidence for such criticism is inevitably drawn from history—both of that nation and of other nations with comparable historical variables. All judgments must be tentative; but there may be better or worse evidence for any point of view, good reasons or no reasons for thinking such-and-such a policy will work. Such argument, to be at all worthwhile, needs to be specific; whereas evolutionary theories pride themselves on their generality, their carefully contrived timelessness and placelessness. Much evolutionary advice consists in showing how far short a country falls of the 'developed' end of an evolutionary scale in sundry respects and prescribing these respects as a solution. It is like a doctor prescribing health as the cure for a disease, rather than something which would actually work on *this* patient in his *present* condition.[21] The answer is not to rely solely on monographs. Monographs are very necessary; but they are already implicitly comparative because of the general concepts they employ, and need to be used in explicit comparisons. In place of evolution we need comparative sociological history, which uses comparison to point up the uniquely crucial. Barrington Moore's *The Social Origins of Dictatorship and Democracy* (1967) is a model for this type of study. It puts the task of the sociology of development succinctly: 'the task is not one of prediction, but merely one of analysing a problem to suggest the range of possible solutions and their relative costs, including the cost of finding no solution'.[22]

Perhaps neo-evolution would have been avoided if its adherents were better acquainted with the nature and the functions of the old evolution. The other attractions of evolution today[23]—its association with more prestigious sciences, its being the way of looking at change which least requires the abandonment of the prevalent forms of functionalism, and perhaps the everlasting appeal of system—would then be less potent. For, as I hope this book has shown, evolution, despite its fatal intrinsic defects, did make much sense in the situation which produced Spencer, when its function was to reconcile men to a process of change which was already well in motion and largely complete. It did not matter that evolution's organic imagery and necessitarian optimism so devalued the interventionary power of thought. But such a type of theory has pernicious consequences when we need to use the critical intelligence to achieve a state of affairs which no one has any right to think inevitable. Social evolution, in any precise sense, is only appropriate when we really are justified in asserting that a particular outcome is necessary—either because it is plausibly believed inevitable in the future or because, as with much recent evolutionary anthropology, the outcome is wholly determined because it exists in the past or present as recorded.

III

This is a lesson which might have been learnt from a consideration of sociology's past. That it has not been is largely due, I believe, to a mistaken general attitude towards that past—an attitude which is part of the enduring scientistic leanings of most sociology. The present irony is that the enslavement of contemporary sociology to this antiquated style of theorizing, evolution, is largely due, not to conscious mental conservatism but to the very modern-sounding notion that the past should be forgotten unless it happens to contain truths which have been unaccountably neglected and need to be restated. How often have sociologists intoned A. N. Whitehead's dictum: 'A science which hesitates to forget its founders is lost'! However interesting the history of sociology, it is irrelevant to the construction of sociological theory. Thus R. K. Merton:

> The attractive but fatal confusion of utilizable sociological theory with the history of sociological theory . . . should long since have been dispelled by recognizing their very different functions. After all schools of medicine do not confuse the history of medicine with current medical knowledge, nor do departments of biology identify the history of biology with the viable theory now employed in guiding and interpreting biological research. Once said, this seems obvious enough to be embarrassing. . . .[24]

Here a persuasive analogy conceals the absence of argument. Merton asks us to assume what most needs to be proved: that what applies to biology also applies to sociology. Is it just an aberration that sociologists pay more attention to Weber than biologists do to Von Baer; or perhaps a sign that the analogy does not hold? The fact that there is a dispute about the relevance of history to contemporary theory is *prima facie* evidence that they are not unconnected.

How ought any community—a tribe, a nation or an academic discipline—to regard its past? It is an open question since though all communities are what their past has made them, they have a variety of options as to what present use they wish to make of it. The capacity to recover the past 'as it really happened' (an inescapable phrase despite its attachment to an unacceptable theory of historiography),[25] and a real need for the past are rarely combined. Among preliterate peoples, particularly, the past is so important that present practices must be justified by it but the means of genuinely recovering it are virtually absent, so that in fact the content of the 'past' is largely determined by the pressures of the present—it becomes myth.[26] At the opposite extreme is the situation of scientific history in modern society. Historical technique is so improved that we have never been better at deciding what really happened; but at the same time, and partly as a consequence, the past has no vital function, except for recreation and escapism (for which it is in increasing demand).[27] Like churchgoing, which used to be a serious and necessary business, history has become optional, to be enjoyed or used as anyone fancies, but not to be binding on anyone.

This outcome derives from two distinct nineteenth-century attitudes to history: historicism and Whiggishness. With historicism (closely allied to evolutionary sociology), past, present and future are bound into an organic pattern which can only be discovered from the analysis of the past. Hence it becomes important to establish the real past and not a 'past' which is just the retrojection of present fancies, in order that its import for present and future may be known. Historicism therefore leads to improved techniques for recovering the past, but errs philosophically in denying the role of the present in selecting the direction of historical research. The 'Whig view of history' is open about this, for it subordinates past to present. The past is not intrinsically valuable, for it is only worth studying as the record of man's striving to realize the present. History is the story of the triumph of progressive forces over reactionary ones; and the present is superior to all. We have combined the historiographical skills, which have helped to undermine their historicist progenitor, with the Whiggish ultimate dismissal of history.

No history is more Whiggish than the history of science, especially when written by scientists inspired by the aim of showing how the present state of enlightenment came about out of errors, obstacles and darkness. Such a history has the subordinate effect of confirming (though everyone knows it already) the legitimacy of present standards and practices. The current practice of any science must be governed by procedures ('the scientific method') and criteria, which are taught to new recruits and whose acceptance marks the true scientist. These criteria and methods are then read back into the history of science, often to the complete denial of the accidents, mistakes, strange obsessions and wrong assumptions which have often lain behind scientific discovery. This occurs both in histories of long-term scientific achievement, as Arthur Koestler[28] and T. S. Kuhn[29] have shown, and in the accounts of experiments given in scientific papers (which, according to Medawar 'not merely conceal but actively misrepresent the reasoning that goes into the work they describe').[30] The Whiggish history of science is matched by its inductivist philosophy, in which the justification of theory (with which working scientists are perpetually concerned) is confused with its origination, which is the historian's interest. Kuhn shows how the history of science, actually marked by a succession of revolutions in which the paradigms which govern 'normal' science are totally overthrown, tends to be seen as a process of steady accumulation, as normal science is.

But what is particularly to be noted is that false theories of knowledge, such as naive Baconian inductivism, and false scientific histories, so far from being detrimental to the practice of science, seem to be positively beneficial for it. Medawar does not remark on this; but though he ridicules the stated epistemology of the scientists, he does not aim to change their practice—indeed his whole point is that what they call 'The Scientific Method' bears little relation to the actual methods of scientists. But T. S. Kuhn (who does not mention Medawar, nor Medawar Kuhn, despite the parallels between their ideas) not only notes the discrepancy between the actual and the believed-in history of science, but explains how the misrepresentation of this history—its portrayal in terms of the current paradigm which is 'true' to the exclusion of all others—supports the successful current prosecution of science.

Now might not this be the case with sociology: that a misleading view of history does not detract from, and may even foster, its successful contemporary practice? Are the assumptions which lie behind the Whiggish-scientistic treatment of sociology's history valid? The commonest assumption is that the 'founding fathers' of sociology are to be considered as contemporaries in intellectual debate, if they are to be considered at all. This is the way in which scientists regard their ancestors, and it means that discarded theories are literally useless except perhaps as aunt-sallies for teaching purposes. They are only worth re-reading if, as Andreski maintains of Spencer,[31] they can be considered true but neglected. Theory is here seen 'flatly', in one dimension only, as true or false answers to the same sociological problems which are our problems too. The problems don't change, merely the attempts of sociologists to solve them. Hence surveys of sociological theory usually discuss the writings of a variety of sociologists, of different times and places, insofar as they contribute to a common focus of debate, the theory of society.[32] The progress of sociology is then seen as a long march towards the perfection of this theory; empirical researches are initiated to test bits of the theory; and as bits of the theory are disproved, they can be discarded and their authors forgotten.

The cumulation model is shared by writers who disagree on whether sociology has hitherto succeeded in being cumulative. The 1940s were a time when there was much talk of convergence and synthesis of various rival approaches with the expectation that real, scientific sociology would shortly commence. Parsons and his collaborators in the 'General Theory of Action' very much conceived of themselves as finally summing up what was good in the past so that the past might be forgotten. R. K. Merton regretted that early sociology was not cumulative, but hoped that his own *Social Theory and Social Structure* (1949) would inaugurate a period when it would become so. An ominously recurrent feature is 'Waiting for Newton': since sociology ought to be, though is not, like other sciences, there should be a great thinker whose theory will furnish the guide-lines for future research; or, in Kuhnian terms, bring to an end the disputes of pre-scientific schools by means of a successful paradigm which will permit 'normal' science.[33] This ambition was first expressed by Locke, when with mock-modesty (as the 'under-labourer') he hoped to do for the 'moral sciences' what 'the incomparable Mr. Newton' had effected for the physical;[34] and at one time Spencer was subject to the same delusion.[35] Who knows which of our contemporaries aspire to the role? Merton opines that 'perhaps sociology is not ready for its Einstein because it has not yet found its Kepler',[36] while Martindale hopes that 'sociology may yet produce a Newton or a Maxwell who will take the materials cast up by chance and worked up with patient labour, clarify them in the crystalline formations of his logic, and fuse them with the fire of his love'.[37] The choice of the scientist whose millennial double is to be awaited is the only thing that varies. A sociological Darwin is no longer in such favour as when Spencer and Marx were each hailed, by different groups of disciples, as he.

There are several variants of the theme. Andreski, introducing a volume of selections from Spencer's *Principles* in which everything 'mistaken or superseded' has been left out, says that it was 'inspired by the desire to show that sociological knowledge has not become cumulative in this generation but has always been so; and that if we cut out from the works of old masters what has become untenable in the light of later studies, their contributions dovetail like parts of a jig-saw puzzle'. It is true, as Andreski says, that much is said today with an air of discovery that was said years ago by 'pre-scientific' sociologists; and that if their works were read the tedious practice of 'rediscovering America' would be avoided. But the fact that it is necessary to say this at all implies that sociology is not in fact cumulative in the required sense. The non-cumulativeness of sociology may be taken as a sickness to be cured by the appropriate methods (finding Newton, more quantification, excluding variable features as inessential, application of the appropriate models drawn from physics and chemistry, concentration on trivial but soluble problems etc.), or it may be seen as a clue to the necessary nature of any systematic study of society.

A further variant, of perennial appeal, is that sociology has had its Newton, and his name is Karl Marx. Sociology fails to develop where Marx is neglected (as in Britain) or where his eternal insights are not sufficiently recast in a 'new reading' (as in France and elsewhere). Thus Perry Anderson, in a most elegant essay, argues that sociology, which considers society in totality, arises as a bourgeois response in societies challenged by Marxist analysis. British society has never produced a totalizing sociology (Spencer?) because, for various reasons, Britain was never obliged to take Marx seriously.[38] Anderson's view of the history of sociology is akin to Zeitlin's in *Ideology and the Development of Sociological Theory*, which maintains that Marx is the true heir of the Enlightenment and that sociology is best seen as a debate with his ghost. This is so partial a truth (for it can be maintained up to a point, of Weber, Pareto and Mannheim) that it amounts to a falsification. Durkheim and the early Americans were much more obsessed with the ghost of Spencer.[39] Zeitlin's thesis is the gross exaggeration of a point made much more acceptably by Wright Mills.[40] A third example which might be mentioned is the attempt by Lefebvre, within the livelier traditions of French Marxism, to establish sociology on the proper Marxian foundation.[41] But such attempts are likely to be futile; for Marx the sociologist was as much a man of the nineteenth century (however timeless we may consider his moral ideals) as was Spencer.

Only if in fact sociology's subject-matter permits it to be cumulative, can these judgments about its theory and history, similar to those which hold for the natural sciences, be true. But, it might be objected, the work of T. S. Kuhn has shown that the progress of the natural sciences are not cumulative, but rather resembles a series of discontinuous revolutions in which one paradigm displaces another. In a way Kuhn encourages those who hope for 'scientific' sociology since he suggests that even physical science is not so unlike other forms of activity. But this is not because Kuhn has any original view about the subject-matter of science, but because he has produced a sociological theory of science—that is, a theory of science as activity—against the customary Whiggish, immanental ones. He never invokes truth or fidelity to nature to explain why a particular paradigm triumphed over its rivals; for such things cannot be a sufficient account of why anyone believes them. Consequently, we are unlikely to get from Kuhn any indications as to how far sociology's own subject-matter will permit it to resemble the natural sciences. In fact even Kuhn does not deny (he *cannot* even do so on his premisses) that each revolution in science represents an absolute improvement over its predecessors in its explanatory and predictive power. Scientific progress necessarily has a constant direction, taken overall, despite the limited backtrackings involved in switching from one paradigm to another, because it is still assumed that nature is there, unchanging, that successive theories approximate to it and that scientists call the most successful ones 'true'. Nature plays a similar role in Kuhn's, or any other socio-historical account of science, as God the First Cause did in Newton's physics: it stands outside the scope of detailed explanation, but is uniquely needed to give it coherence.

But in very important respects the subject-matter of sociology is not an unchanging stuff, as the basic constituents of physical nature are, and so its development cannot be a growing, overall unidirectional approximation to it, nor can it be a process of simple cumulation. Spencer was more perspicacious that many of his successors in fully realizing that a properly cumulative 'scientific' sociology demands such a stuff, and, brushing aside the protean character of actual society, tried to discover 'essential' facts beneath the 'superficial' phenomena about which this kind of theory might be created. In fact, however, each new emerging social context, in all its uniqueness, enlarges sociology's subject and provides not only a new subject-matter but new occasions for theorizing. So there is an important sense in which Marx and Dahrendorf, Spencer and Parsons, Weber and Bendix are neither competitors nor associates in theory-building. Very often the theories of the classical sociologists are neither true nor false in the light of the purposes which have led *us* to theorize; because they are in large measure the attempts to grapple with a different reality, the answers to different problems, the upshot of different purposes. Many 'refutations' of Marx or Weber are not properly such at all, but the discovery that their theories do not fit twentieth-century stratification or certain types of modern organization.

I do not wish to assert that there is no cumulation in sociology. A large number of topics, mostly particular social phenomena, are simply better understood than before. Anyone who wants to know about them would be ill-advised to spend much time reading what Spencer has to say about gift-exchange, intelligent and perceptive though his remarks are, or what Marx has to say about peasant economics. In the same way any history undergraduate can, with some diligent reading, get a better, truer understanding of the French Revolution than such giants as Carlyle or Michelet. There is cumulation too in the variety and the subtlety of the methods available to sociologists—methods including not only research technology but the ideal types and models which we need to guide our perception of social reality. Where cumulation does in fact apply, the advice of the would-be natural scientists of society to forget the past should be good.

But it is because of the final uniqueness of each instance of sociology that it is really worth understanding the history of sociology. This must be history 'as it really happened' (so far as we can honestly achieve it), rather than the Whiggish myths that are so prevalent. We can learn from this past, not because it can tell us directly things that we ought to know, but because we can see in it that theories are the product of particular purposes and a particular subject-matter. We hope to make our own, and can be made more aware of our situation—what our purposes require and what our subject-matter permits—by contrasting it with theirs. Though we have inherited a great deal from Spencer, his interest for us now lies in how different he was from us. It is no less part of the sociological tradition to learn the implications of our purposes better by contrasting them with those of our predecessors.

Notes

1. The Man and his Work

1. William James, *Memories and Studies*, Chap. 6, here p. 126.
2. W. Ross, *Memoirs*, p. viii.
3. Spencer to his father, 1 Apr. 1858, quoted in Duncan, *Life and Letters of Herbert Spencer*, p. 86.
4. *Ibid.*, p. 498.
5. 'Two', *Home Life with Herbert Spencer*, p. 35.
6. See R. Hofstadter, *Social Darwinism in American Thought*, pp. 31–50.
7. Carnegie to Spencer, 14 Sept. 1903, in *Spencer Papers* (at Athenaeum).
8. Jack London, *Martin Eden* (Penguin edn.), Chap. 13.
9. John Fiske, for example, 'feasting [his] soul' on Spencer as a sophomore in the early 1860s, *Essays Historical and Literary*, II, p. 199.
10. I owe this reference to J. Passmore, *100 Years of Philosophy*, p. 39.
11. See Duncan, pp. 292, 319–23, 419, 447.
12. Introduction to his translation of *The Division of Labour in Society* (1933), p. x.
13. On Spencer and Beatrice Webb see Mrs. Webb's *My Apprenticeship*, and the biography by R. Adam and K. Muggeridge, *B. Webb: A Life, 1858–1943*.
14. Crane Brinton, *English Political Thought in the Nineteenth Century*, pp. 226–7, quoted by Talcott Parsons, *The Structure of Social Action*, p. 3.
15. Margaret Cole, *Beatrice Webb*, p. 16.
16. A. O. J. Cockshut, *The Unbelievers*, pp. 73–85.
17. Gertrude Himmelfarb, *Darwin and the Darwinian Revolution*, p. 186.
18. A. R. Wallace, *My Life: A Record of Events and Opinions*, p. 33.
19. Cf. Karl Pearson, *Life of Francis Galton*, pp. 626–8.
20. Sir J. Hooker to Charles Darwin, 26 Feb. 1868, quoted in L. Huxley, *Life and Letters of Sir Joseph Dalton Hooker*, p. 111.
21. P. B. Medawar, *The Art of the Soluble*, pp. 39–58.
22. Huxley to Spencer, 2 Sept. 1860, quoted in L. Huxley, *Life and Letters of T. H. Huxley*, Vol. I, pp. 212–14.

23. Wallace, p. 23.
24. J. S. Mill to A. Bain, 7 Jan. 1863, quoted in H. Eliot, *Letters of J. S. Mill*, p. 273.
25. Quoted in J. W. Cross, *George Eliot's Life as related in her Letters and Journals* (new edn.), pp. 14–15.
26. T. Mozley, *Reminiscences, Chiefly of Towns, Villages and Schools*, pp. 144–74, passim; cf. also L. B. Lamar, 'Herbert Spencer and his Father', *Studies in English* (Texas), XXXII (1953).
27. Mozley wrote that W. G. Spencer taught him 'to believe that what you were simply taught you did not really learn; and that every man who wished to know things really must rummage them out for himself in all sorts of ways, the odder, the more out of the way, the more difficult the better', *Reminiscences, Chiefly of Oriel College and the Oxford Movement*, I, pp. 146–7.
28. H. Spencer, *An Autobiography*, Vol. I, p. 54.
29. Mozley, p. 165.
30. *Autobiography*, Vol. I, pp. 44ff.
31. Cited in Duncan, p. 534.
32. Nottingham was a boom town during 1823–5, when 'Day labourers came from the plough and strikers from the forge, for some of the latter got £5 to £10 a-week. . . . The inflation of the public mind was universal and became a sort of local epidemic—a mania, acquiring the name in after years of the "twist net fever". The whole community was athirst for gain and became intoxicated. . . .', W. Felkin, *History of the Machine Wrought Hosiery and Lace Manufactures*, (1867, new edn. 1967), pp. 331–2. Spencer, *Autobiography*, pp. 67–9.
33. Mozley, pp. 174–85.
34. *Autobiography*, I, p. 28.
35. See, for example *Felix Holt*, Chap. 1. See also H. L. Sussman, *The Victorians and the Machine: the Literary Response to Technology* (1968).
36. C. Gibbon, *The Life of George Combe*, p. 300; on phrenology in general see J. D. Davies, *Phrenology: Fad and Science*, Chaps. 1–2.
37. Wallace, *My Life*, pp. 234–5.
38. J. Morley, *Life of Richard Cobden*, p. 93.
39. Combe, quoted in Gibbon, p. 102.
40. *Autobiography*, I, pp. 140–1.
41. Letter to his father, Duncan, p. 28.
42. The fullest treatment of their relationship is G. S. Haight, *George Eliot: A Biography*, Chap. 4, which is slightly slanted against Spencer.
43. Spencer, Autobiography, I, pp. 394–5.
44. George Eliot to Sarah Hennell, in J. W. Cross, *George Eliot's Life as related in her Letters and Journals*, p. 147.

45. An undated letter from Lewes at the Athenaeum begins 'Dear philosopher' and concludes 'the problematical thinker'.
46. Quoted by G. and K. Tillotson, *Mid-Victorian Studies,* p. 75.
47. Letter to his father quoted in Duncan, p. 75.
48. Letter to his mother, 20 Oct. 1856, in Duncan, pp. 81–2.
49. Says Mozley, a participant, p. 153; H. T. Buckle was present. G. Himmelfarb, *Darwin and the Darwinian Revolution,* p. 107, says that on Darwin's return from the Beagle tour, he spent a lot of time with Buckle, whom Spencer knew well enough.
50. H. Eliot (ed.), *Letters of John Stuart Mill,* pp. 310, 273, 71.
51. *Autobiography,* II, p. 261.
52. Duncan, p. 380.
53. F. W. Hirst, *Early Life and Letters of John Morley,* p. 53.
54. See B. Semmel, *The Governor Eyre Controversy,* E. M. Everett, *The Party of Humanity: The Fortnightly Review and its Contributors 1865–1874,* esp. pp. 15–16, 118–21, and F. W. Knickerbocker, *Free Minds: John Morley and his Friends,* Chap. 4.
55. Huxley to Kingsley, 8 Nov. 1866, cited Semmel, pp. 122–3.
56. Pearson, *Galton,* pp. 67–8.
57. On the X Club see L. Huxley, *Life and Letters of Sir J. D. Hooker,* I, pp. 538–46, *Sketches from the Life of Edward Frankland, edited and concluded by his daughters M. N. W. and S. J. C.,* pp. 148–63, L. Huxley, *Life and Letters of T. H. Huxley,* I, pp. 255–61; and Spencer, *Autobiography,* II, pp. 115–18.
58. J. Fiske, *Essays Historical and Literary,* II, p. 247.
59. *Ibid.,* p. 204.
60. Cf. P. Gaskell, *Morvern Transformed,* Chap. 3.
61. Spencer to Youmans, 15 Feb. 1884, p. 238.
62. See below Chap. 5; also H. George, *A Perplexed Philosopher* (1893).
63. Letter to the Earl of Dysart, 27 May 1892, Duncan, p. 315.
64. James, *Memories and Studies,* p. 140.
65. Cf. a long and careful letter from Clark Maxwell, 12 Dec. 1874 (Spencer papers at the Athenaeum) which for a while (so the letter is noted by H. S.) convinced Spencer of the untruth of his hypothesis: but he later re-adopted it. B. Russell cited in B. Webb, *My Apprenticeship* (Penguin edn.), p. 112.
66. See Duncan, p. 447. A 'Young Syrian' asks to be allowed to spend the summer with Spencer in order 'to accompany you in your daily walks, to hear what you speak, to observe how you act in all the common affairs of life'.
67. Webb, pp. 42 ff.

68. Spencer to Beatrice Webb, 29 June 1903, *Passfield Papers* (at the British Library of Political and Economic Science), II, 4b.
69. Cf. P. Rieff, *Freud: The Mind of the Moralist* (University Paperback edn., 1965), pp. xvii–xviii.
70. James, p. 141.
71. See *Autobiography*, I, pp. 467–8 and Duncan, pp. 77 ff.
72. Spencer to T. H. Huxley, 16 Aug. 1855, *Huxley Papers* (at the Lyon Playfair Library, Imperial College of Science and Technology).
73. *Autobiography*, I, p. 467.
74. See M. P. Medlicott (ed.), *No Hero, I Confess: a 19th Century Autobiography* of C. N. Wright (1790–1871), bookseller of Nottingham, whose wife was a Brettell.
75. Spencer to Huxley, 26 Jan. 1889, *Huxley Papers*.
76. Spencer to Huxley, 16 Nov. 1887, *Huxley Papers*.
77. Spencer to Mrs. Huxley, 12 Dec. 1868, 4 May 1869, *Huxley Papers*.
78. Huxley to Hooker, 22 Sept. 1886, 29 Jan. 1888; Hooker to Huxley, 12 May 1887; *Huxley Papers*.
79. Gertrude Himmelfarb's 'The Victorian Angst', in *Victorian Minds*, touches on this problem; see too W. E. Houghton, *The Victorian Frame of Mind*, Chap. 3, pp. 74–6.
80. Knickerbocker, *Free Minds*, p. 149, quoting Morley's *Voltaire*, p. 44.
81. *Autobiography*, I, pp. 168–9.
82. B. Webb, *My Apprenticeship*, p. 47.
83. *Autobiography*, I, p. 370.
84. Spencer to Richard Potter, 22 Jan. 1856: 'moral and intellectual beauties do not of themselves suffice to attract me; and owing to the stupidity of our educational systems it is rare to find these united with a good physique. Moreover there is the pecuniary difficulty. . . .' (*Passfield Papers* and *Autobiography*, I, p. 476). A curious item in the Spencer papers at the Athenaeum are some 'Definitions', written in a careful adolescent hand, said to be Spencer's, which include the following for Marriage: (1) 'A word which if some people are to be believed should be pronounced *mirage*' and (2) 'A ceremony in which a ring is put on the finger of the lady, and a ring through the nose of the gentleman'.
85. James, p. 141.
86. Beatrice Potter, Diary for 28 May and for 9 June 1886, *Passfield Papers*.
87. B. Webb, *My Apprenticeship*, p. 42.
88. Hooker to Huxley, 2 June 1890, *Huxley Papers*.
89. Cf. Duncan, p. 510.
90. Pearson, *Galton*, II, p. 123.

91. G. P. Gooch, *Life of Lord Courtney*, p. 191.
92. *Autobiography*, I, p. 97.
93. *Ibid.*, I, p. 412.
94. *Ibid.*, I, p. 105. Despite this he seems to have tried to work extraordinarily hard as a youth. There is at the Athenaeum a schedule for the day's work, written in Spencer's hand: rise at 5, 6–8 exercise outside, sketching or any light occupation till breakfast, maths 9–1, electromagnetic experiments 2–3, geometrical drawing 3–4, French 4–6, walking 6–7, tea and conversation on some fixed subject 7–8, reading history or natural philosophy 8–9, writing out diary 9–10½.
95. Spencer to Beatrice Potter, 13 Sept. 1887, *Passfield Papers.*
96. Quoted by B. Willey, *Nineteenth Century Studies*, p. 168.
97. This on the testimony of Galton, who said he owed little to Spencer; Pearson, *Galton*, II, p. 614.
98. Buckle to Spencer, 3 Dec. 1858, cited Duncan, p. 88.
99. Cf. R. Young 'Malthus and the Evolutionists', *Past and Present*, XLIII (1969).
100. This is amply documented by W. F. T. Myers, 'Ideas of Mental and Social Evolution in the Treatment of Character in George Eliot's Novels' (Oxford B. Litt. thesis, 1964).
101. Houghton, pp. 139–40.
102. *Autobiography*, I, pp. 252–3.
103. *Ibid.*, I, pp. 398, 445–6. The same occurred with Buckle, whom Spencer criticized but did not read properly; Wallace, *My Life*, p. 31.
104. *Ibid.*, I, pp. 399–401.
105. Fiske, p. 204.
106. Huxley, quoted by Beatrice Webb, *My Apprenticeship*, pp. 45 ff.
107. On Baconianism see J. W. Burrow, *Evolution and Society*, pp. 34–5; for an example H. G. Atkinson and H. Martineau, *Letters on the Law and Nature of Man's Development* (1851), Chaps. 1–2.
108. *Autobiography*, I, p. 403; Pearson, *Galton*, II, p. 143.
109. Spencer to Huxley, 28 May 1888, *Huxley Papers.*
110. Pearson, *Galton*, pp. 626–8.
111. Eliot, *Letters of J. S. Mill*, pp. 7–8.
112. Wallace, p. 33.
113. Hooker to Huxley, 2 June 1890, *Huxley Papers.*
114. Beatrice Webb's Diary, 3 May 1886, *Passfield Papers.*

2. Enthusiasts and Lunaticks

1. A typical judgment is that of John Bowle in *Politics and Opinion in the 19th Century* (in other respects a good brief account of Spencer),

p. 226: 'The Wesley background . . . was dreary to a degree. . . . It says much for the boy's tenacity and spirit that he ever got out of this environment.'

2. See S. Glover, *The History and Directory of the Borough of Derby intended as a guide to strangers visiting the town* (Derby, 1843), E. Bradbury and R. Keene, *All about Derby: its History, Institutions and Industries* (Derby, 1906).
3. J. R. Vincent, *Pollbooks: How Victorians Voted*, p. 15, Read, *The English Provinces*, pp. 35–7.
4. On Pentrich see M. I. Thomis, *Politics and Society in Nottingham 1785–1835*, Chap. 10 and E. Fearn, 'Reform Movement in Derby and Derbyshire 1790–1832'. (Manchester M.A. thesis, 1964), pp. 124–88, which both differ from the interpretation of E. P. Thompson, *The Making of the English Working Class*, pp. 359–69. It grew out of the Hampden Club membership in the area and according to one confession 'almost all the violent politicians of the lowest class in Derby were members'—including shopkeepers and craftsmen (Fearn, p. 143). On its connection with religious enthusiasm in the area, see below, note 43.
5. Sir R. Philips, *A Personal Tour through the United Kingdom describing living objects and contemporaneous interests, No. II Derbyshire-Nottinghamshire* (1829), pp. 161 ff.
6. See W. A. Richardson, *Citizen's Derby* (1949).
7. See A. Sturgess, *Derby Silk Strike Centenary Celebrations 1834–1934*, for a very brief account.
8. J. A. Hobson, *Confessions of an Economic Heretic* (1938), autobiographical account of mid-late nineteenth century Derby; cf. Birch, *Small Town Politics*, Chap. 2, on Glossop, for a similar picture.
9. Vincent, p. 15.
10. Letter to the *Derby Mercury*, 2 March 1842, referred to in J. D. Standen, 'A Social and Economic History of Derby 1835–1881' (Leeds M.A. thesis).
11. Thus Nottingham Tories, quoted by Thomis.
12. On the Strutts see R. S. Fitton and A. P. Wadsworth, *The Strutts and the Arkwrights 1758–1830* passim; the Strutts' papers are probably the most important single source for Derby social history at this period. Cf. also S. D. Chapman, *The Early Factory Masters*, pp. 195–8.
13. A. Patterson, *Radical Leicester*, p. 340.
14. *Derby Mercury*, 30 Aug. 1848, and 19 March 1848.
15. Spencer, *Autobiography*, pp. 15, 19, and B. A. M. Alger, *King Street Wesleyan Chapel, Derby: A Centenary Memorial 1805–1905* (Derby, 1905), pp. 20–3.

16. Quoted in L. F. Church, *The Early Methodist People*, p. 97.
17. J. C. Weller, 'The Revival of Religion in Nottingham 1780–1850' (Nottingham B.D. thesis, 1957), p. 58.
18. Alger, p. 23; Religious Census of England and Wales (1852), p. 87.
19. A book by a great-nephew, W. Mottram, *The True Story of George Eliot in relation to 'Adam Bede'* (1905) makes these and many other personal and local identifications, with much convincing evidence. It is a pity that G. S. Haight does not refer to Mottram's book to verify the identifications.
20. Cf. Mottram, pp. 249–53, Alger, pp. 20–3, Weller, p. 104. Neither Spencer nor George Eliot, as far as we know, referred to this association between their kinsfolk—they can hardly have avoided knowing of it.
21. *Adam Bede*, Chap. 3.
22. Wesley, *Works* (3rd edn. 1829–30), Vol. VIII, pp. 340–7, 'The Character of a Methodist'.
23. D. Bogue and J. Bennett, *History of Dissenters, from the Revolution in 1688 to the year 1808*, Vol. III (1810), pp. 47–8, 37.
24. A letter of Wesley's quoted by J. Lawson in R. Davies and G. Rupp (eds.), *A History of the Methodist Church in Great Britain*, Vol. I, pp. 198–200.
25. Quoted by Max Weber, *The Protestant Ethic and the Spirit of Capitalism* (English edn. 1930), p. 175.
26. Quoted in R. Currie, *Methodism Divided: A Study in the Sociology of Ecumenicalism*, p. 59.
27. G. B. Macdonald, *Facts against Fiction: or a Statement of the Real Causes which produced the division among the Wesleyan Methodists in Derby*, Derby (1832).
28. Weller, p. 58 quoting a Nottingham Wesleyan in 1847. John Spencer's dissidence, alleges Macdonald, went back some years to a Love-feast at Nottingham.
29. G. A. Williams, *Artisans and Sans Culottes*, p. 18, speaks of Paine's *Rights of Man* as 'in essence the manifesto of the man of small property, big aspiration and broad sympathy'.
30. Bradbury and Keene; Glover.
31. R. E. Schofield, 'John Wesley and Science in 18th Century England', *Isis*, XLIV (1953).
32. *Works*, VII, p. 129.
33. Alger, p. 36.
34. Thus the Methodist historians, Davies and Rupp, p. 297.
35. Cf. L. F. Church, *The Early Methodist People*, pp. 23–4.

36. Andrew Ure, *Philosophy of Manufactures* (1835, 3rd edn. 1861), pp. 14–16, 423.
37. *Autobiography*, Vol. I, pp. 20, 56.
38. E. Halevy, *A History of the English People in 1815* (1924), pp. 371 ff.
39. E. J. Hobsbawn, 'Methodist and the Threat of Revolution in Britain', in *Labouring Men*, pp. 23–33; John Kent, *The Age of Disunity*, Chaps. 3 and 5; E. P. Thompson, *The Making of the English Working Class*, Chap. 11. The controversy is briefly reviewed by G. Himmelfarb, *Victorian Minds*, pp. 292–9.
40. Thompson, p. 381.
41. *Ibid.*, p. 355.
42. *Ibid.*, p. 37.
43. Cf. M. Edwards, *After Wesley*, Chap. 4, and Kent, p. 128. A Nottingham magistrate wrote to Sidmouth after Pentrich that 'the generality of the men taken in arms are religious fanaticks'; quoted by Fearn, p. 177, who suggests a connexion between religious revivalism early in 1817 (Primitive Methodists especially) and Pentrich, pp. 155–6, 178–9.
44. Vincent, *Pollbooks*, p. 18: '. . . the traditional impression that Wesleyan ministers were Tory is not borne out by the limited evidence so far found.' This data relates to *after* 1832, however. But selective quotation from Jabez Bunting will not do.
45. On the D.P.S. see S. Bagshaw, *History, Gazetteer, and Directory* (1846), *Rules and Catalogue of the Library belonging to the D.P.S.* (1835), which contains a report of Darwin's opening speech on 18 July 1784, Glover's *Directory* (1833), p. 430, and an Accounts Book in the Derby Reference Library; see also E. Robinson, 'The Derby Philosophical Society', *Annals of Science*, IX (1953), and R. P. Sturges, 'Cultural Life in Derby in the late 18th century' (Loughborough M.A. thesis), esp. Chap. 6.
46. T. Mozley, *Reminiscences, chiefly of Towns, Villages and Schools* (1885), pp. 171–3.
47. See R. E. Schofield, *The Lunar Society of Birmingham*, and A. E. Musson and E. Robinson, 'Science and Industry in the late 18th century', *Econ.H.R.*, XIII (1960).
48. Quoted by Samuel Smiles, *Lives of the Engineers*, Vol. IV (1865), p. 479.
49. On Erasmus Darwin, see especially Hesketh Pearson, *Doctor Darwin*, D. King-Hele (ed.), *The Essential Writings of Erasmus Darwin*.
50. Quoted by King-Hele, p. 163.
51. Darwin to Boulton, 5 Apr. 1778, quoted Schofield, pp. 143–4.
52. C. C. Hankin (ed.), *Life of Mary Anne Schimmelpenninck* (1858), p. 242.

53. Cited by Hesketh Pearson, p. 197.
54. Schofield, pp. 177–9.
55. Cf. N. Garfinkle, 'Science and Religion in England 1790–1800: the Critical Response to the Work of E. Darwin', *J.Hist. Ideas*, XVI (1955).
56. Fitton and Wadsworth, pp. 166–7.
57. See J. Birks, *Memorials of Friar Gate Chapel, Derby.*
58. *Memoir of the Rev. George Walker* (1809), p. vi.
59. A. Lincoln, *Some Political and Social Ideas of English Dissent, 1763–1800*, Chap. 3.
60. In a letter to Pitt, 1787, quoted in J. A. Passmore, *Selected Writings of Joseph Priestley*, p. 8.
61. See J. M. Colligan, *A History of Arianism in the 18th Century*, and J. Priestley, *Memoirs . . . to the Year 1795* (1809), pp. 48–9, 54.
62. Fitton and Wadsworth, pp. 108–10.
63. Duncan, *Life and Letters of Herbert Spencer*, p. 534.
64. Lincoln, pp. 17 ff.
65. *Ibid.*, pp. 54, 90 ff.
66. D. Read, *The English Provinces c. 1760–1960*, p. 23.
67. J. Pilkington, *The Doctrine of Equality of Rank and Condition examined and supported on the authority of the New Testament and on the Principles of Reason and Benevolence* (1795); this book nearly got Pilkington expelled from Friargate Chapel. Cf. Lincoln, p. 280.
68. Cf. R. B. Rose, 'The Priestley Riots of 1791', *Past and Present*, XVIII (1960).
69. *Derby Mercury*, 29 Sept. 1791. Priestley still replied, *Derby Mercury*, 21 Sept. 1791: 'Excuse me if I still join theology to philosophical study, and if I consider the former as greatly superior in importance to the latter.'
70. Thus Rev. C. S. Hope, in *Address to the Derby Volunteers* (1799), quoted by Sturges, p. 47.
71. Lincoln, p. 50.
72. Passmore, p. 35. Millenialism was, as W. M. Lamont shows in his brilliant *Godly Rule: Politics and Religion 1603–60*, a normal phenomenon in the first half of the seventeenth century. But it was not entirely extinct after 1660, making itself felt, in a semi-secular form, in the reaction of many Dissenters to 1789.
73. Fitton and Wadsworth, pp. 166–7.
74. There was a Derby Society for Political Information, in touch with the London Corresponding Society, with two sections, one for working men with a lower subscription, one for the wealthier; most of the latter members belonged to the D.P.S. See E. Fearn,

'The Derbyshire Reform Societies, 1791–3', in *Derbyshire Archaeological J.*, LXXVIII (1968), p. 51.

75. W. Godwin, *Political Justice* (2nd edn. 1796), p. 205.
76. G. Walker, *Essays on Various Subjects*, Vol. II, pp. 261–336.
77. On Walker, see Thomis, pp. 131–4, on Godwin *Political Justice*, Part II, Chap. 1.
78. Passmore, pp. 31–3.
79. Kent, p. 128.
80. On Wilberforce's influence see Muriel Jaeger, *Before Victoria*, Chap. 2.
81. A. O. Lovejoy, quoted by H. Kearney, 'Puritanism, Capitalism and the Scientific Revolution', *Past and Present*, XXVIII (1965), pp. 96–7.
82. C. Sylvester, *op. cit.*, p. 1.
83. On the Panopticon see G. Himmelfarb, 'The Haunted House of Jeremy Bentham', in *Victorian Minds*, pp. 32–81.
84. Fitton and Wadsworth, p. 181.
85. Himmelfarb, *Victorian Minds*, p. 287.
86. Cf. Noel Annan, *Leslie Stephen*, Chap. 3.
87. Letter to O'Connell, cited R. G. Cowherd, *The Politics of English Dissent*, p. 97.
88. Fitton and Wadsworth, p. 178.
89. T. Mozley, p. 138.
90. Fitton and Wadsworth, pp. 166–7.
91. On the history of the movement see M. Tylecote, *The Mechanics Institutes of Lancashire and Yorkshire before 1851*, and T. Kelly, *George Birkbeck: Pioneer of Adult Education*. The movement began from classes 'abounding with experiments' held by Birkbeck for artisans at the Andersonian Institution in Glasgow in the early 1800s (his successor being Andrew Ure, from 1804). Birkbeck was a Quaker, his family linked with Lunar circles in Birmingham.
92. 22 Aug. 1825, quoted by S. Laughton, *Derby Mechanics' Institution*.
93. Glover, *Directory* (1833), pp. 430–1.
94. Kelly, p. 99.
95. Tylecote, p. 52; cf. A. Ure, *Philosophy of Manufactures*, p. 423.
96. F. Engels, *Conditions of the Working Class in England in 1844*, p. 272.
97. *History of Co-operarton*, Vol. I (1875), p. 142 and Chap. 7.
98. Thus Dr. Fox of Derby; v.s. note 91.
99. Tylecote, pp. 74–5; G. Wallas, *Life of F. Place*, p. 32.
100. Thompson, p. 20, says 'it may be more accurate to think of the L.C.S. as a "popular Radical" society than as "working-class".' G. Williams, *Artisans and Sans Culottes*, p. 105, describes the men with whom Erskine of the L.C.S. stayed in his tour of the country, including Derby, as 'artisans, shopkeepers, Dissenting ministers and

schoolmasters'. For a valuable study using local Nottingham material see R. A. Church and S. D. Chapman, 'Gravener Henson and the Making of the English Working Class', in E. L. Jones and G. E. Mingay (eds.), *Land, Labour and Population in the Industrial Revolution* (1961).

101. Holyoake, *History of Co-operation*, I, p. 9.
102. Holyoake, *Sixty Years of an Agitator's Life*, p. 30.
103. Cf. C. Erikson, *British Industrialists 1850–1950: Steel and Hosiery*, passim, and Chapman, *op. cit.*

3. Anti-Politics of the 1840s

1. Marx, in a letter, quoted by H. Perkin, *The Origins of Modern English Society 1780–1880*, p. 26.
2. This criticism is not intended to dismiss either *The Making of the English Working Class* or *Culture and Society* which are in every way seminal books, invaluable even as foils in debate and quite indispensable for any student of their subject-matter. Chap. 16 of Thompson's book, esp. pp. 711–79, is far and away the best portrayal of this radical culture; for evidence that it was by no means exclusive working class see pp. 724, 726–7. Thompson has presented a clearer, and somewhat modified account of this culture in his 'The Peculiarities of the English', *The Socialist Register* (1965), ed. R. Miliband and J. Saville.
3. On this see C. B. Macpherson, *The Political Theory of Possessive Individualism*, Chap. 3, and B. S. Feinberg, 'The Political Thought of Oliver Cromwell', *Social Research*, XXXV (1968), pp. 445–65.
4. T. Paine, *Common Sense*, p. 1, cited by W. Godwin, *Political Justice* (2nd edn. 1796), p. 125.
5. J. Hamburger, *Intellectuals in Politics*, pp. 276–7.
6. *Ibid.*, p. 23.
7. *Ibid.*, p. 282.
8. J. S. Mill, *The Spirit of the Age* (ed. F. A. Hayek, 1942), Chap. 3, pp. 35 ff. See also I. W. Mueller, *J. S. Mill and French Thought*, pp. 62 ff.
9. J. S. Mill, *op. cit.*, p. 42.
10. *Ibid.*, p. 52.
11. *Ibid.*, p. 59.
12. Cited Hamburger, pp. 217–20.
13. C. Hill, 'The Norman Yoke', in J. Saville (ed.), *Democracy and the Labour Movement*, esp. p. 48.

14. N. McCord, *The Anti-Corn Law League*, p. 185. Cf. 'A Manchester Manufacturer' [Cobden], *England, Ireland and America* (1835): 'There is no remedy . . . but in the wholesome exercise of the people's opinion in behalf of their own interests. The middle and industrial classes of England can have no interest apart from the preservation of peace. The honours, the fame, the emoluments of war belong not to them; the battle plain is the harvest-field of the aristocra cy watered with the blood of the people.'
15. It is extraordinarily hard to plot the spread of this word (with French *classe* and German *Klasse*), and no systematic study has been done, but R. Williams, *Culture and Society* (Penguin edn.), pp. 14–15, though brief is helpful; see also Perkin, pp. 26–32, and S. Ossowski, *Class Structure in the Social Consciousness* (English edn., 1963), pp. 122–5. The greatest eighteenth-century work on social stratification, John Millar's *The Origins of the Distinction of Ranks* (1771) speaks equally of *class* (whether as a general concept or as a particular stratum) and of *order* and *rank*. In Smith's *Wealth of Nations* (1776), the usage is similar and, indeed, *rank* seems to predominate ('the inferior ranks of people', 'middling ranks', 'common people', 'those of better station' and 'men of rank and fortune'). W. C. Lehmann (*John Millar of Glasgow*, p. 139) argues that the terms are not interchangeable, and that *class* bears an 'invidious character', implying a concept of exploitation; but of this, on internal evidence at least, I am dubious.
16. *Memoirs of the Rev. Dr. Joseph Priestley to the Year 1795* (1809), pp. 74–5.
17. Fitton and Wadsworth, *The Strutts and the Arkwrights*, pp. 144–5.
18. D. King-Hele (ed.), *The Essential Writings of Erasmus Darwin*, p. 41.
19. M. I. Thomis, *Politics and Society in Nottingham*, p. 156.
20. A. Briggs, 'The Language of Class in Early Nineteenth Century England', in Briggs and Saville (eds.), *Essays in Labour History*, pp. 43–73, here quoting Southey.
21. See Perkin, esp. Chap. 1.
22. See above, Chap. 2, p. 35.
23. F. E. Manuel, *The New World of Henri Saint-Simon*, Chap. 21.
24. Hamburger, p. 47.
25. R. Owen, *A New View of Society* (Everyman edn.), p. 51.
26. *The History and the Political Philosophy of the Middle and Working Classes.* J. Wade (1788–1875) was 'an industrious writer connected with the press throughout his career' (D.N.B.); his most popular work, which sold 50,000 copies was *The Black Book: or Corruption Unmasked, Being An Account of Persons, Places and Sinecures* (2 vols., 1820–3, reprinted 1831, 1832, 1835).

27. *On the Rise, Progress and Present State of Public Opinion.* W. H. Mackinnon (1789–1870), a son of the chief of the Clan Mackinnon, was elected Tory M.P. in 1830 but later became Liberal, in a long parliamentary career.
28. A. Briggs, 'Middle Class Consciousness in English Politics, 1780–1846', *Past and Present*, IX (1956), esp. p. 69.
29. G. Wallace, *Life of Francis Place*, pp. 217 ff.
30. Hamburger, p. 263, quoting J. A. Roebuck.
31. H. Spencer, *Autobiography*, I, pp. 110–11.
32. *Ibid.*, p. 293, quoting Mrs. Grote.
33. Vincent, *Pollbooks*, p. 18.
34. N. Gash, *Reaction and Reconstruction in English Politics, 1832–1852*, p. 2.
35. R. G. Cowherd, *The Politics of English Dissent*, Chaps. 3 and 9.
36. A. Miall, *Life of Edward Miall* (1884), p. 27.
37. *Ibid.*, pp. 59–71, passim.
38. See *Culture and Anarchy* (C.U.P. paperback edn. 1960), pp. 31, 56, 87.
39. *D.N.B.*, s.v. E. Miall.
40. A. Miall, pp. 151–2.
41. *Ibid.*, p. 140.
42. On Quaker business circles see P. H. Emden, *Quakers in Commerce*, pp. 42–60, on Sturge himself see S. Hobhouse, *J. Sturge: His Life and Work* (1919), and G. D. H. Cole, *Chartist Portraits*, Chap. 2.
43. On Attwood see Briggs, 'Thomas Attwood and the Economic Background of the Birmingham Political Union', *Cambridge Historical Journal*, IX (1948) and Cole, Chap. 4; on Bright, see H. Ausubel, *John Bright: Victorian Reformer*, p. 108.
44. J. Morley, *Life of Richard Cobden*, pp. 662–4.
45. J. Sturge, *Reconciliation between the Middle and Labouring Classes* (Birmingham 1842), pp. 8, 15, 19, 27–32.
46. A. Miall quoting his father, p. 82.
47. Cole, pp. 6–7; see also Lucy Brown 'The Chartists and the Anti-Corn Law League', and A. Briggs 'The Local Background of Chartism', in Briggs, *Chartist Studies*, Chaps. 1–2.
48. See W. Lovett, *Life and Struggles of William Lovett in his Pursuit of Bread, Knowledge and Freedom* (ed. R. H. Tawney, 2 vols. 1920), Cole, Chap. 1; on co-operation, science and Owenism see G. J. Holyoake, *History of Co-operation* (revised edn. 1908), Chap. 9, and, an excellent personal account, A. R. Wallace, *My Life* (1905), pp. 79–105. C. Southwell's periodical, *Oracle of Reason* (1841), is a typical product of this culture; cf. F. B. Smith 'The Atheist Mission, 1840–1900', in R. Robson (ed.), *Ideas and Institutions of Victorian Britain*, Chap. 8.

49. For an account (from the C.S.U. viewpoint) see *The Nonconformist*, 31 Dec. 1842, pp. 873–87; see also 14 Sept. 1842, pp. 618–19, and 7 Dec. 1842, letter of Rev. T. Spencer criticizing O'Connor. Yet when Heyworth stood as Liberal/Radical candidate in Derby in 1848, the Tory *Derby Mercury* (29 March, 30 Sept. 1848) denounced him as a red Republican and dismissed his election address with 'It is Chartism all over, which is description enough.' Sturge stood as a candidate on the platform of the C.S.U. at Nottingham in 1842, against both Liberals and Tories, and very nearly got elected.
50. Cole, *Chartist Portraits*, pp. 6–7, and Briggs, *Chartist Studies*, pp. 1–28.
51. Wallace, *Life of F. Place*, p. 394.
52. See Cole, Chap. 3 and Cowherd, p. 101.
53. See Joy MacAskill, 'The Chartist Land Plan', in Briggs, *Chartist Studies*, pp. 304–41, esp. p. 306.
54. On Thornton see D. E. C. Eversley, *Social Theories of Fertility and the Malthusian Debate*, pp. 129–30; on Bray's scheme see J. Prest, *The Industrial Revolution in Coventry*, pp. 106–12. Similar proposals for allotments were put forward by the manufacturer W. R. Greg, in *Prospects of Industry: being a Brief Exposition of the Past and Present Conditions of the Labouring Classes* (1835); this sees the economic differentiation of industrialism, resulting in 'the breaking up of all home and social affections', as the root of the social problem.
55. Morley, *Cobden*, pp. 662–4.
56. *Ibid.*, p. 305.
57. *Ibid.*, p. 249; McCord, pp. 104–6.
58. Morley, *Cobden*, p. 311.
59. *Ibid.*, p. 395.
60. *Ibid.*, p. 115; McCord, Chap. 5, writing of the 1842 depression. In a letter to Spencer's uncle, he said: 'I look only to the country for any change in our representation', not to Parliament and 'the two aristocratic parties'. Action 'out of doors' was difficult, since the middle classes had had the Charter thrust in their face too often; 'yet out of doors it would be difficult to carry the masses for anything short of it.' 20 Apr. 1848, *Spencer Papers* (Athenaeum).
61. Mackinnon, p. 15.
62. *Ibid.*, p. 1.
63. *Ibid.*, p. 101.
64. Cf. Cobden: 'What brings great changes of policy is the spontaneous [i.e. extra-political] shifting and readjustments of interests, not the discovery of new principles'; Morley, *Cobden*, p. 406.
65. Mackinnon, pp. 17–18. Godwin too took this view: 'the duty . . . of the true politician is to postpone revolution if he cannot entirely

prevent it', (*Political Justice*, p. 284); the whole of Part IV, 'Of the Operation of Opinion in Societies and Individuals', is relevant to the radical ideas on this topic.

66. 2 June 1819, quoted in Fitton and Wadsworth, *The Strutts and the Arkwrights*, p. 191.
67. Letter to Fonblanque, quoted by Hayek in his edition of *The Spirit of the Age*, p. xxxi.
68. Mackinnon, p. 177.
69. Holyoake, *History of Co-operation*, p. 289.
70. *The Economist*, 10 Dec. 1853.
71. Morley, *Cobden*, p. 401.
72. *Spirit of the Age*, p. 42.
73. Mackinnon, p. 18.
74. Cf. the concluding sentence of Spencer's 'Letters on the Proper Sphere of Government' (*The Nonconformist*, 14 Dec. 1842, p. 827): 'if it be conceded that the administration of justice is the only duty of the state, we are at once relieved from one of the greatest objections to the enfranchisement of the working classes.'
75. Edward Miall in 1846, quoted in A. Miall, p. 107.
76. *Felix Holt the Radical*, Chap. 30.
77. *Culture and Society* (Penguin edn.), pp. 112–16.
78. The criticisms of the working class character put by George Eliot into Felix Holt's mouth cannot just be dismissed as another of her prejudices: they can easily be matched by judgments of Owenite co-operators themselves. William Pare, explaining the failure of Owenite labour exchanges, said it was because the members, 'were too ignorant, too selfish, too dishonest; added to which the whole forces of a vast erroneous system were against us' (quoted J. F. C. Harrison, *Robert Owen and the Owenites in Britain and America*), p. 206; cf. the virtues of the co-operator stressed by Holyoake, *History of Co-operation*, pp. 397 ff.
79. F. Rosen, 'Progress and Democracy: William Godwin's Contribution to Political Philosophy' (London Ph.D. thesis, 1965), p. 6, points out that Godwin was much less negative about government in his pamphlets than in *Political Justice*. On the positive side of Paine (esp. *Rights of Man*, Bk. II, Chap. 5), see Thompson, *Making of the English Working Class*, pp. 92 ff.
80. *Wealth of Nations* (Everyman edn.), II, p. 203. Cf. Marx, *Communist Manifesto* (Moscow, n.d.), pp. 89–90: 'When, in the course of development, class distinctions have disappeared, and all production has been concentrated in the hands of a vast association of the whole nation, the public power will lose its political character. Political

power, properly so-called, is merely the organized power of one class for oppressing another.'

81. On this aspect of liberal political theory see S. S. Wolin, *Politics and Vision*, pp. 286–314.
82. Quoted by Wolin, p. 313.
83. J. Hole, *Lectures on Social Science and the Organization of Labour* (London: 1851), esp. Chap. 7; pp. 127 ff. By 'Communism' is not meant Marxism, but a sort of Owenite socialism. James Hole of Leeds (1820–95) was prominent in the Mechanics' Institutes movement; cf. J. F. C. Harrison, *Social Reform in Victorian Leeds*.
84. See R. Miliband, 'The Politics of Robert Owen', *J. Hist. Ideas*, XV (1954).
85. Cobden to Rev. Thos. Spencer, 20 Apr. 1848, *Spencer Papers* (Athenaeum).
86. Thus Cobden; Morley, p. 860.
87. Hamburger, pp. 276–7.
88. J. S. Mill, *The Spirit of the Age*, p. 76.
89. E. Halévy, *The Growth of Philosophical Radicalism* (1928).
90. Morley, Cobden, p. 142.
91. *Rights of Man*, quoted by Rosen, p. 78.
92. On liberalism's sensitivity to pain, see Wolin, pp. 325–31.
93. Quoted in Ausubel, *John Bright*, p. 78.
94. Cobden to James Wilson, 23 Sept. 1856, quoted by McCord, 'Cobden and Bright in Politics 1846–1857', in Robson (ed.), *Ideas and Institutions of Victorian Britain*, p. 113.
95. Ausubel, p. 111. Already in 1848 Cobden complained to Thomas Spencer of 'this wicked attempt to rouse the war spirit against us', letter, 7 Feb. 1848, *Spencer Papers* (Athenaeum).
96. On general historical background see S. Gordon, 'The London *Economist* and the High Tide of Laissez-Faire', *J. Pol. Econ.*, LXIII (1955).
97. *The Economist*, 12 Dec. 1846, 18 June 1853, 31 Dec. 1853, 3 Dec. 1853.
98. *Ibid.*, 13 Oct. 1853.
99. *Ibid.*, 2, 16, 23 Nov. 1844, 18 Oct. 1845.
100. *Ibid.*, 26 Mar. 1853.
101. *Ibid.*, 27 Sept. 1845, 11 Jan. 1843, 14 Nov. 1846.
102. *Ibid.*, 11 Aug. 1846.
103. *Ibid.*, 12 Dec. 1844.
104. *Ibid.*, 8 Feb. 1851, pp. 138–9.
105. J. Wilson, *Influences of the Corn Laws*, pp. 49–50, quoted in Gordon, p. 461.

106. *The Economist*, 13 Feb. 1847.
107. Thomas Hodgskin was so forgotten that he was not even mentioned in the *D.N.B.*, and he owes his present reputation largely to Elie Halévy's *Thomas Hodgskin* (new ed. A. J. Taylor, 1956). For further discussion of Spencer's undoubted indebtedness to Hodgskin see A. J. Taylor, 'The Originality of Herbert Spencer', *Studies in English* (Texas), XXXIV (1955), pp. 101–6.
108. Quoted Halévy, pp. 35–6.
109. Cf. Halévy, p. 116.
110. Quoted by Halévy, pp. 92, 131, and attributed to an article in *The Economist*, 12 Dec. 1846—a reference which seems to be mistaken.
111. *The Economist*, reviewing Harriet Martineau's abridgement of the *Politique Positive*, 10 Dec. 1853.

4. Social Statics

1. Spencer, *Autobiography*, I, pp. 255–6.
2. *The Economist*, 10 Dec. 1853. The earliest book in English to be avowedly sociology was George Fitzhugh's *Sociology for the South* (1854; reprinted with an introduction by H. Wish in *Ante-Bellum: Writings of G. Fitzhugh and H. R. Helper on Slavery*), an extraordinary defence of slavery coupled with an attack on the 'free society' which uses many arguments employed in Europe by socialists. Fitzhugh's ideals are the polar opposite of Spencer's; sociology he sees as the cure for a diseased society, political economy as part of the sickness. Kingsley's combination of Christian socialism and Anglo-Saxon racism he finds appealing, and notes *Alton Locke* (1850) approvingly.
3. On this term's origins see the detailed notes by P. R. Senn in *J. Hist. Ideas*, XIX (1958), pp. 568–70, by J. H. Burns, *Ibid.*, XX (1959), pp. 431–2, and G. G. Iggers, *Ibid.*, pp. 433–6. The earliest use seems to have been by Comte when still a Saint-Simonian in 1822; it was later used by the French Socialist Sismondi, and came thence to England, being used by Mill in 1829 and by Owenites in the 1820s. (Holyoake, in *The History of Co-operation*, attributes its invention to Owen himself.)
4. J. Hole, *Lectures on Social Science and the Organization of Labour* (1851), cf. Chap. 4, note.
5. For example see the work by George Eliot's friend Mary Hennell, *An Outline of the Various Social Systems and Communities which have been founded on the Principle of Co-operation* (ed. with introduction by Charles Bray, 1844), or, an earlier work in the same tradition, Abram

Combe (the brother of George Combe the phrenologist), *The Sphere for Joint Stock Companies* (1825), an account of the principles behind the Owenite community at Orbiston.

6. On the National Association for the Promotion of Social Science (1857–1884) see L. Ritt, 'The Victorian Conscience in Action' (Ph.D. thesis, Columbia 1959). The writing of a leading member, W. R. Greg the industrialist, is typical of the more *laissez-faire* social science: *Essays on Political and Social Science* (1853).
7. *Social Statics* (1st edn. hereafter cited as *S. Stat.*), pp. 66–70, 457, 76–7.
8. *S. Stat.*, p. 1.
9. *Autobiography*, II, pp. 369–70.
10. A. MacIntyre, *Secularization and Moral Change*, pp. 14–15, 24–5.
11. *The Spirit of the Age*, p. 12.
12. Mrs. H. Ward, *Robert Elsmere* (1888), pp. 446–7; see also M. Richter, *The Politics of Conscience: T. H. Green and his Age*, pp. 27–8, 99–100.
13. *The Data of Ethics*, pp. iii–iv. It was much later that Spencer shows symptoms of worrying about the effects of criticism of religion; he described to Youmans his own *Ecclesiastical Institutions* as 'dreadfully destructive', 12 Apr. 1884, in Duncan, *Life and Letters*, p. 251. On the striking unanimity of actual moral judgments of Victorian leaders of opinion in all walks of life see W. E. Houghton, *The Victorian Frame of Mind*, Chap. 10, G. Himmelfarb, *Victorian Minds*, pp. 289–91, 311, and W. S. Smith, *The London Heretics 1870–1914*, esp. on Harrison, Bradlaugh and Holyoake. How far this was the work of evangelicalism alone is difficult to say. Secularists had to show they were as moral as Christians, by the Christians' standards, in order to legitimize themselves.
14. C. B. Macpherson, *The Political Theory of Possessive Individualism*, pp. 81–8.
15. *Ibid.*, pp. 270–7.
16. Quoted by Willey, *The Eighteenth Century Background*, p. 133.
17. See A. MacIntyre, 'Hume on *is* and *ought*', *Philosophical Rev.*, LXVIII (1959); cf. also V. C. Chappell (ed.), *Hume: A Collection of Critical Essays*.
18. On Bentham's relations with Hume, see Mary Mack, *An Odyssey of Ideas: Jeremy Bentham 1784–1792*, pp. 121–2, 184 ff.
19. *S. Stat.*, p. 12.
20. *Ibid.*, p. 15.
21. *Ibid.*, p. 13.
22. Quoted by Spencer, p. 28.

23. *Ibid.*, p. 24.
24. *Ibid.*, p. 32.
25. *S. Stat.*, p. 33.
26. Cf. Burrow, *Evolution and Society*, p. 34.
27. *S. Stat.*, p. 37.
28. *Ibid.*, p. 38.
29. The way in which Spencer, in his early writings, combined evolutionary relativism and absolute standards, is misunderstood by Burrow, p. 217, who quotes *Social Statics* as if it was to be classed with *The Data of Ethics* and his pessimistic later utterances. The change lay in his coming to believe that the fact of men *wanting* freedom did not necessarily mean they were ready to have it; see below pp. 100–2, and on his changing view of human nature, Chap. 7, pp. 144–5.
30. *S. Stat.*, p. 38.
31. *Ibid.*, pp. 40–1.
32. *Ibid.*, p. 51.
33. *Ibid.*, p. 77.
34. *Ibid.*, p. 78.
35. *Ibid.*, pp. 78–9.
36. *Ibid.*, p. 83.
37. Burrow, p. 27.
38. *S. Stat.*, p. 97.
39. *Ibid.*, pp. 114–15.
40. Cf. the Chartist land schemes, Chap. 4 above, notes 50–51.
41. *Ibid.*, pp. 148–53.
42. *Ibid.*, p. 244.
43. *Ibid.*, p. 247.
44. *Ibid.*, p. 274.
45. *Ibid.*, p. 341.
46. Cf. Spencer's earlier remarks in *The Nonconformist*. 19 Oct. 1842, p. 700, and 26 Oct., p. 714, where he opposes state education because it would inevitably encourage conformity: 'Varied mental constitution produces variety of opinion; different minds take different views of the same subject; every side of each question is examined, and out of the general mass of argument, urged forward by all parties, may sound principle be elicited. Truth has always originated from the conflict of mind with mind; it is the bright spark that generates from the collision of opposing ideas; like a spiritual Venus, the impersonation of moral beauty, it is born from the foam of the clashing waves of public opinion.' As often, Godwin is recalled (*Political Justice*, p. 298): 'the moment any scheme of

proceeding gains a permanent establishment it becomes impressed . . . with an aversion to change'—so national education is bad.

47. S. S. Wolin, *Politics and Vision*, Chap. 9, § ii, stresses the pessimistic and tentative aspects of liberalism, citing Locke, Smith and Hume; and he is right to provide a corrective for the opposite stereotype of liberalism as an essentially confident philosophy. Yet the young Spencer was both extremely liberal and extremely confident. What had changed was the estimation of human nature, now assumed to be highly self-controlled. Here, I suspect, we have the moral residue of evangelicalism being taken for granted, and might apply a suggestion of M. Walzer's in *The Revolution of the Saints*, p. 302: 'liberal confidence made repression and the endless struggle against sin unnecessary; it also tended to make self-control invisible, that is, to forget its painful history and naively assume its existence. The result was that liberalism did not create the self-control it required.'
48. Cf. Plato, *Apology* 37a, *Gorgias* 509e, *Republic* 336e.
49. Hume, *Treatise*, II, iii, 3.
50. D. Kettler, *The Social and Political Thought of Adam Ferguson*, Chap. 5.
51. J. Cropsey, *Polity and Economy: an Interpretation of the Principles of Adam Smith*, pp. 2, 45.
52. W. James, *Pragmatism*, subtitle.
53. Most strikingly perhaps E. Durkheim, *The Elementary Forms of the Religious Life* (Collier paperback edn., 1961), pp. 14–15. 'there are no religions which are false. All are true in their own fashion; all answer, though in different ways, to the given conditions of human existence.'
54. Cf. A. G. N. Flew, *Evolutionary Ethics*, p. 32.
55. *S. Stat.*, p. 417.
56. *Ibid.*, p. 419.
57. Houghton, Chap. 9.
58. *S. Stat.*, pp. 59–60.
59. *Ibid.*, p. 65. Godwin (*Political Justice*, p. 1) also used the phrase 'social state' to refer to the consummation of history. It does not look as if Spencer took it in *Social Statics* to be what Rosen says it was for Godwin—an unrealizable ideal to which history would for ever tend, asymptotically ('Progress and Democracy', p. 241); but in the Second Edn. of *Social Statics* (1892), presumably in response to disappointments, he does say that 'perfect adaptation can be reached only in infinite time'.
60. *Ibid.*, p. 409.
61. *Ibid.*, p. 413.
62. *Ibid.*, p. 415.

63. George Eliot to Mrs. Ponsonby, 11 Feb. 1875, quoted in Cross's *Life*, p. 538.
64. *S. Stat.*, p. 475.
65. Quoted in H. George, *A Perplexed Philosopher* (1911), p. 136.
66. *S. Stat.*, p. 474.
67. J. S. Whale, *The Protestant Tradition*, p. 136.
68. See G. Swanson, *Religion and Regime: A Sociological Account of the Reformation*, Chap. 1, for a fuller statement of the meaning of Protestantism's rejection of transcendence.
69. C. Hill, *The Intellectual Origins of the English Revolution*, pp. 180–1.
70. R. K. Merton, 'Puritanism, Pietism and Science', in *Social Theory and Social Structure* (rev. edn 1957), pp. 574–606.
71. Thus Newton's popularizer Maclaurin, quoted by P. Miller, *Jonathan Edwards*, p. 87.
72. Joseph Priestley, quoted by Bogue and Bennett, *History of Dissenters*, II, p. 398.
73. D. P. Walker, *The Decline of Hell*, p. 167.
74. Hume, *On Religion* (ed. R. Wollheim, 1963), p. 167.
75. *Ibid.*, p. 184.
76. M. Weber, *The Protestant Ethic and the Spirit of Capitalism* (English edn. 1930), p. 104; cf. R. Bendix, *Max Weber: An Intellectual Portrait* (Doubleday paperback edn.), p. 59.
77. See, for example, Willey, p. 152.
78. G. R. Cragg, *From Puritanism to the Age of Reason*, p. 16, quoting a correspondent of Archbishop Laud's.
79. Walker, p. 154, quoting Hallywell's *Deus Justificatus* (1668).
80. Miller, p. 57.
81. Quoted by L. S. Feuer, *The Scientific Intellectual*, pp. 27–9.
82. On Hartley, see Willey, Chap. 8.
83. Joseph Priestley, *Memoirs to the Year 1795*, pp. 17, 173, and written by his son, p. iii.
84. Harriet Martineau (1802–76), born of a prosperous Unitarian family at Norwich, perhaps the most celebrated of the early Victorian bluestockings, a prolific author on social, religious and moral topics, translator of Comte; George Combe (1788–1858), son of an Edinburgh brewer, the main British propagator and lifelong adherent of phrenology; Charles Bray (1811–84) radical manufacturer, who progressed from an evangelical phase in which he wondered how 'so large and practical a mind as Benjamin Franklin's could possible doubt' through Unitarianism to philosophical Necessity: H. T. Buckle (1821–62) author of the massive and original *History of Civilization in England*, brought up by a Calvinist mother in London.

85. See R. K. Webb, *Harriet Martineau: a Radical Victorian* (an excellent biography), and A. A. Huth, *The Life and Writings of H. T. Buckle* (2nd edn. 1880).
86. C. Bray, *Phases of Opinion and Experience during a Long Life* (n.d. c. 1884); C. Gibbon, *The Life of George Combe* (1878).
87. Bray, *Philosophy of Necessity* (3rd edn. 1889), p. 10; Webb, p. 244; Buckle, *History of Civilization in England* (new edn. 1882), I, pp. 23–7; Spencer, *S. Stat.*, p. 415.
88. Bray, *Philosophy of Necessity*, pp. 16–23; Webb, pp. 97 ff., referring to Joseph Priestley as the link between Edwards and the Unitarians.
89. Buckle, pp. 9 ff.
90. Bray, *Philosophy of Necessity*, p. 23; K. Erikson, *Wayward Puritans: A Study in the Sociology of Deviance*, pp. 188–205, suggests how Calvinist theology led to a view of human nature which had particular implications for the characterization and punishment of crime.
91. Buckle, p. 18.
92. H. G. Atkinson and H. Martineau, *Letters on the Laws of Man's Nature and Development* (1851), pp. 124 ff.
93. *S. Stat.*, p. 436.
94. Her *Autobiography*, I, pp. 109–11, cited by Houghton, p. 52.
95. Bray, *Phases of Opinion*, p. 5.
96. W. James, *Varieties of Religious Experience*, lectures 7–8, and R. B. Perry, *The Thought and Character of William James*, Chap. 19.
97. J. S. Mill, *Autobiography*, p. 143; on James Mill see Shirley Letwin, *The Pursuit of Certainty*, pp. 195–8. Mill (in *Logic*, 8th edn., 1896, Chap. 2, 'On Philosophical Necessity') says that necessitarians are fatalists, holding that 'our actions follow from our characters and . . . our characters follow from our organization, our education and our circumstances'. He mentions Owenites as holding these views.
98. For Spencer's most formal argument against the freedom of the will, see *P. Psy*[1],. §§ 207–8.

5. From Certainty to the Unknowable

1. On which see R. M. Young, *Mind Brain and Adaptation in the Nineteenth Century* (1970), esp. Chap. 5, and references cited there. This book is the only really full and competent treatment of Spencer's psychology, and especially of his links with Gall and the phrenologists.
2. An excellent example of how the inescapability of predestination leads to psychological explanation rather than moral justification is

Jonathan Edwards' brilliant 'Treatise concerning Religious Affections', in E. O. Winslow (ed.) *Jonathan Edwards: Basic Writings*, pp. 184–95; see also Perry Miller, *Jonathan Edwards*, pp. 139 ff. In other respects Edwards anticipates the nineteenth century—e.g. in his contrast of 'mere notional understanding' to the superior 'sense of the heart': 'when a man smells sweetness, he knows it more accurately than that by which he knows what a triangle is' (Miller, p. 184). Compare Spencer or J. H. Newman, concerned with basically similar problems, in *An Essay in Aid of a Grammar of Assent* (1870).

3. Such as was done in the late seventeenth century, after the fallacies of religious certitude; cf. H. G. van Leeuwen, *The Problem of Certainty in English Thought 1630–1690*.
4. Young, p. 163.
5. 'The Genesis of Science' (1854), in *Essays*, I, Chap. 3, p. 131.
6. *Autobiography*, II, pp. 481–2. See also 'The Origin and Function of Music' (1857), in *Essays*, I, Chap. 5, and 'The Philosophy of Style' (1852) in *Essays*, II, Chap. 1.
7. In *Essays*, III, Chap. 3, and first edn. of *First Principles*; it was omitted from later editions but intended to be put in that part of *P. Soc.* which was to deal with intellectual progress.
8. Letter, 3 Feb. 1851, quoted, without much explanation, by Duncan, *Life and Letters*, p. 67. On 12 March 1852 he wrote saying that he meant 'to produce a sensation', with it.
9. The third edition of Mill's *System of Logic* came out in 1851, being a reply to Whewell's *On Induction* (1849), as the first edition had been stimulated by Whewell's brilliant *Philosophy of the Inductive Sciences* (1840, second edn. 1847). W. Whewell (1794–1866), Master of Trinity College, Cambridge, the author of one of the Bridgewater Treatises (essays in natural theology, 1833), was more distinguished as a historian and methodologist of science than as an original scientist himself, though he did write papers on tides and other topics. He kept up a considerable correspondence with leading specialists, notably Herschel, Faraday and Lyell. To him we owe many scientific terms: 'anode', 'cathode', 'eocene', 'pliocene' and 'miocene', even 'scientist' itself. There has recently been a marked revival of interest in Whewell's ideas. See C. J. Ducasse, 'Whewell's Philosophy of Scientific Discovery', *Phil. Rev.*, LX (1951), A. W. Heathcote, 'Wm. Whewell's Philosophy of Science', *B. J. Phil. Sci.*, IV (1953–4), E. W. Strong, 'William Whewell and J. S. Mill: their controversy about scientific knowledge', *J. Hist. Ideas*, XVI (1955), A. Ellegard, 'The Darwinian Theory and 19th cent. philosophies of science', *J. Hist. Ideas*, XVII (1957), H. T. Walsh,

'Whewell on Necessity', *Phil. Sci.*, XXIX (1962), R. E. Butts, 'On Walsh's Reading of Whewell's view of Necessity', *Ibid.*, XXXII (1965), L. Laudon, 'Theories of Scientific Method', *Hist. Sci.*, VII (1968); also R. Blanché in *The Encyclopaedia of Philosophy* (ed. P. Edwards), s.v. 'Whewell, W.', and I. Todhunter, *Dr. William Whewell: An Account of His Writings*, 2 vols. (1876).

10. Spencer, *Essays*, II, Chap. 11 ('Mill v. Hamilton: the Test of Truth'), p. 413.
11. J. S. Mill, *Autobiography* (2nd edn. 1873), pp. 273–7.
12. W. Whewell, *The Philosophy of the Inductive Sciences* (1847), pp. 1–2, my italics.
13. R. Harré, reviewing reprints of Whewell's work in *B. J. Hist. Sci.*, IV (1969), p. 399.
14. See the 'Inductive Tables' of Astronomy and Optics between pp. 118–9 of *The Philosophy of the Inductive Sciences,* Vol. II.
15. *Ibid.*, Vol. II, Chaps. 1–2.
16. Heathcote, *loc. cit.*, p. 305, quoting Whewell's *Philosophy of Discovery*.
17. *Psychology*,[1] p. 12.
18. *Ibid.*, p. 31.
19. 'Mill v. Hamilton', in *Essays*, II, p. 387.
20. *Psychology*,[1] p. 144.
21. *Ibid.*, p. 126.
22. *Psychology*,[2] p. 449.
23. *Ibid.*, p. 453.
24. *Ibid.*, § 433.
25. *Essays*, I, Chap. 3, p. 119.
26. *Psychology*,[1] p. 51.
27. Whewell, *Philosophy of the Inductive Sciences*, quoted by Ellegard, *loc. cit.*; on Smith see Chap. 4, p. 98 and n. 51.
28. E. Durkheim, *The Elementary Forms of the Religious Life* (Collier paperback edn.), pp. 463 ff.
29. Quoted by P. P. Weiner, *Evolution and the Founders of Pragmatism*, p. 30.
30. *Psychology*,[1] p. 580.
31. *Ibid.*, § 197.
32. *Psychology*,[2] § 431; Vol. II, p. 414.
33. *Psychology*,[1] § 180, p. 526.
34. *Ibid.*, § 208, p. 620.
35. In this account of Spencer's *Psychology* I have drawn on both editions: 1855 and 1870–2 which is about twice the length Nearly all the material of the first is reused, largely without even rephrasing. The main differences are a firmer biological base, connexions with the

metaphysics of *First Principles*, the relocation of the epistemology from the beginning to the middle, and the addition of a final bridge section to sociology. But there is virtually no repudiation of doctrines set forth in the first edition.

36. *Psychology*,[2] Vol. I, p. 184.
37. *Psychology*,[1] p. 265.
38. *Psychology*,[2] § 60.
39. *Psychology*,[1] p. 275.
40. *Psychology*,[2] § 59.
41. *Psychology*,[1] § 105, and [2]§§ 269–72, 475.
42. *Psychology*,[2] Vol. II, pp. 335, 367.
43. *Psychology*,[1] §§ 114–7.
44. *Ibid.*, § 48, p. 188.
45. *Ibid.*, §§ 66, 79, 156.
46. *Psychology*,[2] Vol. II, p. 267.
47. *Psychology*,[1] § 190, p. 561; p. 563.
48. *Essays*, III, Chap. 3, p. 91.
49. *Psychology*,[1] p. 580.
50. *Psychology*,[2] Vol. II, p. 535.
51. *Psychology*,[1] § 157, p. 465.
52. *Psychology*,[2] § 484.
53. *Ibid.*, § 252, I, p. 581.
54. *Psychology*,[1] § 111, p. 350.
55. *Psychology*,[2] § 512, p. 577.
56. *Ibid.*, § 525, p. 609.
57. See S. Eisen, 'Herbert Spencer and the Spectre of Comte', *J. Brit. Stud.*, VII (1967).
58. *First Principles*,[6] § 37, and Chap. 1 of Part II, 'Philosophy Defined'. Four essays are to be considered here: 'The Genesis of Science' (1854) in *Ess.* I, 'Of Laws in General and the Order of their Discovery' (1862) in *First Principles*[1] and *Ess.* III, 'Reasons for Dissenting from the Philosophy of M. Comte' (1864) in *Ess.* III, and 'The Classification of the Sciences' (1871) in *Ess.* III.
59. *Essays* I, pp. 144–5.
60. *Essays* III, p. 96.
61. *Essays* III, Chap. 1.
62. On science and religion see especially A. Ellegard, *Darwin and the General Reader* (1958), G. Himmelfarb, *Darwin and the Darwinian Revolution* (1959), W. Irvine, *Apes, Angels and Victorians* (1955), and C. C. Gillespie, *Genesis and Geology* (1951).
63. On the impact of the higher criticism see Owen Chadwick, *The Victorian Church* (1966), pp. 527–57.

64. *First Principles,*[6] §§ 3–4.
65. H. L. Mansel (1820–71), professor at Oxford of Metaphysics and then of Ecclesiastical History, from 1868 Dean of St. Paul's. Unlike many at Oxford, where the influence of German philosophy was strong, Mansel leant to the French and Scottish schools. Mill attacked him in Chap. 7 of *An Examination of Sir William Hamilton's Philosophy*. Cf. W. R. Matthews, *The Religious Philosophy of Dean Mansel* (1956).
66. *Limits of Religious Thought*, p. 16.
67. *Ibid.*, Chap. 8, p. 57.
68. *Ibid.*, p. 171.
69. *Ibid.*, p. 95.
70. *Ibid.*, p. 98.
71. Quoted by M. St. J. Packe, *The Life of J. S. Mill*, p. 441.
72. J. S. Mill to A. Bain, 22 Nov. 1863, quoted in H. Eliot, *Letters of J. S. Mill* (1910), p. 310; he goes on, '. . . The conservation of force has hardly yet got to be believed and already its negation is declared inconceivable. . . . But this is Spencer all over.'
73. Mill to Bain, 7 Jan. 1863, quoted by Eliot, p. 273.
74. *First Principles,*[6] §§ 39–40.
75. *Ibid.*, §§ 28–29.
76. *Ibid.*, § 32.
77. *Ibid.*, § 31.
78. *Limits of Religious Thought*, p. 000.
79. Those agnostics who liked their Christianity justified in the traditional way were quite puzzled by Mansel. T. H. Huxley, for example, wrote to Charles Kingsley, 23 Sept. 1860: 'When Mansel took up Hamilton's argument on the side of orthodoxy (!) I said he reminded me of nothing so much as the man who is sawing off the sign on which he is sitting, in Hogarth's picture.' L. Huxley, *Life and Letters of T. H. Huxley*, Vol. I, p. 218.
80. See S. Eisen, 'F. Harrison and H. Spencer: Embattled Unbelievers', Victorian *Studies*, XII (1968).

6. Evolution

1. M. Harris, *The Rise of Anthropological Theory*, pp. 108–41, the most detailed recent discussion.
2. See the symposium edited by M. Banton, *Darwinism and the Study of Society*; but for better, negative, assessments see K. E. Bock, 'Darwin and Social Theory', *Phil. of Sci.*, XXII (1955) and D. G. MacRae,

'Darwinism and the Social Sciences' in *A Century of Darwin* (ed. S. A. Barnett), pp. 296–312. But absurdly mistaken judgments such as that of E. S. Corwin ('Spencer's influence is today extinct . . . sociology today owes most of its problems and procedures to Darwinian ideas rather than to Spencerian'), in *Evolutionary Thought in America* (ed. S. Persons), Chap. 5, esp. p. 187, are still common.

3. H. Spencer, *Autobiography*, I, p. 295.
4. 'Progress, Its Law and Cause', *Essays* I, pp. 30–1.
5. See the opening passage of 'The Factors of Organic Evolution' (reprinted as pamphlet from *Fortnightly Review*, Apr.–May 1886), and *Autobiography*, II, pp. 1–14, esp. p. 6.
6. L. Huxley, *Life and Letters of T. H. Huxley*, I, p. 168.
7. *Autobiography*, II, p. 8.
8. Cf. S. Toulmin and J. Goodfield, *The Discovery of Time*, Chap. 8, esp. p. 238, C. C. Gillispie, *Genesis and Geology*, Chaps. 5–6, A. O. Lovejoy, 'The Argument for Organic Evolution before *The Origin of Species*, 1830–1858' in B. Glass, O. Temkin and W. E. Strauss (eds.), *Forerunners of Darwin 1745–1859*, W. F. Cannon, 'The Uniformitarian-Catastrophist Debate', *Isis*, LI (1960).
9. Spencer, 'Factors of Organic Revolution', p. 5. Lyell put it thus: 'all former changes of the organic and physical creation are referable to one uninterrupted succession of physical events, governed by the laws now in operation' (quoted by Gillispie, p. 126).
10. Lyell, quoted by Gillispie, p. 133.
11. Paley's *Natural Theology* (1802) came out a year after the 3rd edition of *Zoonomia*, which it aimed to refute; see F. C. Haber in B. Glass *et al.*, pp. 250–1 and N. Garfinkle in *J. Hist. Ideas*, XVI (1955).
12. Spencer, *Principles of Biology*, I, §§ 143–7.
13. Gillispie, 'Lamarck and Darwin in the History of Science', in Glass *et al.*, pp. 265–91.
14. *P. Bio.*, I, p. 404.
15. *S. Stat.*, pp. 413–5. My italics.
16. P. B. Medawar, *The Art of the Soluble*, p. 45, writing as biologist, suspends judgment on this. In *S. Stat.*, p. 187, Spencer asks why children don't become adults as 'naturally' as acorns become oak trees, and suggests that when adaptation to the social state is complete the socialization process will be automatic.
17. As Burrow, *Evolution and Society*, p. 206.
18. In Glass *et al.*, p. 283.
19. On von Baer see S. J. Holmes, 'K. E. v. Baer's Perplexities over Evolution', *Isis*, XXVII (1947), pp. 7–14, and J. O. Oppenheimer, 'An Embryological Enigma in the Origin of Species', in Glass *et al.*,

pp. 292–322. Von Baer did his most important work in the 1820s and 1830s, and resisted many of the conclusions which were drawn from his discoveries. He was respected by Darwin and Huxley, yet sat on the fence over evolution. Like Oken and other *Naturphilosophen* he thought species neither evolved nor were created, but perhaps emerged in sequence by some sort of spontaneous generation.

20. Cf. Whewell, *Phil. Ind. Sci.* (1847 edn.), II, p. 321, quoting with approval Comte's *Cours de Philosophie Positive*: 'Does not each of us, in contemplating his own history, recollect that he has been a *theologian* in his infancy, a *metaphysician* in his youth and a *physicist* in his ripe age?' (Here the individual's life has the same pattern as humanity's, as Comte sees it). In most cases it is hard to say whether identity or analogy is being asserted, as with the characteristically slippery use of the idea in our own day by Marcuse, who got it from Freud, who got it from late nineteenth anthropology (A. MacIntyre, *Marcuse*, p. 51).
21. 'Progress: Its Law and Cause', pp. 29–30.
22. *First Principles*, p. 291.
23. For a discussion of this essay's background see D. E. C. Eversley, *Social Theories of Fertility and the Malthusian Debate*, pp. 188–92 and R. M. Young, 'Malthus and the Evolutionists', *Past and Present*, XLIII (1969), pp. 109–45.
24. 'Theory of Population', p. 2.
25. *Ibid.*, p. 32.
26. *Ibid.*, p. 33.
27. *Ibid.*, p. 35.
28. 'Progress: Its Law and Cause', pp. 50 ff.
29. The Scottish moralists, Ferguson and Smith, maintained a close association between social progress and population growth, but saw their relationship as reciprocal. Spencer's simpler view—appealing because it makes the social depend on the quasi-natural—was adopted by Durkheim in *The Division of Labour in Society* as the basic explanation of secular social change.
30. *P. Bio.*, I, p. 410.
31. 'Progress', pp. 31–2.
32. *Ibid.*, p. 55.
33. *Autobiography*, II, p. 12.
34. *First Principles*, § 50, pp. 132–3.
35. *Ibid.*, § 188.
36. 25 Nov. 1858, quoted in F. Darwin, *The Life and Letters of Charles Darwin*, II, p. 141.
37. *The Origin of Species* (Penguin edn., ed. J. W. Burrow), p. 348.

38. Cf. T. H. Huxley, *Evolution and Ethics*, pp. 80–1: '"Fittest" has a connotation of "best"; and about "best" there hangs a moral flavour. In cosmic nature, however, what is "fittest" depends on the conditions. If our hemisphere were to cool again, the survival of the fittest might bring about . . . a population of more and more stunted and humbler organisms, until the "fittest" that survived might be nothing but lichens, diatoms and such microscopic organisms. . . .' Even Spencer admitted that 'under its rigorously-scientific form [Darwin's] doctrine [of evolution] is expressible in purely physical terms, which neither imply competition nor imply better and worse'; defending Darwin from James Martineau's criticisms in *Contemporary Review*, XX (1872), p. 147, quoted by A. Ellegard, *Darwin and the General Reader*, pp. 254–5. Ellegard is right to add that in thus denying even competition, Spencer is assimilating Darwin's concept of evolution to his own.
39. *Autobiography*, I, p. 390.
40. *The Origins of British Sociology 1834–1914*, pp. 67–8.
41. *Some Reflexions on Herbert Spencer's Doctrine that Progress is Differentiation*, p. 8.
42. See *P. Bio.*, I, pp. 184–200, pp. 402–42. Here he gives pride of place to what he calls 'direct equilibration' (i.e. Lamarckian adaptation) over 'indirect equilibration' (pp. 443–63, i.e. Darwinian natural selection) which 'does whatever direct equilibration cannot do' in bringing about that process of adjustment to the conditions of existence which is evolution for Spencer. See also 'Factors of Organic Evolution' (1886), *passim*; p. 29; he regrets that 'nowadays most naturalists are more Darwinian than Mr. Darwin himself'. This was true, for Darwin felt natural selection needed supplementing (and not only by sexual selection) and wrote of 'my much despised child "Pangenesis", who I think will some day, under some better, turn out a fine stripling' (letter to E. R. Lankester, 15 Mar. 1870, in *Life and Letters*, III, p. 120). Interestingly, in the same letter Darwin goes on directly to tell Lankester how pleased he is that he appreciates Spencer (and 'I do not think that this is general with the men of science').
43. It is appropriate that in *P. Bio.*, I, p. 248 (in the chapter 'Heredity') Spencer discusses the Americanization of Irish and German immigrants in the same context as the domestication of animals, explicitly to reject the suggestion that spontaneous variation can be responsible for either!
44. *Rise of Anthropological Theory*, p. 118.
45. *Ibid.*, pp. 129–30.

46. *Ibid.*, p. 637.
47. *A New View of Society and other writings* (Everyman edn.), p. 16; cf. also p. 445. Cf. also A. Smith, *Wealth of Nations* (Everyman edn.), I, p. 14: 'The difference of natural talents in different men is, in reality, much less than we are aware of; and the very different genius which appears to distinguish men of different professions, when grown up to maturity, is not upon many occasions so much the cause as the effect of the division of labour. The difference between a philosopher and a common street porter, for example, seems to arise not so much from nature as from habit, custom and education.'
48. Cf. Burrow, pp. 121 ff.: they regarded Spencer's psychology as old-fashioned, *Ibid.*, p. 135.
49. Abram Combe, the brother of George Combe, was the founder of the Owenite community at Orbiston in Lanarkshire, which he proposed to run on phrenological principles; W. H. G. Armytage, *Heavens Below: Utopian Experiments in England*, pp. 96–104. Cf. also F. B. Smith, 'The Atheist Mission 1840–1900' in R. Robson (ed.), *Ideas and Institutions of Victorian Britain*, esp. p. 210.
50. Abrams, pp. 88 ff., is mistaken in seeing eugenics as following from Spencer's theory of evolution, though eugenicists may have seen it like that.
51. G. W. Stocking, 'Lamarckianism in American Social Science, 1890–1915', *J. Hist. Ideas*, XXIII (1962), reprinted with other essays in his important book *Race, Culture and Evolution: Essays in the History of Anthropology* (1968).
52. Letter to Spencer, 22 March 1886; *Life and Letters of T. H. Huxley*, II, p. 126.
53. Harris, pp. 125, 120, 105–6.
54. On whom see W. Stark, 'Natural and Social Selection' in M. Banton (ed.), *Darwinism and the Study of Society*, pp. 49–61.
55. *Mutual Aid* (1915 Everyman edn.), p. 6.
56. 'Theory of Population', p. 34.
57. *The Industrial Revolution*, p. 161.
58. Cf. *Data of Ethics*, Chap. 2, § 6.
59. *The Man v. the State*, p. 61.
60. *The Study of Sociology*, pp. 336–7.
61. *The Man v. the State*, p. 19.
62. *Stud. Soc.*, pp. 347–8.
63. *Ibid.*, pp. 343–4. These are the arguments which were the staple of the opposition to the New Poor Law. Spencer had used them in his Letters to *The Nonconformist*, 13 July 1842, p. 474.
64. *Stud. Soc.*, pp. 199–200.

65. Reprinted in *Evolution and Ethics* (1901), pp. 193–236; see also Spencer's letter to Huxley, 6 Feb. 1888, in Duncan, *Life and Letters of H. Spencer*, pp. 280–1; and L. Huxley, *Life and Letters of T. H. Huxley*, II, p. 187.
66. *Evolution and Ethics*, pp. 46–116, with Prolegomena (1894), pp. 1–45.
67. *Ibid.*, p. 26.
68. *Ibid.*, pp. 81, 83.
69. *Ibid.*, p. 81.
70. Duncan, p. 280. Cf. Huxley's earlier opinion, given to C. Kingsley in a letter of 23 Sept. 1860, on the death of one of his children: 'Science seems to me to teach in the highest and strongest manner the great truth which is embodied in the Christian concept of entire surrender to the Will of God. . . . I have the firmest belief that the Divine Government (if we may use such a phrase to express the sum of the "customs of matter") is wholly just . . . the absolute justice of the system of things is as clear to me as any scientific fact. The gravitation of sin to sorrow is as certain as that of the earth to the sun. . . .', *Life and Letters*, I, pp. 217–22; cf. Burrow, pp. 270–1.
71. Letter to J. A. Skilton, 29 July 1893, in Duncan, p. 336.
72. *P. Soc.*, V (Political Inst.), § 561 and Chap. 18.
73. On this point see C. Brinton, 'Spencer's Horrid Vision', *Foreign Affairs*, XV (1936–7).
74. In *S. Stat.*,[2] p. 31, Spencer actually says that adaptation to the social state can only be complete in infinite time, since it must slow up as the social state is approached and the 'force' of attraction, as it were, gets less.
75. B. Webb, *My Apprenticeship* (Penguin edn. 1938), I, p. 42.
76. *First Principles*, §§ 128–30.
77. *P. Soc.*, I, § 50, p. 106.
78. *First Principles*, Chap. 10, §§ 82–8.
79. *P. Soc.*, VIII (Industrial Inst.), § 852, p. 596.
80. *Ibid.*, § 846, p. 580.
81. *P. Soc.*, II, § 217.
82. N. J. Smelser, *Social Change in the Industrial Revolution*, p. 1, S. N. Eisenstadt, *Modernization: Protest and Change*, pp. 2–7, and 'Social Change, Differentiation and Evolution', *Am. Soc. Rev.*, XXIX (1964), pp. 375–86.
83. Duncan, p. 543.
84. *P. Soc.*, VIII, § 725.
85. Spencer's position, and the debate within American anthropology are well discussed by Harris, *Rise of Anthropological Theory*, pp. 171–3, 637 ff.

86. The argument of this section owes much to K. E. Bock, *The Acceptance of Histories: Towards a Perspective for Social Science* (1956), R. Bendix, 'Tradition and Modernity Reconsidered', *Comp. Stud. in Soc. and Hist.*, IX (1967), and R. A. Nisbet, *Social Change and History: Aspects of the Western Theory of Development* (1969).
87. R. G. Collingwood, *The Idea of Nature*, p. 13, and Toulmin and Goodfield, *The Discovery of Time*, p. 283.
88. 23 Apr. 1852, quoted Duncan, p. 62.
89. *Autobiography*, II, p. 185.
90. Bock, Chap. 4, esp. p. 56.
91. Collingwood, *The Idea of History*, pp. 29–31, on Thucydides. Collingwood dismissed sociology on the same grounds that he criticized Thucydides (and Thucydides' account of early Greek history at I 5–6 is amazingly like a piece of nineteenth century anthropology).
92. C. Kingsley, *The Limits of Exact Science as applied to History* (1860), p. 22, quoted by E. H. Carr, *What is History?* (Penguin edn.), p. 93. Of Kingsley (Regius Professor at Cambridge, 1860–9), Leslie Stephen wrote in *D.N.B.* that 'his lectures . . . were severely criticized by writers of authority as savouring more of the historical novelist than the trained inquirer'. E. S. Beesly, the positivist, attacked Kingsley in 'Mr. Kingsley and the Study of History', *Westminster Review*, XIX (1861).
93. *Stud. Soc.*, pp. 44–7.
94. Sir John Seeley (Professor at Cambridge, 1869–95), was an enthusiastic imperialist; his chief work was *The Expansion of England* (1883), and 'by history he meant political history—not biography, nor history of religion, art or society, but the history of the state' (*D.N.B.*); see the essay by R. T. Shannon in R. Robson (ed.), *Ideas and Institutions in Victorian Britain*, Chap. 9. J. R. Green's *Short History of the English People* (1874), was typical of the quasi-racist Anglo-Saxonism of the history of this period; see J. H. Plumb, *The Death of the Past*, p. 85, and p. 38 on Stubbs.
95. C. P. Gooch, *History and Historians in the Nineteenth Century* (1913), p. 321.
96. *Stud. Soc.*, p. 58.
97. *Ibid.*, p. 50.
98. *Ibid.*, p. 47.
99. *Ibid.*, p. 58.
100. *Ibid.*, p. 70.
101. *Autobiography*, II, p. 253.
102. *Stud. Soc.*, p. 71.
103. *Ibid.*, p. 105.

104. Spencer to W. A. S. Hewins, 24 March 1897, in Duncan, p. 403.
105. According to George Eliot; J. W. Cross, *Life of George Eliot*, p. 538.
106. Spencer to J. A. Skilton, 10 Jan. 1895, in Duncan, pp. 366–7.
107. *P. Soc.*, I, Chaps. 5–26. In this area Spencer can make quite Weber-like noises (e.g. p. 137, 'until we can figure to ourselves . . . the primitive system of thought we cannot fully understand primitive character'; or p. 441, 'this seeming chaos of puerile suppositions and monstrous inferences' become comprehensible when seen 'from the standpoint of the primitive man').

7. The Organic Analogy

1. R. A. Nisbet, *Social Change and History: Aspects of the Western Theory of Development* (1969).
2. Cf. W. Buckley, *Sociology and Modern Systems Theory* (1967), esp. pp. 1–17; two articles by K. W. Deutsch: 'Mechanism, Organism and Society: Some Models in Natural and Social Science', *Phil. of Sci.*, XVIII (1951), and 'Mechanism, Teleology and Mind', *Phil. and Phenomenol. Res.*, XII (1951–2); D. G. MacRae, 'Foundations for the Study of Politics', *Pol. Q.*, XXXVII (1966); W. Stark, *The Fundamental Forms of Social Thought* (1962), and 'Herbert Spencer's Three Sociologies', *Am. Soc. Rev.*, XXVI (1961).
3. See above Chap. 5, p. 123.
4. Cf. Nisbet, pp. 240 ff. I must dissent from Nisbet's excellent discussion over what he calls 'the irrelevance of metaphor'; for metaphor can only become irrelevant when classification is final and human purposes are unanimous.
5. Cf. M. Fortes and E. E. Evans Pritchard, *African Political Systems*, pp. 6–7 and passim.
6. Cf. R. K. W. Hinton, 'Husbands, Fathers and Conquerors', *Pol. Stud.*, XV (1967), p. 291.
7. As P. Laslett, *The World we have Lost* (1965), pp. 170–99.
8. E.g. Spencer, *P. Soc.*, VIII (Industrial Institutions), p. 571.
9. Cf. P. Rieff, *Freud: The Mind of the Moralist*, p. 57. Walzer, *The Revolution of the Saints*, pp. 186–93, notes how the Puritans tended to take the opposite line to Filmer: they did not domesticize the state, but sought to politicize the family.
10. *Culture and Society* (Penguin edn.), p. 146: cf. Nisbet, *The Sociological Tradition*, p. 70, and L. Bramson, *The Political Context of Sociology*, Chap. 8.
11. Cf. the very useful discussion by R. Williams, *op. cit.*, pp. 256–7.

12. Cf. R. G. Collingwood, *The Idea of Nature* (1945), Chap. 1.
13. Cf. C. E. Russett, *The Concept of Equilibrium in American Social Thought*, Chap. 3. It does not follow that, as Mrs. Russett says, p. 28, 'Spencer derived his social theory ultimately from physics'. What 'derived . . . from' implies here is not clear. It is true that in *First Principles* he claimed to 'deduce' everything from the 'Persistence of Force'. (Mrs. Russett casually remarks that this was 'a somewhat old fashioned name for the conservation of energy'—perhaps it was, but the case needs arguing, since Spencer explicitly denied it.) And in any case, organic imagery long antedates the mechanistic language of *First Principles*.
14. A motif found in many industrial apologists of *laissez-faire*, such as Ure, C. Babbage (*On the Economy of Machinery and Manufactures*, 1835) and H. Tufnell (*The Character, Object and Effects of Trades Unions*, 1834), which begins by quoting that old stock item, the Body Politick analogy of Menenius Agrippa in Shakespeare's *Coriolanus*, and goes on to the 'self-acting' mule built by Roberts of Manchester.
15. Bramson, p. 14, regards it as the weapon *par excellence* of conservatives like Burke.
16. Yet he was still very fond of likening legislation to medicine: 'the art of legislation is but the art of healing practised upon a large scale. . . . This is not a mere fanciful analogy' (Mack, *Bentham*, pp. 264 ff.).
17. E.g. ex-President Sukarno of Indonesia, a one-time engineer, liked to see his public role in this way, the directives of the National Planning Council being 'blueprints' for the 'construction' of the nation. See the speech quoted by P. E. Sigmund (ed.), *The Ideologies of the Developing Nations*, pp. 60–1.
18. *Philosophy of Manufactures*, pp. 13, 14–15.
19. *Ibid.*, p. 55.
20. *Ibid.*, p. 453.
21. See Spencer's essays 'Representative Government' (1857) in *Essays*, II, esp. pp. 178 ff., and 'Parliamentary Reform' (1860), *Ibid.*, p. 364.
22. On Carlyle, see R. Williams, *op. cit.*, pp. 85–98.
23. W. R. Greg, *Essays on Political and Social Science* (1853), I, p. 502.
24. *S. Stat.*, p. 390.
25. *Ibid.*, p. 239.
26. *Ibid.*, p. 261.
27. *Ibid.*, p. 315.
28. 'The Social Organism', in *Essays*, I, pp. 384–5.
29. *Stud. Soc.*, pp. 25–30.
30. *Ibid.*, p. 175.

31. *Ibid.*, p. 32.
32. 'Social Organism', pp. 385–6; in 'Representative Government', pp. 199–200, Adam Smith, Cobden and Bright are called the 'unacknowledged legislators' of the age.
33. 'Over-legislation' (1853), in *Essays*, II, p. 63.
34. *Stud. Soc.*, pp. 4, 13, 20–1.
35. 'Specialized Administration' (1871), in *Essays*, III, pp. 129–30.
36. Abrams, *Origins of British Sociology*, p. 74, writes that '. . . it is important to see Spencer did *not* believe he had justified passivity but only a willingness to postpone action until it could be derived from a sociologically adequate analysis of social structure and social causation'. Spencer certainly used this argument from man's ignorance; but he also used other arguments to show that, in industrial society, governmental activity was in principle harmful or superfluous.
37. 'Representative Government', p. 209, archly remarks, 'the metamorphosis we have described is not mentioned in Ovid'.
38. *Ibid.*, pp. 182–3.
39. Such as Bentham employed (Mary Mack, *J. Bentham: An Odyssey of Ideas*, p. 264), or Durkheim (*Rules of the Sociological Method*, ed. Catlin, 1938, pp. 47–75.)
40. 'Social Organism', pp. 388–91; cf. *P. Soc.*, II, §§ 213–22.
41. *Ibid.*, p. 416.
42. 'Specialized Administration', p. 416.
43. E.g. J. H. Goldthorpe, 'Herbert Spencer', in T. Raison (ed.), *The Founding Fathers of Social Science*, p. 79; cf. Deutsch's articles cited above, note 2. Ref. to Spencer is *P. Soc.*, II, § 221.
44. *P. Soc.*, II, § 213.
45. *Autobiography*, p. 433.
46. *Ibid.*, p. 434.
47. *P. Soc.*, II, § 269, p. 613.
48. Cf. Deutsch (1951–2), p. 185.
49. *P. Soc.*, II, § 252.
50. *P. Bio.*, I, p. 160.
51. P. B. Medawar, *The Art of the Soluble*, p. 41.
52. *P. Soc.*, II, § 238.
53. *Ibid.*, § 258.
54. *Ibid.*, §§ 241–55.
55. *Ibid.*, § 254.
56. *Stud. Soc.*, pp. 70–1.
57. *P. Soc.*, II, § 215.
58. *Ibid.*, § 217, p. 469.

59. *Ibid.*, § 234.
60. *S. Stat.*, p. 97.
61. Cf. R. G. Collingwood, *The Idea of Nature*, pp. 16–17.
62. Thus Buckley, p. 18.
63. *P. Soc.*, II, § 228. On Tylor's concept of culture see Stocking, *Race, Culture and Evolution*, pp. 74–81.
64. Cf. Burrow, *Evolution and Society*, pp. 221–2. A typical statement of current sociological orthodoxy is N. J. Smelser and S. M. Lipset, *Social Structure and Mobility in Economic Development*, p. 4, who say that the units of social structure, 'are not persons as such but selected aspects of interaction among persons, such as roles and social organization which refers to clusters of roles'.
65. A. R. Radcliffe-Brown, *Method in Social Anthropology*, pp. 161, 178–89.
66. Russett, *Concept of Equilibrium*, pp. 52, 161–2, seems to associate Spencer's use of equilibrium with an alleged social conservatism.
67. 'Reasons for Dissenting from the Philosophy of M. Comte', *Essays*, III, pp. 75–6.
68. *P. Soc.*, V, § 528, pp. 601–2.
69. *Political Context of Sociology*, p. 22.
70. M. Brodbeck, quoted by W. H. Dray in 'Holism and Individualism in History and Social Science', in P. Edwards (ed.), *Encyclopaedia of Philosophy*. There is a vast philosophical literature on this controversy. See especially E. Gellner, 'Holism and Individualism in History and Sociology', in P. Gardiner (ed.), *Theories of History*, and S. Lukes, 'Methodological Individualism Reconsidered', *Brit. J. Soc.*, XIX (1968).
71. S. Andreski, *Elements of Comparative Sociology*, pp. 173–4.
72. As W. H. Simon, 'Herbert Spencer and the Social Organism', *J. Hist. Ideas*, XXI (1960), pp. 294–9.
73. *Rules of the Sociological Method*, p. 14.
74. Quoted by Lukes, *loc. cit.*, p. 119.
75. *P. Soc.*, II, § 212; also cited by Durkheim, *op. cit.*, p. 100.
76. *P. Soc.*, I, § 6.
77. *Stud. Soc.*, pp. 50–2. By *consensus* Spencer does not mean the value-consensus which is so important in some kinds of contemporary functionalism, but merely fit or correspondence. He admitted to owing the idea to Comte.
78. *P. Soc.*, VIII, § 845, p. 579.
79. 'Railway Morals and Railway Policy' (1854), in *Essays*, II, p. 261.
80. *Essays*, III, p. 443.
81. *Stud. Soc.*, pp. 173–4.
82. *P. Soc.*, V, § 470, p. 327; cf. § 529.

83. *P. Soc.*, I, § 210, p. 460.
84. *Rules of the Sociological Method*, p. 100.
85. Such as Barrington Moore, *The Social Origins of Dictatorship and Democracy*, pp. 240, 281, 286, 291, 308, 334–6.
86. Such as E. E. Hagen, *On the Theory of Social Change*, D. C. McClelland, *The Achievement Motive*, R. E. Levine, *Dreams and Deeds*; or the whole tradition of work in political science on 'political culture', initiated by G. A. Almond and S. Verba, *The Civic Culture*, and heavily influenced by the ideas of T. Parsons.
87. S. M. Lipset in his *The First New Nation* (1963) persuasively attempts to show the enduring force of certain basic cultural values which have informed Americans and their institutions ever since 1776. Their real existence is postulated to explain stability, and may therefore be doubted if sudden contrary changes occur (or else the reality of these must be undermined). As a result of certain political values, Lipset writes (p. 214), 'lower-class individuals and groups which desire to change their social position *need not be revolutionary*: consequently their political goals and methods are relatively moderate'. Can this still be maintained after the politics of the late 1960s? And if not, what becomes of the theoretical premisses? See the criticism of Lipset and the values approach in general by B. M. Barry, *Sociologists, Economists and Democracy*, Chaps. 3–4.
88. J. H. Kunkel, 'Values and Behavior in Economic Development', *Econ. Dev. and Cult. Change*, XIII (1965), pp. 257–77, in attempting to create a 'behavioral' theory of social change, proposes to abolish the dilemma by defining 'personality' as 'the totality of behavior patterns in the individual's repertoire', which are then explained as the result of positive and negative stimuli. But this is to secure more manageable data at the price of disregarding what seems to be a factor in *determining* action, not just a misleading way of describing action.
89. As for example A. MacIntyre, 'A Mistake about Causality in Social Science', in P. Laslett and W. G. Runciman (eds.), *Philosophy, Politics and Society* (2nd series), pp. 48–70, with a closely related issue, that between thought and action.

8. Militancy and Industrialism

1. See D. C. Rapaport, 'Military and Civil Societies: the Contemporary Significance of a Traditional Subject in Political Theory', *Pol. Stud.*, XII (1964), pp. 178–201.

2. See J. Cropsey, *Polity and Economy: an Interpretation of the Principles of Adam Smith* (1957), and A. Smith, *Wealth of Nations* (Everyman edn.), Vol. II, pp. 182 ff.; cf. remarks critical of merchants and favourable to farmers, I, pp. 114, 405–6; II, p. 301.
3. A. Ferguson, *An Essay on the History of Civil Society*, pp. 214, 280–5, and D. Kettler, *The Social and Political Thought of Adam Ferguson*, pp. 204–9.
4. See above, Chap. 3, p. 76.
5. *How to Observe: Manners and Morals* (a handbook on research methodology for the 'science of morals'), pp. 30–8.
6. 'We believe the government of the United States to be at this moment the best in the world; but then the Americans are the best people; and we have a theory that the government of every state is always, excepting periods of actual change, that which is best adapted to the circumstances and wants of its inhabitants': not the young Spencer but 'A Manchester Manufacturer' (i.e. Cobden), *England, Ireland and America* (Edinburgh, 1835), p. 33.
7. *Ibid.*, p. 19.
8. Cf. J. Morley, *Life of Cobden* (1906 edn.), p. 469: 'The *class feeling* amongst the agricultural labourers [of Sussex] is in favour of a cheap loaf. . . . I long to live to see an agricultural labourer strike for wages.'
9. S. Smiles, *The Life of George Stephenson, and of his son Robert Stephenson* (1868), pp. 8, 268.
10. Smiles, pp. 370–81; cf. also A. Ure, *Philosophy of Manufactures* (1835), p. 18.
11. *England, Ireland and America*, p. 6.
12. *On the Rise, Progress and Present State of Public Opinion* (1828), pp. 176–7.
13. *Philosophy of Manufactures*, p. v.
14. H. T. Buckle, *History of Civilization in England* (new edn. 1882), pp. 209–18.
15. *Ibid.*, p. 198.
16. E.g. S. Andreski, introduction to abridged edn. of Spencer's *Principles of Sociology* (1969), p. xxii.
17. On S.-Simon's influence see W. M. Simon, *European Positivism in the Nineteenth Century* (1963), esp. Chaps. 7–8, and on his doctrines F. E. Manuel, *The New World of Henri Saint-Simon* (1956), esp. Chaps. 4, 20–7, and G. Lichtheim, *The Origins of Socialism* (1969), Chap. 4.
18. Buckle, p. 232.
19. See Thorstein Veblen, *The Theory of the Leisure Class* (1899); and

Imperial Germany and the Industrial Revolution (1915). Further discussion below, Chap. 9, p. 241.

20. E.g. Jay Rumney, *Herbert Spencer's Sociology* (1934), p. 22, or J. M. Robertson, *Buckle and his Critics* (1895), maintaining that therefore Buckle was more of a sociologist than Spencer.
21. Cf. Nisbet, *The Sociological Tradition* (1967), pp. 56–61, on Comte's ideals, and his relation to reactionaries such as Bonald and Maistre.
22. *The German Ideology* (1965 edn.), pp. 44–5.
23. *P. Soc.*, I, § 38.
24. *P. Soc.*, III, §§ 317–8. He made the fullest use of Maine's status/contract, however.
25. *P. Soc.*, V, p. 248.
26. *P. Soc.*, III, §§ 278–9, p. 632.
27. *Ibid.*, § 291, p. 661.
28. *Ibid.*, § 288, p. 654.
29. *P. Soc.*, I, § 38, p. 79.
30. *P. Soc.*, IV, § 365.
31. *P. Soc.*, VIII, § 737.
32. *P. Soc.*, IV, § 399.
33. *P. Soc.*, VI, § 627.
34. *P. Soc.*, IV, §§ 429–31.
35. *P. Soc.*, I, § 37.
36. *P. Soc.*, V, § 437, p. 237.
37. *P. Soc.*, I, § 35, p. 70.
38. *P. Soc.*, III, § 282, p. 640.
39. See Chap. 6, p. 156.
40. *P. Soc.*, § 38, p. 78.
41. *Philosophy of Manufactures*, p. 16.
42. Cf. E. P. Thompson, 'Time, Work-discipline and Industrial Capitalism', *Past and Present*, XXXVIII (1967), pp. 56–97, R. Bendix, *Work and Authority in Industry*, Chap. 2, and E. J. Hobsbawn, *Industry and Empire*, pp. 66–70.
43. *P. Soc.*, VI, § 647, p. 811.
44. *Thrift* (1875), p. 179.
45. *Autobiography*, Vol. I, pp. 10–11.
46. Cf. Thompson, *Making of English Working Class*, pp. 776–7, and H. Ausubel, 'The Working Class and Malthusianism', *J. Hist. Ideas*, XIII (1952).
47. *P. Soc.*, II, § 248, V, § 547.
48. *P. Soc.*, V, § 573.
49. *Ibid.*, § 440, p. 244.
50. *P. Soc.*, II, § 257, p. 577.

51. *Ibid.*, p. 578.
52. *Ibid.*, p. 583.
53. *Ibid.*, p. 584.
54. *P. Soc.*, V, § 562, p. 694.
55. *P. Soc.*, II, § 250.
56. *P. Soc.*, V, § 446, p. 257; cf. R. Dahrendorf's 'Out of Utopia', *Amer. J. Soc.*, LXIV (1959).
57. *P. Soc.*, V, §§ 445–6; the attitude is seen clearest in *The Black Book* (several editions from 1820 to 1835), which details aristocratic corruption and sinecures.
58. See Chap. 9, 'An Ecclesiastical System as a Social Bond', in *P. Soc.*, VI, esp. §§ 626–7.
59. *Elementary Forms of the Religious Life* (Doubleday edn. 1961), p. 13.
60. *Community and Association* (Harper Torchbooks edn. 1963), p. 232.
61. *P. Soc.*, IV, § 416.
62. E.g. *P. Soc.*, IV, § 420: 'inconvenient and sometimes painful traits' only to be acquired by those whose wealth makes them useless; VIII, § 738, on the love of appearance before utility, the survival of a militant age with its love of esteem, 'even in our own households'.
63. *P. Soc.*, II, § 247, p. 535.
64. S. Ossowski, *Class Structure in the Social Consciousness* (English edn., trans. S. Patterson, 1963), p. 91.
65. Spencer's model is akin to the official egalitarian ideology of most industrial societies. Its potential remains radical since any realistic social analysis will tend to highlight the discrepancies between ideology and reality. This was Veblen's favourite mode of social criticism; and is an implication of Lipset and Bendix's *Social Mobility in Industrial Society* (1959).
66. *P. Soc.*, IV, § 429.
67. 'Manners and Fashion' (1854), *Essays*, I, pp. 109, 113.
68. W. Bagehot, *The English Constitution* (1865). Cf. Cobden, writing in 1863 to lament the seduction of wealthy manufacturers by the upper classes: 'feudalism is every day more and more in the ascendent in political and social life. So great is its power and prestige that it draws to it the support and homage of even those who are the natural leaders of the newer and better civilization. . . .': J. Morley, *Life of Cobden*, pp. 946–7.
69. *P. Soc.*, VI, § 616.
70. *Ibid.*, § 627, p. 773.
71. *Ibid.*, § 646, p. 808.
72. *Ibid.*, p. 785.
73. *Ibid.*, pp. 824–5, § 660.

74. Veblen echoed them both when he wrote in 1914: 'History records more frequent and more spectacular instances of the triumph of imbecile institutions over life and culture than of peoples who have by force of instinctive insight saved themselves alive out of a desperately precarious institutional situation, as now faces the people of Christendom.' How very American and how close to Spencer's viewpoint, is this combination of sociological pessimism about institutions and psychological optimism about men. It is diametrically opposed to the viewpoints of Weber and especially Durkheim —who incidentally were both enthusiastic about the prospect of war in 1914.
75. *P. Soc.*, V, § 571.
76. *The Man v. the State*, p. 61.
77. 'Over-Legislation' (1853), *Essays*, II, pp. 84, 87, 91.
78. 'Specialized Administration' (1871), *Essays*, III, p. 151.
79. 'Over-Legislation', pp. 101–3. Cf. *P. Soc.*, VIII, p. 402, a typical pro-American outburst: in Britain Sir Henry Bessemer has only been knighted like 'a third-rate public official on his retirement or . . . a provincial mayor on the occasion of the Queen's Jubilee', whereas in America he has one county and six cities named after him.
80. *The Man v. the State*, p. 63.
81. Thus H. M. Hyndman in his pamphlet *Socialism and Slavery* (London, n.d.).
82. E. S. Corwin, in Stow Persons (ed.), *Evolutionary Thought in America*, p. 186.
83. S. E. Finer, *The Life and Times of Sir Edwin Chadwick* (1952), pp. 439–40. To associate Spencer with protectionism is bizarre; and *The Man v. the State* was not 'written when he had just ceased to practise as an engineer' (i.e. 1846) but nearly 40 years later (i.e. 1884).
84. 'Manners and Fashion' (1854), *Essays*, I, pp. 91–2.
85. *How to Observe: Morals and Manners* (1838), pp. 30 ff.
86. *P. Soc.*, II, pp. 595–6.
87. Quoted by S. Avineri, *The Social and Political Thought of Karl Marx*, p. 110.
88. *P. Soc.*, VIII, §§ 819–20; pp. 515–16.
89. E.g. *Stud. Soc.*, p. 199—'the purifying process . . . of industrial war'. His quandary is seen in *P. Soc.*, V, § 582, where, after a passage emphasizing that war has done its work for the 'best races' are the existing survivors, he admits some industrial benefits of war (p. 753), a reluctant concession to the facts of the later nineteenth century.
90. 'Morals of Trade' (1859), *Essays*, II, esp. pp. 134, 137, 146.
91. *Thrift*, p. 290, quoted in K. Fielden's very useful article, 'Samuel

Smiles and Self Help', *Vict. Stud.*, XII (1968). Cf. also A. Briggs in *Victorian People* (1954), Chap. 5, and Bendix, *Work and Authority in Industry*, p. 111.

92. E.g. M. Harris, *Rise of Anthropological Theory* (1969), p. 125, on Spencer's 'condemnation of co-operativism'.
93. Cf. letter of Spencer to H. Seal, 11 July 1893 (Duncan, p. 353), which distinguishes social co-operation from 'state interference' and insists that individualism 'may and does go along with an elaborate form of mutual dependence'. The unhelpfulness of the stereotyped opposition of 'individualists' and 'collectivists' is manifest from the others' side too; see Durkheim's 'Individualism and the Intellectuals', translated and introduced by Steven Lukes in *Political Studies*, XVII (1969).
94. *History of Co-operation*, Vol. II, pp. 275, 299, 582, 666.
95. See D. S. Landes, 'The Structure of Enterprise in the Nineteenth Century', in *The Rise of Capitalism* (1966).
96. S. Pollard, *The Genesis of Modern Management* (1965), pp. 12–13. E.g. Thomas Potter, a successful business man and first Mayor of Manchester, refused to join a public company since 'a man is successful in business only when he can watch with his own eyes everything that is going on' (quoted by J. H. Clapham, *Economic History of Modern Britain*, Vol. I, p. 278).
97. See H. Parris, *Government and the Railways in Nineteenth Century Britain* (1965); G. Todd, 'Some Aspects of Joint Stock Companies, 1844–1900', *Econ. Hist. Rev.* (1st series), IV (1932), and J. Saville, 'Sleeping Partners and Limited Liability, 1850–1856', *Econ. Hist. Rev.* (2nd series), VIII (1956). There were a lot of bankruptcies, due very largely to ignorance, fraud and inexperience on the part of capitalists, who were obsessed with the difficulty and yet the need of creating trust, predictable conditions and norms for industrial organizations. This preoccupation found an echo in Spencer's theory that industrialism needed certain moral and social prerequisites. Opponents of limited liability felt it would sap responsibility (see Saville, p. 425), but when it worked capitalists congratulated themselves that the requisite moral standards were achieved.
98. See J. K. Galbraith, *The New Industrial State* (1967), who develops a long tradition of analysis from Schumpeter, Berle and Means, and others.
99. 'Railway Morals', *Essays*, II, pp. 243–4.
100. *Ibid.*, p. 285.
101. *P. Soc.*, VIII, §§ 838–9. Yet earlier Spencer had said that even in

co-operatives there would always be directors and directed (*P. Soc.*, V, § 578, p. 740), and accused trade unions of wanting to dictate labour relations and bring about 'abolition of free trade between employers and employed': 'Parliamentary Reform' (1860), *Essays*, II, pp. 257–60. I think there is a real change of attitude which Spencer was not wholly aware of and perhaps reluctant to acknowledge.

102. Joint stock companies are 'a point on the way to the transformation of all functions in the process of reproduction hitherto associated with capital ownership into mere functions of the associated producers, into social functions': quoted and discussed by R. Dahrendorf, *Class and Class Conflict in Industrial Society* (1959), p. 22. See also the passages reprinted from *Capital* in T. B. Bottomore and M. Rubel, *Karl Marx: Selected Writings in Sociology and Social Philosophy* (Penguin edn. 1963), pp. 161–4, where Marx quotes Ure.
103. *P. Soc.*, VIII, Chap. 22, pp, 571, 577.
104. *Ibid.*, § 852, p. 595. Cf. Duncan, p. 358, quoting a letter to Holyoake, 10 Sept. 1894, enclosing a subscription for a co-operative venture of the latter's.
105. *The Man v. the State*, Chap. 1.
106. *History of Co-operation*, Vol. II, p. 607.
107. The pioneer was Thomas Spence (1750–1814), schoolmaster of Newcastle, who proposed a land nationalization scheme and a social reorganization. He was repeatedly prosecuted, fined and imprisoned for publicizing his views. The 'Spencean Philanthropists', his disciples, were a link between the radicalism of the 1790s and the later Owenism. See O. D. Rudkin, *T. Spence and his Connections* (1927, repr. 1966).
108. See P. Wiles, writing in G. Ionescu and E. Gellner (eds.), *Populism* (1969), esp. pp. 169–70.
109. For a detailed instance of such a historical irony, see J. Prest's *The Industrial Revolution in Coventry* (1960), on the demise of the craftsman in the lace and stocking trades.

9. History's Revenge

1. See above Chap. 6, p. 156.
2. *The Man v. the State*, p. 5.
3. Cf. S. Avineri, 'Marx and Modernization', *Rev. of Pol.*, XXXI (1969), pp. 172–88; he defends Marx by pointing out, in effect, that like Spencer he wanted to have the benefits but not the disadvantages that accrue to deterministic schemes of history ('tendencies working

with iron necessity towards inevitable results', as the preface to the first edn. of *Capital* puts it).

4. Cf. A. Briggs, *Victorian Cities* (1963), p. 45 and passim.
5. A. V. Dicey, *Law and Public Opinion in England during the Nineteenth Century* (2nd edn. 1914).
6. J. B. Brebner, 'Laissez-faire and State Intervention in nineteenth century Britain', *J. Econ. Hist.* (Supp.), VIII (1948).
7. S. E. Finer, *The Life and Times of Sir E. Chadwick* (1952), p. 20.
8. M. Richter, *The Politics of Conscience: T. H. Green and his Age* (1964), pp. 267 ff.
9. On the railways see H. Parris, *Government and the Railways in Nineteenth Century Britain* (1965).
10. Beatrice Webb, who knew Chamberlain and Spencer equally well, says (*My Apprenticeship*, p. 146), that Spencer described Chamberlain as 'a man who may mean well, but who does, and will do, an incalculable amount of mischief', while Chamberlain said of Spencer: 'Happily for the majority of the world, his writing is unintelligible, otherwise his life would have been spent in doing harm.'
11. Finer, p. 475.
12. 'Parliamentary Reform', *Essays*, II, p. 364.
13. On the Fabians see Mary P. Mack, 'The Fabians and Utilitarianism', *J. Hist. Ideas*, XVI (1955) and E. J. Hobsbawm, 'The Fabians Reconsidered', pp. 250–71 of *Labouring Men* (1964) and D. Roberts, 'J. Bentham and the Victorian Administrative State', *Vict. Stud.*, II (1958–9), pp. 193–210.
14. See H. Perkin, *The Origins of Modern English Society 1780–1880*, pp. 252–70, 428–9, S. Pollard, *The Genesis of Modern Management* (1965). D. Roberts, *The Victorian Origins of the British Welfare State* (1960), and W. J. Reader, *Professional Men* (1966).
15. See C. Bibby, 'T. H. Huxley and University Development', *Vict. Stud.*, II, (1958–9).
16. On A. J. Mundella, manufacturer of Nottingham, and Liberal M. P. for Sheffield, see W. H. G. Armytage, *A. J. Mundella: the Liberal Background to the Labour Movement* (1951).
17. Letter, 15 Feb. 1884, quoted in Duncan, *Life and Letters of H. Spencer*, p. 238.
18. *The Man v. the State*, p. 1.
19. *The Communist Manifesto* (Moscow, n.d.), p. 86.
20. See W. H. Simon, *European Positivism in the Nineteenth Century* (1963), Chap. 8 and W. S. Smith, *The London Heretics 1870–1914* (1967), pp. 84–131.

21. A. M. McBriar, *Fabian Socialism and English Politics 1884–1918* (1962), p. 149.
22. *Ibid.*, p. 242.
23. See Richter, p. 202.
24. Fabian Tract 70, quoted by McBriar.
25. D. G. Ritchie, *The Principles of State Interference* (1902).
26. Letter, 25 May 1902, quoted in Duncan, p. 457.
27. J. A. Hobson, *Imperialism: a Study* (1906); cf. also E. J. Hobsbawm, *Industry and Empire* (1968), Chap. 7 and H. Stretton, *The Political Sciences* (1969), pp. 73–140.
28. B. Semmel, *Imperialism and Social Reform* (1960).
29. Letter to Bright, 2 July 1881, in Duncan, Chap. 16; see too B. Porter, *Critics of Empire*, esp. Chap. 7.
30. Letter to A. Swinburne, 8 March 1881, *Ibid.*
31. Letter to M. D. Conway over the American annexation of the Phillippines, 17 July 1898, in Duncan, p. 410.
32. 26 Aug. 1892, in Duncan, pp. 319–23.
33. 18 Jan. 1904.
34. Cf. A. Briggs, 'The Idea of the Welfare State', *Eur. J. Soc.*, II (1961), pp. 235–6.
35. Semmel, Chap. 4; Halévy, *Imperialism and the Rise of Labour*, p. 24.
36. See G. Himmelfarb, 'Varieties of Social Darwinism', in *Victorian Minds*, pp. 314–32.
37. Such as R. Hofstadter's *Social Darwinism in American Thought* (1944).
38. Penguin edn. (trans. T. W. Tancock), p. 428.
39. See R. M. Young, 'Malthus and the Evolutionists', *Past and Present*, XXXIV (1969), p. 138.
40. But see S. Avineri's 'From Hoax to Dogma: a Footnote on Marx and Darwin', *Encounter*, XXXVIII (1967), pp. 30–2, arguing that the connexion is insubstantial; but he seems to me to have overstated his case, and has to explain away both Marx's own earliest reactions and the later judgments of Engels and other Marxists; cf. G. Lichtheim, *Marxism* (1961), pp. 218–19.
41. E. Ferri, *Socialism and Positive Science: Darwin, Spencer, Marx* (1905, trans. from the French edn. of 1896 by E. C. Harvey).
42. P. Kropotkin, *Mutual Aid.*
43. Ferri, p. 28.
44. *Ibid.*, p. 57.
45. *Ibid.*, p. 75.
46. Halévy, pp. 18–19, Semmel, Chap. 2.
47. Pearson, *Galton*, I, p. 61, II, p. 627.
48. T. Parsons, *The Structure of Social Action* (1937); H. Stuart Hughes,

Consciousness and Society: the Reorientation of European Social Thought 1890–1930 (1959).

49. Abrams, *Origins of British Sociology*, p. 67.
50. See above Chap. 5, p. 121 and n. 41. Huxley once wrote to Spencer: 'you and I are dealt with after the ordinary fashion popular with theologians, who practically say "You shall be materialists whether you like it or not" . . .' (*Life and Letters of T. H. H.*, II, pp. 144–5).
51. See above Chap. 6, n. 107.
52. Hughes, pp. 15–16.
53. *Ibid.*, p. 14.
54. Parsons, p. 697.
55. *Ibid.*, pp. 5, 12, 719–26.
56. E.g. Percy Cohen, *Modern Social Theory*, p. 18.
57. See R. Dahrendorf, *Society and Democracy in Germany*, pp. 33–64; D. S. Landes, in *Cambridge Economic History of Europe*, Vol. VI, pp. 353 ff., and chapters by Landes and Gerschenkron in Landes (ed.), *The Rise of Capitalism*, pp. 99–129.
58. Dahrendorf, p. 42.
59. *Ibid.*, p. 52.
60. *Ibid.*, p. 63.
61. G. Mann, *The History of Germany since 1789*, p. 220; see also J. P. Mayer, *Max Weber and German Politics*, passim.
62. *Imperial Germany and the Industrial Revolution* (1915).
63. Cf. S. Avineri, *The Social and Political Thought of Karl Marx*, pp. 17–31, also pp. 49–50. Whereas, speaking of France in *The Eighteenth Brumaire*, Marx described the bureaucracy as 'the instrument of the ruling class', he also, in *The German Ideology*, put forward another theory, less systematic, that where classes were evenly balanced or deadlocked, bureaucracy might acquire power in its own right. Trotsky's analysis of the Soviet state under Stalin develops from here.
64. See K. Polanyi, 'On the Belief in Economic Determinism', *Sociological Review* (1947), who does not regret its passing with the advent of economic planning. Some modern Marxists wish to deny that Marx was in any very specific sense, an economic determinist, or attribute it to Engels and Kautsky only (e.g. E. Fromm, 'Problems of Interpreting Marx', in I. L. Horowitz (ed.), *The New Sociology: Essays in Honour of C. W. Mills*, Chap. 12 or Z. Bauman, 'Modern Times, Modern Marx', *Social Research*, XXXIV, 1967). They protect Marx from obsolescence by disowning (in a very un-Marxian spirit, it seems to me) the most historically specific, the most sociological, parts of his theory—'economic determinism' becomes a very general theory of man or meta-sociology. It is fair to attribute a general meta-

sociology to Marx—so long as what makes him a proto-sociologist, those theories which express a specific historical reality, are not denied.

65. R. Bendix, *Max Weber: an Intellectual Portrait*, pp. 13–48.
66. Mayer, pp. 45, 57.
67. See Barrington Moore, *Social Origins of Dictatorship and Democracy*, esp. Chap. 1.
68. See S. E. Finer, Introduction to *Vilfredo Pareto: Sociological Writings*, pp. 10–11.
69. E. Durkheim, 'Individualism and the Intellectuals', translated with introduction by S. Lukes in *Political Studies*, XVII (1969), p. 20.
70. Hughes, *Consciousness and Society*, pp. 17, 39, makes the same point about the thinkers of the 1890s. But it was not Darwin's influence which influenced Spencer in this direction, as he maintains.
71. See R. Koebner, 'Adam Smith and the Industrial Revolution', *Econ. H. R.* (2nd series), XI (1959). The point was clearly made by Smith's contemporary Ferguson when he wrote (*History of Civil Society*, 1966 edn., pp. 122–3): '. . . nations stumble upon establishments, which are indeed the result of human action, but not the execution of any human design. . . . Communities . . . admit of the greatest revolutions where no change is intended. . . . No constitution is formed by concert. no government is copied from a plan. . . . The seeds of every form are lodged in human nature; they spring up and ripen with the season.' How Spencerian the sentiments, even to the organic imagery in the last sentence!
72. *Rules of the Sociological Method*, Chap. III.
73. In *Fabian Essays in Socialism* (1889), ed. G. B. Shaw, p. 57.
74. A full recent discussion of Weber's plea for value-free sociology and its social context is T. S. Simey, *Social Science and Social Purpose* (1968).
75. *S. Stat.*, pp. 158–9.
76. H. Sidgwick, *Miscellaneous Essays and Addresses* (1904), Chap. XI, esp. pp. 261, 267–8. Cf. G. E. Moore, *Principia Ethica* (1903), pp. 48–58.
77. Cf. G. Myrdal, *The Political Element in the Development of Economic Theory* (1928).

10. Sociology and its History

1. E.g. L. A. Coser and B. Rosenberg, *Sociological Theory* (2nd edn. 1964), Chap. 6, P. S. Cohen, *Modern Social Theory*, pp. 166–72, J. A. Rex, *Key Problems of Sociological Theory*, Chap. 7.

2. A. R. Radcliffe-Brown, *Structure and Function in Primitive Society*, pp. 6–7.
3. B. Malinowski, *Dynamics of Culture Change*: cf. the trenchant critique of it by M. Gluckman, 'Malinowski's Functional Analysis of Social Change', *Africa*, XVII (1947).
4. For an excellent demonstration of the unwisdom of ignoring history, on 'Yankee City' (Newburyport) itself, see S. Thernstrom, *Poverty and Progress* (1964).
5. Yet see S. M. Lipset and R. Hofstadter (eds.), *Sociology and History: Methods* (1968), one of a series entitled 'The Sociology of American History'; and W. J. Cahnman and A. Boskoff (eds.), *Sociology and History: Theory and Research* (1964).
6. R. F. Bales, *Interaction Process Analysis* (1950), and brief discussion by J. Madge, *The Rise of Scientific Sociology*, Chap. 12, and G. C. Homans, *The Human Group* (1950), and *The Nature of Social Science* (1967).
7. See the autobiographical introduction by Homans to *Sentiments and Activities: Essays in Social Science* (1963), esp. pp. 3–7, and G. C. Homans and C. P. Curtis, *An Introduction to Pareto: His Sociology* (1934).
8. I am indebted for this point to my colleague M. D. King, who applies it to R. K. Merton's famous study of the 'values' which underlay seventeenth-century science and partly stem from Puritanism. A very similar concept of values is employed by L. S. Feuer in *The Scientific Intellectual*, whose detailed opinion as to what these values are is quite different from Merton's.

   The 'values' on which Lipset, in *The First New Nation*, pivots his explanation are likewise extraordinarily constant (see above, Chap. 7, pp. 190–1). They are conceded to be the outcome of historical causes, but for the purposes of analysis of over 200 years of American history, they are taken as givens. It is entirely appropriate that Parsons should get round in the end to comparing 'cultural symbols' (='values') to biological genes—not so much a volte-face as the realization of quasi-biological assumptions which had been there the whole time ('Evolutionary Universals in Society', *Amer. Soc. Rev.*, XXIX, 1964, p. 341).
9. For a more favourable assessment of the pattern variables see L. Sklair, 'The Functional Requisites in Parsonian Sociology', *Brit. J. Soc.*, XXI (1970).
10. E.g. N. J. Smelser, *Social Change in the Industrial Revolution* (1959), R. N. Bellah, *Tokugawa Religion* (1957). Cf. the remarks of Homans about Smelser in his 'Bringing Men Back In', *Amer. Soc. Rev.*, XXIX (1964).
11. See, for example, *Man Makes Himself* (1936), *Social Evolution* (1951).

12. L. A. White, *The Science of Culture: A Study of Man and Civilization* (1949); J. H. Steward, *Theory of Culture Change: the Methodology of Multilinear Evolution* (1955). See also the favourable estimate by M. Harris, *The Rise of Anthropological Theory*, and a further statement by White 'The Concept of Evolution in Cultural Anthropology', in *Evolution and Anthropology: a Centennial Appraisal*, ed. B. J. Meggers (1959).
13. From White (1949), quoted by E. Wolf, 'The Study of Evolution', in S. N. Eisenstadt, *Readings in Social Evolution and Development* (1970), p. 131.
14. T. Parsons, *Societies: Evolutionary and Comparative Perspectives* (1966), p. 109.
15. For three instances see D. B. Barrett, *Schism and Renewal in Africa* (1968), a study of the development of modern African religious movements, and my review in *Sociology*, IV (1970), pp. 249–51; and the discussion of urbanization in developing countries by L. Reissman in *The Urban Process* (1963); or, very markedly, L. W. Pye, *Politics, Personality and Nation-building* (1962), which uses both a model of the necessary transition to modernity (while deprecating the over-simplifications of earlier such schemes), and the notion that the crucial factor is one that is a cultural constant, underlying superficial objective constraints (cf. esp. p. 145)—again, more of Pareto than Weber (cf. above, Chap. 7, nn. 85–8). Much of this work is deeply influenced by Redfield's folk-urban continuum, or variants of it, which are in their turn developments of the classical evolutionary continua like militancy-industrialism. R. Bendix's 'Tradition and Modernity Reconsidered', *Comp. Stud. in Soc. and Hist.*, IX (1967), spells out the unhistorical character of these continua and the dangers of using them as other than non-temporal models.
16. Eisenstadt, *op. cit.*, note 13 above, and H. R. Barringer, G. I. Blanksten, and R. W. Mack (eds.), *Social Change in Developing Areas: a Reinterpretation of Evolution* (1966).
17. J. D. Y. Peel, 'Spencer and the Neo-evolutionists', *Sociology*, III (1969).
18. Parsons, *op. cit.*, note 8 above; and G. L. Buck and A. L. Jacobson, 'Social Evolution and Structural Functional Analysis: an Empirical Test', *Amer. Soc. Rev.*, XXXIII (1968).
19. As, for example, R. D. Schwartz and J. C. Miller succeed in doing in their article, 'Legal Evolution and Societal Complexity' in Eisenstadt, *op. cit.*, pp. 155–72.
20. The general method, which needs to be both committed and in an important sense 'value-free', is that outlined by P. Streeten, 'Programs and Prognoses', *Q. J. Econ.*, LXVIII (1954), and developed

by H. Stretton, *The Political Sciences* (1968); see also Colin Leys, 'The Analysis of Planning', in *Politics and Change in Developing Countries* (1969), pp. 247–75.

21. This is extraordinarily difficult, perhaps most so for economists whose familiar instruments have been adapted for a different social context. See C. Geertz's review of Myrdal's *Asian Drama* in *Encounter* (July 1969), 'Myrdal's Mythology: Modernism and the Third World'; and D. Rimmer, 'The Abstraction from Politics: a critique of economic theory and design with reference to West Africa', *J. Development Studies*, III (1969).
22. B. Moore, p. 387.
23. See further Nisbet, *Social Change and History*, pp. 223–39.
24. *Social Theory and Social Structure* (rev. edn. 1957), p. 4.
25. On which cf. R. G. Collingwood, *The Idea of History* (1961 edn.), pp. 130 ff. and E. H. Carr, *What is History?*, pp. 7–30.
26. Cf. J. Goody and I. Watt, 'The Consequences of Literacy', *Comp. Stud. in Soc. and Hist.*, V (1963),
27. Cf. the main argument of J. H. Plumb's *The Death of the Past* (1969) that 'history' (i.e. what modern historians have achieved) has killed the 'past' (i.e. socially useful versions of what is supposed to have happened). Yet Prof. Plumb still believes that men today 'need an historical past, objective and true' (p. 16) and settles for an eighteenth-century justification of history.
28. A. Koestler, *The Sleepwalkers* (1959).
29. T. S. Kuhn, *The Structure of Scientific Revolutions* (1962).
30. P. B. Medawar, *The Art of the Soluble* (1967), p. 151; cf. his *Induction and Intuition in Scientific Thought* (1969). Medawar, incidentally, rates Whewell's work very highly and follows his approach.
31. Introduction to his edition of Spencer's *Principles of Sociology* (1969), pp. ix, xiii.
32. By some, 'theory of society' is considered distinct from sociological theory, as a kind of philosophical metasociology—e.g. R. Dahrendorf, *Essays in the Theory of Society* (1968), p. vi. I see no harm in this activity provided it is not taken to be more than a conceptual clearing of the ground, prefatory to the real business of sociology.
33. *Structure of Scientific Revolutions*, Chaps. 2–4.
34. *An Essay concerning Human Understanding* (Everyman edn.), p. xxiii.
35. See above, Chap. 1, p. 14.
36. *Social Theory and Social Structure*, p. 7.
37. D. Martindale, *The Nature and Types of Sociological Theory*, p. 542.
38. 'Components of the National Culture', in *Student Power* (eds. A. Cockburn and R. Blackburn, 1969).

39. Cf. R. Bierstedt's remark, reviewing Zeitlin's book in *Am. Soc. Rev.*, XXXIV (1969), p. 402, that Marx is mentioned once in *The Division of Labour in Society*, compared with 43 references to Spencer; a similar picture would emerge if one considered *The Rules of the Sociological Method* or *The Elementary Forms*. Spencer's impact generally in Germany, especially on Toennies, was considerable, and is largely ignored. Dr. E. G. Jacoby of Wellington, N.Z., informs me that Toennies wrote three (untranslated) papers on Spencer.
40. C. W. Mills, *The Sociological Imagination* (Penguin edn.), p. 206.
41. H. Lefebvre, *The Sociology of Marx* (Engl. tr. by N. Guterman, 1968).

Select Bibliography

WORKS BY SPENCER CITED IN THE TEXT

Books

Social Statics: or the Conditions essential to Human Happiness specified, and the First of them Developed, 1850
The Principles of Psychology, first edition 1855
Education: Intellectual, Moral and Physical, 1861
First Principles, 1862
The Principles of Biology, Vol. I 1864, Vol. II 1867
The Principles of Psychology, second edition, Vol. I 1870, Vol. II 1872
The Study of Sociology, 1873
Descriptive Sociology, 1874– (compiled by others on principles laid down by Spencer, and continued after his death)
The Principles of Sociology, Vol. I, Part I, 'The Data of Sociology', Part 2, 'The Inductions of Sociology', Part 3, 'The Domestic Relations', 1876. Vol. II, Part 4, 'Ceremonial Institutions', 1879; Part 5, 'Political Institutions', 1882. Vol. III, Part 6, 'Ecclesiastical Institutions', 1885; Part 7, 'Professional Institutions', Part 8, 'Industrial Institutions', 1897.
The Principles of Ethics, Vol. I, Part I, 1879; Parts 2–3, 1892. Vol. II, Part 4, 1891; Parts 5–6, 1893.
The Man versus the State, 1884
An Autobiography, 1904
The Life and Letters of Herbert Spencer (ed. D. Duncan), 1908

Essays

'The Proper Sphere of Government', *The Nonconformist*, 15 June–14 Dec. 1842
'A Theory of Population, deduced from the General Law of Animal Fertility', 1852
*'Over-Legislation', 1853 (II)
'The Universal Postulate', 1853
*'The Genesis of Science', 1854 (I)
*'Manners and Fashion', 1854 (I)
*'Railway Morals and Railway Policy', 1854 (II)

*'Progress: its Law and Cause', 1857 (I)
*'Representative Government', 1857 (II)
*'The Morals of Trade', 1859 (II)
*'Prison Ethics', 1860 (II)
*'The Social Organism', 1860 (I)
*'Parliamentary Reform', 1860 (I)
*'Reasons for Dissenting from the Philosophy of M. Comte', 1864 (III
*'Specialized Administration', 1871 (III)
*'The Classification of the Sciences', 1871 (III)
*'Replies to Criticisms', 1873 (III)
*'The Comparative Physiology of Man', 1875 (III)
'The Factors of Organic Evolution', 1886

NOTE: Those essays marked * were included in one of the editions of *Essays: Scientific, Political and Speculative.* For Vols. I and II, I have used an edition of 1883, for Vol. III of 1878.

RECENT REPRINTS AND SELECTIONS

The Study of Sociology, 1961; entire with brief introduction by T. Parsons
The Principles of Sociology, 1967; mostly Part 5, with long introduction by R. L. Carneiro
The Principles of Sociology, 1969; about half of the original, with introduction by S. L. Andreski
The Man versus the State, 1970; and four other essays, with long introduction by D. G. MacRae

NOTE: There is a complete bibliography of Spencer's writings in J. Rumney, *Herbert Spencer's Sociology*.

OTHER WORKS PUBLISHED BEFORE 1920†

Alger, B. A. M., *King St. Wesleyan Chapel, Derby: a Centenary Memorial 1805–1905*, Derby, 1905
Arnold, M., *Culture and Anarchy*, 1869, new edn. Cambridge, 1960.
Atkinson, H. G. and Martineau, H., *Letters on the Laws of Man's Nature and Development*, 1851
Babbage, C., *On the Economy of Machinery and Manufactures*, 1835
Bagehot, W., *Physics and Politics*, 1869, 4th edn. 1876
Bradbury, E. and Keene, R., *All about Derby: its History, Institutions and Industries*, Derby, 3rd edn. 1906

† Unless otherwise stated, the place of publication is London

Bray, C., *The Philosophy of Necessity: or Law in Mind as in Matter*, 1841, 3rd edn. 1889
Phases of Opinion and Experience during a Long Life, n.d. (*c.* 1884)
Bogue, D. and Bennett, J., *History of Dissenters, from the Revolution in 1688 to the Year 1808*, Vol. III 1810, Vol. IV 1812
Buckle, H. T., *The History of Civilization in England*, Vol. I 1857, new edn. 1882
Clifford, W. K., *Lectures and Essays*, Vol. II 1901
Combe, A., *The Sphere for Joint-Stock Companies*, Edinburgh, 1825
Combe, G., *The Constitution of Man*, 1828
Cross, J. W., *George Eliot's Life as related in her Letters and Journals*, Edinburgh, n.d. new edn.
Darwin, C., *The Origin of Species*, 1859, Penguin edn. 1968
Darwin, E., *Essential Writings*, ed. D. King-Hele, 1968
Zoonomia: or the Laws of Organic Life, 2nd edn. 1796
Darwin, F., *The Life and Letters of Charles Darwin*, 1887
Dicey, A. V., *Law and Public Opinion in England during the Nineteenth Century*, 1919
Durkheim, E., *The Division of Labour in Society*, 1893, trans. G. Simpson, New York
The Rules of the Sociological Method, 1895, trans. S. A. Solovay and J. M. Mueller, New York
'Individualism and the Intellectuals', 1898, trans. and ed. by S. Lukes, *Political Studies*, XVII, 1969
The Elementary Forms of the Religious Life, 1912, trans. J. W. Swain, New York, 1961
Edwards, J., *Basic Writings* (including parts of 'Treatise Concerning Religious Affections', 1746, and 'Freedom of the Will', 1754), ed. E. O. Winslow, New York, 1966
Eliot, H., *Letters of J. S. Mill*, 1910
Eliot, G., *Adam Bede*, 1859
Felix Holt: the Radical, 1866
Economist, The, 1843–
Engels, F., *The Condition of the Working Class in England in 1844*, 1845, new edn. 1892
Ferri, F., *Socialism and Positive Science (Darwin, Spencer, Marx)*, 1896, English edn. 1905
Ferguson, A., *An Essay on The History of Civil Society*, 1767, new edn. Edinburgh, 1966
Fiske, J., *Essays: Historical and Literary*, Vol. II, New York, 1902
Fitzhugh, G., *Sociology for the South*, 1854, reprinted in *Ante-Bellum*, ed. H. Wish, New York, 1960
Frankland, E., *Sketches from the Life of Edward Frankland* (ed. and concluded by his daughters M. N. W. and S. J. C.), 1902
George, H., *A Perplexed Philosopher: being an Examination of Mr. H. Spencer's Various Utterances on the Land Question*, 1893
Gibbon, C., *The Life of George Combe*, 1878
Glover, S., *The History and Directory of the Borough of Derby*, Derby, 1843
Godwin, W., *Enquiry Concerning Political Justice*, 2nd edn. 1796
Greg, W. R., *Prospects of Industry: being a Brief Exposition of the Present Conditions of the Labouring Classes*, 1835
Essays on Political and Social Science, Vol. I, 1853

Hall, C., *The Effects of Civilization on the People in European States*, 1805, new edn. New York, 1965
Hennell, M., *An Outline of the Various Social Systems and Communities which have been founded on the Principle of Co-operation*, 1844
Hobhouse, S., *Joseph Sturge: his Life and Work*, 1919
Hobson, J. A., *Imperialism: a Study*, 1906
Hodgskin, T., *Labour Defended against the Claims of Capital*, 1825, new edn. 1963
Hole, J., *Lectures on Social Science and the Organization of Labour*, 1851
Holyoake, G. J., *The History of Co-operation*, Vol. 1875, Vol. II 1879, new edn. 1908
Sixty Years of an Agitator's Life, n.d. (*c.* 1885)
Hume, D., *Dialogues concerning Natural Religion*, 1779, reprinted in *Hume on Religion* (ed. R. Wollheim), 1963
Huth, A. H., *The Life and Writings of H. T. Buckle*, 2nd edn. 1880
Huxley, L., *The Life and Letters of T. H. Huxley*, 1900
The Life and Letters of Sir J. D. Hooker, 1918
Huxley, T. H., *Evolution and Ethics and Other Essays*, 1901
Hyndman, H. M., *Socialism and Slavery*, n.d.
James, W., *The Varieties of Religious Experience*, 1902, new edn. 1960
Pragmatism, New York, 1907
Memories and Studies, 1911
Kidd, B., *Social Evolution*, 1894
Kropotkin, P., *Mutual Aid*, 1902, popular edn. 1915
Lovett, W., *The Life and Struggle of William Lovett in his Pursuit of Bread, Knowledge and Freedom*, 1876, 2nd edn. 1920
Mackinnon, W. H., *On the Rise, Progress and Present State of Public Opinion*, 1828
'Manchester Manufacturer' (Cobden), *England, Ireland and America*, Edinburgh, 1835
Mansel, H. L., *The Limits of Religious Thought*, 4th edn. 1859
Martineau, H., *How to Observe, Manners and Morals*, 1838
Marx, K., *Selected Writings in Sociology and Social Philosophy* (ed. T. B. Bottomore and M. Rubel), 1961
Marx, K. and Engels, F., *Manifesto of the Communist Party*, 1848, Moscow edn. n.d.
Miall, A., *Life of Edward Miall*, 1884
Miall, E., *The Franchise as the Means of a People's Training*, 1851
Mill, J. S., *The Spirit of the Age*, 1831, new edn. 1942
A System of Logic, 1843, People's edn. 1896
An Autobiography, 1873, new edn. Chicago, 1954
Millar, J., *The Origin of the Distinction of Ranks*, 1771, reprinted in W. C. Lehmann *John Millar of Glasgow*, Cambridge, 1960
Mottram, W., *The True Story of George Eliot in relation to 'Adam Bede'*, 1905
Morley, J., *The Life of Richard Cobden*, 1879, 13th edn. 1906
Recollections, 1917
Mozley, T., *Reminiscences Chiefly of Oriel College and the Oxford Movement*, 1882
Reminiscences, Chiefly of Towns, Villages and Schools, 1885
Newman, J. H., *An Essay in Aid of a Grammar of Assent*, new edn. 1895
Nonconformist, The, 1842–
Owen, R., *A New View of Society, and Other Writings*, 1813, new edn. 1927

Paine, T., *Common Sense*, 1776, new edn. 1792
The Rights of Man, 1791, new edn. 1915
Pearson, K., *Life of Francis Galton*, 1914–30
Phillips, R., *A Personal Tour through the United Kingdom. . . . Vol. II, Derbyshire-Nottinghamshire*, 1829
Pilkington, J., *The Doctrine of Equality of Rank and Condition . . .*, 1795
Priestley, J., *Writings on Philosophy, Science and Politics*, selected by J. Passmore, New York, 1965
Memoirs of the Rev. Dr. J. Priestley to the Year 1795, 1809
Ritchie, D. G., *The Principles of State Interference*, 1902
Robertson, J. M., *Buckle and his Critics*, 1895
Shaw, G. B. (ed.), *Essays in Fabian Socialism*, 1889
Sidgwick, H., *Miscellaneous Essays and Addresses*, 1904
A. S. and E. M. S., *Henry Sidgwick: a Memoir*, 1906
Smiles, S., *The Lives of Boulton and Watt*, 1865
The Life of Geo. Stephenson and of his Son Robert Stephenson, 1868
Thrift, 1875
Smith, A., *The Theory of Moral Sentiments*, 1759, 11th edn. 1808
The Wealth of Nations, 1776, new edn. 1910
Spencer, T., *Pamphlets*, including 'The People's Rights and How to Get Them', 'The Pillars of the Church of England, or are Intemperance and Ignorance, Bigotry and Infallibility, Church Rates and Corn Laws Essential to the Existence of the Establishment?', 'Remarks on National Education', 'Religion and Politics: or Ought Religious Men to be Political', all 1843
Sturge, J., *Reconciliation between the Middle and the Labouring Classes*, Birmingham, 1842
Toennies, F., *Community and Society (Gemeinschaft und Gesellschaft)*, 1887, trans. C. P. Loomis, Michigan, 1957
Tufnell, H., *The Character, Object and Effects of Trades Unions*, 1834, new edn. Manchester, 1933
Two, *Home Life with Herbert Spencer*, Bristol, 1906
Veblen, T., *The Theory of the Leisure Class*, New York, 1899
Imperial Germany and the Industrial Revolution, New York, 1915
Wade, J., *The History and Political Philosophy of the Middle and Working Classes*, Edinburgh, 1833, 4th edn. 1842
Walker, G., *Essays on Various Subjects*, 1809
Wallace, A. R., *My Life: a Record of Events and Opinions*, 1905
Wallas, G., *The Life of Francis Place*, new edn. 1918
Webb, B., *My Apprenticeship*, 1926, new edn. 1938
Weber, M., *The Protestant Ethic and the Spirit of Capitalism*, 1904–5, English trans. 1930
Wesley, J., *Works*, 3rd edn. 1829–30
Whewell, W., *The Philosophy of the Inductive Sciences*, 1840, 2nd edn. 1847
Ure, A., *The Philosophy of Manufactures*, 1835, 3rd edn. 1861
Zola, E., *Germinal*, 1865, English trans. L. W. Tancock, 1954

MODERN WORKS ON THE SOCIAL-HISTORICAL BACKGROUND

Annan, N., *Leslie Stephen*, 1951

Armytage, W. H. G., *A. J. Mundella, 1825–1897: the Liberal Background to the Labour Movement*, 1951

Heavens Below: Utopian Experiments in Britain, 1961

Ausubel, H., *John Bright: Victorian Reformer*, New York, 1966

Bendix, R., *Work and Authority in Industry*, New York, 1956, new edn. 1963

Birks, J., *Memorials of Friar Gate Chapel, Derby*, Derby, n.d.

Brebner, J. B., 'Laissez-Faire and State Intervention in 19th Century Britain', *J. Econ. Hist.* (Supp.), VIII, 1948

Briggs, A., *The History of Birmingham*, Vol. II, 1952

Victorian People, 1954

'Middle-Class Consciousness in English Politics 1780–1846', *Past and Present*, IX, 1956

(ed.), *Chartist Studies*, 1959

Victorian Cities, 1963

'The Language of Class in Early 19th Century England', in Briggs and Saville

Briggs, A. and Saville, J., *Essays in Labour History*, 1960

Chadwick, O., *The Victorian Church*, Vol. I, 1966

Chapman, S. D., *The Early Factory Masters*, Newton Abbot, 1968

Checkland, S. G., *The Rise of Industrial Society in England, 1815–1885*, 1964

Church, L. F., *The Early Methodist People*, 1948

Cole, G. D. M., *Chartists Portraits*, 1941

Colligan, J. M., *A History of Arianism in the 18th Century*

Cowherd, R. G., *The Politics of English Dissent*, New York, 1956

Cragg, G. R., *From Puritanism to the Age of Reason*, Cambridge, 1966

Currie, R., *Methodism Divided: a Study in the Sociology of Ecumenicalism*, 1968

Dahrendorf, R., *Society and Democracy in Germany*, 1968

Davies, J. D., *Phrenology: Fad and Science*, New Haven, 1955

Davies, R. and Rupp, G. (eds.), *A History of the Methodist Church in Great Britain*, Vol. I, 1965

Edwards, M., *After Wesley*, 1935

Erickson, C., *British Industrialists: Steel and Hosiery*, Cambridge, 1959

Erikson, K., *Wayward Puritans: a Study in the Sociology of Deviance*, New York, 1965

Everett, E. M., *The Party of Humanity: the Fortnightly Review and its Contributors 1865–1874*, Chapel Hill, 1939

Fearn, E., 'Reform Movements in Derby and Derbyshire 1790–1832', M.A. thesis, Manchester, 1964

'The Derbyshire Reform Societies, 1791–93', *Derb. Archaeol. J.*, LXXVIII, 1968

Fielden, K., 'Samuel Smiles and Self-Help', *Victorian Studies*, XII, 1968

Finer, S. E., *The Life and Times of Sir Edwin Chadwick*, 1852

Fitton, R. S. and Wadsworth, A. P., *The Strutts and the Arkwrights 1758–1830*, Manchester, 1958

Gash, N., *Reaction and Reconstruction in English Politics 1832–1852*, Oxford, 1965

Haight, G. S., *George Eliot: a Biography*, Oxford, 1968
Halévy, E., *A History of the People of England in 1815*, English trans. 1924
Imperialism and the Rise of Labour, English trans. 1926
Harrison, J. F. C., *Robert Owen and the Owenites in Britain and America*, 1969
Hill, C., 'The Norman Yoke', in J. Saville (ed.), *Democracy and the Labour Movement*, 1954
Intellectual Origins of the English Revolution, Oxford, 1965
Hobsbawm, E. J., *Labouring Men: Studies in the History of Labour*, 1964
Industry and Empire 1750–1960, 1968
Hobson, J. A., *Confessions of an Economic Heretic*, 1938
Holt, R. V., *The Unitarian Contribution to Social Progress in England*, 1938, 2nd ed. 1952
Houghton, W. E., *The Victorian Frame of Mind 1830–1870*, New Haven, 1957
Jaeger, M., *Before Victoria: Changing Standards and Behaviour 1787–1857*, 1956, new edn. 1967
Kelly, T., *George Birbeck: Pioneer of Adult Education*, 1857
Kent, J., *The Age of Disunity*, 1966
Kitson-Clark, G., *The Making of Victorian England*, 1962, new edn. 1965
Knickerbocker, F. W., *Free Minds: John Morley and his Friends*, Cambridge, Mass., 1943
Landes, D. S., 'Technological Change and Development in Western Europe 1750–1940', in *The Cambridge Economic History of Europe*, Vol. VI, Cambridge, 1965
(ed.), *The Rise of Capitalism*, New York, 1966
Lincoln, A., *Some Political and Social Ideas of English Dissent 1763–1800*, Cambridge, 1938
McBriar, A. M., *Fabian Socialism and English Politics 1884–1918*, Cambridge, 1962
McCord, N., *The Anti-Corn Law League 1838–1846*, 1958
MacLeod, R.M., 'The X Club, a Social Network of Science in Late-Victorian England', *Notes and Records of Roy. Soc.*, XXIV, 1970
Mann, G., *The History of Germany since 1789*, 1968
Mineka, F. E., *The Dissidence of Dissent: 'The Monthly Repository' 1806–1838*, Chapel Hill, 1944
Musson, A. E. and Robinson, E., 'Science and Industry in the late 18th Century', *Econ. Hist. Rev.* (2nd Series), XIII, 1960–1
Parris, H., *Government and the Railways in Nineteenth-Century Britain*, 1965
Patterson, A. T., *Radical Leicester*, Leicester 1954
Perkin, H., *The Origins of Modern English Society 1780–1880*, 1969
Pollard, S., *The Genesis of Modern Management*, 1965
'Nineteenth Century Co-operation: from Community Building to Shopkeeping', in Briggs and Saville
Porter, B., *Critics of Empire: British Radical Attitudes to Colonialism in Africa, 1895–1914*, 1968
Prest, J., *The Industrial Revolution in Coventry*, Oxford, 1960
Read, D., *The English Provinces c. 1760–1960: a Study in Influence*, 1964
Roberts, D., 'J. Bentham and the Victorian Administrative State', *Vict. Stud.*, II, 1958–9
The Victorian Origins of the British Welfare State, New Haven, 1960

Robinson, E., 'The Derby Philosophical Society', *Annals of Science*, IX, 1953
Robson, R. (ed.), *Ideas and Institutions of Victorian Britain*, 1967
Rose, R. B., 'The Priestley Riots of 1791', *Past and Present*, XVIII, 1960
Rowe, D. J., 'The London Working Men's Association and the People's Charter', *Past and Present*, XXXVI, 1967
Rudkin, O. D., *Thomas Spence and his Connections*, 1927, new edn. New York, 1966
Saville, J., 'Sleeping Partners and Limited Liability, 1850–1856', *Econ. Hist. Rev.* (2nd Series), VIII, 1956
Schofield, R. E., 'John Wesley and Science in 18th Century England', *Isis.*, XLIV, 1953
The Lunar Society of Birmingham, Oxford, 1963
Semmel, B., *Imperialism and Social Reform: English Social Imperial Thought 1895–1914*, 1960
The Governor Eyre Controversy, 1962
Smith, W. S., *The London Heretics 1870–1914*, 1967
Standen, J. D., 'The Social, Economic and Political Development of Derby 1835–1888', M.A. thesis, Leeds, 1959
Sturgess, R. P., 'Cultural Life in Derby in the late 18th Century c. 1770–1800', M.A. thesis, Loughborough, 1968
Swanson, G. E., *Religion and Regime: a Sociological Account of the Reformation*, Ann Arber, 1967
Thomis, M. I., *Politics and Society in Nottingham 1785–1835*, 1969
Thompson, E. P., *The Making of the English Working Class*, 1963
'The Peculiarities of the English', *Socialist Register*, 1965
'Time, Work-Discipline and Industrial Capitalism', *Past and Present*, XXXVIII, 1967
Todd, G., 'Some Aspects of Joint-Stock Companies 1844–1900', *Econ. Hist. Rev.* (1st Series), IV, 1932
Tylecote, M., *The Mechanics' Institutes of Lancashire and Yorkshire before 1851*, 1957
Vincent, J. R., *Pollbooks: How Victorians Voted*, Cambridge, 1967
Walker, D. P., *The Decline of Hell*, 1963
Walzer, M., *The Revolution of the Saints*, 1966
Webb, R. K., *Harriet Martineau: a Radical Victorian*, 1960
Weller, J. C., 'The Revival of Religion in Nottingham 1780–1850', B.D. thesis, Nottingham, 1957
Williams, G. A., *Artisans and Sans-Culottes*, 1968
Williams, R., *Culture and Society 1780–1950*, 1958, new edn. 1961

HISTORY OF SOCIOLOGY, INTELLECTUAL HISTORY

Abrams, P., *The Origins of British Sociology 1834–1914*, Chicago, 1968
Anderson, P., 'Components of the National Culture', in *Student Power*, eds. A. Cockburn and R. Blackburn, 1969

Bibliography

Avineri, S., *The Social and Political Thought of Karl Marx*, Cambridge, 1968

Banton, M. (ed.), *Darwinism and the Study of Society*, 1961

Barnett, S. A. (ed.), *A Century of Darwin*, 1959

Bendix, R., *Max Weber: an Intellectual Portrait*, New York, new edn. 1962

'Tradition and Modernity Reconsidered', *Comp. Stud. in. Soc. and Hist.* IX, 1967

Bock, K. E., 'Darwin and Social Theory', *Phil. of Science*, XXII, 1955

The Acceptance of Histories: Towards a Perspective for Social Science, Berkeley, 1956

Bowle, J., *Politics and Opinion in the 19th Century*, 1954

Bramson, L., *The Political Context of Sociology*, Princeton, 1961

Brinton, C., 'Spencer's Horrid Vision', *Foreign Affairs*, XV, 1936–7

Burrow, J. W., *Evolution and Society: a Study in Victorian Social Theory*, Cambridge, 1966

Carneiro, R. L., 'Spencer, Herbert', *International Encyclopedia of the Social Sciences*

Cannon, W. F., 'The Uniformitarian-Catastrophist Debate', *Isis*, LI, 1960

Cockshut, A. O. J., *The Unbelievers*, 1964

Cowles, T., 'Malthus, Darwin and Bagehot: a study in the Transference of a Concept', *Isis*, XXVI, 1936

Cropsey, J., *Polity and Economy: an Interpretation of the Principles of Adam Smith*, The Hague, 1957

Ducasse, C. J., 'Whewell's Philosophy of Scientific Discovery', *Phil. Rev.*, LX, 1951

Eisen, S., 'Herbert Spencer and the Spectre of Comte', *J. Brit. Stud.*, VII, 1967

'Frederic Harrison and Herbert Spencer: Embattled Unbelievers', *Victorian Stud.*, XII, 1968

Ellegård, A., 'The Darwinian Theory and 19th Philosophers of Science', *J. Hist. Ideas*, XVIII, 1957

Darwin and the General Reader, Goteborg, 1958

Ensor, R. C. K., *Some Reflection on Herbert Spencer's Doctrine that Progress is Differentiation*, Oxford, 1946

Eversley, D. E. C., *Social Theories of Fertility and the Malthusian Debate*, Oxford, 1959

Fine, S., *Laissez-Faire and the General-Welfare State*, Ann Arbor, 1956

Finer, S. E., Introduction to *Vilfredo Pareto: Sociological Writings*, 1966

Garfinkle, N., 'Science and Religion 1790–1800: the Critical Response to the Work of Erasmus Darwin', *J. Hist. Ideas*, XVI, 1955

Gillispie, C. C., *Genesis and Geology*, Cambridge Mass., 1951

Glass, B., Temkin, O. and Straus, W. E. (eds.), *Forerunners of Darwin 1745–1859*, Baltimore, 1959

Gordon, G., 'The London *Economist* and the High Tide of Laissez-Faire', *J. Pol. Econ.*, LXIII, 1955

Greene, J. C., 'Biology and Social Theory in the Nineteenth Century', in M. Clagett (ed.), *Critical Problems in the History of Science*, Madison, 1962

Goldthorpe, J. H., 'Herbert Spencer', in *The Founding Fathers of Social Science* (ed. T. Raison), 1969

Halevy, E., *Thomas Hodgskin*, new edn. A. J. Taylor, 1956

The Growth of Philosophical Radicalism, 1928

Hamburger, J., *Intellectuals in Politics: J. S. Mill and the Philosophical Radicals*, New Haven, 1965

Harris, M., *The Rise of Anthropological Theory*, 1969
Hearnshaw, F. J. C., *The Social and Political Ideas of Some Representative Thinkers of the Victorian Age*, 1933
Hearnshaw, L. S., *A Short History of British Psychology, 1840–1940*, 1964
Heathcote, A. W., 'W. Whewell's Philosophy of Science', *Brit. J. Phil. Sci.*, IV, 1953–4
Himmelfarb, G., *Darwin and the Darwinian Revolution*, 1959
Victorian Minds, 1968
Hinton, R. K. W., 'Husbands, Fathers and Conquerors', *Pol. Stud.*, XV, 1967
Hofstadter, R., *Social Darwinism in American Thought*, 1944, new edn. Boston, 1955
Holmes, S. J., 'K. E. von Baer's Perplexities over Evolution', *Isis*, XXVII, 1947
Hughes, H. S., *Consciousness and Society: The Reorientation of European Social Thought 1890–1930*, 1959
Kardiner, A. and Preble, E., *They Studied Man*, New York, 1961
Kettler, D., *The Social and Political Thought of Adam Ferguson*, Ohio, 1965
Koebner, R., 'Adam Smith and the Industrial Revolution', *Econ. Hist. Rev.* (2nd Series), XI, 1959
Lamar, L. B., 'Herbert Spencer and his Father', *Studies in English*, XXXII, 1953
Lehmann, W. C., *John Millar of Glasgow 1735–1801*, Cambridge, 1960
Letwin, S. R., *The Pursuit of Certainty*, Cambridge, 1965
Leeuwen, H. G. van, *The Problem of Certainty in English Thought 1630–1690*, The Hague, 1963
Lipset, S. M., 'Harriet Martineau: a Pioneer Comparative Sociologist', in *Revolution and Counterrevolution*, 1969
Lovejoy, A. O., *The Great Chain of Being*, 1936, new edn. New York, 1961
MacIntyre, A., 'Hume on *Is* and *Ought*', *Phil. Rev.*, LXVIII, 1959
Mack, M. P., 'The Fabians and Utilitarianism', *J. Hist. Ideas*, XVI, 1955
Jeremy Bentham: An Odyssey of Ideas 1748–1792,
Macpherson, C. B., *The Political Theory of Possessive Individualism*, Oxford, 1962
Manuel, F. E., *The New World of Henri Saint-Simon*, Cambridge Mass., 1956
Martindale, D., *The Nature and Types of Sociological Theory*, 1961
Mason, S. F., 'From Hierarchy to Evolution in the Theory of Biology', in Saville, *Democracy and the Labour Movement*
Matthews, W. R., *The Religious Philosophy of Dean Mansel*, 1956
Mayer, J. P., *Max Weber and German Politics*, 2nd edn. 1956
Meek, R. L., 'The Scottish Contribution to Marxist Sociology', in Saville
Meggers, B. J. (ed.), *Evolution and Anthropology: a Centennial Appraisal*, Washington, 1959
Miliband, R., 'The Politics of Robert Owen', *J. Hist. Ideas*, XV, 1954
Mueller, I. W., *J. S. Mill and French Thought*, Urbana, 1956
Myers, W. F. T., 'Ideas of Mental and Social Evolution in the Treatment of Character in George Eliot's Novels', B. Litt. thesis, Oxford, 1964
Nisbet, R. A., *The Sociological Tradition*, 1967
Social Change and History: Aspects of the Western Theory of Development, New York, 1969
Packe, M. St. J., *The Life of J. S. Mill*, 1954

Parsons, T., *The Structure of Social Action*, Glencoe, Ill. 1937
Pearson, H., *Doctor Darwin*, 1930
Peel, J. D. Y., 'Spencer and the Neo-Evolutionists', *Sociology*, III, 1969
Persons, S. (ed.), *Evolutionary Thought in America*, New Haven, 1950
Rapoport, D. C., 'Military and Civil Societies', *Pol. Stud.*, XII, 1964
Rieff, P., *Freud: the Mind of the Moralist*, 1959, new edn. 1965
Richter, M., *The Politics of Conscience: T. H. Green and his Age*, 1964
Rosen, F., 'Progress and Democracy: W. Godwin's Contribution to Political Philosophy', Ph.D. thesis, London, 1965
Rumney, J., *Herbert Spencer's Sociology*, 1934
Russett, C. E., *The Concept of Equilibrium in American Social Thought*, New Haven, 1966
Simon, W. M., 'Herbert Spencer and the Social Organism', *J. Hist. Ideas*, XXI, 1960
European Positivism in the Nineteenth Century, Ithaca, 1963
Stark, W., 'Herbert Spencer's Three Sociologies', *Am. Soc. Rev.*, XXVI, 1961
The Fundamental Forms of Social Thought, 1962
Stocking, G. W., *Race, Culture and Evolution*, New York, 1969
Strong, E. W., 'W. Whewell and J. S. Mill: their Controversy about Scientific Knowledge', *J. Hist. Ideas*, XVI, 1955
Taylor, A. J., 'The Originality of Herbert Spencer', *Studies in English*, XXXIV, 1955
Toulmin, S. and Goodfield, J., *The Discovery of Time*, 1965
Weiner, P. P., *Evolution and the Founders of Pragmatism*, Cambridge Mass., 1949
Willey, B., *The Eighteenth Century Background*, 1946
Wolin, S. S., *Politics and Vision*, 1960
Young, R. M., 'Malthus and the Evolutionists', *Past and Present*, XLIII, 1969
Mind, Brain and Adaptation in the Nineteenth Century, Oxford, 1970
Zeitlin, I. M., *Ideology and the Development of Sociological Theory*, Englewood Cliffs, 1968

OTHER WORKS

Andreski, S. L., *Elements of Comparative Sociology*, 1964
Barringer, H. R., Blanksten, G. I. and Mack, R. W. (eds.), *Social Change in Developing Areas: a Reinterpretation of Evolution*, Cambridge Mass., 1966
Bellah, R. N., 'Religious Evolution', *Amer. Soc. Rev.*, XXIX, 1964
Buck, G. L. and Jacobson, A. L., 'Social Evolution and Structural Functional Analysis', *Amer. Soc. Rev.*, XXXIII, 1968
Buckley, W., *Sociology and Modern Systems Theory*, Englewood Cliffs, 1967
Cahnman, W. J. and Boskoff, A., *Sociology and History: Theory and Research*, 1964
Carr, E. H., *What is History?*, 1961, new edn. 1964
Childe, V. G., *Social Evolution*, 1951
Cohen, P. S., *Modern Social Theory*, 1968
Collingwood, R. G., *The Idea of Nature*, Oxford, 1945
The Idea of History, 1946, new edn. Oxford, 1961

Coser, L. A. and Rosenberg, B., *Sociological Theory*, 2nd edn. New York, 1964
Dahrendorf, R., *Class and Class Conflict in Industrial Society*, 1959
'Out of Utopia', *Amer. J. Soc.*, LXIV, 1959
Essays in the Theory of Society, 1961
Deutsch, K. W., 'Mechanism, Organism and Society', *Phil. of Sci.*, XVIII, 1951
'Mechanism, Teleology and Mind', *Phil. and Phenom. Research*, XII, 1951–2
Dray, W. H., 'Holism and Individualism in History and Social Science', in P. Edwards (ed.), *Encyclopedia of Philosophy*, 1967
Eisenstadt, S. N., *Modernization: Protest and Change*, Englewood Cliffs, 1966
(ed.), *Readings in Social Evolution and Development*, 1970
Etzioni, A., *The Active Society*, New York, 1969
Flew, A. G. N., *Evolutionary Ethics*, 1967
Geertz, C., 'Myrdal's Mythology: Modernism and the Third World', *Encounter*, July 1969
Gellner, E. A., 'Holism and Individualism in History and Sociology', in P. Gardiner (ed.), *Theories of History*, Glencoe, Ill., 1959
Thought and Change, 1964
Gluckman, M., 'Malinowski's Functional Analysis of Social Change', *Africa*, XVII, 1947
Hagen, E. E., *On the Theory of Social Change*, 1962
Homans, G. C., *Sentiments and Activities*, 1963
Kuhn, T. S., *The Structure of Scientific Revolutions*, Chicago, 1962
Kunkel, J. H., 'Values and Behaviour in Economic Development', *Econ. Dev. and Cult. Change*, XIII, 1965
Lefebvre, H., *The Sociology of Marx*, 1968
Levine, R. A., *Dreams and Deeds: Achievement Motivation in Nigeria*, Chicago, 1966
Lipset, S. M., *The First New Nation*, 1963
Lipset, S. M. and Hofstadter, R., *Sociology and History: Methods*, New York, 1968
Lukes, S. M., 'Methodological Individualism Reconsidered', *Brit. J. Soc.*, XIX, 1968
MacIntyre, A., *Secularization and Moral Change*, 1967
Malinowski, B., *Dynamics of Culture Change*, New Haven, 1946
Medawar, P. B., *The Art of the Soluble*, 1967
Induction and Intuition in Scientific Thought, 1969
Merton, R. K., *Social Theory and Social Structure*, 2nd edn. Glencoe, Il.., 1957
Mills, C. W., *The Sociological Imagination*, 1959, new edn. 1970
Moore, B., *The Social Origins of Dictatorship and Democracy*, 1967
Myrdal, G., *The Political Element in the Development of Economic Theory*, 1929, English edn. 1953
Asian Drama: an Inquiry into the Poverty of Nations, 1968
Ossowski, S., *Class Structure in the Social Consciousness*, M. S. Patterson, 1963
Parsons, T., *The Social System*, Glencoe, Ill., 1950
'Evolutionary Universals in Society', *Amer. Soc. Rev.*, XXIX, 1964
Society: Comparative and Evolutionary Perspectives, Englewood Cliffs, 1966
Plumb, J. H., *The Death of the Past*, 1969
Polanyi, K., 'The Belief in Economic Determinism', *Soc. Rev.*, XXXIX, 1947

Pye, L. W., *Politics, Personality and Nationbuilding*, New Haven, 1962
Radcliffe-Brown, A. R., *Structure and Function in Primitive Society*, 1952
Rostow, W. W., *The Stages of Economic Growth: a Non-Communist Manifesto*, Cambridge, 1960
Sigmund, P. E. (ed.), *The Ideologies of the Developing Nations*, New York, 1963
Simey, T. S., *Social Science and Social Purpose*, 1968
Smelser, N. J., *Social Change in the Industrial Revolution*, 1959
Smelser, N. J. and Lipset, S. M. (eds.), *Social Structure and Mobility in Economic Development*, 1964
Steward, J. H., *Theory of Culture Change*, Urbana, 1955
Streeten, P., 'Programs and Prognoses', *Q. J. Econ.*, LXVIII, 1954
Stretton, H., *The Political Sciences*, 1969
Thernstrom, S., *Poverty and Progress*, Cambridge, Mass., 1964
White, L. A., *The Science of Culture*, New York, 1949

Index

Index

Index